MW00424103

Pacific Gibraltar

ADST-DACOR DIPLOMATS AND DIPLOMACY SERIES

Since 1776 extraordinary men and women have represented the United States abroad under widely varying circumstances. What they did and how and why they did it remain little known to their compatriots. In 1995 the Association for Diplomatic Studies and Training (ADST) and Diplomatic and Consular Officers, Retired, Inc. (DACOR) created the Diplomats and Diplomacy book series to increase public knowledge and appreciation of the professionalism of American diplomats and their involvement in world history. Professor William M. Morgan's *Pacific Gibraltar*, the forty-sixth volume in the series, combines historical scholarship and graceful writing with new insights into the political, military, and diplomatic dimensions of the annexation of Hawai`i.

OTHER TITLES IN THE SERIES

Gordon Brown, *Toussaint's Clause: The Founding Fathers and the Haitian Revolution*

Charles T. Cross, *Born a Foreigner: A Memoir of the American Presence in Asia*

Michael P. E. Hoyt, *Captive in the Congo: A Consul's Return to the Heart of Darkness*

Stephen H. Grant, *Peter Strickland: New London Shipmaster, Boston Merchant, First Consul to Senegal*

Dennis Kux, *The United States and Pakistan, 1947–2000: Disenchanted Allies*

Jane C. Loeffler, *The Architecture of Diplomacy: Building America's Embassies*

Terry McNamara, *Escape with Honor: My Last Hours in Vietnam*

Robert H. Miller, *Vietnam and Beyond: A Diplomat's Cold War Education*

David D. Newsom, *Witness to a Changing World*

Richard B. Parker, *Uncle Sam in Barbary: A Diplomatic History*

Ralph Pezzullo, *Plunging into Haiti: Clinton, Aristide, and the Defeat of Diplomacy*

Nicholas Platt, *China Boys: How U.S. Relations with the PRC Began and Grew*

Howard B. Schaffer, *Ellsworth Bunker: Global Troubleshooter, Vietnam Hawk*

Ulrich Straus, *The Anguish of Surrender: Japanese POWs of World War II*

William G. Thom, *African Wars: A Defense Intelligence Perspective*

Nancy Bernkopf Tucker, Ed., *China Confidential: American Diplomats and Sino-American Relations, 1945–1996*

Pacific Gibraltar

U.S.– JAPANESE RIVALRY OVER
THE ANNEXATION OF HAWAI'I, 1885–1898

WILLIAM MICHAEL MORGAN

NAVAL INSTITUTE PRESS
Annapolis, Maryland

An ADST-DACOR Diplomats and Diplomacy Book

This book has been brought to publication with the generous assistance of Marguerite and Gerry Lenfest.

Naval Institute Press
291 Wood Road
Annapolis, MD 21402

Library of Congress Cataloging-in-Publication Data
Morgan, William Michael.
  Pacific Gibraltar: U.S.–Japanese rivalry over the annexation of Hawai`i, 1885–1898 / William Michael Morgan.
    p. cm. — (ADST-DACOR diplomats and diplomacy series)
  Includes bibliographical references and index.
  ISBN 978-1-59114-529-5 (hardcover : alk. paper) 1. Hawaii—Annexation to the United States.
2. Hawaii—History—Overthrow of the Monarchy, 1893. 3. Hawaii—History—1893–1900.
4. Hawaii—Emigration and immigration—History—19th century. 5. Japan—Emigration and immigration—History—19th century. 6. United States—Foreign relations—Japan. 7. Japan—Foreign relations—United States. I. Title.
  DU627.4.M58 2011
  996.9'028—dc22

                                                                        2010049923

Printed in the United States of America.

19 18 17 16 15 14 13 12 11   9 8 7 6 5 4 3 2 1
First printing

To my wife, Valerie

Contents

Acknowledgments

NO PROJECT SUCCEEDS WITHOUT HELP, and I benefited greatly from the counsel of many people. My teacher, the late Dr. Charles S. Campbell Jr., of the Claremont Graduate University, sparked my interest in the topic. My old friend Dr. Stuart Anderson warmly encouraged the project, as did Margery Thompson at the Association for Diplomatic Studies and Training. Professor David Painter gave helpful advice on early draft chapters. Dr. Henry J. Hendrix, Ambassador William Bodde, Professor Edward P. Crapol, and Professor Charles W. Calhoun read the entire manuscript, offering detailed advice and corrections. Despite all their help, remaining errors are of course my responsibility.

I received generous assistance from many archivists and librarians, especially at the U.S. National Archives, the manuscript division of the Library of Congress, the State Archives of Hawai`i, the Bishop Museum in Honolulu, the National Archives of the United Kingdom at Kew, and the National Diet Library of Japan. The staff of the Massachusetts Historical Society, the Minnesota Historical Society, and the Oregon Historical Society made it easy to sift through their valuable manuscript collections. Historians at the Naval Historical Center (NHC) in Washington, D.C., educated me about relevant files, especially those without finding aids. The cartography sections of the NHC and of the University of Hawai`i dug up many useful maps. Greg Olson, then a graduate student in history at the Claremont Graduate University, diligently tracked down a number of documents and articles that I could not find in Budapest during my assignment there. While I was assigned to Japan, reference librarians at the San Francisco Public Library repeatedly answered e-mail queries about U.S.–Hawai`i trade, most of which passed through San Francisco, and about travel and immigration with Honolulu.

Mark Wnukowski, former supervisor of the operations laboratory of the Brooklyn refinery of the Domino Sugar Corporation, educated me about sugar processing in general and helped me locate descriptions of the Dutch Standard System of grading sugar and late-nineteenth-century sugar-refining techniques. *Diplomatic History*, the journal of the Society for Historians of American Foreign Relations kindly permitted me to include an enlarged and revised version of my article "The Anti-Japanese Origins of the Hawaiian Annexation Treaty of 1897," from the winter 1982 edition.

Over the years of researching, writing, and revising, squeezed around my "day job" in various American embassies, I appreciated the continual interest and support from my Foreign Service colleagues, several of whom read draft chapters and tried hard to straighten out my arguments.

Last, but above all, I thank my wife, Valerie, for her unstinting love and encouragement from the moment, many years ago, when I first put words on paper.

A NOTE ON NAMES AND TERMS

With respect to participants in the story of annexation, I used the version of their names most commonly appearing in documents and letters. For example, the rebel Honolulu lawyer known to his friends as Bill Smith is W. O. Smith or William O. Smith in nearly all archival material, and therefore in my narrative. Japanese names are presented Japanese-style, family name first, unless the person in question, often a Japanese American scholar, has chosen to write the family name last.

Any description of Hawai`i's complex ethnic and national mix demands a definition of terms. I chose terms purely for descriptive convenience; they imply no political or other judgments. "Native Hawaiian" means pure-blooded descendents of the original Polynesian settlers of the islands. Part-Hawaiians, an important political group, were persons of mixed race, Native Hawaiian and some other. The monarchs and their supporters are called royalists. While I understand the argument that persons of any race or ethnicity born in Hawai`i can be considered Hawaiian, for clarity I do not refer to Hawaiian-born whites or Asians as "Hawaiian." The term "white rebels" refers to those whites who opposed the monarchy, especially during the revolution of 1893 and the period of the provisional government. Whites came from all over: North America, Europe, Australia, New Zealand. The term "Asian" refers almost exclusively to Chinese and Japanese because few persons from other Asian countries resided in Hawai`i in the 1890s.

Pacific Gibraltar

Introduction

HAWAI`I IS BOTH FAMILIAR AND, strangely, unknown. Few places are as recognizable to the entire world as Hawai`i. To Finns, Lebanese, and Kenyans, Hawai`i calls to mind a tropical paradise synonymous with fine weather, beaches, Polynesian culture, and the place where President Barack Obama spent many of his formative years. Tens of millions of tourists throng to the islands yearly. Hundreds of millions have seen popular Hawaiian-themed TV shows, such as *Magnum P.I.* and *Hawai`i Five-O*, and the dozens of movies filmed there.

Behind this common picture of a tropical paradise lurks a martial image, a less happy remembrance of war and death, of smoking, half-sunk metal giants burning alongside Ford Island. If the number of tourists who have visited Hawai`i is staggering, so too is the number of U.S. troops who have passed through Hawai`i in peacetime and during the country's wars. The huge O`ahu bases, among them Schofield Barracks, Hickam Air Force Base, Kāne`ohe Bay Marine Corps Air Station, and Wheeler Army Airfield, give Hawai`i the densest concentration of military might of any state or territory. Hawai`i has the most famous base in American history, and the most important American military outpost of the twentieth century—Pearl Harbor. There, astride the sunken battleship *Arizona*, the small white memorial, visited by many Japanese as well as Americans, commemorates the resting place of those killed during the surprise attack of December 7, 1941. Few Americans, indeed few humans, do not know of Hawai`i.

Yet despite the familiar twin images of paradise and war, Hawai`i is often unknown, unfamiliar. It seems to have appeared from nowhere, to have no history beyond our parents' or, at most, our grandparents' generations. When one thinks of Boston, one recalls the *Mayflower* and the Pilgrims. Virginia recalls Pocahontas, tobacco plantations, George Washington, and Thomas Jefferson. Pennsylvania

evokes Quakers, the Liberty Bell, and Benjamin Franklin. But who recalls pre–
World War II Hawai`i, much less the great warrior king, Kamehameha, a contemp-
orary of the Founding Fathers and, like them, a creator of a country?

Remote in historical memory, the islands are geographically isolated as well.
Most people do not realize that among places with a significant population,
Hawai`i is the most remote spot on the earth. Lodged in the middle of the vast
Pacific Ocean, Hawai`i is far from everything. Halfway into a flight from the
American mainland—two hours out, perhaps a thousand miles from takeoff—an
airliner is as far from a landing field, even an emergency field, as on any commer-
cial flight path in the world.

Not only is Hawai`i's isolation unnoticed, but its precise geographical location
is dimly grasped. Most people mistakenly believe the islands lie in the tropical
South Pacific. Hawai`i lies far to the north of the equator, roughly the latitude of
Hanoi or Mexico City. Because the North American mainland stretches westward across the northern ocean—a reach easily seen on a globe but not on our
schoolhouse Mercator maps—few people, aside from geographers and mariners,
realize that Hawai`i is closer to Eureka, California, near the Oregon border, than
to Los Angeles.

Put crudely, the Hawaiian chain lies in the middle of a vast watery no-man's
land in the north-central Pacific. Imagine a great circle with a radius of 2,200
miles and with Hawai`i at its center. Only on the rim of the circle, more than
2,000 miles distant, lie habitable areas of any significance. To the north lies the
nearly deserted Aleutian chain. More than 2,000 unbroken miles to the east lies
the American West Coast. Far to the south and southwest lie Samoa and the
Marshalls and Gilberts, and far to the west lies the Japanese archipelago. Aside
from lush Hawai`i, the great circle encompasses only atolls or mini-islands such as
Midway, Wake, and Johnston, which are only a few miles across, sparse of vegetation and water, incapable of supporting a population of any size, and devoid of
first-class harbors. Only at Hawai`i—with arable land, a fine climate, abundant
water, and a land area about the size of Connecticut's—could a sizable population
live. Only at Hawai`i could whalers rest and replenish in comfort. Only from Pearl
Harbor could a fleet protect the U.S. West Coast and project power westward
across the Pacific.

Beginning in the late nineteenth century, Hawai`i's commanding, unique
geographical position—a lush oasis in the midst of a watery desert—gave it an
unparalleled geostrategic significance, particularly in the days of coal-fired armored
warships. A fleet based at Hawai`i could control a huge expanse of the earth. The
Pacific Ocean is the largest geographical feature on the globe, covering 64,186,000

square miles, more than all the land area of the earth combined. That circle centered on Honolulu with a radius of 2,200 miles—roughly the distance from Hawai`i to the U.S. naval bases at San Francisco—contains 15,205,344 square miles. This represents, amazingly, about a twelfth (7.5 percent) of the earth's entire surface, and almost a quarter of the vast Pacific Ocean.[1] No other geostrategic position on the globe dominates so absolutely such a vast, heavily trafficked, and vital area. Other great bases, such as Gibraltar or Singapore, are either constricted by nearby land, or, like Malta, Scapa Flow, or Norfolk, control smaller areas. Yes, there is much that we do not know about Hawai`i.

I seek to explain the acquisition of what might be called America's Pacific Gibraltar, a prized naval bastion. Why, for the first time, did the United States acquire territory outside of North America? And why did that occur in July 1898, during the Spanish-American War? Did the war cause annexation? Was Hawaiian annexation unique, or similar to other 1890s American imperialist episodes? To answer these questions, I explore the interactions of the peoples, governments, and economies of the United States, Hawai`i, Japan, and Britain. I have not intended a general history, so the reader will not find much in the book about Hawai`i before King David Kalākaua. Nor have I written about the impact of annexation on the Hawaiian people. Instead I focus on causation, on forces and events and actions that bore directly on the 1893 revolution and the acquisition of the islands almost six years later.

Hawaiian annexation was the complex product of broad, global forces and local, individual actions. Working over many decades, transnational forces pulled Hawai`i into global economic flows, imperialist rivalries, immigration flows, technological developments, and disease migration. These broad forces—it seems obvious to label them globalism—significantly shaped the story of annexation. National factors, usually operating in one country, were also important. In the United States, a strong anti-imperialist tradition, the rise of a new, technology-driven navalism, a peculiar intellectual climate, and a desire to increase exports to absorb domestic overproduction affected the strength of the annexation drive and the timing of its ultimate success. International rivalries—traditional worries about British schemes in Hawai`i and a later, intense concern about Japanese intentions—caused constant policy adjustments. So did unexpected local developments, such as the 1893 Hawaiian revolution.

Explaining annexation, therefore, requires analysis at more than one level. Examining only broad global or transnational forces can yield conclusions that do not fit a particular event or episode, blurring or ignoring significant differences among them while forcing everything into an overarching pattern that supposedly "explains everything." Conversely, scrutinizing the details and emphasizing the differences among events leads to a string of episodes without a pattern, a kind of "explains nothing" interpretation. Both approaches have merits and flaws. Therefore, I have attempted an interlocking analysis on three levels: global, national, and local.

People populate all three levels. Global and national forces affect history through the actions of individuals. Hawai`i was brought into the global trade and economic system not by impersonal, invisible "forces" but by people such as the captains of trading vessels, the buyers of whale oil, and the sugar barons. The terrible scourges that decimated the Native Hawaiian people were brought by other humans, in their blood, in their lungs, on their skin. The huge increase in the Japanese population that scared Hawai`i's white minority government grew from decisions by government officials who decided that contract workers were the salvation of the sugar industry, and from the decisions of Japanese to leave their homeland to improve their economic position.

I have structured the book in rough chronological order. Some chapters focus on broad themes, such as trade reciprocity and the rise of the sugar industry, the emergence of new naval technologies and strategies, and Japanese immigration. Other chapters are chronological narratives where that level of detail is required to fully understand events. Like most tidal shifts in old patterns of behavior, Hawaiian annexation had multiple causes. Hawai`i's desire to be annexed and America's desire to do so emerged from different impulses on the American and Hawaiian sides, modified constantly by interaction with each other and with Japan and Great Britain. The mix and strength of those impulses changed over time.

Although I have certainly relied on the vast secondary literature, I have made fresh, provocative analyses of the most disputed episodes in the story of annexation: the revolution of 1893 and the landing of American troops, the abortive restoration attempt, the uproar over Japanese immigration and the 1897 U.S.-Japan crisis, and the consummation of annexation in the middle of the Spanish-American War.

A constant theme of this book is that, although economic and ideological arguments facilitated annexation, even more important on the U.S. side was a new and enhanced appreciation for Hawai`i's strategic value that emerged from the revolution in naval technology and strategy in the final two decades of the century. I define strategic factors as the nexus of (a) naval modernization and expansion; (b) the implications for tactics and strategy of advances in naval technology, especially coal-fueled steam propulsion, armor, and long-range guns with explosive shells; and (c) the growing military value of the only protected harbor in the North Pacific.

Another enduring topic is the competition for power among the Native Hawaiian, white, and Asian communities. The white-dominated Republic of Hawai`i's desire to be annexed grew not from the strategic, economic, ideological, and other themes that motivated the United States but from the struggle for power and wealth in the islands.

A final persistent theme is a growing American rivalry with Japan over Hawai`i that underlay the final annexation drive. Japan's place in annexation is often overlooked. Indelibly linked to Hawai`i by the Pearl Harbor attack of 1941, Japan played a central role in the American acquisition of the islands forty-three years before the strike on Battleship Row.

This is a work of history, not of public policy. Of course the two are related. The making of public policy is often informed by what participants accept as the most important and relevant historical facts. From that factual array they forge historical judgments on which public policy may rest.[2] Hawaiian annexation is intertwined with twenty-first-century Hawaiian politics, and with the present Hawaiian sovereignty movement. In that political drama, the political views of individual actors and the actions of the federal government rest on historical judgments about how and why annexation occurred. For example, the 1993 congressional "Apology Resolution," which offers an apology to Native Hawaiians for the overthrow of the Kingdom of Hawai`i, rests on several historical assessments. The resolution says that American officials "conspired" with white rebels and landed troops ("invaded") intentionally to "intimidate" the royalists, and that the insurrection would have "failed" without that American support.[3] Testing those assertions is the task of the historian. My analysis shows these assertions are wrong in an absolute sense but sometimes partly right in a larger sense. U.S. minister to Hawai`i John L. Stevens did not conspire, but his interaction with white rebels was close and highly improper. The United States did not land troops to intimidate the queen—they were landed to position themselves ashore to maintain public order if needed—but the way in which American officials handled the details of the landing caused timid royalists to feel intimidated.

Some in 1898 and some today assert that annexation was illegal because most Native Hawaiians opposed it and because no popular referendum was held in Hawai`i. That no referendum was held is incontestably true. It is virtually certain that a big majority of Native Hawaiians preferred an independent monarchy. A historian might also point out that although some antiannexationists, including President Grover Cleveland, called for a referendum, polling the inhabitants of targets for acquisition was definitely not the practice of nineteenth-century European, Japanese, or American imperialists.

In the twenty-first century, with differing sensibilities and standards, whether the federal government should do something about all this is the realm of politics. It is the task of politicians to determine whether a corrective is required and, if so, to devise an appropriate remedy. I leave this present-day arena to others.

❦

CHAPTER 1

Hawai`i on the Cusp of Revolution

A s the USS *Boston* approached O`ahu early on Saturday, January 14, 1893, the crew's first glimpse of land had been the 1,208-foot summit of Koko Head. The warship would soon be in the middle of a political struggle every bit as fiery as that ancient volcano had once been. The *Boston*'s central place in the overthrow of Queen Lili`uokalani three days after its arrival would make it the best-known warship put in the service of American gunboat diplomacy. Carrying the U.S. minister to Hawai`i, the elderly and irritable John L. Stevens, the *Boston* was returning from a ten-day voyage to Hilo and Lahaina. As the cruiser rounded the O`ahu coast south of Diamond Head and neared Honolulu's tricky, twisting channel, edged by sharp reefs and marked by buoys, the murky ocean depths changed to clear, emerald water, beneath which could be seen glistening rocky sand and living coral. At the bell buoy a mile out from the channel's entrance, the water was about seventy feet deep. The water was so clear that the men could see starfish on the bottom and schools of brightly colored fish. To port, a wooden pedestrian causeway stretched from a landing pier in the inner harbor over a kilometer of mud flats, bare at low tide, to the immigration station. This causeway was called the China Bridge because tens of thousands of Chinese and Japanese immigrants had marched across it to present their papers. To starboard was the Marine Railway and the small boathouse of the late king, David Kalākaua. Off-watch sailors lining the rails inhaled perfumed breezes redolent of moist vegetation and plentiful spring blooms, even on that winter day. Mabel Craft, an observant twenty-six-year-old whose book about her 1898 visit is one of most illuminating traveler's accounts, said the breezes carried the scent of "a land of a thousand Junes," locked perpetually in late spring.[1]

Moored at last, the *Boston*, like all arriving vessels, had been surrounded by young Hawaiian boys who dove for coins. At the boat landings were the customary structures of a bustling port: warehouses, shipping companies, machine shops, law offices, and bars. Looking from the cruiser's deck over the port buildings and toward the mountains, Honolulu appeared far less an urban metropolis than a sprinkling of two- and three-story buildings poking out of thick vegetation. Nevertheless, amid the greenery was a modern downtown area of four square miles occupied by nearly thirty thousand people. Honolulu had macadamized streets, an opera house, street trams, electricity, and telephone service. Given its perfect weather and newfangled amenities, for people with money it was surely one of the most comfortable places to live in the world.

But the modernity and pleasant living conditions that surprised white visitors were not the reality for all, or even most, Honolulu residents. Honolulu's smiling public face masked deep antagonisms. The city mirrored the incredible economic, political, and demographic changes that swept Hawai`i in the nineteenth century. Honolulu had been, and would soon be again, the setting for potentially dangerous confrontations between great powers. For centuries peopled solely by hundreds of thousands of Polynesians, Hawai`i suddenly became one of the most ethnically diverse societies in the world. Polynesians now comprised only about a third of the population, due to the rampaging of smallpox, typhoid, cholera, and other diseases to which the long-isolated Native Hawaiians had little resistance, and to the massive, recent immigration of Asians and whites drawn by the booming sugar industry's need for workers.

That morning, Queen Lili`uokalani made a fateful move. She had just skillfully maneuvered into office a cabinet of four hand-picked men. Around ten o'clock, she told them she would proclaim on her own authority a new constitution to strengthen royal powers. Three hours later, her attempted proclamation triggered a revolution that cost her throne.

As she talked with her ministers, the *Boston*, moored three hundred meters from Brewer's Wharf, lay literally and figuratively in the very middle of the uproar. Its return to Honolulu with the American minister aboard and at the precise moment the revolution began has always been highly suspect. Its role in the revolt would give the *Boston* and its crew a place in virtually every history written about nineteenth-century American imperialism.

But the steam-powered cruiser was already well known when it arrived in the islands in August 1892. It was the "B" of the famous "ABCD" ships—the cruisers *Atlanta*, *Boston*, *Chicago*, and the dispatch boat *Dolphin*—the first modern vessels of the New Steel Navy authorized in the mid-1880s. The *Boston* fell into a class called a "protected cruiser" because immense coal bunkers surrounding the steam propulsion system, magazines, and other critical internal spaces protected these vital innards, as did an internal horizontal armored deck. Unable to fight toe to toe with fully armored vessels, protected cruisers were a short-lived design. The Navy built only a dozen. Indeed the *Boston*, somewhat obsolete only six years after its 1887 commissioning, would be decommissioned in December 1893 for an extensive refitting. If not a high-seas warrior, the cruiser had substantial ability to project power ashore, less by its two 8-inch and six 6-inch guns than by a 269-man crew from which Captain Gilbert Wiltse could assemble a sizable landing party, called "the battalion," and put them ashore with the ship's boats: a steam launch, a sailing launch, two cutters, and several smaller craft.[2]

The most famous vessel to call at Hawai`i, however, was not the *Boston* or even Captain James Cook's *Resolution;* it was a giant canoe whose name, if it had one, has disappeared into the mists of time. Historians sometimes write, as a kind of shorthand, that Cook, the legendary British explorer of the Pacific, "discovered" Hawai`i. Even as they pen those words, they know very well that Cook found the islands teeming with people whose ancestors had arrived long before. Cook's 1778 voyage represented the second or so-called European discovery of Hawai`i. The islands were first discovered in the third or fourth century AD by several Polynesian explorers, or even a single expedition sailing huge canoes from the Marquesas Islands. As a demonstration, Fijians built a replica of those ancient canoes in 1842. The replica suggests that at least some Oceanic peoples, and likely many of them, possessed skills needed to construct large craft capable of long voyages. The Fijian replica was a huge double canoe, 118 feet long, 24 feet wide, with a 6-foot-deep hull made of heavy planking with carefully carved joints. The monster had a weather deck and shelter for passengers. The 50-foot mast had a boom about 75 feet long supporting a triangular lateen sail of matting. Capable of a steady seven knots, the huge vessel could easily carry several dozen people with supplies enough to colonize new lands.

Michael Dougherty speculates that drought-caused famine or the pressures of overpopulation drove Marquesans to attempt a long, perilous voyage to a new land. They did not know that Hawai`i existed; they did not know that they would have to cross 2,500 miles of ocean, navigating by the stars, the sun and moon, and by wind and wave action when clouds obscured the heavens. Loaded in their canoes were nutritional building blocks for a new life: sugarcane, taro and breadfruit roots, banana shoots, sweet potatoes, coconuts, chickens, hogs, and dogs.[3] And there was no going back if things went badly. Winds and currents in the north-central Pacific made a return voyage to the Marquesas almost impossible, though there is some evidence of bilateral trade between Tahiti and Hawai`i during the twelfth to fourteenth centuries, which allowed additional immigration and technology imports. One can imagine how joyous the first journeyers, in the vast Pacific, must have been when, after anxious weeks of sailing northward, they spied the great Hawaiian mountains jutting above the horizon. Whoever these first Hawaiians were, they did not lack bravery and a sense of adventure, and they were clearly among the greatest seamen in human history.

Over their centuries of isolation, Hawaiians developed a carefully ordered society based on the `ohana, or extended family. At the top of each `ohana was the high chief, or ali`i. The ali`i and family were the hereditary rulers of the group. The land was divided into ahupua`a, or large strips running from the inland peaks to the sea. Each `ohana's chief held title to the group lands. Agriculture and fishing, though low-tech, employed a sophisticated system of collective effort. Lacking metal tools and large animals, Hawaiians used their hands and wooden digging sticks. Nearly all the population settled on the lowlands, near the sea. Freshwater, wood, and fertile ground allowed cultivation of taro, sweet potatoes, and other crops. Fish formed the main protein of their diet, but pigs, dogs, and chickens were occasionally consumed. The kapu (taboo) system determined tasks. Men raised taro, a complex process in a land where rainfall and water courses varied wildly due to winds and altitude. Men built networks of dams, irrigation ditches, and terraces. Women and men both raised sweet potatoes, the second-most important crop. Skilled craftsmen built the heavy canoes used for deep-sea fishing, itself a specialized occupation. Hawaiians built many fish ponds along the tidal flats. At high tide, the seawater covered the low, hand-built stone walls. As the tide ran out through openings in the walls, Hawaiians netted the openings and snared many fish. The historian Edward Beechert noted that Kamehameha I needed ten thousand men just to repair the mile-long wall of one huge fish trap.[4]

Centuries of a healthful lifestyle of strenuous work and play and a good diet made the Hawaiians a large, powerful people. The wonderful climate and a love of swimming, surfing, and canoeing also helped mold the impressive Hawaiian physique. For all their power, the Hawaiians could be gentle as well. Hawaiians were unique among Polynesians by making their supreme deity, Lono, the god of peace and rainfall and crops, rather than the god of war. Ancient Hawaiians disliked aggressiveness and acquisitiveness.[5] This cultural inheritance later worked to their disadvantage when dealing with westerners with unlimited aggression and lust for possessions. Whatever its supposed flaws by present-day standards—the subordination of women via the taboo system is perhaps the most discordant to modern ears—Old Hawai'i functioned well and gave order and structure and meaning to the lives of the populace. People had enough to eat, and their health was generally good.

The unified Kingdom of Hawai'i, which Queen Lili'uokalani ruled, or over which she reigned—this was the essence of the struggle between royalists and rebels—did not exist when Cook called at Kealakekua Bay. But the kingdom's legendary founder, the great Kamehameha, was among the chiefs who met Cook. Over many years of warfighting and politicking, Kamehameha I became ruler of the island of Hawai'i, vanquished the leaders of the other islands, and by 1810 welded their domains into one country. Even as he forged his kingdom, the diseases and social and economic disruptions of Western intrusion began to work their immensely destructive course.

Few if any isolated communities survived intact their collision with the rest of the world.[6] Hawai'i was no exception. During the century following Cook's arrival, much of traditional Hawaiian civilization was destroyed. Despite positive achievements, missionary activity helped delegitimize traditional values. This made it easier for disease, imperialist pressure, and the attraction of the new to destroy the old way of life, both enticing and compelling Native Hawaiians to enter, first, the Western economy of the port cities and, through them, the global economy. Hawaiians were ill prepared—by their upbringing, by their leaders, and by their self-appointed teachers, the whites—to adapt quickly to the globalized political economy. They lacked capital and appropriate skills. Racial prejudice made it very difficult for them to get a fair shake in either the local or global economies. So rapidly thrust into the urban lifestyle, they were vulnerable to many "outsider" diseases as well as unhealthful temptations such as excess drink.

As contact with Hawai'i deepened, U.S. policy rested on the principle that no foreign nation should interfere with Hawaiian independence or, better said, with American influence. In 1842, watching the strong British and French presence in the Pacific, President John Tyler and Secretary of State Daniel Webster formulated the first explicit policy toward Hawai'i. Tyler declared that the United States would look with "dissatisfaction" upon any foreign move to control the islands. Webster quickly informed Great Britain and France of America's new policy of noninterference.[7] He instructed the first U.S. commissioner to monitor foreign agents and warn King Kamehameha III to avoid antagonizing "powers whose policy is to . . . multiply their colonies abroad."[8]

As Webster penned those words, the British had already seized Hawai`i. In February 1843, when the king declined an ultimatum to settle unresolved disputes, Lord George Paulet's troops forced the king to cede the islands to Britain. Paulet ruled from February to July. The United States warned Britain that "there is something so entirely peculiar in the relations between this little commonwealth and ourselves that we might even feel justified . . . in interfering by force."[9] Britain, with no immediate designs on the islands, disavowed Lord Paulet and ended the occupation.[10] In 1843 Britain and France jointly declared that they would never seize of any of the Hawaiian Islands, thereby avoiding a challenge to Tyler's doctrine that no foreign power, other than the United States, should control Hawai`i.

Despite their declaration, the French soon threatened Hawaiian independence. To force Hawai`i to settle several disputes, Admiral Legoarant de Tromelin issued the "Ten Demands" in 1849. The demands were mostly minor—for example, the use of French to transact diplomacy and the discipline of schoolboys who disrupted a French church service. When Hawai`i refused, the French occupied the old fort, the customs house, and other waterfront buildings for ten days. Having suitably punished the Hawaiians, Tromelin departed. A Hawaiian delegation went to France but failed to settle the dispute. In December 1850 a new French commissioner, Emile Perrin, with whom the Hawaiians had negotiated fruitlessly in Paris, pressed the ten demands, backed by the corvette *Serieuse*. The tone grew so nasty that the king and privy council sought U.S. help. On March 11, 1851, two of the king's ministers gave U.S. commissioner Luther Severance a document placing the islands under American protection. If necessary, the *Vandalia* would land U.S. troops and confront the *Serieuse*. The French moderated their demands and settled with Hawai`i.[11]

Tyler's successors upheld his noninterference policy. James Polk pushed a treaty of amity and commerce finally ratified in 1850 in Zachary Taylor's administration.[12] Taylor reaffirmed that no foreign power could possess Hawai`i.[13] Franklin Pierce's secretary of state, William Marcy, believed strategic acquisitions helped expand American trade. Marcy had his commissioner negotiate an annexation treaty in 1854 with King Kamehameha III, an ardent advocate of immediate statehood for Hawai`i.[14] The king's death aborted the annexation effort as his successor, Kamehameha IV, sought instead a guarantee of independence from the United States, Britain, and France. The United States squelched this multilateral approach and declared it would protect Hawai`i by keeping warships near the islands.[15] With annexation dead, the Pierce administration thought a reciprocity agreement would boost U.S. influence.[16] But domestic sugar planters opposed duty-free Hawaiian sugar and killed an 1856 reciprocity treaty.[17] Henceforth, the United States adhered to the Tyler Doctrine: that no foreign power should have a paramount interest. This commitment never wavered an inch and was still American policy in 1893 as the *Boston* moored in Honolulu harbor, in a city that did not exist a hundred years before.

Although Honolulu was already an important port, it was brand new. Unlike Venice, Alexandria, London, and other ancient ports, or younger ones such as Boston and Baltimore, Honolulu was a nineteenth-century artifact. Until deep-draft western traders arrived, no port was needed. O'ahu is fringed with coral reefs lying slightly below the ocean's surface. Ancient Hawaiians easily crossed the reefs in their shallow draft canoes. In 1792 or 1793, Captain William Brown discovered a small harbor where the Nu'uanu River's strong flow of cool water retarded coral growth and created a narrow path to the sea, eighteen to forty-two feet deep. Currents and winds made it impossible to sail heavy vessels directly into the port. For many years, ships were warped into port by a line attached to an anchor dropped ahead of the ship, or to a point on shore. The crew then winched the ship up to the anchor and repeated the process. Sometimes ship's boats towed the mother vessel into port, but as traffic increased, Hawaiians seized a business opportunity. A Russian ship calling in 1816 recorded being pulled into port at a speed of three knots by eight double canoes, each with twenty brawny Hawaiian paddlers. Later a small steam tug, the *Pele*, came into service. Even for the tug, the morning calm was the easiest time to enter the channel, and the tug's crew and other port workers started work early. Catering to the early risers was H. J. Nolte's Beaver Saloon, a favorite waterfront bar open from three o'clock in the morning for hot and cold meals; tea and coffee; ginger ale and soda water; and cigars, cigarettes, pipes, and tobaccos.

In Honolulu's first century, traders, whalers, and sugar magnates successively influenced its development. In the 1790s Hawai'i became an essential stop in a triangular fur trade route. Traders spent the summer collecting beaver and other furs along the North American coast, then sailed to Honolulu to replenish for the onward voyage to China to sell the pelts. Fur traders spurred the development of the port services, such as mechanics, sail makers, carpenters, longshoremen, and harbor pilots. Sandalwood exports to China became a good business for the ten to fifteen years it took to cut down the accessible trees. As foreign commerce bloomed, the harbor area attracted more residents, although it was dry and dusty compared to Waikīkī, where many *ali'i* lived.[18]

More than five hundred whalers based in Hawai'i in the early 1850s. They procured whale oil for lamps, candles, soap, and leather waterproofing. They had an outsized economic impact because of the quantity and quality of their purchases.

While traders took on provisions for two or three weeks' onward sailing, whalers loaded vast amounts for their months at sea. Many goods had to be imported from the United States, and Hawaiian retailers profited. Blacksmiths, sail makers, mechanics, and carpenters flourished. Whalers under refit remained for weeks or months, so bars, brothels, and eateries sprang up to cater to the hundreds of sailors ashore at any given time. Whaling infused a lot of money into the economy, but competition from other oils soon curtailed the industry. In 1852 the whaling fleet took 373,450 barrels of oil; eight years later, only 63,000.

The Civil War dramatically but temporarily increased the demand for Hawaiian sugar. It substituted for Louisiana sugar in the kitchens of the North and in the rations of its blue-coated soldiers. When southern sugar returned to the postwar market, the sugar price plummeted and the Hawaiian industry withered. The problem was that Hawaiian sugar was foreign, subject to duty, and distant, with high transportation costs. Although sugar remained Hawai`i's chief export, and despite small successes in exporting coffee and other agricultural products, the economy muddled along for some years.

`Iolani Palace, the queen's residence, was the city's spiritual heart. Completed in 1882 at the then-astounding cost of $350,000, `Iolani Palace was a gorgeous piece of craftsmanship, the city's most famous building. The grounds occupied one city block. Among the outbuildings were a large bungalow used as a guesthouse and stone-walled barracks for the king's household guard. King, Richards, and Merchant streets merged in a triangular area oddly called Palace Square, often used for public gatherings.

Across King Street from the palace stood Ali`iōlani Hale, often called the Government Building, an ornate stone edifice housing the legislature, the judiciary, and the royal bureaucracy. Beside Ali`iōlani Hale but separated by a small lane called Mililani Street was the large Music Hall, or Opera House.[19] Just south of the Music Hall was a much smaller building, Arion Hall. The palace, Ali`iōlani Hale, and Arion Hall would become key sites in the revolution.

At first glance, Honolulu appeared a pleasant, tree-lined city with most of the modern conveniences—electricity, ice, telephones—of San Francisco, Paris, or Boston, though on a much smaller scale. Few tourists, and not many white residents, looked closely at the way most people lived, though no one could miss the ethnic diversity of the bustling streets. Honolulu was the most diverse town in an archipelago whose population of 109,000 was itself one of the world's most diverse. In 1896 Honolulu had 29,920 people, of which 11,386 were Native Hawaiians and part-Hawaiians. Whites, usually labeled simply Europeans but made up mostly of Americans, Portuguese, British, Germans, Frenchmen, and Norwegians, totaled

9,573. There were 2,174 Japanese and 6,484 Chinese. Most Asians jammed into Chinatown, roughly between Nu`uanu Street and the Nu`uanu River and mountainward from King Street.[20]

Honolulu's social life, distorted by differences in wealth, ethnicity, class, and occupation and rarely rejuvenated by visitors, was akin to that of a cliquish, snobbish mainland town of perhaps 5,000 persons. Georges Sauvin observed that "everyone keeps an eye on everyone else, criticizes, is jealous, invents tales about neighbors, falls to quarreling, becomes reconciled."[21] Wealthy Native Hawaiians and white foreigners dominated the social life of the elite. The most influential Native Hawaiians were royalty—the *ali`i*—along with well-to-do or politically influential pure-blooded Hawaiians and part-Hawaiians, such as two of the queen's January 1893 cabinet, Samuel Parker and John Colburn. White businessmen, lawyers, and bankers tended to be part of the elite.[22]

Native Hawaiians filled many jobs: civil servants, perhaps clerks or road repair supervisors, or, occasionally, cabinet ministers. A few became lawyers, preachers, or teachers. Most worked as laborers. Nearly two thousand worked on sugar plantations, many as *luna*, or overseers of labor gangs. Many port stevedores were powerfully built Hawaiians. Several thousand were sailors. The extensive interisland commerce conducted by steamers and sailing vessels was chiefly crewed by Hawaiians, as were the hordes of low-draft rowboats that ferried sugar, carted to the water from mills scattered around the archipelago, to ships outside the reefs.

Many still lived by subsistence, much as they had lived before the whites came. Largely beyond the white man's economy and rarely observed by journal-keeping travelers, they were not much thought about by the white community. Lamenting the loss of the old ways, Sauvin was among the few who did not consider what he called the Americanization of Hawai`i a wonderful process. He said Americans "impose upon the other people their own customs, their religion, and a large measure of their American laws and institutions."[23] One might argue that this romantic view conflicted with the hard fact that the nineteenth-century world was not as God fashioned it. Parts of the earth had been conquered again and again, and the inhabitants of a given spot in the 1890s were quite likely not the inhabitants of earlier millennia, or even preceding centuries. Even the climate changed, as shown by the increasing aridity of what was once the fertile crescent of the Middle East. An observer was merely taking a snapshot of an unending process of change. To this argument Sauvin had a good retort. He questioned the "rightness" of the process by the standards of his own day: "We have the right to ask whether progress is a positive thing or merely relative. . . . It will prove difficult to explain on what grounds of superiority one people should absorb another—claiming 'civilization' as the pretext." He concluded: "It is utterly inexcusable to destroy the customs and traditions of a race."[24]

His criticism did not go nearly far enough, for the processes of "civilization," "modernization," and "globalization" did more than destroy traditional Hawaiian values and force Native Hawaiians, in the name of "progress," to convert to a new way of life. Whites liked to think benignly of Hawai`i as simply a harsh school for discarding old ways and learning new ones. It was much, much worse than that. It was literally a land of death, where Western encroachment caused the near physical extinction of the Hawaiian people. From 1778 to 1898 and after, Native Hawaiians disappeared at a horrific rate. Reeling from Western diseases, they died in multitudes, not only in dreadful epidemics, such as one in 1804 that killed ten thousand people in two months, but also in thousands of lonely individual illnesses. Survivors, weakened by repeated microbial invasion and psychic distress at the loss of family and friends as well as their old system of values, produced few children. Many of those youngsters sickened and died before adolescence.

Measuring the loss of life is difficult. No one knows how many lived in Ancient Hawai`i; there is only the imprecision of travelers' accounts, beginning with Cook's journals and those of crew members such as the *Resolution*'s sailing master, William Bligh. New England missionaries conducted rough counts in 1831 and 1835. More accurate surveys began in 1850, usually at six-year intervals.

Given scanty evidence, a noisy debate rages about the size of the pre-Cook Hawaiian population. Estimates emerge not only from physical evidence but also from analysts' assumptions, such as when the islands were settled, how many settlers came, and whether there were subsequent immigrants. Anthropologists Tom Dye and Eric Komori studied the residues of ancient cooking fires from 606 sites. They assumed that these sites represented permanent camps, dated the samples by carbon-14 analysis, and plotted their geographic distribution. They found no evidence of fires before AD 300. They concluded that the number of inhabitants, based on the number of cooking fires, increased sharply from AD 900–1300, grew more slowly during 1300–1600, and then leveled off. Their analysis suggests that Hawai`i was not settled by a couple of canoes full of adventurers but by skilled sailors guiding many canoes over a long period, perhaps even making round trips from the Marquesas. Their study suggests that the pre-1778 population grew 0.27 percent annually. At this rate, 771 persons in AD 300 would produce 100,000 inhabitants in 1778.[25]

David Stannard asserts a 1778 population of at least 800,000. He reviewed traveler's reports, calculated the potential productivity of the land and the sea— what he called the land's "carrying power"—and used theories and facts about massive declines in other indigenous populations suddenly exposed to European civilization.[26] Critics of Stannard's powerful work take issue with the conclusions he drew from the writings of early visitors, and with the reliability of theories about supposedly similar experiences of American Indians, Africans, or Polynesians. The critics doubt Stannard's assertion that 400,000 Hawaiians, half the population, perished in the first twenty-five years after Cook's arrival. The argument goes on, although most writers still accept a figure of 200,000–300,000 for the pre-Cook population.

Whatever the number of inhabitants in 1778, there is no doubt that the Native Hawaiians suffered a catastrophic decline after that date. They began to sicken and die almost immediately. By 1823, only forty-five years after whites came, the population dropped to about 135,000, which means that more than half of all Hawaiians perished (assuming a pre-Cook population of 300,000). A hundred years after Cook, in 1878, there were only 44,088 pure-blooded Polynesians, and this number fell again to 31,019 just before annexation. It matters little whether those alive in 1896 represented 3.8 percent of the original inhabitants (Stannard's estimate) or 10.3 percent (using the most common estimate). Whatever the starting point, the process was the same, and just as horrific. Hawaiians perished by many tens of thousands for more than a century.

Why did they die so rapidly? Oswald A. Bushnell, in his masterful work *The Gifts of Civilization*, theorizes that centuries of isolation and inbreeding made them extraordinarily vulnerable to new diseases. The small number of the first Polynesian settlers created a tiny gene pool. Within a few generations, it would have been very hard to find mates who were not at least distant blood relatives. The lack of social taboos against marriage between blood relatives that visitors noticed after 1778 was almost certainly in place over the preceding centuries. Interbreeding, through a process called gene drift, may have enhanced both weaknesses and strengths in the gene pool, although Bushnell cautions that gene drift may not influence human populations as significantly as it affects plants, animals, and microorganisms. Gene drift may have given a large fraction of the population unhelpful traits such as agammaglobulinemia, an inability to produce enough gamma globulin, from which the body derives disease-fighting antibodies. During centuries of isolation, the absence of new diseases hid this immune system defect, but those Native Hawaiians with the trait would have been helpless before newly introduced diseases.[27]

For perhaps fifteen hundred years, the ocean's expanse spared Hawai'i most of humankind's worst diseases. The ancient Hawaiian language lacked words to describe the diseases that decimated the people after 1778, powerful evidence that those maladies were not present in Hawaiʻi. The first voyagers surely brought disease with them, but as the centuries passed, their virulence abated as the population adapted. They suffered considerably from fleas, lice, and especially from scabies mites. They were bothered by rheumatism, arthritis, and dental disease. But before 1778, they were free of syphilis, gonorrhea, bubonic plague, cholera, typhoid fever, smallpox, influenza, malaria, typhus, yellow fever, dysentery, measles, and leprosy. Foreigners brought all of these.

The passing of the old social order increased the risk of Native Hawaiians. They entered the money economy, mixing with disease-carrying foreigners. Some abandoned, in the congested towns, healthy habits developed over the centuries, such as the practice of eliminating body waste far from dwellings and water sources. They were exposed to venereal disease brought by whites. Women retained the habit of feeding babies by prechewing food and placing it, mixed with saliva, into their infants' mouths. With mothers ill themselves, this custom accelerated infant mortality. Even so-called childhood diseases were deadly, such as measles, which killed Kamehameha II and his queen during their state visit to Britain in 1824. As Bushnell explained, "explorers, traders, trappers, and missionaries have been much more effective as sowers of diseases than as sharers of knowledge or savers of souls."[28] The interaction of foreigner and Native Hawaiian, given the latter's unequal economic and social position and enhanced vulnerability to new diseases, was a great human tragedy—the near destruction of a people. As Robert Louis Stevenson put it: "The white man's civilization was scarcely less fatal than the white man's bullet."[29] Medical science could not help because physicians did not know that microorganisms caused disease, and few medications were effective against the scourges.

The demographics of the population changed rapidly, but in ways not immediately obvious. Between 1850 and 1896 the total island population grew from 84,165 to 109,020. This 30 percent increase masked massive population loss and gain. The Native Hawaiian population continued to collapse while the white and Asian population soared. In 1850 only 1.9 percent were foreign-born, but by 1896 the foreign-born represented 51 percent, and an additional 13 percent were people of foreign (non-Polynesian) ancestry born in Hawaiʻi. On the cusp of the revolution, Native Hawaiians constituted only about a third of the people, greatly weakening their political power.[30]

The sad and terrible decline of Native Hawaiians to minority status greatly shaped the environment in which the revolution would occur. Equally important was a rise in the power of foreigners, itself the consequence of the Hawaiian-American Reciprocity Treaty of 1876 that allowed the creation of the world's most efficient sugar industry.

CHAPTER 2

Pearl Harbor and Reciprocity

Zephaniah S. Spaulding's career in secret intelligence lasted less than a year. Arriving in Hawai`i in December 1867, he posed as an investor in cotton lands while he wrote confidential reports for Secretary of State William Seward. No one paid any attention to the young man with curly blond hair, acne-scarred skin, and ears that lay close to his head. But he elicited the first serious American interest in the Pearl River lagoon, several miles west of Honolulu. In the 1870s and 1880s, the right to develop a base at the Pearl River, and the right to deny it to other powers, became a key factor in the debate over reciprocity, the chief politicoeconomic issue driving Hawaiian–American relations.

While preparing a reciprocity treaty for the Senate, Seward wondered what Hawai`i thought about outright annexation. Perhaps Seward believed a private citizen could gather information more freely than the American legation, or perhaps he was simply finding a job for the son of an influential congressman. He gave Zephaniah Spaulding a secret mission: assess how passage of the reciprocity treaty might affect Hawai`i's political and economic situation. Spaulding's masquerade ended when he took a regular job in the legation until the incoming Grant administration replaced him in 1869. Liking the islands, he bought a Maui sugar plantation with two other men, married the daughter of one, and remained active in Hawaiian politics well into the 1890s.

Hawaiian reciprocity meant waiving American duties on Hawaiian sugar in exchange for Hawaiian concessions on imported American goods. But political considerations were also important, for in economic terms the United States would benefit far less than Hawai`i. Tariff revenue would drop and American sugar growers would complain about increased competition. Hence, many politicians saw little commercial advantage in Hawaiian reciprocity.

After the reciprocity treaty failed in June 1870—only half the Senate voted for the pact—Spaulding knew that reciprocity must grab Washington's attention to succeed. In letters to President Ulysses S. Grant and Secretary of State Hamilton Fish, Spaulding linked reciprocity to a new naval station. Spaulding claimed Hawai`i would gladly grant a ninety-nine-year lease for a naval yard.

The military potential of the vast Pearl River lagoon so fascinated foreigners that even professional strategists began to speak of "Pearl Harbor" when, in reality, Pearl Harbor did not exist. It was merely a notion, a name attached to a place that was far from being a usable harbor, for the reefs at its mouth allowed entry only by small sailing craft that drew little water. Military men took an early interest. The British warship *Blonde* surveyed the Pearl River in 1824–25 and informed the Admiralty that if an entrance were cut through the coral reefs, the entire British Navy could anchor. In 1840 U.S. explorer Lieutenant Charles Wilkes found that the coral bar at the mouth of the lagoon, where it opened to the sea, lay only fifteen feet deep. Once past the bar, the water was deep. Once developed, the lagoon would be the "best and most capacious harbor in the Pacific." Not that the United States itself was moving any faster to develop bases on its own soil. As late as 1851 the Navy had no naval base on the West Coast.[1]

As coal-fired ships became more common, the Navy sought overseas coal depots, if not full-fledged bases. The Confederate raider *Shenandoah*, which captured or destroyed fifty-six ships, could have done much more damage if it could have recoaled at Hawai`i instead of distant Sydney. In 1867 the United States claimed Midway, an atoll a thousand miles northwest of Honolulu. Tiny Midway, only two square miles, proved inadequate as a harbor.[2] The American legation in Honolulu often urged reciprocity. Secretary Fish read these dispatches to the cabinet, but the only reaction was silence. Fish grumbled: "A matter must be imminent to engage attention."[3]

In mid-1872, something "imminent"—a dangerous crisis with Great Britain— impelled the first serious examination of the military aspects of Hawaiian ports.[4] Several grievances poisoned U.S.–British relations. First, the Fenians, a U.S.-based Irish group, hoped to free Ireland by provoking war. They raided into Canada. The American government seemed unwilling to stop them. Second, because the 1846

Oregon Treaty did not detail the Puget Sound border, both nations claimed the San Juan Islands and stationed troops there. A third dispute grew from U.S. abrogation in 1866 of the Marcy-Elgin Treaty, which gave Canadians some free trade provisions for allowing Americans to fish Canada's rich waters. The Canadians withdrew the privileges and patrolled the fishing grounds, but Americans armed their boats and continued to fish.

The fourth issue was the touchiest: the *Alabama* claims. During the Civil War, Britain's public neutrality masked a pro-Southern bias, or so went the accusations. London allowed shipwrights to build Confederate cruisers. Worse, the British permitted the ships—including the *Alabama*, *Florida*, and *Shenandoah*—to leave port to attack American shipping. The raiders, including those not built in Britain, destroyed 257 Union ships and forced 700 others under foreign flags. The merchant marine shrank by two-thirds. After the war, the U.S. demanded compensation for "direct claims" for the merchanters lost to the raiders.

These four irritants contained the potential for civilian violence and military action. Negotiations went in fits and starts. Seward negotiated the Johnson-Clarendon Convention to address the claims issue, but the Senate rejected it 54–1. Charles Sumner, the chair of the Foreign Relations Committee, blasted the pact for failing to address "indirect claims." He charged that unneutral British behavior not only caused direct losses, which he pegged at a wild $125 million, far more than other estimates, but also prolonged the Civil War. Sumner held the British liable for these "indirect claims" of more than $2 billion, roughly the cost of the war after Gettysburg.

Sumner demanded a settlement of indirect as well as direct claims. In 1871, an American-British-Canadian Commission hammered out the Treaty of Washington, creating arbitration panels for most trilateral disagreements. A German arbitrator decided the San Juans belonged to the United States. Another arbitrator set a price for Americans to fish Canadian waters and allowed Canadians to fish the less rich American waters. Britain abandoned claims for damages for Fenian cross-border raids. Most importantly, the Treaty of Washington created a commission to arbitrate direct and indirect claims.

Unfortunately, the treaty's imprecise text, endorsed by Sumner himself, masked a hidden flaw. The flaw was inadvertent ambiguity, as rare in a diplomatic agreement as intentional ambiguity is not. Britain and the United States each thought the other had accepted its position on the indirect claims. Both charged the other with trickery. Tensions skyrocketed as the arbitrators gathered. No British government could assent to an open-ended arbitration that might result in responsibility for half the cost of the Civil War. Neither could the Grant administration, in an election year, back down in the face of anti-British feeling at home. As Anglo-American amity teetered on the brink, behind-the-scenes negotiation produced compromise. The United States would not formally abandon the indirect claims but assented privately to remove the arbitrators' jurisdiction over them. The arbitrators addressed the direct claims alone. Only in the case of the *Alabama*, *Florida*, and *Shenandoah* had Britain failed to exercise due diligence, the arbitrators declared in September 1872, and assessed $15.5 million in damages.

In the summer of 1872 the *Alabama* claims war fever peaked. If war broke out, the British navy would surely attack America's Pacific interests. Secretary of War William Worth Belknap, fretting about war with "a powerful maritime nation," ordered a study of the defensive capabilities of Hawaiian ports.[5] Belknap selected Major General John M. Schofield, commander of the Army's Military Division of the Pacific, and Lieutenant Colonel Barton Alexander of the Army Corps of Engineers. Although only forty-two years old, Schofield was one of the most senior officers in the Army. He looked bookish rather than martial—in a photo from later in his life he had soft lips and a little black moustache framed by huge white muttonchops and a bald head—but he was a warrior. He went into the Civil War a captain and came out of it, like other capable officers, a general. Unlike nearly all of them, he was awarded the Medal of Honor for gallantry. After Appomattox, he called for armed intervention against the French in Mexico, went on a diplomatic mission to Paris during the subsequent revolution against Maximilian, and served briefly as secretary of war in 1868. Alexander was a fortifications expert.[6]

The selection of Army officers shows that the administration was not thinking about offensive naval operations from the Pearl River. That concept of power projection would not appear until the late 1880s and would not be broadly accepted until the end of the 1890s. Rather, in 1873, Washington wanted a fortified harbor of refuge, where weak navies and merchant fleets could hole up during wartime.

Schofield and Alexander reported that Honolulu, the only existing harbor, could not be defended by shore batteries. Only a few coral reefs protected the harbor from the sea. The report noted: "An enemy could take up his position outside of the entrance to the harbor and command the entire anchorage, as well as the town of Honolulu itself. This harbor would therefore be of no use to us as a harbor of refuge in a war." Only the Pearl River had all the properties of an excellent naval port. It had abundant deep water extending six miles from the mouth of the lagoon, or estuary, which had three portions or "locks" (lochs), like a three-fingered hand. The lagoon's entrance was the problem. Only twelve to eighteen feet of water covered the reef at low tide, much too shallow for warships. But a cut two hundred yards wide and twenty-six feet deep was feasible, making the "Pearl

River Harbor" perfect. It could be defended easily by shore batteries. It had thirty miles of sheltered shoreline for the ammunition depots, coal dumps, and machine shops of a major naval station. The officers knew the planters wanted duty-free entry for their sugar. Perhaps the Pearl River might be traded for duty-free sugar.[7]

King Kalākaua opposed any surrender of sovereignty, but he visited the United States in 1874 to pursue reciprocity.[8] He was the first king ever to visit. The Navy transported the royal party to San Francisco, where General Schofield, who had become friends with the king, hosted him for a pleasant week. The king departed in a luxurious Pullman car provided by the United States. So special was this first visit of a reigning monarch that the secretaries of state, war, and the navy escorted him to his government-provided ten-room suite at the Arlington Hotel. The king appeared at a joint session of Congress, and Grant hosted a plush state dinner.

Kalākaua refocused attention on reciprocity. As the king charmed his way home, generating reams of coverage in media-rich cities across the United States, Secretary Fish and the Hawaiians completed a draft treaty in January 1875. The king arrived home to a big thank you party. The Government Building was festooned with red, white, and blue lanterns, and candles burned in every window. A great decorative crown with the word "Kalākaua" topped the building. Anna Dole wrote: "Rockets and fireballs were sent up, a torchlight procession came into the palace yard ... and listened to a few words from the king." Afterward, everyone watched a hula at the monarch's house.[9]

But in Washington the pact was in trouble. A simple reciprocity treaty would not pass the Senate, which previously had killed three similar treaties. Senate negotiators extracted an additional concession from the Hawaiians and passed the revised treaty 51–12. It bound Hawai`i not to lease or grant any "port, harbor, or territory" to a foreign power. This caused some grumbling in Honolulu, but others pointed out that if Hawai`i was not going to cede territory to the United States, there was little harm in ruling out cession entirely. Hawai`i surrendered no sovereignty; it merely promised not to surrender it to a third party. The Reciprocity Treaty took effect September 9, 1876. It allowed duty-free entry of Hawai`i's chief exports: sugar (by far the largest export), hides and skins, rice, bananas, nuts, and vegetables. All U.S. products currently imported into Hawai`i, such as agricultural implements, animals and animal products, grain, cotton goods, lumber, machinery, and tobacco, received duty-free entry. The treaty's term was seven years, after which it could be abrogated on a year's notice, making the earliest possible end September 8, 1884.

Everyone understood the bargain: economic concessions, significant to Hawai`i though insignificant to the United States, for increased U.S. influence—

the "intimacy of our relations," as Grover Cleveland later put it. Annexation was impossible; King Kalākaua and his subjects opposed it, as did many Americans. Reciprocity was the perfect middle ground.

The treaty was a good trade deal for Hawai`i. Sugar received free entry, and duties were waived on most items that Hawai`i needed to import. Local industry benefited from cheaper imported materials and parts. The Chinese tailors who produced the colorful cotton goods favored by Hawaiians faced a little competition from imported goods, but they could now import their cotton cloth duty-free. The Honolulu Iron Works, which fabricated machinery for the sugar industry, faced a bit more competition, but the Iron Works specialized in customized machinery built from American components, which could now be imported duty-free. Reciprocity boosted the whole economy, not just the infant sugar industry.[10]

The reciprocity treaty governed the sugar trade until annexation. Because reciprocity was a poor economic bargain for the United States, abrogation was a possibility. Critics charged that unscrupulous Honolulu businessmen imported cheap Asian sugar and reexported it to the United States duty-free. Treasury officials found no fraud but reported that Hawaiian sugar hurt southern sugar growers. Nor did consumers benefit much. Before reciprocity, West Coast refineries bought dutiable Hawaiian sugar because transporting southern sugar by train was costly. After reciprocity, Hawaiian sugar entered duty-free, but refiners kept the price just under that of eastern refined sugar and pocketed the windfall.

The federal government never considered abrogation because reciprocity enhanced American preeminence.[11] In 1883 the Hawaiian government decided the treaty should be renewed.[12] Another seven-year term would entice bigger capital investments than if reciprocity could be terminated on a year's notice. In 1884 the Senate Foreign Relations Committee recommended renewal for another seven years coupled with an increase of duty-free articles and "the privilege of establishing permanently a proper naval station in the vicinity of Honolulu."[13]

Grover Cleveland, who took office in 1885, opposed reciprocity in principle. He even withdrew from the Senate a reciprocity treaty with Spain. But he left the Hawaiian pact alone, seeing it as a special case. Resolutions calling for termination went nowhere.[14] Opponents could not kill the treaty but they could prevent a seven-year extension unless the United States gained the right to build a naval station at Pearl Harbor. Hawai`i opposed granting that right.[15]

Cleveland's secretary of state, Thomas F. Bayard, sought to bridge the gap. Rumors of foreign machinations during 1886 spurred Bayard's concern about preserving influence in Hawai`i. Newspapers reported talk of a reciprocity pact between Hawai`i and Canada. There were discussions about a 2 million dollar

British loan for a telegraphic cable from Canada to Australia through Hawai`i. But what truly alarmed Bayard were German intrigues in Samoa.

The Samoan islands lie in the South Pacific, roughly twenty-three hundred miles southwest of Hawai`i. The capital was Apia, on the island of Upolu. Because a Hamburg company traded with the islands since 1847, Germany's influence exceeded that of the United States and Great Britain. Squabbling chiefs ruled different islands. Chiefs opposed to German meddling sent an emissary to ask Washington for annexation or at least a protectorate. In early 1878, the United States pledged its good offices if Samoa had a diplomatic dispute. In return, the United States received the right to build a naval station in Pago Pago. The Senate approved the agreement. The Navy stored coal but did not construct a naval station. The consuls of the United States, Britain, and Germany formed a ruling body not only for Apia but for all of Samoa. This tripartite system, undemocratic and, in the American consul's case, against his own government's desire that Samoans govern themselves, soon broke down. In 1885, to maintain economic interests, the German consul had German troops seize Apia and the Mulinuu peninsula, where King Malietoa lived. Germany sent additional troops and may well have fomented a rebellion against Malietoa. America was caught up in what Paul Kennedy called the "Samoan tangle."[16]

The blatant German aggressiveness shocked Cleveland and Bayard, who declared German occupation unacceptable even if U.S. commercial activity went unhindered. In May 1886, responding to Malietoa's plea, the U.S. consul put Samoa under American protection, greatly increasing the chances of a clash with Germany. Bayard swiftly disavowed the protectorate. Although Germany and Britain accepted Bayard's call for three-power talks, negotiations collapsed in July 1887 because Germany, claiming its interests dwarfed those of the other two, insisted on ruling Samoa itself. Four German warships landed troops at Apia. Germany declared war on Malietoa and soon captured and deported him, to great public dismay. Only German troops saved their puppet king Tamasese from a popular uprising. Americans railed against Germany's meddling. Bayard sent the *Adams* to Apia as an expression of concern. Rebels attacked a German force, killing twenty and wounding thirty more. Germany burned and shelled Apia. When the Germans seized an American boat, public outrage obliged the Navy to send Admiral Lewis Kimberley to Samoa along with two more warships. Cleveland and Bayard could not accept a "preponderance of German power." Inflammatory, posturing statements flew around the Congress. In February 1889, just before he left office, Cleveland signed bills appropriating $500,000 for defending U.S. interests in Samoa and $100,000 to enlarge the Pago Pago coal dump into a naval station.[17]

Bismarck saw the crisis getting out of hand and invited British and American representatives to Berlin to work out a compromise. Before the conference opened, a massive hurricane struck Apia, sinking all the American and German warships, damaging the sole British vessel, and killing many sailors. The storm highlighted the value of a protected anchorage. (Apia was not one, which explains the American focus on Pago Pago.) The Berlin conference rapidly reached agreement. Germany restored Malietoa as king. A chief justice jointly appointed by the three powers would advise Malietoa and rule on disputes between the king and any one or all three of the powers.

The Samoan agreement was a departure from traditional American policy. Never before had the United States involved itself in governing another people. American diplomacy in the Samoan affair was very sensitive to foreign intervention in the Pacific. Because the United States considered the renewal of Hawaiian reciprocity during the low point of the Samoan tangle, the hard lessons learned in Samoa were swiftly applied to Hawaiian policy. Excluding foreign influence in Hawai`i was crucial. So was strengthening American influence by extending reciprocity, especially with a clause allowing a U.S. base at Pearl Harbor.

Hawai`i's reluctance to accept a Pearl Harbor clause ended abruptly on July 1, 1887, when a bloodless coup toppled the cabinet. Under pressure, King Kalākaua accepted a new cabinet and the so-called Bayonet Constitution, which limited his powers. In elections held under the new constitution, the white-dominated Reform Party won handily. A Reform cabinet requested that Bayard stipulate that Hawai`i merely allowed the use, not cession, of the Pearl River. Bayard produced the stipulation. In November 1887, the two nations extended reciprocity indefinitely but with an initial seven-year term. Lili`uokalani, the future queen, wrote: "King signed a lease of Pearl Harbor to U. States for eight years to get R. Treaty. It should not have been done."[18] She did not record her reasons for opposing the Pearl River clause. Hawai`i got renewal of the reciprocity treaty in return for a temporary privilege that the United States never used. No land was ceded; Hawai`i surrendered no sovereignty.

Critics could not claim that reciprocity damaged the American economy when it was growing so fast and generating such huge federal surpluses. Tariff revenues rose so much that reduction of the surplus became a major political issue. Once politicians began to tinker with the tariff, they used it to protect the industrial and agricultural interests of their constituents. In 1888 Republicans won the presidency and Congress, and prepared "An Act to Reduce the Revenue," the McKinley Tariff of 1890, named after the chair of the Ways and Means Committee.

The McKinley tariff stripped Hawaiʻi of its advantages, putting foreign sugar on the duty-free list, just like Hawaiian sugar. Worse, the act authorized a bounty of two cents per pound for U.S. producers. There was no violation of reciprocity because Hawaiian sugar still entered duty-free. When the bounty provisions took effect in April 1891, the price of Hawaiian sugar dropped, costing Hawaiʻi millions per year in lost profits. Island producers did not regain their level playing field until the low-tariff Democrats returned to power in 1892. In 1894 the Wilson-Gorman Tariff eliminated the bounty and reimposed duties on foreign sugar, restoring Hawaiʻiʻs equality with domestic sugar.

The United States never developed a coaling station at the Pearl River. The Navy gathered data useful in the later annexation debate. In 1894 the *Philadelphia*'s survey crew discovered that the bar was not coral but sand, which might be dredged or suctioned, leaving a deep, one-hundred-meter-wide entrance. The Navy filed and forgot the report. Nevertheless, reciprocity achieved American aims of closer ties between the mainland giant and the tiny kingdom.

On the Hawaiian side, the economic gains were paramount. Sugar planters were far less concerned about the treaty's political benefits than its economic ones. Everyone knew reciprocity would jump-start the sugar industry. Businessmen lined up credit and planned to enlarge existing plantations and build new ones. For Hawaiʻi, reciprocity and sugar were inseparable. King Cane, as the sugar industry was soon called, would dominate the economy and distort politics and foreign relations as well.

CHAPTER 3

The Empire of Cane

Fourteen days after Senate passage of the Reciprocity Treaty, the *City of San Francisco* ferried the good news, appearing off Diamond Head on August 24, 1876, "decked with bunting from bowsprit to spanker boom."[1] Aboard was a passenger whose impact on the sugar industry would be exceeded only by the Reciprocity Treaty itself. Claus Spreckels, the forty-eight-year-old San Francisco sugar refiner, was making his first Hawaiian visit. He stayed three weeks, bought up about half the prospective sugar crop for his mainland refineries, and invested in the sugar industry. He quickly became the biggest player in what was probably the world's most sophisticated and efficient sugar industry. Soon, when people thought of sugar, they thought first of Spreckels, the Sugar King.

Born in Germany in 1828, Spreckels arrived in South Carolina—flat broke— at age eighteen. By hard work and thrift, he soon owned his own grocery store. He went to California, where in the 1850s he got rich selling groceries, dry goods, and beer. A sale of his various businesses brought more than $100,000. In 1863 he and some relatives founded the Bay Sugar Refinery. Although the venture grew rapidly, Spreckels was restless; he had even bigger plans. He returned to Germany, whose refinery technology was then considered the best. The story goes that he worked as a common laborer to learn the process inside out, but whether the wealthy Spreckels actually drew a laborer's salary or not, he mastered every nuance of German refining. In 1868 he founded the California Sugar Refining Company, processing raw sugar from Hawai`i and the Far East. He introduced techniques, some invented in Hawai`i, for cutting the refining time from three weeks to less than twenty-four hours.[2]

A burly, energetic man with pale gray eyes, a salt-and-pepper beard, and thinning hair sometimes gathered in a tiny pigtail, Spreckels was a master schemer. His close association with King Kalākaua was less friendship than design. He obtained cheap land and water rights by manipulating the king and other officials with loans and bribes. Spreckels loved big projects. Spreckelsville plantation in Maui became the world's largest; his sugar beet refinery near Salinas, California, was the world's biggest. The Spreckels Building was San Francisco's tallest. Spreckels was stubborn and vindictive. When the owner of the San Francisco Gas and Electric power plant refused to curb smoke that bothered tenants in the Spreckels Building, Spreckels founded his own electric company and started a rate war. Eventually, he sold his company to the San Francisco utility for a tidy profit.[3]

After reciprocity, sugar drove the Hawaiian economy. Sugar was by far the leading export. Shipping and trading companies, machine shops and ironworks that built cane presses and vacuum pans, shops catering to sugar workers: all connected to sugar. Tiny Hawai`i sent all its sugar to the United States, supplying one-eighth of the market, taking share from domestic producers as well as giant exporters such as Cuba.

The rise of sugar connected directly to the fragmentation of Hawaiian politics, to the 1893 revolution, and ultimately to annexation in 1898. White businessmen, managers, and mechanics benefited most from sugar. As white businessmen became richer and paid most of the taxes, they sought political influence commensurate with their dominant economic position. Native Hawaiians, benefiting far less from sugar, felt their country slipping away as their numbers continued to drop and as whites sought to curb the monarchy's power. Politics polarized into two camps. Royalists, composed mostly of Native Hawaiians, part-Hawaiians, and a few whites, opposed curbs on royal powers. So-called Reformers—mostly whites, part-Hawaiians, and a few Native Hawaiians—wanted a constrained monarchy in which the king would reign but not rule, leaving the management of the country to the business and professional community.

Sugar radically changed the demographic balance, sucking in so many sugar laborers of various nationalities that the newcomers, mostly Chinese and Japanese who could not vote, soon became a majority of the adult population. The recruitment and importation of these laborers became a central focus of the government. The sugar industry could not grow without them, but the Asian majority, if ever granted suffrage, would mean the end of white rule.

In short, sugar created a powerful economy but polarized island politics helped to cause the revolution, oriented economic and political life to the United States, and created a huge immigrant population that might someday seek—perhaps with the help of home governments—political control. But as Spreckels stood on the deck of the *City of San Francisco* and gazed at the crowded Honolulu waterfront, it was clear to no one, not even to the future Sugar King, that the sugar industry would expand so rapidly, and would so powerfully shape the political future of the islands.

Although cane had been grown in Hawai`i for decades, the Civil War jump-started the industry. Northern consumers, cut off from traditional suppliers in Louisiana, demanded Hawaiian sugar. Sugar production soared during the war but plunged when southern producers reentered the market and drove down the price. At normal peacetime pricing, perhaps six to seven cents per pound, only growers planting on the most fertile, well-watered land could pay the U.S. duty of three cents per pound and still profit. The 1876 reciprocity treaty leveled the playing field for Hawaiians, giving them equal access to the consumer but no more than that. The real job lay ahead. The vast empire of cane would have to be built stalk by stalk, acre by acre, mill by mill.

Why sugar? From a purely commercial aspect, sugar was a smart choice, leaving aside, for the moment, the adverse social and political consequences of a sugar economy. What else but sugar could have produced such large export earn-ings? The islands possessed no basics for heavy industry—no iron, coal, or oil—and, most damaging, no large internal market for industrial products. The climate was unsuited to wheat and corn. Rice was commonly grown but was bulky and not a high-value crop. A shipload of rice brought less money than a shipload of sugar. Few believed that Hawai`i could grow enough coffee at low enough production costs to make a lot of money. The slowness of the transport system and its lack of widespread refrigeration (from Hawaiian farm to the mainland consumer's table) made it impossible to reap substantial earnings in fruit, meat, or dairy products. With arable land so limited, it was wise to concentrate on a high value-added product easy to store and ship. Reciprocity gave entrepreneurs confidence to make the huge investments necessary for the production efficiencies and economies of scale that allowed Hawai`i to compete with Louisiana cane and California sugar beets.

The Polynesians who originally settled Hawai`i brought cane with them. The word "sugar" comes from India, where producers labeled pebble-like sugar crystals as *sarkara*, or gravel. When sugar manufacture migrated to Europe, *sarkara* trans-muted into the English word "sugar." The sucrose-rich "Lahaina Cane" variant, brought from Tahiti in the modern era, was a perennial grass, growing in clumps of huge stalks eight to twenty-five feet tall and one to two and a half inches in diameter. Hawaiian cane was mostly grown from cuttings, or "slips," of mature plants. The top of the plant provided the best slips, soft and quick to germinate. A twelve-inch-long slip was pushed into the earth, ideally tilled twenty to twenty-four inches deep. To mature, the average stalk needed about eighteen months and as much as two years at higher elevations. Sometimes planters "ratooned," letting new stalks grow from the roots of cut cane. Although the planter avoided the expense of furrowing and planting, ratooning produced slightly lower yields.[4]

Cane was best cut by hand. Workers wielded cane knives eighteen inches long, broader at the tip than the base, and with a hook on the back to strip leaves and manipulate the stalk. They cut and trimmed the stalks and stacked them for transport to the mill. There huge rollers crushed the cane to extract the sap, which is about 80 percent water, 16 percent sugar, and 4 percent other by-products. In the old days, sugar sap was simply left in the open air for weeks to evaporate the water. To speed up the process, sugar workers boiled the sap, but if the sugar scorched (caramelized), it ruined the taste. Technology soon provided the vacuum pan, monstrous steel urns that would hold several thousand gallons of sap. Under partial vacuum, boiling occurred at lower temperatures, 140 to 160 degrees instead of 230 to 260 degrees, which greatly decreased the risk of scorching. When the water boiled off, workers shoved the lumpy mixture of sugar crystals and dark molasses into squat centrifugal separators. The "centrifugals" looked like overgrown versions of the top-loading household washing machine of the late twentieth century. Inside were large, whirling, finely perforated drums, usually about thirty inches in diameter. The machines spun out the thick liquid molasses through the holes, leaving sugar crystals. Mark Twain described the process: "The nasty-looking grained sugar—it is about half black molasses, and looks like an inferior quality of mud—is dumped in . . . the tub is set to spinning around at the rate of ten to twelve hundred revolutions per minute—the mud begins to retreat from the center and cling to the sides—and in about three minutes the bottom is as clean as a dinner plate; the sides are packed with a coating two or three inches thick of beautiful light straw-colored sugar ready for the table, and all the disagreeable molasses has been expressed through the innumerable pinholes by the frightful velocity of the machine."[5]

The sugar's color and fineness varied with the molasses residue, a function of the speed of the centrifuge, the viscosity of the molasses, and the amount of trace nonsugars. Workers abraded the golden sugar between metal screens to achieve the fine-grained texture consumers wanted, and then placed the sugar in barrels for transport.

The reciprocity negotiators confronted a knotty problem. What exactly was raw sugar? This crucial treaty definition would not only determine whether Hawaiian exporters paid U.S. duties but would have also a huge effect on investment in island sugar mills. Hawaiian growers, seeking to keep value-adding work, would surely build facilities that processed sap to the highest quality level that still permitted waiver of duties.

Traditionally, neither grower nor refiner could afford to duplicate the efforts of the other. Plantations prepared raw sugar from cane juice. Refiners processed raw sugar into refined white sugar. This division of labor blurred as plantation sugar mills adopted much refinery technology, such as vacuum pans and centrifuges. The industry used the Dutch Standard System to grade sugar.[6] The whiter the sugar, the less molasses it contained, and the better its quality and grade. Dutch Standard Number 25—fine-grained and pure white—was the best, and the rawest was DS 6, deep brown with the consistency of thick mud. Grades DS 16–25 were "refined sugar," grades DS 6–15 were raw sugar.[7]

The problem was, both plantation mills and mainland refiners produced plenty of medium-quality sugar in grades DS 13–15. Half the Hawaiian production was this pale yellow "coffee" or "grocery" sugar. The refiners argued that because Hawaiian coffee sugar went directly to consumers, it was dutiable refined sugar. But the alert Hawaiian negotiators succeeded in labeling coffee sugar as duty-free raw sugar. The reciprocity treaty applied no duty to "muscovado, brown, and all other unrefined sugar, meaning hereby the grades of sugar heretofore commonly imported from the Hawaiian Islands and now known in the markets of San Francisco and Portland as 'Sandwich Island sugar.'"[8]

This great negotiating coup enticed mainland refiners to invest in Hawaiian plantations, cutting out the middlemen, vertically integrating their businesses, and reaping profits at each level of the industry. Americans (including naturalized Americans such as Spreckels and Hawaiian-born whites of American ancestry) owned 75 percent of roughly sixty-seven plantations in 1890. British money constituted 18 percent and German investment most of the rest.[9]

The United States produced only an eighth of the raw sugar it used, importing the rest from low-cost producers, chiefly Cuba but also the West Indies. To enter this huge, competitive sugar market, Hawaiian entrepreneurs built a world-class industry. When reciprocity took effect in 1876, producers planted more land, bought extra milling equipment, and hired additional workers. In a single year, exports increased 50 percent. This strong growth continued year after year. In 1881, 46,894 tons were produced; 70,826 tons in 1884; and 129,899 tons in 1890. In 1899, when planters harvested the final crop planted before annexation, production totaled 282,807 tons, a staggering 2,200 percent increase over 1877.[10]

What accounts for such phenomenal growth in a highly competitive global sugar market? First, Hawai`i had plenty of managerial and technical expertise. Many men knew how to grow sugar efficiently and find mainland buyers for the crop. Second, an immense fundamental advantage was the magnificent island climate, ideal for cane. The Hawaiian growing and harvesting seasons were longer than in most cane-growing regions.[11] Plantations operated year-round with cost-efficient use of labor and equipment. Third, by extensive irrigation, growers increased acreage tenfold between 1874 and 1898, far exceeding even expert predictions.[12] Finally, productivity—yield per acre—doubled. Roughly a ton of sugar per acre was produced in 1874; this reached a little over two tons per acre by the end of the 1890s, although some plantations produced four or five tons per acre.[13] The productivity stemmed from widespread irrigation, introduction of hybrids, planter cooperation in disseminating technical advice, scientific soil analysis and the use of fertilizer, increases in mill efficiency, better transport of the cane to the mill, and the acquisition of a skilled labor force efficiently used year-round. All of these factors linked to good management.

No country had better mill technology.[14] Engineers steadily increased the size and pressure of the rollers. A second and—in the 1890s—a third set of rollers squeezed out even more sap. Before pressing, workers shredded the stalks with massive toothed wheels or used a locally designed "Smith's Cane Cutter." Locally invented "Messchaert Grooves" in the rollers let pressed sap run out freely, preventing reabsorption. A Honolulu engineer invented "maceration," rinsing the shredded stalks with hot water to flush out the last of the sweet sap. Sugar mills in the 1850s pressed out 60 percent of the sap; in the 1890s they extracted more than 90 percent.[15] Plantations became so mechanized that they were akin to factories. Engineers designed machinery for plowing, unloading harvested cane from wagons, and feeding dried, pressed cane to the boilers for fuel.[16] Plantations moved cane with narrow-gauge locomotives and portable track.[17]

By augmenting rainfall, irrigation provided exactly the right amount of water to the crop, increasing the yield. Cane is 87 percent liquid and only 13 percent woody fiber, so the stalks were always thirsty. Planters had a rule of thumb that it took a ton of water to produce a pound of refined sugar. About half the cane lands received the seventy-five inches of rain, which made irrigation unnecessary, but to bring additional lands into production, the planters undertook vast water projects.[18]

The most famous of these, the Hamakua Ditch, was the first to carry enough water for a large plantation. The ditch tapped the streams cascading down the northern slopes of the giant volcano Haleakalā in East Maui.[19] The ditch curved seventeen miles from central Maui up and around Haleakalā's massive shoulder.[20] Where it ran across land it was six feet wide at the top, three and a half feet wide on the bottom, and three and a half feet deep. It dropped fifteen feet per mile, creating a swift flow of 40 million gallons per day. The ditch was a complex of trenches, flumes, tunnels, and piping. Timbered flumes carried the water across small gullies. Tunnels burrowed through rocky escarpments. Rather than massive and expensive wooden trestles, giant siphons were used to cross broad, deep gorges.[21]

Claus Spreckels soon built a bigger ditch. In 1878 he bought 16,000 central Maui acres and leased 24,000 acres of Crown lands at a pittance, only $1,000 per year for the entire property. Certainly the lands were arid and currently uncultivable, but the exceedingly low price was best explained by Spreckels' "loan" of $35,000 to Walter Murray Gibson, his "gift" of $10,000 to King Kalākaua, and smaller payments to the attorney general as legal retainers. Spreckels' 30-mile ditch girdled Haleakalā's northern slopes, lower on the mountain than the Hamakua Ditch. It carried 3,600 gallons per a minute, enough to irrigate even Spreckels' extensive lands.[22] With both land and water secured, Spreckels built Spreckelsville, the biggest sugar plantation in the world.

Even more important than famous water projects were countless smaller ones scattered around the islands. And when aboveground water sources approached full utilization in the 1890s, planters drilled artesian wells to tap the plentiful groundwater in the volcanic soil. For example, when Koloa plantation in Kauai could extract no more water from streams, ten pump-driven wells three hundred feet deep provided 10 million gallons of water per day.[23]

In 1888, with sugar at 6 cents per pound and an average yield of 4 tons per acre, Spreckelsville's per acre profits were $222. Given that Spreckels had 40,000 acres, total profits were enormous. For the Hawaiian industry overall, the break-even point was $3.23 per pound paid to the planter (the Honolulu price). Honolulu sugar brokers took 20 percent of the final delivery price for finding a buyer and shipping the sugar. For the grower, the lowest price was in Honolulu: no shipping needed. The San Francisco delivery price was higher, and the New York delivery price higher yet.[24]

In sum, the Hawaiian sugar industry was blessed by a good climate and an immense nearby market. It innovated constantly and relentlessly used the best technology. It recruited sufficient workers and used them more efficiently. It had great internal cohesion and a willingness to share good ideas. It made itself into the equivalent of a late-twentieth-century agribusiness, becoming the most sophisticated, albeit small, sugar industry of its time. But the crowning of King Cane had negative as well as positive effects.

On the positive side, sugar pumped a great deal of money into the Hawaiian economy, increasing the overall wealth of the country. Even at the lowest price point in 1891, under the impact of the McKinley tariff, sugar exports were about $8 million. Even in those depressed times, some planters still made money, and many came close to breaking even. Despite some layoffs, most everyone else— laborers, overseers, machinists, lawyers, shippers, shopkeepers—received wages and fees, though at lower levels. Over the whole reciprocity period, profits were big enough to finance the industry's incredible growth. Merze Tate estimated that Spreckels, in the best years, made profits of 50 percent of sales.[25] In more normal years, 20 percent annual profit seems close to the mark.

Sugar made Hawai`i a great export engine, a tiny trade superpower. It outper-formed the United States in export earnings and balance of trade. In 1897 the United States exported about $14.40 of goods per person and imported about $9.95. Hawai`i did much, much better. Per capita exports were $147 per person. What is striking is the trade surplus, an astounding $77 per capita in Hawai`i compared to $4.45 per capita in the United States, the latter a fine showing that seemed low only when compared to Hawai`i's.[26] During the reciprocity period, Hawai`i generated some $229 million in exports and a trade surplus of $101.5 million, an incredible amount for a nation with a population measured in the tens of thousands.[27]

But sugar had downsides as well. The booming industry oriented the economy on the United States. Sugar represented 95 percent of the value of Hawaiian exports, and 99.04 percent of Hawai`i sugar went to the United States.[28] A few believers in the Jeffersonian ideal of a nation of small farmers pondered alterna-tives. To prevent "bloated monopolists" from hogging the good sugar lands, in 1876 the *Hawaiian Gazette* proposed a sugar industry of thousands of small farms of a hundred or so acres, all feeding cane to mills owned by the farmers cooperatively or by outside investors.[29] That same year a government commission observed that by distributing Hilo sugar lands to small farmers, "an admirable opportunity would be given to parties of small means and to the Native Hawaiians in the vicinity."[30] Such advice, which might have made a valued place in the sugar industry for Native Hawaiian farmers, went unheeded.

Large plantations became the norm. Admittedly, it would have been very difficult to produce sugar for export on plots of ten to one hundred acres. The huge investment in machinery was impossible for a small farmer, and the equip-ment was best suited to working large plots. Large water projects were beyond the reach of small concerns. In theory, small farmers might have organized into giant cooperatives, jointly working their lands and sharing equipment and irrigation systems to achieve economies of scale. Cooperatives would have needed a very high degree of farmer organization and cooperation and government loans for the initial purchases of milling machinery and field equipment. This was certainly contrary to the go-it-alone entrepreneurial spirit of Claus Spreckels and others, and perhaps to the economic thinking of the Gilded Age. In any event, it did not happen. Sugar caused some environmental damage as well, including the drying up of some small streams sucked dry by big irrigation systems. This hurt Native Hawaiian subsistence farmers who depended on the streams.

As the economy developed, the old Hawaiian way of life further withered. Most loss of Hawaiian traditions occurred before the sugar industry began its rapid growth in 1876, but even after that date, Native Hawaiians saw little financial benefit. Small farming by Hawaiians wasted away. Thousands of Hawaiians worked in the fields and mills, as port laborers, and as seamen, but the majority of field and mill jobs, and especially mid-management jobs such as overseers—went to new immigrants.

Worst of all, sugar distorted Hawaiian politics. As the business community, dominated by whites, became wealthier, it sought influence in the government equivalent to its financial might and its contribution to government coffers. Many whites complained of mismanagement of their tax dollars. They thought they should dominate the government, though they composed only a fraction of the voters. Sugar's rise paralleled white demands for what they called "reform." The rise of sugar accelerated the fracturing of politics during the final ten years of King Kalākaua's reign.

❦

CHAPTER 4

The Beginnings of Japanese Immigration

R obert Walker Irwin and his 17-year-old bride were not, in the opinion of Japanese law, man and wife. A tall, long-faced Pennsylvanian, Irwin sought his fortune in Japan during the Meiji Restoration, when opponents of the stultified Shogunate, the military government that ruled Japan for 250 years, revolted under the banner of the young emperor Meiji to bring Japan into the nineteenth century. The Meiji Revolution had two years left to run in 1866, when, at age 22, Irwin became the agent of the Pacific Mail Company in Yokohama. There he met the diminutive Iki, age 17. Japan, opened to the world only 13 years before, did not yet recognize marriage between Japanese and westerners. Whatever its clouded legal status, Robert and Iki's relationship was strong enough that when in 1869 he took a job in Nagasaki, Iki went along. Fortunately, the modernization wave that swept Japan in the early Meiji era aided the Irwins; in 1873 the law was changed and in 1882 their union was officially recorded.[1]

By 1872 Irwin was working for a Yokohama trading company. He became friends with two men destined for great influence in Meiji Japan, Masuda Takashi and Inoue Kaoru. A legendary businessman, Masuda had picked up a little English working for the American consulate in 1863 at age fourteen. Within a year, the youngster used his fledgling language skills to get himself into a delegation to Europe to get agreement to the Shogun's plan to stem foreign "pollution" by closing Yokohama port. The mission failed. Yokohama, the vibrant new gateway to Japan, was too important to close. Masuda—like Irwin—was soon working in a foreign trading house. His talents were quickly noticed by Inoue Kaoru, a rising star who would become one of the most powerful men in Japan. Inoue found Masuda a job in the Finance Ministry. For the rest of their careers, Masuda and Inoue were close. They formed a company to export rice to London and hired their friend Irwin as chief financial advisor. In 1876 this company evolved into Mitsui Trading, which Masuda built into a massive trading company and eventually into the largest pre–World War II industrial conglomerate. It is still one of the world's largest trading companies. Like many Japanese, Masuda absorbed Western ways without losing his Japanese soul. At work, he looked like a rich American corporate chief, with meticulously parted short hair, a small mustache, and a white pocket handkerchief poking out of a finely tailored Western suit. But after retiring from Mitsui in 1915, he spent his final twenty-three years in kimono as a famous master of tea ceremony.

In 1876 Inoue led an official delegation abroad to study currency markets and other government-supervised financial systems. Inoue asked Irwin to plan and lead the study trip. Irwin escorted the group to London and New York, adding visits to San Francisco, Niagara Falls, and the magnificent Philadelphia Centennial Exposition. In 1877 Irwin set up Mitsui Trading's London office, returning to Tokyo in 1879 as senior counselor.

That same year Inoue Kaoru became foreign minister, serving until 1887. Inoue hailed from the famous castle town of Hagi, from the feudal domain of Choshu, now part of Yamaguchi Prefecture. Choshu men led the successful rebellion against the Shogunate in the 1860s. Severely wounded in battle, Inoue afterward rose quickly in the new Meiji government. After leaving the foreign ministry in 1887, he headed three other ministries, becoming a genro, one of the handful of very senior and respected "supreme advisors" to the throne. He served as the crucial go-between for his friend Robert Irwin and Iki's family and assisted them in negotiating the final legal hurdles in recording their marriage.

Irwin was a rarity, a longtime resident of Japan when less than a thousand foreigners lived there, fluent in Japanese, and extremely well connected. When the Hawaiian consul general took an extended leave in 1880, Irwin became acting consul, then minister.[2] Concurrently, Irwin served as special commissioner of the Hawaiian Board of Immigration. A somewhat prickly man, Irwin was very proud of his position. In an 1889 official portrait the immaculate white-gloved, splendidly uniformed Minister Plenipotentiary, his handlebar mustache carefully trimmed and graying hair cut short, stands regally beside the slim, dignified Iki.

Irwin's ties to the Japanese establishment greatly helped him obtain labor for Hawaiian agriculture. From 1884 he was the key player in the flow of the Japanese to the booming sugar industry, a flow that became a torrent by the late 1890s. The huge demand for sugar workers could not be met without immigration, given the horrendous decline in the numbers of Native Hawaiians. The immigration issue embraced the true immigration of people intending to stay permanently in Hawai`i with the admission of contract laborers for three-year periods. Locals loosely called both inflows "immigration," partly because some laborers did not return home at the end of their contracts and settled permanently, thereby becoming true immigrants. Most people blurred the difference between "immigrate" (to enter a new country to settle there) and "emigrate" (to leave one's native country to go and live elsewhere). Thus "immigrants" usually meant both persons arriving in Hawai`i and those still in Japan intending to go to Hawai`i.[3]

Japanese immigration would have immense consequences for eventual annexation. Over the years immigration radically changed Hawai`i's demographics and enabled the incredible growth of sugar. Eventually the cumulative effect of Japanese immigration on island politics and power relationships in the Pacific would become a spur to annexation. But in the mid-1880s Japanese immigration was seen only as a lifeline for labor-starved sugar plantations.

Immigration to Hawai`i went through two stages. During the first century after Cook's arrival, a trickle of whites and Chinese came to Hawai`i for missionary work or employment. Meanwhile, the Native Hawaiian population declined catastrophically from several hundred thousand to fewer than fifty thousand by 1876. Even in that year, there were so few foreigners in Hawai`i that Native Hawaiians still represented about 90 percent of the total population. During the second, shorter period, roughly 1876–98, rapidly rising Asian and Portuguese immigration significantly altered the demographic makeup, doubling the island population. By 1896 Native Hawaiians constituted only 36 percent of the population, greatly weakening their political power.[4]

The Japanese were latecomers among immigrant groups. The first foreigners to settle in modern times were a handful of white men who arrived during Kamehameha I's reign. More beachcombers than true immigrants, many were regarded by Native Hawaiians as curiosities and occasionally as intermediaries who could show them some of the supposed advantages of Western life and technology. Kamehameha I used several in his drive to modernize weaponry and to construct a Western-style ship.

American missionaries were the first organized group of white immigrants. The first group of twenty-three arrived in April 1820, and their number—preachers, doctors, printers, teachers—slowly increased over the years. Missionary children and grandchildren entered other fields, such as the law and business. Business opportunities lured whites in the fur and sandalwood trades. From the 1840s whaling enticed immigrants who ran the businesses that serviced the whaling fleet. A few entrepreneurs invested in sugar and coffee plantations, though neither industry prospered much except during the Civil War, when Hawaiian sugar temporarily replaced Louisiana sugar in the North. While these white immigrants were politically, economically, and spiritually influential, their numbers were quite small. In 1853 whites totaled 1,687, a tiny 2.3 percent of the population. In 1878, the white population still numbered only 3,748.

The cataclysmic collapse in the Polynesian population dwarfed immigration's tiny contribution to population growth. From several hundred thousand, the Native Hawaiian population dropped so swiftly that in 1878, census takers counted only 44,014 Hawaiians, a tenth or perhaps even a twentieth of their number a century earlier.[5] The government attempted repopulation by infusing immigrants from "cognate races." More than 2,000 South Sea islanders came during 1878–84, but their dissatisfaction with working conditions caused most to return home. Hawai`i vainly tried to import Malaysians, Javanese, and Indians from the Raj.[6]

The government sought whites who would work under contract, then remain as permanent residents. In 1880 the Board of Immigration recruited six hundred Norwegians but most were not farmers and soon quit the plantations. Nearly a thousand Germans arrived in 1881–82, but many moved to the mainland when their contracts expired.

Portuguese were the only whites successfully recruited in large numbers. Over the years, several hundred Portuguese dribbled in, building a reputation as law-abiding and industrious. In 1876 William Hillebrand, living temporarily in Madeira, recommended bringing Portuguese from the Azores, thinking that farmers from semitropical islands would adapt swiftly.[7] The Board asked Hillebrand to recruit families for permanent settlement. Under three-year contracts, men earned $10 a month plus food allowances, lodging, and medical care. Women and working children received lower wages. During 1878–86, 10,216 Portuguese arrived. Kuykendall notes that men composed 30 percent, women 22 percent, and children 48 percent. Portuguese immigration was expensive and provided fewer field-workers than hoped. The 2,752 Portuguese who came in 1884–86 cost $89 per passenger for transportation and other expenses, and only about one in three became a laborer.[8]

A cheaper alternative was already at hand: the Chinese. Several Chinese visited Hawai`i in 1788 as crew on the trader *Felice*, and by 1794 a handful, probably shipwrights or carpenters, were among Kamehameha's foreign advisors. Several hundred arrived in the 1830s and 1840s and worked primarily as shopkeepers and craftsmen.[9] Over the next quarter century, 2,625 Chinese entered Hawai`i. When the sugar industry expanded after 1876, Chinese immigration soared. Within two years, they composed 10.4 percent of the population.[10] From 1878 through 1885, 23,715 Chinese arrived, mostly as "free immigrants," not bound by contract, therefore not compelled to leave afterward. The 5,605 Chinese sugar workers in 1886 were chiefly free immigrants who sought work and signed contracts only after arrival. Other Chinese went directly into town jobs dominated by whites— shopkeepers, small businessmen, craftsmen, and mechanics. A white anti-Chinese movement sprang up, advocating an immigration cut-off.[11] Chinese immigrants should work only as agricultural laborers or domestic servants, avoiding competition with blue-collar whites. A legislative committee charged that "the competition of other races with Chinese is impossible, and that whenever other races are forced into such competition the result is not competition but the substitution of the Chinese for their competitors."[12] Until 1884 Chinese entered without documentation, but from that year entry required travel documents. The Hawaiian consulate in Hong Kong stopped issuing such documents and convinced the British to do the same. These measures ended the inflow. Over the next eight years, only 911 Chinese immigrants entered.[13] By 1894 the Chinese population shrank to 15,000.[14]

Given the expense of the Portuguese, white opposition to Chinese, and the failure of other recruitment efforts, Japan seemed the best source of low-cost, high-quality laborers who would return home and not displace blue-collar whites. Hawai`i thought Japanese immigration would be controllable if carefully coordinated by the two governments. The plantations would calculate the number of workers needed, and only that number would be recruited, bound by preapproved contracts issued by the Board of Immigration. Money would be withheld from their wages to offset the ticket home, making it likely that they would leave.[15]

Hawai`i had some experience with Japanese. In 1868 Eugene Van Reed, the Hawaiian Consul General at Yokohama, recruited 148 plantation workers. He told them little about the work and rushed them off without official permission to emigrate, angering the Imperial Government. In Hawai`i, the tough fieldwork and insensitive treatment from overseers shocked the Japanese. Japan brought home 40 workers and got better treatment for the rest.

While checking on this first batch of immigrants, Japanese officials suggested a treaty to regularize bilateral relations. Hawai`i asked the American minister to Japan to negotiate on its behalf because the Japanese refused to deal with the duplicitous Van Reed. The Treaty of Amity and Commerce of 1871 allowed nationals of both countries to trade and reside freely on the other's soil. While Article 2 mentioned unimpeded residence in connection with commerce, Article 4 stipulated that Hawaiian subjects shall enjoy all "privileges, immunities, and advantages" that Japan gave to subjects of other nations. The treaty did not address privileges and immunities that the Japanese would enjoy outside of commercial pursuits.[16]

During his 1881 world tour King Kalākaua visited Mutsuhito, the Meiji Emperor. Kalākaua offered his niece, Ka`iulani, as the future wife of a Japanese prince. The Japanese declined, but Kalākaua impressed them. In 1882 Hawai`i sent John Kapena to discuss immigration with Foreign Minister Inoue Kaoru. Inoue promised to consider the matter soon. To smooth the way, Hawai`i appointed Irwin to the concurrent post of special commissioner for Japanese immigration.[17] In April 1884 the king's emissary, Curtis Iaukea, suggested to Inoue that if enough Japanese immigrated, no Chinese would be needed, a provision sure to please the Imperial Government. With a straight face, he reminded Inoue that Irwin was now special commissioner. Inoue replied that a man "so well acquainted with the affairs of Japan as Mr. Irwin cannot but be satisfactory to His Imperial Majesty's government."[18] Although not ready to commit to a convention, Inoue agreed to a trial.

Irwin sprang into action. He explained to Hawaiian officials and planters how to avoid the problems of the 1868 Van Reed episode. He returned to Tokyo with a list of sugar plantations that desired workers and with a model labor contract. The immigrants would sign an initial contract with Irwin and a more detailed one in Hawai`i, once assigned to a specific plantation. The Hawaiian government committed three hundred thousand dollars to the project and gave Irwin fifty thousand dollars for a recruitment drive. Irwin placed advertisements in newspapers and printed flyers.[19]

The Japanese government helped enormously. Foreign Minister Inoue guaranteed the success of Irwin's effort by distributing to government offices throughout Japan a detailed description of the immigration program. This gave recruitment the government's imprimatur. The ministry issued guidelines for what people should take to Hawai`i: "three sets of ordinary wearing apparel, a short-sleeved kimono, a pair of tight fitting trousers, a set of summer nightwear, summer bedding and mosquito netting . . . and perhaps pots and pans."[20] Playing off his connections with the foreign minister, Irwin met with prefectural and local officials to gain their assistance and gathered immigrant applications. The recruitment effort took on the appearance of official policy.

During 1885–94 most immigrants came from four prefectures in southwestern Japan where Irwin's Japanese friends had the strongest connections.[21] Inoue was from Yamaguchi and urged Irwin to recruit there. Masuda, Mitsui's president, recommended Hiroshima, Yamaguchi's neighboring prefecture. Mitsui employees went to various prefectures to help recruit. Mitsui ran newspaper advertisements. Many thousands of Japanese applied for the first shipload. Irwin went to great lengths to avoid problems. He arranged for Japanese food on the ship. He built strong personal ties with Nakamura Jiro, who would set up a consulate to look after the immigrants.[22]

On February 8, 1885, the *City of Tokio* docked with 943 immigrants, 676 men and 267 women and children. This was the first of dozens of shiploads over the next thirteen years until Hawai`i passed under the American flag in 1898, although immigration continued to increase after that date and remained high until the anti-Asian exclusion laws of the 1920s. Irwin was aboard as well. The first shipload met a warm welcome. The *Pacific Commercial Advertiser* proclaimed that their arrival was—next to the signing of the Reciprocity Treaty—the most important event of Kalākaua's reign. The paper praised the emigrants' "sturdiness and healthy appearance." "Not only are they attractive physically, but their bedding, being aired outside on thin ropes, look clean and give a pleasant impression," the paper reported.[23]

On the slow nineteen-day voyage, the Japanese met the quarantine requirement that, from the time the ship left Yokohama, no smallpox cases emerged among the passengers for at least eighteen days. Having satisfied the health requirement at sea, they immediately went sightseeing ashore while awaiting transportation to their plantations. They were soon peering in the windows of mansions, guzzling soda water (rare in Japan), and smoking American cigarettes. At the Royal Hawaiian Hotel, they shed their footwear, arranged the various *geta* (wooden clogs), slippers, and shoes neatly at the entrance, and strolled about "as if they were in a public hall," Consul Nakamura wrote disdainfully. Most wore the same farm clothing that they wore in Japan. Nakamura remarked condescendingly: "I cannot but feel ashamed when I meet them in the streets." (The consul seems to have internalized a view that civilization meant Westernization.)[24]

In the Queen's Hospital on the day after arrival, Iida Hisano gave birth to a girl, probably the first Japanese born in Hawai`i. King Kalākaua and his sister Lili`uokalani became godparents for the infant, named Lydia after Lili`uokalani's

Christian name. The king gave a party at `Iolani Palace, where forty men staged a sumo tournament. The delighted monarch gave each participant a silver dollar, and everyone guzzled sake, which Irwin wisely imported, and crunched the seasoned rice crackers (*senbei*) that Hawaiians called "Japanese snap biscuits."[25]

Irwin escorted a second shipload in June 1885. Inoue Katsunosuke, Inoue Kaoru's stepson, came along to investigate ill treatment of laborers in the first shipload. Although Hawai`i employed a few Japanese as interpreter-inspectors for the Board of Immigration, Inoue Katsunosuke requested an independent office of inspection and interpretation headed by Nakayama Joji as well as the hiring of many more Japanese inspectors and doctors. The Hawaiian government agreed to act as the laborers' guardian, remove Japanese from Paia Plantation where they suffered abuse, and ensure that overseers did not use violence against the workers.[26]

Foreign Minister Inoue now asked Hawai`i to empower Irwin to conclude a formal convention. Hawai`i complied. Inoue allowed a third shipload to be recruited while he crafted an agreement that incorporated Katsunosuke's recommendations. This was hardly a negotiation because Inoue and Irwin were close friends. An agreement was in the personal and professional interests of each man as well as the two countries. They signed the Convention of 1886 just before the *City of Peking* departed with 927 immigrants.[27]

The convention governed virtually all Japanese immigration to Hawai`i. In Article II, Japan allowed unhindered emigration to Hawai`i but reserved the right to regulate the flow if "the exigencies of the state or the welfare of Japanese subjects justifies such action." The only route was Yokohama to Honolulu. The Kanagawa prefectural government (Yokohama is in Kanagawa) would be Japan's agent. A special agent of the Hawaiian Board of Immigration would reside in Yokohama. Article III stipulated that Japan must approve the agent's appointment. This amazing infringement of Hawai`i's right to appoint its own officials emerged from Inoue's desire to protect Irwin, the current special agent. Article IV stated that all emigration would be by contracts not to exceed three years between immigrants and the special agent, and approved by Kanagawa authorities. Hawai`i guaranteed the "full and perfect protection of the laws of the Kingdom" and promised to promote the immigrants' "welfare and comfort … at all times and under all circumstances." Hawai`i provided free steerage passage and a "sufficient" number of inspectors, interpreters, and Japanese physicians. Article I applied these provisions retroactively to immigrants already in Hawai`i.[28]

Given later disputes, it is worth noting what the convention did not stipulate. First, because Article II described actions and authorities of Japan only, the provision that Japanese might freely emigrate referred to their ability to leave

Japan, not to freely enter Hawai`i. Hawai`i did not surrender its right to regulate immigration. Article IV's stipulation that "all emigration under this Convention shall be by contract" meant that Japanese who arrived in Honolulu without signed contracts—that is, free immigrants—fell outside the pact's purview. Finally, Hawai`i's guarantee that immigrants would receive the "full and perfect protection" of Hawaiian law did not, in itself, guarantee voting rights, as some later claimed. Under the 1864 Hawaiian constitution, only citizens (royal subjects) or denizens (foreign citizens with a royal grant of the privileges of a citizen) could vote. For a Japanese to vote, the king would have to naturalize the laborer or award the status of denizen. This had been done with many whites and a handful of Asians. But the Convention of 1886 did not guarantee naturalization, denization, or the vote. However, under the later 1887 constitution, which limited citizenship to Hawaiians and Europeans, Japanese lost the potential to become citizens, even through naturalization. This violated the 1871 Treaty of Amity and Commerce, which said Japanese would enjoy "the same privileges as may have been, or may hereafter be granted to the citizens or subjects of any other nation." Although the treaty was principally concerned with the treatment of traders and merchants, it could be argued that the traders, if not all Japanese, should enjoy most favored nation treatment.[29]

A side agreement stipulated that males would be paid fifteen dollars per month (nine dollars wage plus a six dollar food allowance) and females ten dollars (six dollars wage and four dollars food allowance). All would receive free firewood, lodging, and medical care. The agreement demanded twenty-six workdays per month at ten hours per day in the fields, or twelve hours if assigned to an easier mill job. Irwin paid for passage to Honolulu—reimbursed by the Hawaiian government—but male laborers had to pay their return passage. To make sure workers saved return fare, Japan required workers to deposit a quarter of their wages with its consulate.

During the 1885–94 convention period, the two nations occasionally adjusted wage levels and transport allowances. After three shiploads, Hawai`i convinced Japan to charge males $65 for passage home and the cost of entry processing and additional doctors and interpreters. In 1891, when the sugar price dropped precipitously due to the McKinley tariff, Hawai`i won a reduction of monthly wages from $15.00 to $12.50, partially offsetting this pay cut by reducing the charges for return passage and doctors and interpreters. Hawai`i always paid costs for the laborers' wives, who composed only 16 percent of the newcomers, because there were fewer field jobs for women.[30]

The tough economic conditions in the 1880s as Japan transformed into a modern state impelled the authorities to allow emigration. Ernest Wakatsuki quotes an 1884 government report that many poor Japanese were not living a life befitting human beings. Farmers, the vast majority of the population, suffered greatly as the price of rice, their main crop, dropped by a stunning 50 percent between 1881 and 1886. Bankruptcies increased among village shopkeepers and small businessmen. Hunger was common. A later survey reported that the average farmer ate taro root and loquat dumplings with gruel for breakfast, rice and barley in hot water for lunch, and the same for dinner. To this basic fare were added beans, radishes, turnips, and a few seasonal vegetables, leavened rarely with fish or chicken. Sugar was served only to guests. Full stomachs were so rare that the privilege of eating at the company dining hall was a major inducement for young women to take factory jobs.[31]

Pushed to look abroad by tough conditions at home, immigrants were also pulled to Hawai`i by comparatively higher wages for a roughly similar workweek. Work hours in Japan were long, both on and off the farm. Not until 1911 did Japanese law limit to twelve hours per day the work hours of women and children fifteen and under, though fourteen-hour days were permitted on occasion. The sixty-hour workweek on Hawaiian sugar plantations (seventy-two hours for mill workers) was brutal but no worse than back home. And Hawaiian wages were higher. The convention wage rate—$15 a month with free lodging and medical care—looked good to suffering Japanese, despite tough Hawaiian working conditions. Male farm workers in Japan made $1.72 per month and females $0.95 in the 1880s, rising to $1.99–$3.19 per month in 1899. That same year, the Japanese Consulate in Seattle listed $17.00–$18.00 as the monthly wages of an American farmhand and $12.00–$13.00 for an apprentice laborer. Hawaiian (or mainland) wages were about four to five times greater than those in Japan.[32]

The possibility of returning with money for a better life was an irresistible attraction. Emigrants had an ambitious slogan: "Four hundred yen in three years." One immigrant said if he returned home with 500 yen (about $250), he could marry into a propertied family. Alan Takeo Moriyama points out the impossibility of saving that much from three years' gross salary of roughly 650 yen, but it was easier to save on Hawaiian wages than on Japanese wages.[33]

A traditional Japanese labor practice called *dekasegi rodo* (seasonal labor away from home) made it easier for people to bring themselves to leave their villages. Three years in Hawai`i was a big leap, but it was still temporary work, and the emigrants did not have to make the difficult psychological commitment to abandon Japan permanently. Indeed, Japanese officials often described immigrants as *dekasegi-nin* (a person employed away from his home) instead of *kanyaku-imin* (government-sponsored emigrants).[34]

Even in the first years of immigration, various levels of the Japanese government were intensely interested in the money flowing back from Hawai`i. Departing laborers received written guidance from their prefecture on how to handle savings: "It is necessary for those departing on *dekasegi* to bear in mind that they should not waste money, should accumulate savings and should return to Japan three years hence with a large amount of money, that they should use it to buy land or regain land lost to debtors and thus return home in glory."[35] Yamaguchi prefectural officials told immigrants to bring back two hundred dollars from a three-year Hawaiian stint. In the early years, laborers deposited remittances with the Japanese consulate, which passed the money through prefectural, district, and village officials to the intended recipient. Later, Hawaiian branches of Japanese banks took over transmission of funds, but the foreign ministry carefully tracked and regularly reported the amounts to the finance ministry.[36]

Remittances were the eighth-leading source of Japan's overseas revenue in 1892. During 1885–94, Japanese workers sent home more than $2.6 million dollars—$459,778 in 1894 alone. Given that immigrants usually brought back as much or more money than they remitted, it is clear that immigration to Hawai`i generated a good deal of money for the Japanese economy, perhaps as much as $5 million over the ten-year period. By way of comparison, Japan's chief export— tea—earned less than half that amount in 1892.[37] The Japanese government paid a lot of attention to the benefits to Japan and its people flowing from immigration to Hawai`i.

The immigrants obtained passports from prefectural authorities and made their way to Yokohama. The transpacific voyage usually took ten to fourteen days. They disembarked onto a small dock at the edge of the deep water in Honolulu harbor. Shouldering their baggage, they walked across a narrow causeway built of planks laid on top of pilings driven into the tidal sand flats, bare at low tide. The causeway stretched a kilometer to the reception station on Sand Island, barely above high tide level itself. There they lodged in the *sennin-goya*, or "hut of a thousand people." In reality, the hut was a collection of large government buildings, though these quarters were indeed cramped and the amenities few. One immigrant described the *sennin-goya:* "It had rough boards for beds and looked like a jail. Rice and beef, etc., were provided, which we cooked ourselves. If there was any case of contagious disease among us, our stay would be prolonged. So, we all hoped that nobody would become sick while there."[38] A justifiable fear of disease underlay Hawaiian insistence on eighteen days of quarantine, the presumed incubation period of smallpox, from the time they left Yokohama. Assuming a journey of ten to fourteen days, contract workers remained in quarantine four to eight days. If necessary, the authorities extended the quarantine until no disease appeared for eighteen consecutive days.

During 1885–94 the two governments arranged 26 shiploads totaling 28,691 immigrants, 23,071 men, 5,487 women, and 133 children. Despite the mandatory payroll deductions for return tickets, roughly half the immigrants remained after their three-year stints. Why some returned and others remained is not clear. Likely some workers had not saved enough to return to Japan and buy land, so they kept working. Others probably thought their lives, though hard, would be better in Hawai`i.[39]

By the late 1890s, a large plantation was often much like a mainland company town. Living conditions varied according to the quality of the white management. One of the best, the Brewer Halawa Plantation, had a cluster of multistoried mill buildings around a giant ten-story smokestack. Near the mill were barracks for single workers and several rows of two-room worker huts with tiny porches. Communal bath and toilet buildings were nearby. In the center of the housing complex lay a small, classically designed Japanese temple, with its steep roof and broad eaves.[40]

Plantation life was hard at best and terrible on the worst plantations in the early years of immigration. Workers received metal identification tags called *bango*, after the Japanese word for number. Their contracts stipulated free housing, medical care, and cooking fuel. Housing varied from rude huts built by workers themselves from plantation supplies to large barracks with single men and families jammed into tiny rooms. Besides working in the fields, women cooked for their own families and often, for a fee, for the bachelors. Some plantations had central cookhouses. Given low wages and a desire to save, workers economized on food. Their diets were likely as good as or better than back home but no more lavish than needed to sustain their tough physical labor. Rice was a staple, along with fish, tofu, small portions of chicken or pork or beef, and vegetables such as squash, turnips, onions, green beans, and Japanese radishes. Medical care was mediocre at best and often substandard.

Daily life commenced at four thirty in the morning with the dreaded camp whistle. After a light breakfast of rice, miso soup, and tea, workers were in the fields by six o'clock for a ten-hour day, six days a week, with a half hour to eat prepacked lunches (*bento*). To protect their skin from the sun, insects, and the cane, workers wore hats and scarves, gloves, long pants or skirts, leggings, and sturdy footwear. Hawai`i's fine weather felt much worse when heavily dressed and hacking one's way through the sun-baked, breezeless middle of a cane field. After the four-thirty whistle, they headed home to bathe, eat supper, tend gardens, wash clothes, and socialize a bit before retiring early. Not surprisingly, Japanese tried to impose a semblance of normality to their lives; hence customs such as Japanese style bathhouses (*ofuro*), occasional sumo and baseball tournaments, and Japanese festival days crept into plantation life, especially after annexation.

The Convention of 1886 satisfied both Hawai`i and Japan. It met Hawai`i's desire for diligent workers who would go home after the contract expired. It allowed Hawai`i to stop the politically unpopular Chinese immigration. It produced significant remittances for Japan's economy and a better life for thousands of its people. Both countries addressed, if not always solved, problems such as the lack of enough interpreters or doctors, or the mistreatment of laborers on the plantations.

Above all, the convention made the inflow predictable and controllable. This was acutely important for Hawai`i. Immigrants arrived only in the numbers requested. Because the Japanese government controlled passport issuance, virtually no Japanese went to Hawai`i except as contract laborers.

After 1885 Japanese immigrants supplied the vast majority of new fieldworkers. The Portuguese and Native Hawaiian labor force was stable and the number of Chinese laborers declined until 1894. For now, no one worried about the political implications of the dramatic demographic change and the evergrowing interest of the Japanese government in Hawaiian affairs. Everyone regarded Japanese immigration as a lifeline, rescuing the sugar-centered Hawaiian economy from labor shortages.

CHAPTER 5

The Fragmentation of Hawaiian Politics

For a century, Native Hawaiian monarchs wielded supreme authority. Kings often appointed foreigners to cabinets and consulted white advisors, but royal authority was unquestioned. Missionaries and other foreigners taught Hawaiians that the modern era required education, piety, and good government. For a long time, Native Hawaiians saw their future as intertwined with that of foreigners. Both would prosper together, or so went the theory. Over the years, as the Native Hawaiian population shrank and many more foreigners came to the islands, foreigners' influence rose. The white business community grew richer. Their taxes funded the government; their businesses employed most of the population. They wanted political influence commensurate with their economic position.

During the reign of King David Kalākaua, Hawaiian politics fragmented. Hawaiians and foreigners ceased to share common interests and similar visions of the future. Native Hawaiians felt their country slipping away and strongly supported the monarchy as the last bulwark of Polynesian predominance. Whites wanted an efficient government nurturing an Anglo-American style of politics and economic development. They wanted the king to follow their advice. They wanted an Americanized or Europeanized country. In a compelling analysis, Jonathan Osorio concludes that nineteenth-century Hawaiian history was "a gradual accommodation of the haole, first their presence, their religion, their legal system, and finally their economics, into a national order that was designed to separate the Natives from their traditional reliance on the *ali`i* (high chief) and on the *`āina* (the land or earth), transferring them to a reliance on western law, education, and capitalism. Intrinsic to this transformation was the haole claim that it was necessary for the kingdom and its Native inhabitants to embrace, or at least deal with, Western conceptions of modernity for it and them to survive."[1]

The booming sugar industry had little room for Hawaiians in middle management, certainly none in the lily-white top levels. The white-dominated business community did nothing to help Hawaiians advance in the economy. Instead they occupied the bottom rungs. The situation cried out for what would later be called affirmative action. Moreover, there were no longer enough Polynesians to supply plantation needs, which meant turning to immigrants. The kingdom expended a good chunk of money to facilitate the growth of sugar by subsidizing immigration and funding internal improvements. Wasn't it unfair to complain about taxes on wealth when the public purse contributed to the creation of that wealth? A feeling of alienation from the sugar industry made it easier to support taxes on the whites who were getting rich from it.

Political fragmentation began from the very moment of Kalākaua's ascension. King Lunalilo died in February 1874 without an heir.[2] For the first time, the legislature would select a monarch. Many Native Hawaiians and the British community strongly supported Queen Emma, widow of Kamehameha IV. Other Hawaiians and the rest of the foreign community, especially the Americans, backed David Kalākaua. The legislature voted for Kalākaua 39–6, triggering a riot. Several hundred of Queen Emma's supporters trashed the courthouse where the legislature met, injuring more than a quarter of the legislators. One died and another was seriously wounded when he was tossed out of a second story window. American and British landing parties restored order, remaining ashore more than a week. More than fifty persons paid fines or served jail time. The disorder foreshadowed the constant political troubles that followed, including a revolution in 1887 that set the stage for a second rebellion in 1893 that overthrew the monarchy

Kalākaua initially pleased the whites, with his successful push for reciprocity, and Native Hawaiians, with his encouragement of Hawaiian arts and culture. A congenial man, he mixed easily with everyone. He loved music, literature, and good conversation. Henry Adams claimed the king knew Hawaiian arts and history like a professor. He founded the *Hale Naua* (Temple of Science) to encourage the study of Native Hawaiian history and genealogy. He collected stories and tales from oldsters, and he published *The Legends and Myths of Hawai`i* in 1886. In his younger days, he surfed and wrestled, and loved to be at sea throughout his life. A powerful, big-chested man with long sideburns and a droopy mustache, he had a melodious voice and was almost as good at composing songs as his sister Lili`uokalani.

It is doubtful that Kalākaua was quite as much a womanizer, drinker, and gambler as his critics claimed. It is clear that he was quite attractive to women. Kalākaua's friendship with a pretty Danish woman he met in Vienna on his world tour was noticed by his wife, Queen Kapiolani. But perhaps his greatest attraction, to both men and women, was his good nature and courtesy. People might disagree with him, but they liked him. Even rebels such as Samuel Damon, William O. Smith, and Sanford Dole liked the king personally. When the cabinet recommended Dole for a Supreme Court vacancy in 1887, he had to interview with Kalākaua for final approval. Kalākaua knew Dole was a rebel sympathizer, inclined to restrict royal powers. But Dole recalled a "pleasant interview," given the king's "disposition to greet both friends and foes courteously and with kindliness of demeanor, whatever the feelings in his own heart."[3] Riding once with his retainers, Kalākaua discovered a young boy, Austin Strong, near the royal duck ponds in Waikīkī. Austin had stolen a large Japanese goldfish from the ponds and was fearfully hiding it under his hat. The genial king swept up both boy and fish, depositing them in front of the Strongs' house where Austin dropped the parched but still-wriggling fish in the horse trough. The next morning Austin received, by royal messenger, a note granting him the perpetual right to fish in the royal ponds, signed: "Kalākaua Rex."[4] It was hard to dislike a man like that.

As he grew older, Kalākaua's drinking hurt his health. He liked to hole up in the King's boathouse with friends, cards, and alcohol. When Robert Louis Stevenson came to Hawai`i in 1889 on doctor's orders, the two became close friends. "A fine, intelligent fellow," Stevenson wrote, "but what a crop for drink!"[5] The king's face and body grew thinner and he moved more slowly, though his mind stayed sharp.

Kalākaua always needed more money than the legislature gave the Crown. This need allowed Claus Spreckels to manipulate him with gifts and loans. When the cabinet denied Spreckels' application for water rights on Maui royal land, the sugar baron used a personal loan to get the king to appoint pliable new ministers, who sold the license for five hundred dollars a year. In 1880 the king again dismissed the cabinet and named as prime minister Celso Caesar Moreno, an Italian adventurer with big ideas for enriching himself and Kalākaua by setting up a steamship line to Asia. Moreno sought a public subsidy for his line and a $10 million foreign loan, which would give the Crown more funds without having to balance the annual budget. Moreno lasted five days in office before the popular uproar forced the king to sack him.

King Kalākaua knew that, for his Native Hawaiian subjects, the monarchy defined their identity. A rich, powerful, respected monarch helped his people feel they were still in control of their destiny, even as their numbers dropped and they fell behind in the economy. The king tried to portray Hawai`i, and himself, as important international players. He took a trip around the world in 1881. Kalākaua stopped first in Japan, where he met a warm welcome. It did not seem to matter that all of Hawai`i had fewer people than one administrative division of Tokyo. Kalākaua was a royal head of state, the first Christian king to visit from what Japanese thought of as "The West," and that was enough. Soon after his return, Kalākaua arranged a lavish coronation for himself to attract international attention and also confirm his family as the dynasty replacing the Kamehamehas. The expense of the coronation and of `Iolani Palace, the recently completed masterpiece where the coronation occurred, bothered white businessmen, whose taxes paid for it. Two more of Spreckels' schemes further outraged them. For his giant Maui plantation, Spreckels bought property but also leased 24,000 acres of Crown lands. After he manufactured a bogus claim against other royal lands, he got the legislature to give him title to his leased Crown lands in exchange for dropping the bogus claim. It was obvious that bribes had been involved. The tainted legislature later approved the king's request to mint in San Francisco a million dollars of silver coins bearing Kalākaua's likeness. Spreckels pocketed $150,000 in fees for handling this transaction. All this manipulation went to the Sugar King's head. He put on such airs that the real king decided to dump him. The government borrowed a million dollars from London bankers and paid off Spreckels. He returned to the mainland, where from then on, he spoke ill of the king. He kept his enormously profitable sugar operations.

The king's appointment of Walter Murray Gibson further dismayed much of the white community. Gibson was an adventuring opportunist with a big brain and big ambition, who dominated the cabinet from 1882 to 1887. With the king's tacit approval, Gibson rammed controversial measures through the legislature. The cabinet received the right to sell an opium import license for $30,000 annually. This upset moralistic whites, not just because the measure involved an evil drug but because bribes might influence the license sale. In fact, some government jobs were sold outright. It appeared the king used his privilege of importing personal items duty-free to evade custom charges on goods later sold to others. Gibson pandered to the king's dream of becoming the most influential leader in Oceania. Kalākaua unwisely intervened in the Samoan tangle, greatly upsetting Germany. He sent to Samoa a little steamer fitted out with a few guns and crewed with nonsailors and a drunken captain. Though perhaps partly motivated by excessive self-regard, he also sought to increase the monarchy's prestige to balance the wealth and stature of the sugar barons.[6]

By early 1887 the white business community, along with a few Native Hawaiians and part-Hawaiians, thought that Kalākaua and Gibson were corrupt and bad managers of the country. That was probably true, though they did forge the useful immigration convention with Japan. Nor did the opposition offer anything to substitute for the king's appeal to the Native Hawaiian electorate. The white business community offered little but trickle-down economics. Few Native Hawaiians could get bank loans to start a business or buy an interisland steamer, and none was able to scrape up the capital for a sugar plantation. Whites turned to other whites to borrow money and share the costs of new ventures. To whom would a Hawaiian turn? Hawaiians had little faith in the white-run system to give them a better life. No whites made a major, conscious effort to involve Hawaiians in the sugar business and ensure some possibility of advancement. Given their educations and privileged social and economic positions, white opponents of the king might have come up with better ideas for constructing a better future for all peoples. Instead, they embraced the same pedestrian idea found on the mainland: that economic development driven by the well-to-do—and primarily benefiting them—would improve the lot of everyone else.

Admittedly, Native Hawaiian leaders themselves came up with few sound schemes for improving people's lives. During the final years of the monarchy, it seemed mere control of the government was the end in itself. Certainly many Native Hawaiians linked preservation of the monarchy with preservation of a Native Hawaiian nation, but could the monarchy have been more than a symbol? One looks in vain for the economic development program behind Queen Lili`uokalani's determination to restore royal prerogatives. For what useful end, besides power itself, did she wish greater authority? While regaining control of the legislature and the courts was a necessary first step, she laid out no program beyond that, as a visionary leader might have. That said, Native Hawaiians identified with the monarchs, even if the royals occasionally disappointed them with human frailties. The white community never understood that the monarchy was the last remaining symbol of the greatness of Old Hawai`i. Most whites did not appreciate that, for Native Hawaiians, turning their faces from the throne meant abandoning their identity. That lack of understanding, that dearth of shared destiny, bedeviled and fragmented island politics. Jonathan Osorio persuasively argues that the haole did not share the same deep faith in the legitimacy of the Hawaiian kingdom as did Native Hawaiians. Haole, even those born in the islands, had an ancestral home that was more real to them than the kingdom. For Native Hawaiians, the monarchy "symbolized their very survival as a people."[7]

Many opposed to the Gibson government coalesced into the Hawaiian League. One of the leaders, Lorrin Thurston, would become the arch-rebel. No other rebel would be as influential over so many years.[8] Born in O`ahu of a missionary family, Thurston was a fluent Hawaiian speaker. His memoirs record a lively childhood, diving for "pearls" (bits of colored rock) in Nu`uanu stream, playing and quarreling with white and Native Hawaiian playmates, and running afoul of Hawaiian royalty, a trait he would continue into adulthood. After he was thrown out of Punahou School for repeated pranks and taking his studies lightly, he worked for Judge Alfred Hartwell for three years, learning enough law to hang out his own shingle. He worked fifteen months as the chief accountant of the Wailuku Sugar Company, then studied at Columbia University Law School, where his classmate was Theodore Roosevelt. Back in Honolulu in 1881, Thurston built his own law practice, partnering with William O. Smith, and entered the legislature in 1884 as a rabid opponent of the Gibson government.

Thurston was brash and stubborn. His memoirs record a boyhood run-in with Princess Ruth Ke`elikōlani, who loved Waikīkī's trees as much as her godchild Ka`iulani did. Thurston and his friend Akono Akau drove an oxcart to Waikīkī to get sand for Punahou School. They had just filled the cart when they were told "the chief" forbade them to remove the sand. The chief was the formidable Princess Ruth, sitting cross-legged on a mat beneath a coco palm and gazing at the ocean. One of the last of the Kamehamehas, she was an immense woman, six feet tall and four hundred pounds, so heavy that she could not mount a horse and had great difficulty entering a carriage. She rode around the city sitting in the back of a low wagon driven by retainers.

The princess took no note of the boys as they approached. In fluent Hawaiian, Thurston twice explained their task, and twice the huge princess, still staring at the water, grunted "no!" Thurston, as quick with a rude retort as a boy as he would be as an adult, told the princess that she was stingy for hoarding sand when it was so plentiful. Slowly the massive head turned and pinned Thurston with a glare. "Who," she roared, "is this impudent white boy?" A nearby woman identified Thurston as the grandson of the respected Reverend Andrews. Princess Ruth digested this fact—it may have saved Thurston from being the *late* grandson of Reverend Andrews—pointed away from the beach with her arm (it was the size of a tree limb), and commanded: "Ku! A hele!" Thurston and Akono wisely slunk away as ordered. But, typical of the obstinate Thurston, the boys went to another part of Waikīkī and got their sand there.

Thurston had a lifelong fascination with Hawai`i's volcanoes. For several years he lived in Maui and attended the Haleakalā Boarding School, nine miles from

Haleakalā's 10,032-foot summit. He loved to hike and began leading tourists up the volcano and into the crater. Later he became entranced with the volcano Kīlauea on the big island and tried to build up tourism there. While he was minister of the interior in 1887, he appointed his Haleakalā schoolmate Robert Kalanipo`o as chief engineer of a wagon road from Kona into the interior. In 1889 Thurston ordered construction of a carriage road from Hilo, where steamers called, to Kīlauea. When the Hilo road opened in 1894, stagecoaches reached the Volcano House, a hotel on the rim of Kīlauea's crater, in only four hours. Thurston presented, in his 1891 book, *Vistas of Hawai`i*, an idyllic and largely true picture of Hawai`i as an undiscovered tourist paradise. Thurston spent much time and money producing the "Cyclorama of Kīlauea," a multimedia extravaganza he displayed at the World Columbian Exposition in Chicago in 1893 and at the San Francisco Fair in 1894–95. Later, as publisher of the *Pacific Commercial Advertiser,* he spearheaded the 1916 creation of Hawai`i Volcanoes National Park.

Only twenty-eight years old in 1887, Thurston had piercing black eyes and an attitude that could only be described as "intense." He strongly supported annexation. He hated the pomp and ceremony of the Crown almost as much as he disliked what he saw as the mismanagement and corruption of the royal government. Thurston was not a planter, but like William O. Smith, Sanford Dole, and others, he bought and sold a few shares of plantation stocks. But like virtually all white people in Hawai`i, Thurston made a living in an economy shaped and dominated by sugar. The plantations depended on the lawyers to write their contracts and settle their disputes, and on the bankers to loan money for improvements and manage the money flows. Mechanics built centrifuges and vacuum pans, shopkeepers sold goods to the plantation workers, prostitutes catered to the young, predominately male labor force. When sugar made money, whites made money. But the revolutionists and the planters were hardly in perfect agreement. Many American planters, such as Claus Spreckels, feared that American law would strip away the foreign workers without whom the industry would collapse. Some British planters preferred an independent Hawai`i. Other planters focused on their business interests. Whoever ran the country would still nurture and protect the sugar industry.

Thurston's burnished, selective memoirs, written more than forty years later, are the only source of information about the Hawaiian League. Several hundred whites of American or German birth or descent joined. They were not planters but clerks, mechanics, tradesmen, lawyers, and shopkeepers. They agreed to support potential paramilitary actions "to protect the white community against arbitrary or oppressive action of the Government."[9] A radical faction wanted to topple the monarchy by force and annex Hawai`i to the United States. The much larger, less radical group wanted a new constitution to constrain the king's authority and make him reign in a fashion similar to British monarchs. Some men, such as Sanford Dole, left the League because they could not stomach the radical proposals. The League midwifed the birth of the Honolulu Rifles, a militia composed largely of Americans and one German company, the Drei Hundert.

King Kalākaua realized that disaster approached. On June 27, 1887, he talked with his friend George Merrill, the American minister, who advised that Gibson was driving League members toward revolt. Merrill reported that the king agreed to dismiss Gibson on the grounds that those who paid the kingdom's taxes should have confidence in the cabinet.[10]

Under the Rifles' threat, the king accepted the "Bayonet Constitution" that curtailed royal powers. Previously the king had appointed the upper house and the cabinet. Universal male suffrage had elected the lower house. Under the Bayonet Constitution, voters elected both houses, but property or income qualifications restricted suffrage. Candidates for office had to meet income or property qualifications as well. The legislature assumed responsibility for naturalizing and enfranchising residents. Thus, Americans and Europeans could remain citizens of their home country and benefit concurrently from Hawaiian citizenship. Native Hawaiians, Europeans, and Americans could be citizens, but not Asians. Royal decrees now required consent of the cabinet. These constitutional changes could have been made by amending the 1864 constitution, but with no hope of obtaining a two-thirds vote of both houses, the white rebels resorted to extralegal methods.[11] As Merze Tate noted, the Bayonet Constitution took no individual rights from Native Hawaiians but greatly weakened their relative power by boosting the political power of the propertied whites.[12] The new constitution brought the relative powers of the king and legislature closer to the practice of Britain and other parliamentary democracies. That said, in the 1887 Hawaiian context, the new constitution took power from the monarchy—the institution used by Native Hawaiians to control their homeland—and increased the power of a small group.

The Bayonet Constitution kicked off five and a half years of discord, a long semirevolution culminating in the overthrow of the monarchy in 1893. The king tested the constitution's limits wherever he could. Native Hawaiians frequently petitioned the king for a new constitution or a constitutional convention. Some unhappy Native Hawaiians, persons of mixed race, and a few whites looked to Robert Wilcox, a part-Hawaiian with some military training and with a bent toward action if not sound judgment.[13] Born in Maui in 1855, Wilcox won a seat in the legislature in 1879 when his opponent was convicted of stuffing the ballot box. Wilcox aligned himself with royal interests. The king immediately rewarded him by sending him for military training in Italy. Wilcox spent seven years on a lavish government subsidy, attending the basic officer course, earning a commission, and completing an advanced artillery course. As soon as Gibson was forced from office, the new cabinet recalled all Hawaiians studying abroad at government expense. Wilcox returned in the fall of 1887 and immediately entangled himself in a scheme to have Kalākaua abdicate in favor of his sister. Wilcox could not find work and even lived with his Italian wife at Lili`uokalani's residence for a time. His anti-Kalākaua scheming forced him to go to California. Upon his return in April 1889 he instantly plunged into another plot against the king. Wilcox's biographer, Ernest Andrade Jr., notes his constantly changing motivations, grudges, and alliances. Thurston called him a chronic revolutionist because he did not care which side he was on, so long as he was leading a fight.[14]

Wilcox's group wanted a new constitution as well, but one that suited their purposes. Even Thurston's white Reform Party, which won the first elections under the Bayonet Constitution, became unhappy when the suffrage limitations did not guarantee white supremacy. Before long, the Reform Party lost control of the legislature and was turned out of the cabinet.[15]

On July 15, 1889, rumors flew that agitators planned to depose Kalākaua, install his sister and heir, Lili`uokalani, and proclaim a new constitution. Soon Wilcox and one hundred Native Hawaiians and part-Hawaiians attempted a coup. They occupied the Government Building and the palace grounds. (The king was not in the palace.) Hawaiian government troops surrounded the area, trapping Wilcox and his men. Sharpshooters picked off insurgents who were attempting to operate their three cannon on the palace grounds. Troops landed from the *Adams* to guard American citizens and "as a precautionary measure in the event any assistance to preserve order might be required."[16] The government did not ask for help, and American troops took no part in the fighting. Government forces killed six insurgents and wounded twelve before Wilcox surrendered. He was later acquitted of treason by a Native Hawaiian jury sympathetic to his testimony that the king had somehow blessed his rebellion.

In the summer of 1890 another revolt looked possible. Wilcox and his followers demanded a new constitution via a convention. Wilcox proclaimed that "if the people are not granted their rights, the streets will be sticky with blood . . . , many people killed, and I myself will take a hand in it."[17] The new U.S. minister, John L. Stevens, and British commissioner James Wodehouse prepared to land troops to quell rioting.[18] The near revolt may have scared Kalākaua into considering a new constitution, either by convention or by proclamation. At the request of prominent whites, Stevens and Wodehouse told the king that to proclaim a new constitution would be "fatal."[19] The king backed off.[20] Wodehouse and Stevens agreed to keep warships in Honolulu to deter any outbreak.[21]

While in California to rest, the king died suddenly on January 20, 1891. His sister Lydia Kamaka`eha Dominis Lili`uokalani became queen at age fifty-two.[22] A dignified woman with a squarish face, Lili`uokalani studied at the Chiefs' School for children of high chiefly rank. She had been a regent during Kalākaua's 1881 trip around the world. She had been to the United States twice and visited Britain for the Queen's Jubilee. Her husband, John Dominis, whose infidelity and other behavior caused her much pain over the years, was a white businessman and governor of O`ahu until his death in the early months of her reign. A devout Christian, the queen had many social connections through the church. She participated intimately with Native Hawaiian societies, supported Polynesian culture and welfare, and sometimes endorsed hot issues such as constitutional reform. Like her brother, Lili`uokalani was well read and a great lover of music. Among her many compositions is the famous song "Aloha `Oe." Like her brother, she relied too often on inept advisors with their own agendas. Her occasional consultations with Fraulein Wolf, a German mystic, illustrated her tendency to have things be what she wished or hoped, rather than what they were.

She was very close to her sister Likelike, mother of Princess Ka`iulani, but had much rockier relations with her brother, especially after 1887. It was common knowledge that she felt Kalākaua yielded too easily to his opponents. By such actions as turning a willing ear to occasional suggestions that the king should abdicate in her favor and letting Robert Wilcox live in her unoccupied house in Kapalama, she allowed herself to be associated with anti-Kalākaua forces.

Like her brother, Lili`uokalani hated the Bayonet Constitution's restraints on royal power. She would eventually act on those feelings. An early sign came on January 29, 1891, when the chief justice administered the oath of office, required by Article 24 of the Bayonet Constitution, that legally put Lili`uokalani on the throne. She swore "to maintain the Constitution of the Kingdom whole and inviolate, and to govern in conformity therewith."[23] Wodehouse said she initially balked at the oath but gave in only when the chief justice explained she could not become queen without it.[24] The queen later wrote that her opponents callously forced her to take the oath:

So dazed with the suddenness of the news that had come upon us in a moment, that I hardly realized what was going on about me, nor did I at all appreciate for the moment my situation. Before I had time to collect myself, before my brother's remains were buried, a trap was sprung upon me by those who stood waiting as a wild beast watches for his prey. The ministers, who were apparently of one mind with the justices of the supreme court, called together the members of the council, and when all had taken their seats, sent for me. I turned to Governor Dominis before entering the chamber, and inquired of him, "what is the object of this meeting?" He said that they had come together to witness my taking of the oath of office. I told him at once that I did not wish to take the oath just then, and asked why such proceedings could not be deferred until after my brother's funeral. He said that others had decided that I must take my official oath then and there. Few persons have ever been placed without a word of warning in such a trying situation, and I doubt if there was any other woman in the city who could have borne with passable equanimity what I had to endure that day. I will scarcely limit the comparison to my sex; I doubt if many men could have passed successfully through such an ordeal. Ere I realized what was involved, I was compelled to take the oath to the constitution, the adoption of which had led to my brother's death.[25]

The queen's recollection of her oath-taking reveals much. She was understandably distraught by her brother's death, but the cabinet and chief justice did their constitutional duty, albeit by a constitution she hated.

The queen portrayed herself as coerced in order to mitigate her violation of the oath in January 1893, when she attempted to proclaim a new constitution. Lili`uokalani's real complaint was against the constitution itself, not the timing of the oath. Despite the extralegal imposition of the Bayonet Constitution, the white community considered the queen bound by it. These sharply conflicting views signaled trouble ahead.

The government disbanded the Native Hawaiian Rifles, including the Kamehameha Guards, after the 1889 rebellion proved that Wilcox supporters had infiltrated the Guards. The white Honolulu Rifles disbanded not long after. With the two militias gone, the King's Royal Household Guards were the only organized military force in the islands when Lili`uokalani ascended to the throne.

In 1892 the political fragmentation worsened. Wodehouse reported that Wilcox again plotted revolution, joined by Volney Ashford, a white architect of the Bayonet Constitution, who now wanted to destroy it.[26] Stevens noted impatience with the monarchy among white businessmen and the "less responsible of the foreign and native population of the islands."[27] In March 1892 tension grew to the point where Marshal Charles Wilson ordered the Household Guards to sandbag the palace grounds.[28] On March 8 Stevens described a secret group of revolutionists "hostile to the Queen and to her chief confidants," and especially opposed to the future accession of the "half-English" Ka'iulani. He asked Secretary of State James G. Blaine outright for guidance if the Hawaiian monarchy were threatened. Would he be justified in helping the royal government, or should he confine himself to protection of American property, the lives of American citizens, and, vaguely, "the prevention of anarchy?" On March 25, in a private letter to "Bro. Blaine," Stevens asked, "I want you to write me in as few or many words as you please—are you for annexation?"[29] Blaine did not reply.

Based on his talks with Blaine, Mott Smith did not think the secretary sought overthrow of the queen. The United States would support the queen in

> her authority and in the preservation of internal order, with the view that
> our native Sovereigns and our native government should stand in the front
> as long as possible. You may rest assured that the United States will not
> interfere in our affairs, except by desire of the Queen, in times of [trouble],
> and then only to withdraw when order shall have been restored. . . . What
> the United States wants in our Islands is preservation of law and order, and
> no changes but such as may come about through Constitutional means.[30]

U.S. admiral George Brown apparently offered to aid the queen if there was a revolt. He landed three hundred sailors for a drill that British commissioner Wodehouse complained was a "naval demonstration" when the troops paraded in front of the palace to show that they stood behind the monarch. Wodehouse feared Brown's support would curry favor with the queen.[31]

Although the queen may have appreciated Brown's support, she certainly did not enjoy her interactions with John Stevens, whose behavior toward the Crown was overbearing and rude. Stevens and Secretary of State Blaine were old friends, who in the 1850s helped found the Republican Party in Maine and from 1854 jointly edited the *Kennebec Journal*. Later Blaine entered national politics while Stevens worked in state politics and then served as minister to Norway, Sweden, Paraguay, and Uruguay. Seventy-two years old in 1892, he was a tall, thin patrician who usually wore a pained expression on his face. He spoke slowly and condescendingly to the queen. He was quarrelsome with her supporters, partial to her white opponents, and convinced that the Crown was holding back Hawaiian development. Once a practicing minister, Stevens took an excessively moralistic and critical view of the royals and identified strongly with royal opponents, many the descendants of Maine immigrants. Unlike his predecessor, George Merrill, who earned the trust of both the Crown and its opponents, Stevens had terrible relations with Lili`uokalani and especially with her marshal, Charles Wilson.

Meanwhile, Wilcox plotted. In April he told a rally that the monarchy should go because the queen paid no attention to Native Hawaiians. In May he termed the queen the enemy of the Hawaiian people and declared a republic preferable, with only Native Hawaiians allowed to hold the important government posts. Marshal Wilson used undercover police officers to track the plotting. When Wilcox proclaimed that Hawaiians should abandon the current regime and impose a new constitution, Wilson jailed him for treason, along with seventeen others, including the incendiary Volney Ashford. Judge Sanford Dole released most arrestees for lack of evidence but bound over Wilcox and five others for trial because the judicial hearings showed they planned to overthrow the government. Before long, the attorney general dropped the charges against Wilcox, who returned to his legislative seat. The government did not think a Native Hawaiian jury would convict the rabble-rouser.[32]

During the Wilcox hysteria in May, Thurston went to Washington to sound out policy makers and promote the idea of annexation. (He spent most of his visit to the United States in Chicago making preparations for Hawai`i's Kīlauea Volcano pavilion at the Chicago World's Fair, dedicated in October 1892 with the pavilion opening in May 1893.) It is worth remembering that his trip occurred when the royal government feared a coup attempt not by Thurston and the Reform Party but by Wilcox and his followers. The arrests came while Thurston was abroad. Thurston believed that annexation was the long-term solution to internal political squabbles. Thurston saw Cushman Davis, a senior Republican on the Senate Foreign Relations Committee; James Blount, the Democratic chair of the House Committee on Foreign Affairs; Secretary of the Navy Benjamin Tracy; and Secretary of State Blaine. Thurston wrote many years later that all were sympathetic to his story of progressive white elements struggling against evildoers. They remembered being noncommittal. Blount thought Thurston was full of himself.

The arrests of the Wilcox plotters ended the immediate threat of rebellion, but the queen's camp sought to undercut Wilcox's popularity among Native Hawaiians by embracing his issues, including a "new and more liberal constitution."[33] Queen Lili`uokalani secretly worked on a revised constitution with three advisors, probably the legislators Joseph Nāwahī and William White as well as the captain of the guard, Samuel Nowlein. On August 2, 1892, she wrote: "our work is completed and only waits for the Proroguing of the Legislature."[34] (Prorogation was the sovereign's formal closing of the legislative session.)

Thus the queen decided well before the January 1893 revolution—even before the *Boston* was deployed to Hawai`i—to promulgate a new charter, largely to preempt an immediate threat to her political base. Sudden unilateral promulgation would likely please Native Hawaiians and decrease Wilcox's appeal, but it would certainly trigger a political clash with whites, perhaps one more severe than 1887. Given the deeply held and relatively unalterable positions of the major political groups, once the queen committed to unilateral promulgation in the summer of 1892, the January 1893 revolution became virtually inevitable, barring a last minute change of plans by the monarch.

While the queen prepared her constitution, the political discord increased. Three groups—the queen's supporters, the white-led faction, and Wilcox's followers—struggled in the legislature. An August 1892 no-confidence vote turned out the Samuel Parker cabinet that Lili`uokalani had appointed eighteen months earlier. For three months, no cabinet could be formed. British practice was to form cabinets from leaders of the majority party or coalition. But the Bayonet Constitution empowered the queen to appoint new men she liked, though they could be turned out by a no-confidence vote. For three months, that is exactly what happened. She appointed her favorites and the legislature voted them out.[35]

Finally, she summoned Wodehouse, who spent the summer persuading the queen that Stevens and Admiral Brown in particular were not acting in her best interests.[36] Perhaps this disposed the queen toward Wodehouse, for she asked him what to do about the cabinet. They discussed four men who were respected enough not to be turned out. Wodehouse urged her to select them. "I will make the appointments," she said. She complained about Stevens and asked if he would interfere in her struggle with the legislature. Wodehouse replied that Stevens needed a pretext, and appointing her new cabinet would not provide one.[37]

The Wilcox cabinet took power on November 8. George N. Wilcox (no relation to Robert W. Wilcox) was minister of the interior. A wealthy sugar grower from Kauai, Wilcox was born in Hawai`i of missionary parents. The minister of foreign affairs was Mark Robinson, of mixed parentage, whom even Stevens declared was highly capable. The minister of finance was Peter Jones, who had arrived in Hawai`i twenty-five years before. Cecil Brown, born in the islands of British parents, was attorney general. A gleeful Stevens saw the new cabinet as the "triumph of the better citizens over the worse, and especially a proof of American ascendancy over ultra English and other anti-American elements and sentiments."[38] (He might have been less thrilled if he knew that the queen had consulted the British minister about the cabinet.) The *Boston*'s captain concurred that "the danger of a political crisis seems to have passed."[39]

The Wilcox cabinet skillfully managed affairs. Politics seemed to settle down. Wodehouse predicted an attempt to turn out the cabinet because, being moderate, it was not completely satisfactory to either extreme. "As the session is drawing to a close," he wrote, "if the cabinet can hold their position a little longer, they will be safe for two years." After the planned dissolution of the legislature in January 1893, the legislature would not reassemble for almost two years, making a no-confidence vote impossible.[40]

About the same time, Stevens learned the Democrats won the 1892 presidential election. He turned his mind to his impending departure. He wrote a long briefing paper for the incoming administration and his unknown successor. (He had promised this overview to Blaine but, after Blaine's June resignation and replacement by John Watson Foster, never got around to writing it.) Stevens predicted that U.S. policy "will soon demand some change, if not the adoption of decisive measures, with the aim to secure American interests and future supremacy by encouraging Hawaiian development and aid to promote responsible government in these islands." Stevens urged the old stand-bys: annexation or a protectorate, forging a customs union, laying an undersea cable to the west coast, and obtaining cession of Pearl Harbor.[41]

Stevens initially favored a military protectorate but by 1892 preferred annexation. Outright ownership would place Hawai`i inside the U.S. tariff wall, rectifying the loss of reciprocity benefits caused by the McKinley tariff. This would reenergize the sugar industry. And after annexation, U.S. law enforcement would prevent rebellion. Annexation did present one tremendous complication. American law would prevent planters from importing the contract laborers who were essential to the sugar industry. Stevens knew no way around that huge obstacle to annexation.[42]

Throughout 1892 Stevens' behavior toward the Crown worsened. This grew partly from a hatred of the new marshal, Charles Wilson, spurred by Wilson's arrest of one of Stevens' Chinese servants for gambling. Partly it grew from Stevens' anger at an ugly newspaper story about him that he thought royalists had planted. Partly it was his affinity for whites, and partly it was his inability to take a powerful female seriously.[43]

Worst of all, Stevens let these irritants distort his behavior. Diplomats should be familiar with all elements of their host country. It was reasonable for Stevens to know people who favored annexation as a theoretical position, but he had no business hobnobbing with declared enemies of the queen. His close association with annexationists colored the course of events. His dispatches were so full of brutal remarks, innuendos, and character assassinations that Foster chastised him for incendiary language and directed him to separate his reports into two classes, a "narrative of public affairs in their open historical aspect," and the other a confidential channel for commentary on personal intrigues and other matters that would give the secretary a full understanding of the situation.[44] Was Foster beginning to worry about Stevens' ranting? Did he expect that Stevens was doing something that Foster did not want reported fully and openly? Those questions remain unanswered, though it is very likely that the punctilious Foster simply found Stevens' reports unprofessional.

Charles S. Campbell Jr. argues that Stevens exceeded his written instructions by overly close relations with Reform Party annexationists in 1892 and then by inappropriate actions during the January 1893 revolution. Campbell asserts that, by an astute reading of what instructions Stevens did *not* receive, he complied with the administration's intent to succor the annexationists. Blaine's silence to Stevens' messages in the spring of 1892 signaled approval: "A highly intelligent man, the Secretary obviously saw the drift of his protégé's queries and comments. Had he disapproved he should have sent a strong caution. By not so doing Blaine in particular, but also Foster and President Harrison, incurred a clear responsibility for Stevens' actions when the revolution occurred."[45]

Campbell is correct that—especially during the revolution—Stevens exceeded instructions. But it is doubtful that Blaine's (and Foster's) silence was a wordless message to act. First, Stevens knew his friend was ill. Blaine's health had been weakening for years. He took six months' sick leave in 1891 but continued to lose strength. Stevens might well have thought Blaine's silence was due to inattention from failing health. Blaine resigned on June 4, 1892, to challenge Harrison for the presidential nomination at the Republican convention.

Second, if Stevens knew Blaine's mind so well, why was the query necessary? If Stevens felt obliged to check with his mentor, silence must have left him uncertain about Blaine's wishes. Stevens could easily have interpreted silence as no change in policy; that is, no support for those who might topple the government.

Third, Blaine's resignation, shortly after Stevens' spring 1892 letters asking for guidance, should have had a deterrent effect. For if Stevens thought silence signaled "proceed but don't tell me the details," then how could Stevens not be stymied by Blaine's resignation? Without Blaine there to provide backup and move annexation along quickly, it would have been too risky to proceed.

Fourth, Blaine and Foster were busy and distracted. The potentially violent fur seal dispute with Britain consumed their attention during 1891–92. Even while at home sick, Blaine worked with Sir Julian Pauncefote, the British ambassador, to forge an arbitration treaty signed in February 1892. The treaty established a

seven-person panel—two Americans, two British, and three neutral Europeans—
to arbitrate the fur seal dispute once and for all. In the meantime, violence threatened again because the 1892 sealing season would occur before the arbitration.
The stopgap modus vivendi would expire in May. Blaine was again ill, and from
his sickbed in March had his secretary warn President Harrison against sending
warships to the Bering Sea. When Blaine staggered back to work at the end of
March, he and Sir Julian devised an extension of the modus vivendi, signed on
April 18, 1892. It was quite understandable that Blaine concentrated his limited
energy on the fur seal issue without intending to signal anything by not replying
to Stevens' dispatch. Foster was similarly distracted. Before becoming secretary, he
worked on the fur seal issue for months as the chief lawyer for the American side.
Because changing agents so close to the arbitration hearing, scheduled for Paris in
the spring of 1893, would have greatly damaged the American position, President
Benjamin Harrison asked Foster to handle both jobs. For eight months, Foster
acted in a dual capacity, spreading himself very thin.

Finally, rather than intentionally allowing Stevens to exceed instructions,
it is more likely that Blaine, ill and with a great deal on his plate, was simply
monitoring events. He rarely gave feedback, even before the crucial year of 1892.
During almost three years while Blaine was secretary and Stevens was in Hawai`i
(1889–92), Blaine wrote not a single substantive instruction or reply. As he saw it,
the trend of events ultimately favored annexation, whatever the royal government
did in the short term. The real danger was Robert Wilcox, whose coup might
strengthen Native Hawaiian control. To that threat, Blaine paid attention. After
receiving Stevens' query about his position on annexation, Blaine told Mott Smith
in early April that "I expect to hear of a revolution there" based on Stevens' report
of "an organized revolutionary party," that, given the Wilcox rabble-rousing of the
spring, surely referred to Wilcox, Ashford, and the other firebrands.[46]

What was Blaine's Hawaiian policy? His 1881 dispatch to Minister James
Comly laid the base: "The situation of the Hawaiian islands, giving them the
strategic control of the North Pacific, brings their possession within the range of
questions belonging to purely American policy, as much so as that of the Isthmus
itself. Hence the necessity, as recognized in our existing treaty relations, of drawing
the ties of intimate relationship between us and the Hawaiian Islands so as to
make them practically a part of the American system without derogation of their
absolute independence." Although the United States did not desire to possess
Hawai`i, "under no circumstances can the United States permit any change . . .
which would cut it adrift from the American system." The United States would
view with concern the introduction into Hawai`i of "new social elements destruc-

tive of its necessarily American character." By "American character" Blaine clearly meant a Native Hawaiian monarchy with wealthy whites exercising great influence. The remedy for the decline in the Native Hawaiian population, Blaine wrote, was not Asian immigration. "The Hawaiian Islands cannot be joined to the Asiatic system. If they drift from their independent station it must be toward assimilation and identification with the American system, to which they belong by the operation of natural laws and must belong by the operation of political necessity."[47] In 1891, at home on sick leave, he commented to President Harrison "there are only three places that are of value enough to be taken, that are not continental. One is Hawai`i and the others are Cuba and Porto Rico. Cuba and Porto Rico are not now imminent and will not be for a generation. Hawai`i may come up for decision at any unexpected hour and I hope we shall be prepared to decide it in the affirmative."[48] In Albert Volwiler's collection of Harrison-Blaine correspondence, this is the only substantive mention of Hawai`i, hardly a sign of intense interest by either Blaine or Harrison.

What was the situation as 1892 ended? Stevens was mentally packing his bags. His overview closed with a section called "What Should Be Done?" Clearly, he thought nothing would happen before his own departure.[49] Captain Wiltse of the *Boston* noted a "large and growing sentiment, particularly among the planters, in favor of annexation, but . . . the leaders do not think an opportune moment will arrive for some time to come. However, everything points to an eventual request for annexation."[50]

There was no reason to rush anything. The incoming Cleveland administration looked friendly. Grover Cleveland followed a steady course in his first term (1885–89), accepting reciprocity and even negotiating the treaty's extension. Importantly, the Democrats disliked high tariffs and were not beholden to the sugar trust. Their 1892 platform denounced the McKinley tariff and promised its repeal. It seemed certain a new tariff would restore Hawai`i's advantages under the reciprocity treaty.[51] There was no reason to foment a revolution, with all its attendant risks, to regain the duty-free status for sugar that Democratic victory would soon restore.

Sugar planters played no discernible role in fomenting revolution. Significantly, the turmoil of 1887–93 grew from political and constitutional dissatisfactions and rivalries for power among the royalists, Wilcox's supporters, and the white group opposed to both of them. The rebellions of 1887 and 1889 and the threatened rebellion of 1890 took place before the McKinley tariff took effect in April 1891. After that date, the sugar industry stagnated, but the tripartite political battles continued as before.

The Harrison administration did nothing to promote revolution. The Washington agent of the Annexationist Club, Archibald Hopkins, whom Thurston paid seventy-five dollars a month, seems to have done little while rumormongering incessantly. He claimed to have talked with administration officials, but there is no record of a meeting in the papers of any key policy maker—not in those of John Watson Foster, John Tyler Morgan, Robert Hitt, Cushman Davis, or anyone else. Hopkins surely started the newspaper rumors that Hawaiian minister Mott Smith talked secretly with Secretary of State Foster about annexation. Foster angrily denied any contacts.[52] Minister Smith told his foreign ministry, which opposed annexation, that he did nothing to advance it.[53] Probably Hopkins simply wanted to convince Thurston that he had done something. The newspaper barrage was twaddle, and bad twaddle at that. Even Wodehouse, never slow to imagine American mischief, told Lord Rosebery in December 1892 that the stories misrepresented the situation. There was no possibility of violent overthrow of the government.[54]

As the legislature prepared to end its work, the cabinet seemed stable. Whites were happy with it. Nobody was plotting, not even Wilcox, who had temporarily quieted down. The queen faced no immediate threat, but she still wanted to undermine Wilcox's appeal to her base. Hence, the only specific item to be implemented in the next few months was the queen's new constitution. She was the only principal with a timetable. Whether she would stick to it would determine the fate of the monarchy.

❧

CHAPTER 6

The Revolution Begins

Within two weeks, the USS *Boston* would become the most famous warship ever put in the service of American gunboat diplomacy. But on a crisp morning on January 4, 1893, the *Boston*'s sailors were simply readying the cruiser for sea. They were excited at the prospect of a trip to Hilo. Aside from a brief voyage to rescue some shipwrecked mariners, the *Boston* had not left port at Honolulu since its arrival the previous August. The deckhands worked rapidly in the predawn chill. The temperature dropped into the fifties overnight, unusually cold, even for a winter day in Hawai`i. The men loaded 160 pounds of fresh beef, 160 pounds of fresh vegetables, and 132 pounds of soft bread, enough for 250 hungry sailors for a day or two. Deep within the steel hull, men methodically coaled and fired the six boilers that drove the 3,500-horsepower engines and the single screw. At 9:35 AM, three civilian passengers came aboard: Minister John L. Stevens, his youngest daughter, and her friend Mrs. E. K. Martin. The large Marine contingent "paraded" in a formal welcoming ceremony for the minister. By this time, the sun was up and the chill was long gone. The officer of the deck recorded "fair, bright, pleasant weather," 71 degrees Fahrenheit with gentle breezes from the northwest. At 10:25 AM the cruiser departed for Hilo. Over the next 22 hours, the ship steamed 184 nautical miles at a little over 8 knots, about half its top speed, arriving at nine o'clock the next morning, January 5.[1]

Nine days later, on January 14, the *Boston*, and Stevens, returned to Honolulu precisely when the revolution began. On January 16, in the midst of the rebellion against the queen, the *Boston* landed troops and bivouacked them near the royal palace and across the street from Ali`iōlani Hale (popularly called the Government Building) from whose front steps the rebels proclaimed a new government a day later. Minister Stevens quickly recognized the new government. The queen's forces surrendered within a few hours, claiming a need to avoid conflict with the *Boston*'s landing party. The role of warship and sailors in the overthrow has always been murky and controversial. Cleveland's investigator, James Blount, compiled a detailed report on the revolution, as did the Senate Foreign Relations Committee, chaired by John Tyler Morgan, in 1894. Neither the Blount nor the Morgan report, nor several dozen subsequent histories have conclusively settled the controversy.

THE *BOSTON'S* VOYAGE

A central question is whether the *Boston*'s voyage was part of a conspiracy between white rebels and U.S. government representatives. If the *Boston* had not returned when it did, American troops could not have been landed and Minister Stevens could not have meddled.

Some writers have seen conspiracy in the warship's return just as the queen tried to promulgate the new constitution, triggering the revolt. Robert McElroy, an early Cleveland biographer, argued that the ship's return "just as the revolution needed the support of American marines" was the minister's attempt to create a "psychological moment for a brilliant stroke" to push annexation.[2] Merze Tate, author of the classic *The United States and the Hawaiian Kingdom*, argued that Stevens improperly conspired with white rebels to create a revolution. Stevens and Wiltse were "thoroughly acquainted with the explosive situation and knew exactly why the *Boston* left naval row that Wednesday [January 4]. . . . The annexationists, aware that no proposal for union with the United States would ever receive the approval of the electorate, and cognizant of their inability to carry a project of annexation through the Hawaiian legislature, deliberately lured the queen into a trap: they enticed her into committing a rash act which radically changed the political situation." Tate concluded: "the departure of the *Boston* certainly appears to me to have been arranged to test or aggravate the political situation."[3]

Helena G. Allen, who wrote biographies of Lili`uokalani, Kalākaua, and Dole, asserted that "Mr. Stevens, usually so knowledgeable about affairs of state, seemed determined to appear ignorant of what he later accused the queen of knowing:

that the opposition had enough votes lined up" to oust the Wilcox cabinet. "It was, however, extremely important that everything on the surface should appear as if neither Stevens nor Thurston anticipated anything but harmony."[4] Rich Budnick in *Stolen Kingdom* argued that the voyage "may have been a carefully planned maneuver intended to prepare U.S. marines and the ship's cannons for combat."[5]

Did Stevens take the *Boston* out of Honolulu to entice the queen into a rash act that would justify her overthrow? If so, we should expect to see evidence that Stevens, Wiltse, and the future rebels thought the political situation was unstable, knew that the new constitution was ready, and believed that the queen intended to impose it if the *Boston* left port. We should also expect a connection between the *Boston*'s trip and the intended provocation. There should be signs that Captain Wiltse rushed the cruiser back to Honolulu and prepared to land troops soon after the cruiser's return, in anticipation of a rash act by the queen. No reliable evidence has yet been found to support any of these points.

First, in early January, nearly everyone, aside from the queen's innermost circle, believed the political situation was stable. After months during which no party could form a government, George Wilcox formed a cabinet in November 1892 that seemed acceptable to all. The *Advertiser* doubted the royalists could gather the twenty-five votes needed to turn out the cabinet: "The opposition is not strong enough to carry *poi* to a Chinese restaurant."[6] John Stevens too thought the Wilcox cabinet safe. Stevens had been in Hawai`i three and a half years. Knowing the incoming Democratic administration would replace him, he relaxed and prepared to depart. When Captain Gilbert Wiltse invited him to join a training cruise, Stevens decided to go along, taking one of his daughters and her friend, hoping to see a bit of the islands he would soon leave.

Stevens' presence in Honolulu was not militarily significant. The warship that could land troops to restore order or influence political developments was militarily significant. Captain Wiltse, not Stevens, controlled the cruiser's movements and the activities of its crew, though he would certainly give due weight to the minister. Wiltse had joined the Navy at age seventeen, and over the next thirty-eight years slowly climbed the ranks. Short, thick-bodied, with bushy white muttonchops and pale skin that constantly reddened in the sun, Wiltse was not brilliant but thorough and diligent. He had commanded *Boston* for four years.[7] The crew was long overdue for gunnery practice and sea-keeping exercises. The executive officer, Lieutenant Commander William Swinburne, said, "On the first of January Captain Wiltse began to talk about his target practice; we had had no target practice for nine months. Minister Stevens was anxious to visit Hilo and other places on the islands and would not have another opportunity, as he expected to go home in April, and he thought that would be a good opportunity to visit Hawai`i, which he had not seen."[8]

Aboard the warship, Stevens told several people that the situation was quiet, and it was safe for the *Boston* to leave port. He dismissed Lieutenant Lucien Young's observation that there might be an effort to turn out the Wilcox cabinet.[9] Stevens later told a Senate investigating committee: "I did not dream of any revolution that the Queen had on foot."[10] He told Lieutenant Charles Laird that the Wilcox cabinet would remain in power for two years after the legislature disbanded. A senator asked, "So that at the time you left [Honolulu] you had no apprehensions of a civil outbreak or political disturbance?" Laird: "None whatever."[11] Nor did Captain Wiltse have doubts about leaving. When Lieutenant Commander Swinburne suggested that the voyage could wait until the legislative session ended, Wiltse said everything was "as quiet as possible, and it was as good a time to go as could be."[12]

Stevens would not have left the city if he feared the collapse of the Wilcox cabinet, the promulgation of a new constitution, and revolution. He thought the cabinet's establishment represented the "triumph of the better citizens of Hawai`i . . . this new cabinet is justly considered the most positively American there has been since the Reform ministry went out two and a half years ago."[13] He would not have risked its survival by intentionally provoking the queen to move against it while the *Boston* was gone. What was the point? The white clique was in the driver's seat. For Stevens, there was much more to lose than to gain. If the queen succeeded and a white counterrevolt did not materialize or was put down, the situation would have been grim for the white clique, out of power and unlikely to get back into power because of the new constitution. Under that scenario, the queen would have won, though conceivably the whites could have re-formed the Honolulu Rifles and intimidated the Crown as had been done in 1887. Conversely, if it continued in office, the Wilcox cabinet would not derail the so-called Americanization process that Stevens thought would inevitably lead to annexation or a protectorate. Stevens and Wiltse did not believe that leaving Honolulu put the cabinet at risk.

Examination of the cruise reveals no connection with a conspiracy to provoke the queen into a rash act, then return just in time to rescue the white rebels. If that theory were true, we should see signs that the ostensible reasons for the voyage— training for the ship's crew and vacation for the minister—were phony. Yet the ten-day voyage was remarkably free of political overtones. If Stevens expected a sudden need for a quick return to Honolulu, he would have remained on board or in Hilo. Rather, he and his party, joined by several naval officers, left the ship for a week of sightseeing on the Big Island, including a trip to the volcano. Stevens took himself out of easy communication with the ship and enjoyed the sightseeing and relaxation—including a January 11 picnic on tiny Coconut Island in the bay of Hilo—that were his declared reasons for the journey.[14]

Meanwhile, the *Boston*'s crew went back to sea and carried out the drill and target practice that were Captain Wiltse's expressed reasons for the cruise. The big guns were fired as well as the 37-mm and 47-mm deck guns. Back at Hilo on January 12, the three civilian passengers reboarded. The sea off Hilo had been too rough for the rolling and pitching ship to complete gunfire training, so Wiltse changed his plans, returning to Honolulu via Lahaina so he could repeat target practice in the smoother waters southwest of the old whaling port. The guns finally secured, the warship entered Lahaina at 5:35 PM on Friday, January 13. Stevens remained aboard. Wiltse ordered a midnight departure so the cruiser could enter Honolulu harbor the following day during the calm morning hours, as all ships tried to do.[15]

Therefore, it was at Lahaina, not Hilo, that Stevens and Wiltse learned by happenstance about recent political developments in Honolulu. No telegraph cable connected Oʻahu to the other islands or, for that matter, to North America or Asia. Interisland news moved by boat.[16] About ten o'clock the steamer *Kinau* made its normal Lahaina stop on the way to Hilo. The purser brought word that the Wilcox cabinet had been voted out the previous afternoon. Wiltse and Stevens expressed surprise, though not alarm. Swinburne recalled that "of course everyone was quite taken aback; still we did not anticipate any particular trouble."[17] The incoming premier, the well-known Samuel Parker, was hardly a rabble-rouser and headed the queen's first cabinet during 1891–92.

If the conspiracy theory were true, Wiltse should have rushed back to Honolulu, arriving just in time—"conveniently," to use Helena Allen's word—ready to land troops.[18] But Wiltse and Stevens had no inkling that the queen planned to proclaim a new constitution or that her move would provoke a revolt; these events would not occur until the following afternoon. Hence the *Boston* steamed back to Honolulu under "very leisurely, half-steam power," even departing Lahaina a bit late. At 8:05 Saturday morning, January 14, just off Diamond Head, the ship's dog fell overboard. The crew dropped a cork life raft, hoping the dog would crawl onto it. The kindly Captain Wiltse, in no rush to return to Honolulu nor being nagged by Stevens to hurry, indulged his crew by lowering a boat and vainly searching for the mascot. The *Boston* finally moored in Honolulu at 9:56 AM. Stevens debarked an hour later, hardly a sign of worry about what was happening ashore. Wiltse too seemed unconcerned about developments in town. Among the messages brought

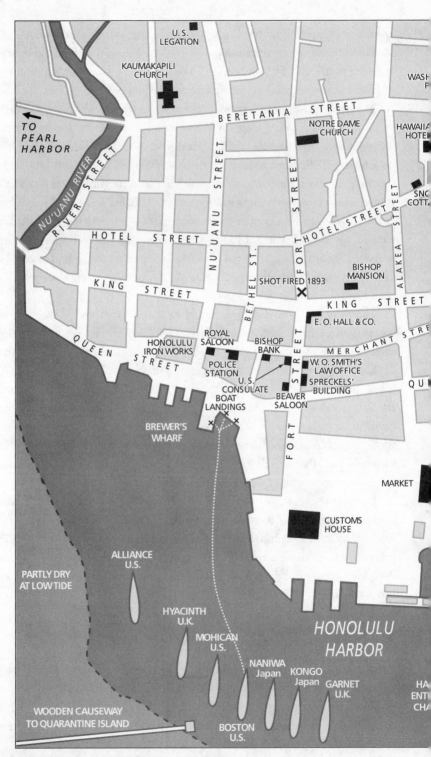

Map 1. Honolulu, 1893

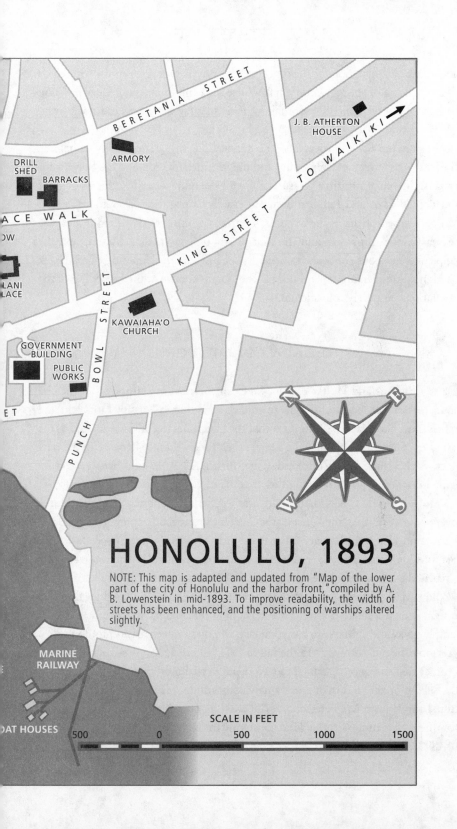

BERETANIA STREET

J. B. ATHERTON
HOUSE

DRILL
SHED

ARMORY

BARRACKS

TO WAIKIKI

ACE WALK

OW

KING STREET

LANI
LACE

BOWL STREET

KAWAIAHA'O
CHURCH

GOVERNMENT
BUILDING

PUBLIC
WORKS

PUNCH

ET

N
E
W
S

HONOLULU, 1893

NOTE: This map is adapted and updated from "Map of the lower
part of the city of Honolulu and the harbor front," compiled by A.
B. Lowenstein in mid-1893. To improve readability, the width of
streets has been enhanced, and the positioning of warships altered
slightly.

MARINE
RAILWAY

OAT HOUSES

SCALE IN FEET

500   0   500   1000   1500

aboard was an invitation for the officers to attend the prorogation (the sovereign's formal closing of the legislature), but Wiltse sent only Lieutenant Lucien Young because the other officers "were taking their midday meal, and did not care to go."[19]

In sum, the *Boston*'s voyage had no connection with an impending coup. The Stevens party's week of sightseeing and the later debarkation of Miss Stevens for more sightseeing confirm a pleasure cruise for the minister and his friends. Target practice off Hilo and Lahaina occurred exactly as planned. Even after Captain Wiltse learned of the Wilcox cabinet's ouster, the cruiser's dawdling return, the search for the ship's dog, and the lack of any urgency among Stevens and the ship's officers about going ashore strongly suggest that the ship did not rush back to Honolulu expecting to land troops. The *Boston*'s return at the beginning of the revolution was purely coincidental.

THE NEW CONSTITUTION

Clearly Stevens and Wiltse did not know of the new constitution, but did the soon-to-be rebels know of it? Merze Tate claimed that in "gossipy Honolulu" the rebels must have learned of the draft that the queen and her advisors crafted in the summer of 1892.[20] Although the future rebel leaders did not know of it, the new pact was not completely concealed. Chief Justice Albert F. Judd likely received a copy from young Willie Kaae, whose fine handwriting caused the queen to ask him to pen several copies.[21] But Judd later testified that although he "heard hints over some years that the Queen was anxious to proclaim a new constitution," he had no idea until January 14 that she intended to do it.[22] Associate Justice Sanford Dole was similarly in the dark. If Attorney General Arthur Peterson had circulated the draft in legal circles, as Lili`uokalani said he did, surely Dole or Judd would have caught wind of it. Probably Peterson took some kind of draft from the queen, kept it a while, and returned it, hoping that the provocative issue would simply go away. Similarly, in early January, when the queen asked him to write a preamble, he did nothing.[23] In the fall of 1892, John McCandless heard from his brother that the queen planned to pass controversial bills legalizing a lottery and the sale of opium and then grant a new constitution. "This information came to him, I think, from Mr. Peterson. . . . But we did not believe it," McCandless said, for "there were rumors of that kind constantly through the term of the Legislature of 1892."[24]

After the *Boston* sailed, a few more hints slipped out. On January 11, Peter Jones, finance minister in the Wilcox cabinet, got an unsigned note, apparently drafted by John Colburn, saying: "If you don't get out of office, and a new Constitution is shoved on this country by the Queen, you four men and your hypocritical supporters will be to blame for it."[25] Jones did nothing. The message did not make sense. Jones did not expect his cabinet to be voted out, nor did he think a new cabinet would stop a new constitution. Indeed, the reverse was true: new ministers might support it. In fact, that was exactly the queen's strategy. On January 12, the day the royalists toppled the Wilcox cabinet, John Emmeluth awaited Marcus Colburn at the Lewers & Cooke warehouse just outside John Colburn's office. Emmeluth overheard Arthur Peterson ask John Colburn if he would join a cabinet as minister of the interior on the queen's condition that he help promulgate a new constitution. Colburn agreed, said Emmeluth.[26] On Friday night, January 13, when royalist John Kalona proclaimed at a party that he would die happy if he could get the new constitution proclaimed and kill a few white men at the same time, his words were dismissed as alcohol-induced bluster.[27] Even on the morning of January 14, when Chief Justice Judd heard that a new constitution would be proclaimed that very afternoon, he passed the news to his fellow justices but "they didn't credit it," he said later.[28] The hints of impending promulgation were too bizarre to be taken seriously.

Even had the queen's opponents known of the new constitution, that knowledge would not have triggered a revolt. Everyone knew she disliked the 1887 constitution and that Native Hawaiian groups several times petitioned her for change. Rather, the trigger would be the queen's attempt to proclaim the pact unilaterally. Only at that point, as we shall see, did the rebels begin to organize themselves.

But before she could proclaim the constitution, the queen had to oust the Wilcox cabinet and install a pliable one, prorogue the legislature, get her new ministers to endorse the new constitution (or so she thought), and finally promulgate it. These steps were unpredictable. No antiroyal plotters could have reliably foreseen them. The Wilcox cabinet might not fall. The date of prorogation was unsettled. On January 7 the legislature said business was complete and the queen could close the session on January 12. Had they been plotting to provoke the queen to a rash act, the rebels would not have taken the risk that the queen could have announced the new pact and put down any rebellion while the *Boston* was two days out. Instead, the attempted constitutional proclamation caught all parties by surprise.

Did the queen have an alternative? Her most promising method to obtain a new constitution was constitutional. Articles 47 and 82 of the 1887 Bayonet Constitution gave amendment power solely to the legislature. If a majority approved an amendment, it would be referred to the next legislative session, in this case mid-1894. In the second stage the amendment had to receive a two-thirds majority to become law. The Hawaiian amendment procedure was easier than the American law, which required proposed amendments from two-thirds of the Congress or from a convention called by two-thirds of the states. In the American case, the second stage was ratification by the legislatures or conventions in three-fourths of the states.

With the Parker cabinet installed and the legislature controlled by royalists, the queen's supporters could have pushed through before the end of the session a proposal to adopt a new constitution or significantly amend the old one. Only a majority vote was needed to start the amendment process. Then the sovereign and her new cabinet could have campaigned over the next thirteen months to increase, via the February 1894 election, the royalists in the legislature. The royalists had twenty-five votes when they ousted the Wilcox cabinet in January 1893. Another seven seats would provide the two-thirds majority needed to amend the constitution or install a new one. Getting those seven seats would have been quite difficult, given the party balances and the voter qualifications for the upper house, but acting in accordance with existing amendment provisions would not trigger a revolt and offered a slight but practical chance for amendment. This course would have left the queen on the moral high ground and left the white opposition in the untenable position of standing against constitutional reform in accordance with the white-imposed Bayonet Constitution. Even if the queen could not get a new constitution, she might have been able to negotiate agreement, given her new cabinet and a legislative majority, on amendments to strengthen royal powers or weaken voter qualifications. But the queen gambled that she could best attain her goals by unilateral promulgation on January 14.

The queen's new constitution would have greatly strengthened her authority. Although the original disappeared (the Blount Report contains a close copy), it was largely cut and pasted from earlier charters. The new draft dropped the 1887 provision requiring the monarch to act with the advice and consent of the cabinet. Instead, ministers would serve "during the queen's pleasure," meaning she could fire them, but they were still subject to a vote of no confidence. Upper house members would be appointed by the queen for life terms instead of being elected, but the Supreme Court justices would be elected instead of appointed for life. In both cases the queen could replace incumbents she disliked. Last, only Hawaiian-born or naturalized male subjects could vote. This latter change would have eliminated the strange practice of "denization" (allowing resident foreigners to vote), thereby stripping the franchise from some Americans and other foreigners. Kuykendall concluded the changes would have given the queen "more power and more influence over the government than had been possessed by Kalākaua at the beginning of his reign" in 1874.[29] Importantly, the queen could have established a government dominated by Native Hawaiians, thereby destroying Robert Wilcox's main issue and eliminating him as a political threat, her main goal in the whole process.

History was repeating itself. Kamehameha V unilaterally promulgated the Constitution of 1864 to increase royal authorities weakened in the previous pacts. Now Queen Lili`uokalani too tried to restore royal powers compromised in a previous (1887) pact. But economic and demographic changes had diluted royal clout. The queen lacked Kamehameha V's unquestioned personal authority. She faced a more powerful white element than he did. She had challengers—Wilcox and his crowd—even within the Native Hawaiian community.

It is easy to see why the white faction saw the new constitution as a political attack. They ignored the fact that royalists were merely doing what white rebels did in 1887: promulgating a new constitution by unilateral action.[30] As a practical matter, the key question facing the queen was not her theoretical or moral right to do what the whites did in 1887, or what her predecessor did in 1864. Instead it was what practical measures might be best to advance her political position and that of her people, given the circumstances in 1893. By choosing to move arbitrarily and without notice, she made a major strategic error. That her other choice—attempt to persuade the entire country that a new pact should be ratified by the legislature—had little chance of success helps explain why she chose a more risky option.

THE FALL OF THE WILCOX CABINET

Before the queen could announce a new charter, she had to oust the Wilcox cabinet. She thought, mistakenly, that her cabinet must endorse any new pact. Therefore, she needed pliable men. In late December, Representative Joseph Nāwahī threatened to oppose the cabinet if they did not support a constitutional convention to replace the 1887 Bayonet Constitution.[31] Rumors circulated about a want of confidence vote.[32] A mainland reporter predicted that a new cabinet would be voted into office just after the *Boston* departed. His story turned out half right. Just after the cruiser cleared the harbor, the opposition introduced a no-confidence vote, but it failed nineteen ayes to twenty-two nays with seven absent or not voting. This was approximately the party breakdown, and seemed unlikely to change. Twenty-five ayes, a majority of the forty-eight-seat legislature, were needed for passage. The *Advertiser* declared that "the cloudburst has passed and hurt nobody, and the Cabinet is safe."[33]

The legislature, with royalists cooperating, spent three days cleaning up pending matters. On January 7, the queen was told that she could prorogue the legislature on January 12 or after. She chose January 14.[34] She needed time to orchestrate the downfall of the Wilcox cabinet, either by pressuring legislators to change their votes on a no-confidence measure or by stalling until some pro-Wilcox legislators returned home after real business ended but before the formal end of the session on the fourteenth, thereby putting royalists in the majority of any quorum. She clearly felt no pressure to wrap up her power play before the *Boston* returned. She intended to move regardless. She did not anticipate, or was not deterred by, possible intervention by U.S. forces or she would have moved earlier.

First she needed control of the legislature. On January 12, a want of confidence measure passed twenty-five ayes to sixteen nays, with seven members absent or not voting. Six Native Hawaiians who voted in favor of the cabinet on January 4 voted against it eight days later.[35] Likely this was the result of royal arm-twisting, for the cabinet had taken no controversial steps during the period that could conceivably have alienated six supporters. The Wilcox cabinet resigned immediately. Queen Lili`uokalani appointed a new cabinet with Samuel Parker as minister of Foreign Affairs, John Colburn as minister of the Interior, William Cornwell as minister of Finance, and Arthur Peterson as attorney general. The *Advertiser* noted that "this change of ministry will not, however, lead to any political disturbance or unrest.... There is absolutely no excitement of any kind."[36] The Parker cabinet was not disliked enough for a successful no-confidence vote. On Saturday morning, January 14, the legislature met briefly with the new ministers in place, and then at noon the queen dissolved (prorogued) the legislature. The new cabinet would not be vulnerable to a no-confidence vote until the legislature reconvened in mid- to late-1894.

Around January 8, the queen told Marshal Charles Wilson and possibly Captain Samuel Nowlein of the Household Guards that she intended to promulgate the constitution. She ordered them to prepare to put down any disturbances. Wilson objected to her plan and made no security arrangements, hoping the monarch would drop the idea. On January 13, she mentioned it again and again the marshal objected, successfully, he thought. In her book and diary, the queen recollected no objections from Wilson, recording only that on Saturday, January 14, Wilson told her that the requested security measures were in place.[37] If the queen expected civil disorder to result from the announcement, it is not hard to imagine why the white clique interpreted her tactics as an assault on them, and as a step away from a white-dominated system where she would reign and they would rule.

THE QUEEN ATTEMPTS TO PROCLAIM
THE NEW CONSTITUTION

About nine o'clock Saturday morning, January 14, the new cabinet learned the queen intended to proclaim a new constitution that afternoon.[38] She requested that her ministers be present to sign the new charter, either because she believed the signatures were necessary to make the proclamation legal, or, more likely, because she wished to show that the ministers endorsed the new constitution. Peterson refused to sign because the cabinet had not read it. Lili`uokalani reminded him that she had given him a draft to revise. Colburn immediately asked why the rest of the cabinet had not been informed of the existence of the draft. The queen later claimed that her new ministers were well aware of her intent to promulgate a new constitution. "Mr. Parker and Mr. Cornwell had given me assurances of their support as ministers, while Mr. Peterson understood that such was my intention, and although I had not mentioned it to Mr. Colbourn, he had heard of it already from Mr. Peterson."[39] If, as John Emmeluth's affidavit suggests, Colburn and Peterson entered the cabinet by promising to support the constitution, why did they change their minds? Perhaps they hoped the queen would change her mind or that Wilson would talk her out of it. Clearly, the cabinet did not want to endorse the constitution, or at least its arbitrary imposition.[40]

The worried ministers crossed to the Government Building for the wrap-up of the legislative session. They expected that the queen's opponents would react strongly, perhaps militarily, as they had in 1887 and 1889. The legislature quickly adjourned until the formal dissolution at noon. Around ten o'clock, Parker returned to the Palace to reconfirm the queen's intentions, but she was unavailable. An anxious Colburn hurried downtown to get advice—the queen later called his behavior treasonable—from his old friend Alfred Hartwell, who listened to the story and then asked if he might invite Thurston and William O. Smith to hear it too. By now Arthur Peterson had joined the group. Hartwell, Thurston, and Smith urged the two ministers to resist the queen.[41] They also urged the ministers not to resign in protest, for with the legislature on the verge of dissolution—it was now about eleven thirty in the morning—the queen could appoint any new cabinet she wanted without fear of its being overturned by a vote of no confidence. One of the three men (Thurston, Hartwell, or Smith) apparently drafted an undated note from the four ministers asking Stevens to land troops to support the cabinet against the queen.[42] It is not clear whether any of the ministers authorized or even saw this note, which has never surfaced. Meanwhile, the *Boston* moored in the harbor and Stevens left the ship, ignorant of events ashore.

Peterson and Colburn rejoined Parker and Cornwell at the Government Building just before noon. Precisely at twelve o'clock, the queen prorogued the legislature and immediately went across the street to the palace. Hartwell went to the American legation, where Stevens just arrived from the *Boston*, and asked him to join British minister Wodehouse in dissuading the queen from promulgating the constitution. Unable to see the queen, Stevens, Wodehouse, and other foreign representatives met the cabinet in the Government Building around one o'clock.[43] Wodehouse asked about the draft constitution. Parker said they had heard rumors of it and intended to oppose it. The conversation explored the queen's motivation. The cabinet said it must be her desire to respond to petitions from the Hawaiian people. Stevens, who obviously had his priorities askew, asked if the queen had signed the lottery bill. Parker explained that she had signed it because she felt bound to follow the wishes of the majority of the legislature and that the cabinet concurred. Stevens pounded on the floor with his cane, declared that the lottery bill was a direct attack on the United States, and stalked from the room after demanding that he be informed if the queen pursued the new constitution.[44]

The cabinet went over to the palace, where the queen waited with members of the legislature, representatives of Native Hawaiian political societies, and members of the public. She said nine thousand persons had petitioned for a new constitution. She thought this was an appropriate time to honor their request. She wanted the ministers to sign the document with her. They refused and urged her to abandon the idea. Thus the Samuel Parker cabinet—the handpicked one she worked so hard to get into place—decided it could not support her new charter, at least not one unilaterally promulgated. The unpopularity of her plan, even among her cabinet and a close advisor such as Marshal Wilson, says much about her neglect to form a base of support among senior royalists and her lack of judgment in proposing the new pact in an arbitrary manner. Why did she do it? She was responding to Native Hawaiian requests, to her dislike of the Bayonet Constitution, and to Wilcox's threat to her political base. Theo Davies thought she acted "foolishly," but he noted she "hardly knew who to trust and fell back on her own bad judgment and probably felt like a bull in a net."[45]

Parker continued to try to talk her out of promulgation. The other three went back to the Government Building. Although Stevens had left, diplomats and politically active whites such as Thurston were still there. Thurston said the foreign community opposed a new constitution and would back the cabinet in their resistance, even deposing the queen if necessary.

Soon a large crowd gathered, by the queen's invitation, in the Throne Room of the palace. Across the central hallway, in the intimate Blue Room, the queen and her ministers acrimoniously debated their refusal to sign the constitution. This lengthy argument was interrupted frequently as ministers went out into the hall to converse with diplomats and influential white residents. Finally, the queen reluctantly agreed to withhold the document, based, she said, on Peterson's proposal that she could announce a revised version within two weeks. Visibly angry, she passed through the Throne Room and went out on the balcony to speak to a crowd in the palace yard. She told them that she could not issue a new constitution now but would do so before too long. Accounts differ on whether this period was to be days, weeks, or longer. Although upset, the crowd dispersed without incident.[46]

THE REBELLION BEGINS . . . WITH MINISTER
STEVENS' INVOLVEMENT

Had the political climate been less partisan, the queen's change of mind might have defused the crisis. But her promulgation attempt was like match to tinder. Her opponents instantly turned irrevocably against the monarchy. American diplomatic and naval representatives were quickly drawn into the political crisis, or, better said, willingly involved themselves in it. Henry Cooper came aboard the *Boston* about eleven thirty in the morning, just after Stevens disembarked, to inform Captain Wiltse that the queen intended to proclaim a new constitution. Cooper later claimed that Wiltse said that if violent protests occurred, he might have to land troops to protect American citizens and their property.[47] Normally, the *Boston*'s crew would have received liberty after a cruise, but Wiltse kept them aboard because of his worries about trouble ashore. He did not share his fears with his officers nor did he make any preparations for landing troops. The executive officer made the crew spend the weekend cleaning the ship. On the morning of the eventual landing—Monday, January 16—the crew had not yet made any preparations for going ashore and were still mending rigging and sanding the wooden decks.[48]

While Wiltse cautiously waited, Minister Stevens moved to center stage. From Saturday afternoon, Stevens was deeply and inappropriately involved in the revolution. Although there is no convincing evidence of a conspiracy between Stevens and the rebels, the events of January 14–17 show a high degree of mutual understanding and an array of simultaneous or complementary actions typical of a unified group rather than two distinct camps. Stevens' improper actions, intimations, and suggestions significantly influenced events, aiding the rebels and intimidating the royalists and possibly keeping the revolution alive. Certainly his active opposition—a declaration that American forces would support the royal government—would have squelched it.

Although there had been no conspiracy to entice the queen into a rash act, once she made a tactical misstep, the rebels moved immediately to oust her. They had scant loyalty to the monarch. White antiroyal sentiment had crystallized against Lili`uokalani long before January 1893. Whites believed they had made a bargain with the Crown in 1887. They felt the attempted promulgation was a "last straw" in six years of royal attempts to restore the monarch's power. Whites were blind to the pressures on the queen from Robert Wilcox's supporters and from Native Hawaiian petitioners. They were oblivious to Lili`uokalani's well-founded conviction that if something were not done, Native Hawaiians would have a second-rate future in the land of their birth. They did not trust the queen. Their swift move against her demonstrated how much patience had been exhausted on both sides for "offenses" committed by the other. Peter Jones spoke for many rebels: "While the Queen professed to take back all she had said and done about a new constitution I felt it was only to gain time to make better preparations to carry out her designs."[49]

The rebellion grew quickly. Here is where the members of the Annexationist Club become crucial to the story, not because they were members of the club, for they had not conspired together, and not because the club was secret, for it was not. Some writers have overemphasized the supposedly secret nature of the club, probably to convey a stronger aura of conspiracy. However, no close observer of island politics, especially the queen and her allies, had any doubt about who their opponents were and whether they supported annexation. Such men as Thurston and Smith were well-known opponents of the monarchy and had often made clear their desire for annexation. They forced the Bayonet Constitution on Kalākaua. They forced the resignation of royalist cabinets in 1892. Who the rebels were and what they believed was common knowledge. Had these men not been members of the Annexationist Club, it would have made no difference in January 1893. The important aspect was not their club membership, secret or not, but their common thinking. They knew each other well; they were friends and colleagues. They were of one mind about getting rid of the queen.

That Saturday afternoon of January 14, in the Smith-Thurston law offices, the queen's overthrow got under way. As men gathered, some wanted the queen's overthrow but most had no concrete plan. The comings and goings slowly coalesced into a large meeting run by Henry Cooper. A smaller group, the so-called Committee of Safety, was established with Cooper as chair. He appointed twelve others, eleven of them, like him, members of the Annexationist Club. Among the thirteen were four Americans, three Hawaiian-born whites of U.S. descent, three naturalized whites of American ancestry, a naturalized Australian, a Scot, and a German. (The German, Crister Bolte, soon resigned because he thought his membership incompatible with being consul of Germany.) Thurston, William O. Smith, and William Castle were the Hawaiian-born whites. The chair, Henry Cooper, had arrived from California in 1890. Thirty-six years old, he had received denizen status from the queen only the previous July. A lawyer, he owned what today would be called a title company. A forceful personality, he quickly bonded with Thurston, Smith, and other aggressive rebels.[50]

There were no sugar planters in the group. That said, because the entire Hawaiian economy revolved around sugar, most members connected to the industry through their own businesses. The Committee of Safety quickly adopted Thurston's proposal to replace the monarchy with a provisional government. The committee declared its intent to depose the queen before the rebels approached Stevens, though they surely anticipated that he would support them. They most certainly did not think he would suppress their movement. Thurston and two others were directed to seek military assistance from Stevens.

Most improperly, Stevens received the little delegation on Saturday afternoon. He knew of the political ferment in the city, the attempt to promulgate the constitution, and the white opposition to it. He knew Thurston's stance regarding the monarchy and annexation. Despite his personal displeasure with the queen's actions, he was accredited to her government and absolutely should not have met its declared opponents. Yet he did so. Several senators hammered at this point during his testimony to the Senate Foreign Relations Committee in early 1894. "Did you state to Mr. Thurston . . . that troops would have to be landed from the *Boston*?" asked Senator George Gray. "Not at all," said Stevens, "my answer was the same—when the troops landed it would be for the purpose of protecting life and property." Gray pounced: "You say you made no statement to Mr. Thurston about landing troops?" Stevens: "I do not remember any. I may have stated—as I did to other gentlemen—that the troops might be landed. . . . I was quite as courteous to the royalist emissaries as I was to the others."[51]

Stevens could not see his egregious error. He patted himself on the back for treating the legal government as courteously as rebels planning its overthrow. Senators grilled him about whether he told the rebel trio that he would recognize any government in possession of the archives and other buildings. Stevens insisted no such question was asked of him because the rebels would not "embarrass" him with questions like that. He said they knew a de facto government would be recognized.[52] Whatever Stevens said, and that was surely much more than he admitted even under oath, what the rebels heard was quite comforting. That Saturday evening, Thurston told Smith and Castle, both members of the Committee of Safety, and four others who were not—Sanford Dole, Alfred Hartwell, Fred Wundenberg, and Charles Carter—that Stevens promised to recognize whatever government exercised the powers of government; that is, was in control of the city and in possession of the major government buildings. De facto control of the government would bring American recognition.[53]

Stevens' partiality—he somehow considered it as evenhandedness—made it clear that the Crown was on its own, unlike 1874 and 1889, when American troops landed to support the monarch. Stevens believed that the cabinet (while it resisted the queen) and what he called the people—in his mind only the white rebels, not the great mass of Native Hawaiians—were right and the queen wrong. By ruling out support for the Crown, Stevens encouraged the rebels to continue their rebellion. By describing conditions needed for recognition, Stevens made it much more likely that those conditions would develop. Stevens should not have met with the plotters, much less speculated about conditions for recognition. His behavior was highly improper, even by the permissive nineteenth-century tradition of meddling by American emissaries.

With Stevens' moral support, by Sunday morning the rebels were moving swiftly toward overthrowing the queen at the very time that the Parker cabinet began backing away from them. As the threat of a royalist constitutional coup faded, the cabinet ceased cooperation with the plotters, preferring to maintain the monarchy. Parker himself returned to the fold on Saturday. On Sunday morning the other ministers cut off contact with the rebels when Thurston told them that the Committee of Safety still intended to overthrow the monarchy.[54]

No one knows why the royal government did not arrest the plotters during January 15–17. Marshal Wilson suggested arresting them, but Peterson and the cabinet objected. They claimed they feared U.S. intervention, but in postrevolution affidavits, they also claimed that they could have easily coped with "any insurrection of a few malcontents." When warned on Monday that the rebels intended to set up a new government, the cabinet professed confidence that "no such attempt could succeed if the insurgents depended on their own forces."[55] But the *Boston* had not yet landed troops. If the government was really so much stronger than the rebels, it could have jailed them and suppressed the revolution before Stevens and Wiltse even learned of the arrests. The cabinet was far too timid and overly worried about potential American intervention. Arresting rebels might provoke a revolt they still hoped to avoid. The government declared on Monday that the queen promised that no constitutional changes would be made. The proclamation had no effect because the rebels were fixed on overthrow.

The government tried again to deter rebellion by lining up American support. Parker and Cornwell called on Stevens on Sunday evening. Quite properly, he received them. They were the legal government. Parker asked for support while simultaneously saying the government was "perfectly capable of dealing with the situation." Stevens said he desired to protect the cabinet and that it should not resign. Parker asked directly: Would Stevens respond to a plea for help? Stevens said he could not assist while that "scoundrel" Charles Wilson remained marshal.[56] This was another awful error that contributed to the royalists' conviction that the minister was hostile. Now that Stevens declared he could not support the monarchy, if U.S. troops did land, the royalists might understandably assume the troops would support the rebels, rather than preserve order as a neutral party.

After Parker and Cornwell left, Stevens once again seriously violated diplomatic propriety by meeting with Thurston and Smith, back for another visit. Stevens told them he could not recognize any government until actually established. American troops would protect life and property but not take sides in the dispute. He should not have speculated about the landing of troops at all, although the rebels probably would have abandoned their plans only if Stevens had told them that American troops would support the queen.

But the bottom line was that the rebels left this second meeting with Stevens confident that they had a free hand. They had nothing to fear from U.S. troops. This was an immense advantage. By Sunday night, Stevens had eliminated rebel fears that he would intervene on behalf of the queen and had boosted royalist fears that he might support the rebels with a landing.[57] To that momentous event we now turn.

❦

CHAPTER 7

The Landing of U.S. Troops

Marshal of the Kingdom Charles Wilson was the only royalist feared by the rebels. Born at sea as his mother, a Tahitian princess, and father, a British-Tahitian captain, sailed to Fanning Island, Wilson settled in Hawaiʻi as a young man. He became a highly skilled blacksmith and mechanic. Powerfully built, he was for a time the heavyweight boxing champion of Honolulu. With intense coal-black eyes and coal-black hair and massive shoulders, he cut a striking, magnetic figure. Lorrin Thurston said Wilson was one of the handsomest men in town. Wilson successfully wooed Kitty Townsend, a beauty to whom Liliʻuokalani was a kind of godmother, and the Wilsons remained close to her when she became queen. Charles and Kitty's son Johnny would be a famous mayor of Honolulu in the twentieth century. Wilson was well known to the white rebels. He and Thurston knew each other as children in Maui. Wilson worked for Thurston as chief of the waterworks while the lawyer was minister of the interior. Sanford Dole had been Wilson's legal representative in an abortive venture to build a Honolulu tram system. Wilson loved guns and hunting. He joined the Honolulu Rifles when it was formed as a gun club in 1884 but dropped out when it transmuted into an antiroyal militia. He was a tough man, brave and aggressive.[1]

Marshal Wilson tried to head off the revolt. On Monday morning, things were coming to a head. Each side scheduled an afternoon mass meeting to test their support. The rapidly rearming rebels had not yet written a proclamation of a new government nor picked the men who would head it. The Committee of Safety met in the Thurston-Smith law offices at nine o'clock to take stock. Wilson appeared and proposed to Thurston that the two sides make up. He guaranteed the queen would not bring forth her constitution again. Thurston said the rebels intended to settle things for the last time. Wilson said later that a fearful and timid cabinet refused his request to arrest the plotters.[2]

That same morning, the Committee of Safety asked Stevens to land troops for their protection.[3] This note seemingly weakens the rebels' later claim of military superiority. But on January 16, the Honolulu Rifles were still re-forming. They had nothing to lose by asking for assistance. McCandless and others thought the request unnecessary: "We were making such rapid progress with our organization and the other people so completely cowed, we thought probably it would precipitate a crisis as soon as the troops came ashore, and in a day or two we would be better prepared to resist it than then."[4] The committee retracted its landing request.[5] Stevens' response, if any, is unknown.

At two o'clock a thousand rebels jammed into the armory. Thurston harangued the crowd, which by acclamation gave the Committee of Safety a free hand. The royalists gathered more sedately at Palace Square. There was no disorder, but the atmosphere was tense. Businesses closed at midday, men thronged the streets heading to and from the mass meetings, and anxious Americans gathered at the legation.[6]

The Committee of Safety reconvened after the mass meeting, a little past three o'clock. The group conclusively decided to establish a provisional government.[7] There was rash talk of immediately occupying the Government Building, so Thurston penned another note asking for a landing. Cooler heads pointed out their unreadiness to bring matters to a head. Not a single paper had been written, not even the proclamation of a new government. There were no proposed officials. It was too late in the day to begin the endgame. There was little chance the intimidated royalists would take action. The committee decided to "get everything in shape."[8] About four thirty, three rebels went to the legation to ask Stevens, just returned from the *Boston*, to delay a landing. But the troops were already in their boats.[9]

The landing was Wiltse's decision, not Stevens'. The captain made his own evaluation of the situation.[10] Over the weekend, Wiltse talked frequently to people on the streets and conferred with Stevens. When he went ashore Monday morning and learned of the impending mass meetings, he grew alarmed. Consul General Henry Weld Severance claimed the royalists would break up the rebel mass meeting.[11] Around noon, Wiltse told his executive officer, Lieutenant

Commander Swinburne, to prepare to put the troops ashore. The men ate lunch, assembled their gear, and by two thirty were ready. Swinburne planned to land at four o'clock, when Wiltse guessed the two mass meetings would break up. The *Boston's* troops would be able to stop trouble in the streets from brawling partisans.[12]

At two thirty Stevens came aboard to request a landing only to find that Wiltse already decided to deploy troops. The captain gathered his senior officers. Stevens said there might be trouble after the mass meetings.[13] Wiltse reiterated that he had already ordered the battalion ashore to protect "our legation, consulate, and the lives and property of American citizens, and to assist in preserving public order. Great prudence must be exercised by both officers and men, and no action taken that is not fully warranted by the condition of affairs, and by the conduct of those who may be inimical to the treaty rights of American citizens."[14] Wiltse stressed the landing party's neutrality. Lieutenant Laird asked about Wiltse's goal. Wiltse said, "My desire is that you remain neutral; you are to protect the lives and property of American citizens."[15]

Discussing protection of the legation, Stevens said only fifteen to eighteen men could camp in the yard.[16] Swinburne asked where the rest of the landing force should bivouac. Neither Wiltse nor Stevens had considered the matter. (The decision to land before identifying a bivouac area is additional evidence that Wiltse decided to land on very short notice.) Swinburne recalled:

> Mr. Stevens said he did not know where we would be able to go; he had not thought the matter over; that he would have to have some large building somewhere; and he thought the opera house would be a good place if we could get it. The opera house faces the palace. I said that my own desire and preference would be to be near the landing [wharf], because I would be nearer my base, and nearer the liquor stores. My idea was, if there was an outbreak of any kind, my first move would be to close all liquor stores, and if necessary leave a guard there, or nail them up, to prevent people from getting liquor. Mr. Stevens said he did not know of any building around the waterfront, but he thought we could get the opera house. Then he said: "By the way, there is a Mr. Atherton, an American, who lives down on King Street; suppose you let the troops go there." That was to the captain. So that was finally decided upon in an unofficial sort of way. The captain said: "You can stop at the consulate and send half the marines to the minister's: leave the other half in charge of Lt. Draper at the consulate and march on, and by that time we will be able to tell you where you are to go." I said: "In the

event of not getting any orders—I wanted to get the men off the street so soon as possible—I will go to Mr. Atherton's." The captain said: "Yes."[17]

Stevens debarked at 3:40 PM. In an earlier note, Consul General Severance said he would lower the consulate flag to half-mast if there was trouble ashore.[18] Stevens stopped at the consulate to let them know Marines were coming their way. He likely told Severance to lower the flag. At 4:20 PM, the officer of the deck observed the consulate flag being lowered. By 4:25 PM, the troops were in the boats.[19] Delayed by the extended discussion with Stevens, Wiltse landed troops almost two hours after Swinburne readied them, and more than an hour after the mass meetings broke up. Even had he known that there was no trouble, he probably would have landed troops anyway because he expected the situation ashore would get worse. During Monday's preparations for landing, the ship had no contact with the Committee of Safety. In fact, by the time of the landing, the committee preferred that it occur on Tuesday, hardly a sign of a tightly coordinated conspiracy.

Using eight boats, the battalion formed on Brewer's Wharf by five o'clock. The force totaled 164: 109 naval "bluejackets" broken into three companies, one Marine company of 30, 11 officers, and a color guard of 14 men, including drummers and buglers. Swinburne commanded, with Lucien Young, the senior lieutenant, and lieutenants Charles Laird and De Witt Coffman heading the bluejacket companies and First Lieutenant Herbert Draper the Marines.[20] The presence of musicians with instruments indicates that Wiltse did not expect trouble. The battalion was a formidable professional force, about the size of a modern infantry company. Once the troops were ashore, Wiltse searched for a bivouac location. The sailors remaining on ship "organized on board to repel an attack," surely a routine precaution.[21]

The men carried standard equipment for landing parties, small arms and two heavier weapons, a 37-mm cannon and a Gatling gun. Men carried eighty to one hundred rounds for each rifle and pistol and shouldered knapsacks. A photo in the Library of Congress shows the *Boston*'s crew practicing riot control at the Brooklyn Navy Yard, equipped as they were in Honolulu on January 16.[22] Young said he had landed in Nicaragua, Venezuela, and Panama, and "we simply did here what we have done before in other places."[23]

Stevens claimed the landing occurred during an "interregnum" in government authority, that "the Queen's government ended on Saturday afternoon."[24] The interregnum was a preposterous fiction of Stevens' partisan thinking. Lieutenant Laird and Lieutenant Commander Swinburne noticed "a great many more people on the street at that time of the evening than . . . under ordinary circumstances," but they were not rowdy or threatening. A clerk at the U.S. consulate attended the rebel mass meeting and saw no disorder.[25] John McCandless admitted that police "were on the streets just as common as they were ordinarily."[26]

Swinburne moved immediately to protect American property. The battalion marched in a column—without apparent concern for their safety, and with rifles slung across their shoulders—along Queen Street to Fort Street, turned left and went to the U.S. consulate at Fort and Merchant. Swinburne posted a reinforced Marine squad at the consulate and sent the rest of the Marines to the legation (Stevens' residence and office) on upper Nuʻuanu Avenue. Swinburne therefore used a quarter of his force to protect the two most important American properties.

The three naval companies with the musicians playing merrily marched east on Merchant Street through Palace Square, past ʻIolani Palace on the left of the column and the Music Hall and Government Building on the right. The troops found no discord whatsoever. As the sailors passed the palace, they saw the queen standing alone on the balcony and gave her a military salute: a droop of the colors, a trumpet blast, ruffles on the drums, and the men at port arms. Either from unfamiliarity with military salutes—unlikely, as she watched troops drill ashore for decades—or, more likely, to portray the landing force as intimidating her, she claimed they drew up in a line in front of the palace gates and pointed their guns at her and her supporters.[27] This was untrue. However, as we shall see, it was understandable that the queen felt the troops threatened her throne, if not her person.

Swinburne stopped the column just east of the palace at J. A. Hopper's house and phoned the ship. No bivouac had been identified so, as planned, Swinburne marched farther out to Atherton's house, where the troops rested under the trees, amid gentle evening showers, and drank lemonade and ate bananas. Swinburne phoned Wiltse "two or three times when it got dark" to check on a hall.[28] The most likely halls were unavailable. The American owner of the Music Hall declined permission, recalling that his building suffered considerable damage in 1889, when government sharpshooters used its second floor to duel with Robert Wilcox's cannoneers in the palace grounds. The owner of the old armory near the waterfront was off the island. The re-forming Honolulu Rifles were already using the big, newer armory at Beretania and Punchbowl.

THE POSITIONING OF U.S. TROOPS

About nine thirty that evening, Wiltse or Stevens, it is not clear who, secured Arion Hall, an American-owned building behind the Music Hall. Swinburne did not know where Arion Hall was. He used a guide to find it. The battalion walked quietly: "In order not to make any disturbance, the music was stopped." At Arion Hall, the men spread blankets—they brought no tents—on the floor of the one large room and the broad verandas. They stacked rifles and pulled the two guns into the yard.[29]

Placing the troops at Arion Hall, close to the palace and the Government Building, occurred simply because it was the first hall that was available, although an unnamed building near the legation was known to Stevens and would have been considered if Arion Hall had not been available. Lieutenant Coffman said another building was suitable, on upper Nuʻuanu Avenue and managed by John Waterhouse, brother of rebel Henry Waterhouse. When Coffman mentioned the Nuʻuanu building to his seniors, they paid no attention. The officers might simply have thought Arion Hall more central. Marines had been dispatched to the legation and the consulate, and the Nuʻuanu building as well as the building known to Stevens were between those small detachments. Perhaps Wiltse believed that part of town could be handled by the two Marine parties. Or perhaps he thought lodging at a building managed by a leading rebel's brother would appear too partial. The likeliest explanation is that the troops were already at Atherton's, it was late, and Arion Hall was available and close.[30]

If lodging troops at Arion Hall was not intended to intimidate the queen's supporters, some thought so. Asked by Blount months later for a military man's evaluation, Admiral Joseph S. Skerrett, commander of the Pacific Station, said an Arion Hall bivouac was "inadvisable" for protecting American citizens and property, but a "wise choice" to support the provisional government.[31] Blount's stay in Honolulu overlapped that of Stevens and Wiltse, but he never asked them why the troops lodged in Arion Hall because he was certain the troops lodged there to intimidate the royalists. Blount wrote that, with American troops in nearby Arion Hall, royalists could not have attacked the rebels in the Government Building for fear of hitting the Americans inadvertently, but Arion Hall had not been damaged in the 1889 crossfire between government troops in the Government Building and Music Hall and Wilcox's supporters on the palace grounds. Lieutenant Young exaggerated when he claimed, "They could have fought all they pleased in Palace Square and out in the Government grounds without ever affecting us in the slightest."[32] Lieutenant Commander Swinburne thought his force in Arion Hall would have been in a precarious position if government troops attacked the rebels in the Government Building. "I thought at the time that it was untenable in the event of a fight between the two factions; I expected to have to withdraw my men from that position . . . at least I was not in a good position in the event of an outbreak."[33]

If intimidation was the purpose, lodging U.S. troops close to the main bodies of royalists in the barracks and the police station would have been more intimidating. In a military sense, the precise location of the troops was unimportant, despite Admiral Skerrett's declaration. Distances in downtown Honolulu were short. The principal buildings were in the same area, only a few blocks apart. Arion Hall was only a few hundred meters from `Iolani Palace; it was a little over twice that far to the American consulate, the police station, the barracks, and other key spots. From Arion Hall, and from secondary positions at the consulate and legation, U.S. troops could have rapidly deployed anywhere in downtown Honolulu. If they had bivouacked at the old armory near the waterfront, at the consulate (had there been room), or simply remained in Atherton's yard, they were still only minutes away from likely trouble spots. Any downtown bivouac would have sufficed. Swinburne noted: "So far as American property is concerned, I should say that Arion Hall is as good as any other place. There were as many Americans on one side as on the other."[34] The troops simply occupied their best bivouac location without regard to its proximity to the queen's forces and without intending to support the rebels. Neither Stevens nor American naval officers told the rebels where the bivouac location would be—they did not know themselves—nor did they consult the rebels about potential locations. The selection of Arion Hall was purely a question of availability.

The positioning of the troops was far less important than the landing itself, which made the royalists much less likely to challenge the rebels. Stevens made it abundantly clear that he would not support the queen. When the troops landed, some royalists therefore assumed they threatened the monarchy. The queen's aide, Colonel Curtis Iaukea, said the queen and her staff became uneasy when they heard American troops had landed. "This feeling soon turned to one of grave alarm and apprehension when, a few minutes later, the troops were seen moving in the direction of the palace, and without warning, immediately take a position a short distance from, and in full view of, the Palace and the Government Building," Iaukea told Blount. "This unexpected show of force right under the Palace walls"—Iaukea was apparently referring to the troops' pause near the palace while Swinburne phoned the ship—and the later encampment at nearby Arion Hall convinced many royalists that the troops were landed "for some other purpose than the protection of life and property." Iaukea claimed this feeling deterred the queen from offering resistance to the rebels when they later occupied the Government Building.[35]

Thus the unannounced troop landing, the failure of Stevens and Wiltse to explain the reasons for it to the royalists in advance, the psychological effect of the troops passing in front of the palace, and, to some degree, their lodgment at nearby Arion Hall accentuated the fears of the royalists. The royalists perceived a pattern of American military support for the rebels. Even the short pause near the palace so that Swinburne could phone the ship from Hopper's residence was somehow seen, in Iaukea's words, as a "show of force." Stevens intentionally did not offer to the queen assurances of American neutrality, and although Wiltse and Swinburne were trying to be neutral, they were oblivious to how their actions might be perceived. To the naval officers, American movements were neutral and logical, completely routine, but the queen and her supporters, timid and fearful, understandably interpreted them as threatening.

THE PROCLAMATION OF A PROVISIONAL GOVERNMENT

That Monday night, the Committee of Safety met at Henry Waterhouse's residence.[36] Thurston and two others were home, sick with flu. The committee asked Sanford Dole to head a new government. Dole was forty-eight years old in 1893. His gentle eyes and benign expression emphasized the mild manner and cool reserve remarked upon by everyone who met him. He was a bit high-strung and prone to moodiness. His long beard, stretching well down his chest, was already white. Born to missionary parents in Honolulu and fluent in Hawaiian, he studied at Punahou-O`ahu College and then at Williams College. He read law in Boston and returned to Hawai`i to set up his own practice. Sanford Dole was not a planter himself, though he held shares in Grove Ranch plantation until 1888. Dole's brother George managed Koloa sugar plantation and his younger cousin James founded the family's famous pineapple business in 1901. Sanford Dole's first foray into politics was his public opposition to the king's appointment of Cesar Moreno in 1880. Dole opposed other Gibson policies while serving in the legislature during 1884–86. He helped Thurston draft the Bayonet Constitution. By the January 1893 revolution, Dole had been for several years an associate justice of the Supreme Court. Royalists somehow thought Dole was a moderate. Although he did not want to eliminate the monarchy, he wanted it subordinated to the legislature. To the Committee of Safety's proposal to eliminate the monarchy and make him president, Dole vainly argued that Princess Kai`ulani should reign under a regent until she came of age. Dole went home to ponder. The next morning, Tuesday, he decided to accept the committee's suggestion and headed downtown, stopping at Stevens' house, where the minister yet again improperly meddled and told him, "I think you have a great opportunity."[37]

Dole hurried to the Thurston-Smith law office where, by ten or eleven o'clock, the proposed appointees and rebel leaders gathered. They prepared Dole's appointment and other papers. Thurston was still home, sick, and would miss the day's events. About one thirty, the Committee of Safety signed the proclamation of a provisional government. As McCandless put it, "there was nothing to do then but to go to the Government Building and take it, and launch the new Government." McCandless went to the Armory to order the assembling rebel troops to the Government Building. A rebel reported that all was quiet at the Government Building, though some Native Hawaiians were in front of the Music Hall across the street.[38]

About 2:20 PM, peering out the law office door, Dole saw six Hawaiian policemen across the street. Thirty years later, he recalled: "We had no inkling of their instructions. We were for the most part unarmed. Our pockets were filled with documents of a seditious nature. Those were critical moments for both sides. Success or failure . . . of our movement seemed equally balanced."[39]

Meanwhile, McCandless hurried toward the armory at the corner of Beretania and Punchbowl, the rallying point for the re-forming Rifles. The streets were full of government supporters and rebels. McCandless heard a policeman's whistle and ran to the spot. John Good and other rebels purchased guns and ammunition at the E. O. Hall and Sons hardware store and loaded them on a wagon. A valiant police officer named Leialoha grabbed the bridle of the team of horses. Good shot Officer Leialoha in the shoulder. (The only casualty of the revolution, Leialoha recovered fully and received a two-hundred-dollar payment and get-well letter from Dole.)[40] The other police officers fell back. The wagon headed to the armory. As McCandless reached the armory, Captain C. W. Zeigler's Company A hustled toward the Government Building.[41]

As the Committee of Safety filed out of the Thurston-Smith office, they heard Good's shot, fired only two blocks off. The loud report drew everyone to the spot of the shooting. The police officers across the street disappeared. The committee split into two groups and hurried via different streets to the Government Building. They were surprised to find it unguarded aside from J. C. McCarthy.[42] Shortly after two thirty, in the presence of McCarthy and a few clerks, Henry Cooper read a short proclamation abrogating the monarchy and establishing a provisional government. During the reading, about 2:40 PM, Company A arrived.[43] Dole requested royal officials to remain in their posts, except for the queen, her cabinet, and Marshal Wilson. The rebel government set up shop in the Government Building. John Soper organized street patrols. Dole invited the *Boston*'s troops to participate, but "this invitation met a curt refusal."[44]

Why did the rebels proclaim the new government at the Government Building? Most of the answer is that it was undefended. Secondly, it was the seat of the legislature, the counterpoint to the monarchy, and the seat of the cabinet ministries. To antiroyalist rebels, the symbol of political legitimacy was not `Iolani Palace—that was the monarchy's crown jewel—nor the police station and the barracks, for those were bastions of the queen's forces. The rebels viewed the legislature as the counterpoint to royal power. It was natural to read the proclamation at the legislative building.

THE BEHAVIOR OF U.S. TROOPS

Although most saw their presence ashore as support for the rebels, the American troops tried to remain neutral. Charles Carter rode to Arion Hall to alert Swinburne that a proclamation would soon be read, and to gain a sense of Swinburne's orders. Swinburne showed Carter his orders and said, "You see my orders are to protect the legation, the consulate, and the lives and property of American citizens, and to assist in preserving order: I do not know how to interpret that; I can do it but one way. If the Queen calls upon me to preserve order, I am going to do it." Swinburne asserted that he had neither orders nor intent to support the rebels. At the Senate hearings, Morgan asked if Swinburne interpreted the landing order to mean support for the existing government or any other government. Swinburne said, "I supposed it to mean the Queen's Government; that was my interpretation. There was no other government when I landed." But, he continued, he was not there "to fight her battles any more than anyone else's. I was there to preserve order; protect the peaceful rights of citizens in the town." "You were going to prevent fighting?" Morgan asked. Swinburne replied, "I was going to prevent any fighting that endangered the Americans in the town." Swinburne denied that he would have "felt called upon" to stop the queen's troops from firing on the rebels.[45] By now Wiltse too was at Arion Hall checking on his troops.

Throughout the turmoil, the American troops never left Arion Hall. Swinburne knew, from Carter's tip, that the rebels would soon read the proclamation. He did not tell the other officers.[46] The *Boston*'s troops heard Good's shot. Given the crowds on the street, the shooting, and the prospective reading of the proclamation, Swinburne expected a riot. He had his men stack arms and form in ranks in the rear of Arion Hall so that they were out of sight.[47] The men kept breaking formation to peer over the fence to see what was going on, and Swinburne had "great difficulty keeping them in the ranks."[48] Swinburne did not deploy a patrol or investigate the shot, hardly the actions of a man determined to support the rebels.

Soon Dole and others arrived at the Government Building and Cooper read the proclamation.[49] Samuel Damon, one of the rebel party, sent a messenger asking Swinburne for protection. The reply: "Capt. Wiltse's orders are 'I remain passive.'"[50] Not long after—Swinburne guessed it four thirty or five o'clock—Dole asked Wiltse to come over to the Government Building for a talk. Wiltse and Swinburne met with Dole, Peter Jones, William O. Smith, and others. The Government Building was well garrisoned. Swinburne remembered a big store of guns and ammo piled in the room, guards at every building entrance, and "at least 100 men under arms." Smith and Jones did most of the talking and requested that Wiltse recognize them as the de facto government because they occupied the Government Building, the archives, and the treasury. Wiltse asked if they controlled the police station and the barracks, and whether they could guarantee the safety of life and property. Dole admitted that the rebels as yet did not control the police station or the barracks. Wiltse said he could not recognize them, and the two officers returned to Arion Hall by six o'clock. Legally, with an American minister posted in Honolulu, Wiltse lacked authority to recognize anyone, but it is worth noting the vast difference between Wiltse's criteria for recognition and Stevens' much looser standard.[51]

STEVENS' RECOGNITION OF THE REBEL GOVERNMENT

Amazingly, while Wiltse and Swinburne discussed recognition with rebel leaders at the Government Building, Stevens had already recognized the provisional government as the de facto government of Hawai`i. Word had not yet reached the naval officers, nor Dole and Jones and Smith. (Why ask Wiltse for recognition if Stevens had already given it?) Not until after six thirty that evening did the naval officers learn of Stevens' action.[52]

There has been considerable debate over the timing of recognition and whether Stevens recognized the provisional government before it had effective control of the facilities and functions of government. Royalist participants and historians persuaded by their recollections assert that Stevens recognized the provisional government almost as soon as the rebel party read its proclamation in front of the Government Building. The government had sensed the crisis coming to a head. When Stevens did not attend the cabinet's meeting with the diplomatic corps at midday, the cabinet went to his residence, where Parker and Peterson

THE LANDING OF U.S. TROOPS

talked with him briefly. (Like Thurston and others, Stevens had the flu and was lying on a couch.) Peterson claimed Stevens said he could offer the Crown no support because a respectable group of citizens had asked for his help. Stevens later denied this, but it is nearly certain that Peterson's account is correct. In any event, the royalists believed Peterson's version, strengthening their conviction that, at the least, they were on their own. Back at the police station, where they had holed up, the cabinet learned, about 2:45 PM, that the rebels proclaimed a provisional government. The cabinet sent Charles Hopkins back to Stevens to get an answer "in black and white," as Cornwell put it. The ailing minister had his daughter tell Hopkins that he was incapacitated, but Hopkins would not go away. Finally, Stevens gave Hopkins a note saying he had recognized the provisional government. Hopkins stated that he carried this note to Samuel Parker at 3:10 PM; Marshal Wilson said it was between 3:30 and 4:00 PM. John Colburn says the cabinet received it at 3:55 PM and "concluded to surrender and yield to America."[53] Though the royalists differed on the exact time of receipt, they very likely received the note by 4:00 PM.

Rebel participants and not a few historians claim that recognition came one to three hours later, only after Stevens verified that the provisional government controlled the city. Stevens sent another note, this one to Dole, saying, "A Provisional Government having been duly constituted in the place of the recent Government of Queen Liliuokalani and said Provisional Government being in full possession of the Government Building, the Archives, and the Treasury and in control of the capital of the Hawaiian Islands, I hereby recognize said Provisional Government as the de facto government of the Hawaiian Islands."[54] William Wilder stated that shortly after the reading of the proclamation, Stevens sent someone to see if the rebels possessed the Government Building. A couple of hours later, about 5:30 PM, Wilder said, a formal missive saying Stevens had recognized the provisional government arrived at the Government Building.[55] Peter Jones testified that about 4:00 PM the rebels sent a notice to Stevens that they possessed the Government Building. Senator George Gray asked when an answer came back: "Very soon," Jones replied. "Before dark?" Gray asked. "I think it was just about dark," Jones said. On January 17, 1893, sunset was at 6:13 PM and twilight ended at 6:37 PM. "About dark" must have been roughly 6:00 PM to perhaps 6:40 PM. Jones also testified that Wiltse and Swinburne's visit to the Government Building—a visit that concluded at 6:00 PM—occurred before the rebels received Stevens' note of recognition.[56]

The apparently contradictory evidence on the timing of recognition is easily explained. The first expression of Stevens' recognition of the provisional government was his reply carried to the cabinet by Charles Hopkins between 3:15 and 4:00 PM. Thereafter, other persons, including rebel leaders, learned of the American recognition at different times and by different means. Several heard of it from royalist leaders, others heard it in the streets, still others did not know of it until Stevens formally communicated it to the provisional government officials at the Government Building. Last to learn of it were the U.S. naval forces; Swinburne did not learn until sometime after 6:00 PM. All the evidence shows that Stevens recognized the provisional government very soon—within an hour—after it occupied the Government Building. From that time, roughly 4:00 PM, it took a couple more hours before everyone in town knew.

Stevens' recognition was very premature and mightily improper, violating the practice that a rebel government must be in control and executing the functions of government. Stevens himself never fully understood his error, and to the degree that he did understand, he tried to cover it up. At the Morgan hearings, senators grilled him mercilessly about the timing of recognition and whether he first verified that the rebels possessed most government facilities or, more generally, controlled the situation. In fact, when Stevens recognized the rebels, they occupied only the Government Building. Yet Stevens said, in his recognition letter, that the rebels controlled the capital of the Hawaiian Islands. But the palace, station house, and barracks were not controlled, and the government's forces had not been beaten. The rebels did control the streets by late afternoon because the police holed up in the station house and the royalist troops hunkered down in the barracks. The royal ministers were cowed—taking cover in the police station—and not in full control of the situation either. Stevens should have waited to see which group would win, but as a practical matter Stevens' highly partisan behavior (and the U.S. landing, a decision he did not make but did not try to stop) made him a participant, rather than a neutral diplomatic observer.

When Senator Morgan asked what information from the provisional government impelled recognition, Stevens waffled: "I could not say, but there is probably a note on file in the legation in Honolulu, I presume there is—stating that they were constituted. But I learned of it in very many ways outside of that. There was a complete want of government, an interregnum, from Saturday afternoon, and my purpose was to recognize the first real government that was constituted, and if Mr. Wilson had gone forward and shown any force and organized a government I should have recognized that."[57] Preposterous on its face, this lie deceived no one.

Despite his evasions and lies, Stevens surely remembered when he recognized the provisional government. Recognition was his single most significant act on January 17, perhaps of his time in Hawai`i. Morgan: "When did you write that note?" Flustered, Stevens replied: "I could not say." Morgan pressed harder: "About what time?" "I could not swear to that," Stevens stammered, and then he blurted the truth: "I prepared a note before; had it in readiness, because it was as open as any railroad meeting would be in your city or mine; and I probably got the note ready without signature beforehand."[58] Stevens prepared an unsigned recognition note, probably on Sunday or Monday, as he learned via his rebel contacts and their visits to his residence that they planned a provisional government. He was ready to recognize any rebel government immediately without truly verifying its control of the situation. This was not only a severe breach of diplomatic practice but also revealed his extreme prorebel bias. Although Stevens had made up his own mind, he had not fully communicated his sentiments to the rebels. They were not absolutely certain how much control they had to demonstrate before Stevens would recognize them. When Senator Gray asserted that the Committee of Safety thought all they had to do was seize the Government Building, John McCandless disagreed. The rebels expected only "when we had the upper hand he would recognize us."[59] But to Stevens, having the upper hand meant merely occupying the Government Building. As we have seen, this was not Captain Wiltse's position. Wiltse and Swinburne tried to adhere to the accepted standard of control of the city, including the royalists' strong points.

THE SURRENDER

The rebels sent Samuel Damon and Crister Bolte to the police station to demand a royalist surrender. The ministers were afraid to leave, but Parker and Cornwell finally came to the Government Building when their safety was guaranteed. They declined to surrender without talking to the queen. Samuel Damon went with them to the palace to present the provisional government's demands. Damon had already seen the queen that day. That very morning he had decided to join the rebels. As he had long supported the Crown, he felt obliged to inform the queen of his decision. He advised her that resistance was hopeless. She should surrender to prevent bloodshed. The conversion of a former ally may have added to the queen's distress. American troops had landed, her former allies were leaving her, and she knew the rebels were rapidly reconstituting their militia. She may have begun to think of surrender even on the morning of January 17.[60]

At the palace, the queen gathered her four cabinet ministers, two royal princes, and four trusted royalists: Ned Macfarlane, Joseph Carter, Hermann Widemann, and Paul Neumann. Damon alone represented the rebels. He said he had been sent to inform the queen that she was deposed and that a provisional government, recognized by Stevens, had replaced the monarchy. Damon requested her surrender. He said the queen might prepare a protest if she wished. This broadside, though in polite language, produced what Carter called "an awkward pause," which he broke by expressing sympathy but reiterating that her situation was hopeless and that she should surrender. Carter knew the rebels held the Government Building, he knew the *Boston*'s troops were nearby, and he heard that Stevens recognized the provisional government. He thought surrender the only prudent course.[61] Widemann concurred. Carter said she should make a formal protest, and Widemann added that the British reversed their seizure of the islands in 1843. The queen agreed to surrender without much persuasion. Damon said it was "the Queen's idea that she could surrender pending a settlement at Washington, and it was on that condition that she gave up."[62]

Her protest, drafted by Paul Neumann with Carter's help, said she was coerced by the "superior force" of the United States, whose minister landed troops to support the rebels. To avoid fighting and loss of life, she would "yield my authority until such time as the Government of the United States shall, upon the facts being presented to it, undo the action of its representatives and reinstate me."[63] Tactically, this was the only option left. If she surrendered to the provisional government, her power was gone for all time. By surrendering to the United States, she preserved a small chance of regaining the throne. Oddly, her protest was duly delivered not to Stevens, the U.S. representative, but to Dole, who accepted it without comment. The rebels wanted capitulation. If the queen wanted to appeal to the United States, it was not a concern of theirs. The queen drafted a note to Marshal Wilson directing him to surrender, not to U.S. officers at Arion Hall, nor to Stevens, but to the provisional government forces, which, after all, were the only ones demanding it. Wilson refused to surrender and did not until the cabinet appeared personally and commanded him.[64]

Royalists later claimed that U.S. backing of the rebels was the chief reason for the surrender and for the government's timidity.[65] Cornwell claimed they did not put troops in the Government Building because a clash there might endanger the *Boston* men, "and the Government desired, at all hazards, to avoid giving Minister Stevens any excuse or pretext for his hostile actions." (This begged the question of why no forces were posted there before the U.S. landing.) Cornwell felt intimidated by the troops at Arion Hall. Their placement "so far from the center of the property of Americans and so very close to the property of the Hawaiian Government was both very remarkable and very suggestive."[66] The royalists would undercut Lili`uokalani's appeal to Cleveland if they attributed their surrender to anything other than U.S. backing of the rebels. They had much to gain from sticking to that argument.

It is striking that none of the nine senior royalists had any ideas beyond surrender.[67] The royalists understandably felt intimidated by the American landing and by the deployment nearby. But they were not just intimidated or pressured; they were completely paralyzed and strongly predisposed to surrender. Strong leaders do not cave immediately under pressure; rather, they attempt to devise counterstrategies. Not so with the royalist leaders. At the queen's "surrender" conference, the four ministers had nothing to say; they had given up. The invited advisors—Carter, Macfarlane, Widemann, Neumann—offered reasonable but extremely timid advice. Nor did the queen inspire the others. Four days earlier, on January 14, she had Marshal Wilson and Captain Nowlein prepare to suppress forcibly any protest of her constitutional promulgation. That Saturday afternoon she had armed guards lined up before the palace while arguing whether to issue the pact. But her resolve withered when faced with a real dilemma. She produced no useful ideas about how to deal with the rebellion, nor did she insist that her advisors generate options other than capitulation. No one in the royalist camp had any imagination. They were paralyzed by their assumptions about the possibility of bloodshed, the extent of Stevens' backing for the rebels, and the possibility of American military support for the rebels. They did not test their assumptions. Even after American recognition, the royalists could have waited to see if the rebels attacked their strongholds and gauged the American response. In the best case, the stalemate might have continued until Washington reversed Stevens' hasty recognition. By folding their hand so early, they lost any chance for a negotiated settlement.

The royalists put themselves in a difficult position. Before the landing, the royalists were unjustifiably passive. Why did royalist forces not control the streets better? Why did they not arrest the rebel ringleaders? Why did they not seize the Armory to prevent its use by the rebels? Why did they not seal the public buildings and post armed guards at the entrances? Why did they not declare a state of emergency and close the hardware stores that were selling guns and ammunition to the rebels? Why did they not institute a curfew to hinder rebel communications? A more aggressive police and military stance might have headed off the rebel declaration, deterred a landing, and perhaps prevented American recognition. That the royalists took none of these steps, before or after the U.S. landing, demonstrates weak leadership and poor judgment. All reflect badly on the royalists as an effective military and police force.[68] Albert F. Judd said, "no one of the Queen's party dared to strike a blow. . . . If Marshal Wilson and the cabinet ever intended to resist the movement, they had ample time to do so . . . before troops from the *Boston* had landed."[69] Royalist weaknesses were extremely important in their rout.

Beginning with the earliest postmortem of the revolution—that of President Cleveland's investigator, James Blount, in the spring of 1893—far too much attention has been paid over a century of historical writing to the U.S. troop landing and the timing of Stevens' recognition of the provisional government, and far too little attention given to the military strengths and leadership of the contending parties. Blount's approach emerged from two bedrock assumptions, one wrong and the second beside the point, though technically correct.

First, Blount wrongly assumed that the rebels were militarily inferior. Only the presence of U.S. troops, he assumed, prevented the royalists from suppressing the revolt. His assumption led him to focus on the intimidation effect of the landing and of Stevens' behavior, and to neglect the strength and determination of rebel forces. In fact, the rebels had clear military superiority, despite roughly equal numbers, and despite royalist claims to the contrary. John Colburn told Blount that "we would have annihilated them were it not for the United States troops and Minister Stevens."[70] This was postsurrender bluster. There was no chance the royalists could put down the rebellion when Cooper proclaimed a new government. Despite having a minimum of 496 armed men from the Royal Guard, regular police, and volunteers, the royalists failed to garrison key points around town. Instead, they barricaded themselves in the police station and the barracks. How could they put down a rebellion if they would not control the streets? After the queen's capitulation, Captain Nowlein, commanding the troops at the barracks (and a few at the palace), surrendered 272 men armed with either Springfield army rifles or Winchester repeating carbines, 12 breech-loading rifled cannon, and 1 Gatling gun. With rebels using the armory just a block away, and the unguarded Government Building across from the palace, none of Nowlein's 272 men did anything to suppress rebel activity or even to guard a key facility like the Government Building, even before the *Boston*'s troops were ashore.[71] Marshal Wilson surrendered 224 armed men and 1 Gatling gun at the police station. Aside from Officer Leialoha and Wilson himself, none of the 500 men in the queen's forces did anything to suppress the rebels before or after the Americans landed.[72] W. D. Alexander said the cabinet, cowed by the rebels' determination, used the landing and Stevens' partiality as an excuse for inaction.[73] Henry Waterhouse said, "We knew the feeling of those who were in power then—that they were cowards— that by going up with a bold front, and they supposing that the American troops would assist us, that would help us out."[74] Blount heard those words but did not believe them.

The rebels had strong will to fight. John Good's shooting of Officer Leialoha is typical of the rebel resolve. The rebels rapidly rebuilt the forces that backed the Bayonet Revolution of 1887 and suppressed the Wilcox Rebellion in 1889. The case of Joseph Fisher illustrates how rapidly the rebels were rearming. Fisher had been captain of Company B of the Honolulu Rifles, disbanded in August 1890. On January 14, 1893, he and other ex-captains began recruiting their old comrades, using old rosters. Nearly all the former Rifles and many new men joined. By Monday evening, January 16, he had forty-five armed men in his reconstituted company, and other captains were filling their units too. Fisher's affidavit said, "Orders were issued to assemble at the old Rifles Armory promptly at 3 o'clock on January 17. Matters were precipitated by the shot fired by Ordnance Officer Good on Fort Street about 2:20 o'clock. Was at the armory immediately after, and at the request of the members of the new Government sent men as fast as they arrived in squads to the Government Building, the first sent being Captain Zeigler with about 36 men. Had not been told nor did not believe the United States marines would take part one way or another."[75] John McCandless said his brother went out to his ranch and brought back his weapons, a phenomenon occurring all over town.[76] McCandless did not think the government could suppress the rebels after Monday morning, January 16. With a rapidly growing force of determined volunteers, experienced in the crises of 1887 and 1889, "there was no reason why we should not win again."[77]

Royalist military inferiority would have cost them the struggle even had the *Boston* still been at sea when the revolt began. The battle might have taken several days and shed some blood, but the rebels would definitely have won. Swinburne testified that if the *Boston* had stayed out longer "they would have deposed the Queen and had the whole business settled before we got there, as they were capable of doing."[78]

The second assumption that underlay Blount's investigation was his belief that Stevens' premature recognition of the provisional government forced the queen's capitulation. While he was correct in the strictest sense, he overlooked the fact that royalist leadership failures and tactical errors had lost the revolution even before Stevens' recognition and indeed even before Henry Cooper read the proclamation at the Government Building. Blount found it significant that the rebels did not attack the royalist strong points, the barracks and the police station, which did not surrender until the United States recognized the provisional government. They would not have surrendered, Blount declared, without that recognition.

It is true that American recognition made it impossible for the queen to win, at least until Washington responded to the queen's protest, but Blount's observation missed the point. If her forces had not surrendered, they would have remained confined to the police station and barracks and eventually would have surrendered for lack of food and water whether or not Stevens recognized the provisional government. Once the royalists holed up, they lost the military phase of the revolution. Their major tactical error allowed the rebels to cover the building exits by fire and prevent reinforcement and resupply. Why didn't the rebels attack? They saw no need to storm the barracks and the police station when little blood would be shed by simply waiting until trapped royalists capitulated. That the queen surrendered before the rebels needed to take this step did not mitigate the royalist error.

Blount made a strong, valid point that while the royalists were uncertain about the role of U.S. troops, the rebels never thought those troops would be used against them.[79] Lieutenant Coffman said, "Everybody believed that the entire American force and American minister were in accord and sympathy with the movement, and I do not think the movement would have been undertaken had they not thought so beforehand." Surely, Coffman continued, the rebels "thought and felt that if there was necessity our troops would aid them. I do not say they would have done so by firing." Senator Morgan asked, "How could you aid them except by firing?" Coffman replied, "The moral presence of the troops, which is very great in an occasion of that kind, and the position in which they were placed." Senator Gray asked, "Your position is, that while these troops were there to protect life and property there was a general impression in Honolulu that carried the purpose of their presence far beyond that." Coffman: "Yes, I believe that."[80] Samuel Damon told Blount the rebels tried to convey the impression that American troops landed to support them.[81]

Blount said the rebels and royalists believed that the troops would prevent fighting between the parties. But the melee in front of E. O. Hall and Sons showed that U.S. troops would not deploy in all circumstances. U.S. troops heard the shot and soon learned that there was a clash between police and rebels. Their reaction was not to deploy to preserve public order but to tighten discipline and remain within the boundaries of Arion Hall. The incident also showed that rebels were ready to resort to violence without the physical backing of U.S. troops.

Certainly the presence of the ship had an effect: the troops might be landed and, once ashore, might intervene. The U.S. minister's well-known bias in favor of the white rebels might mean he would conspire with them. He might recognize their government early. Each of these situations, when confronted, demanded a different analysis by the royalists. Overall, it is clear Stevens' improper actions and Wiltse's landing of troops significantly influenced events and greatly complicated the political and tactical situation facing the weak royalist leadership. The royalists needed a skillful, confident, aggressive leader to devise counterstrategies. That leader was lacking anywhere in royalist ranks, aside from Marshal Wilson.

STEVENS: INDEPENDENT ACTOR OR POLICY TOOL?

Old and irascible, Stevens disliked dealing with a female leader. He was condescending and impatient with the queen. Lili`uokalani recalled him visiting the
palace and lecturing her while sitting with one leg over the arm of his chair.
Stevens' memory and veracity were poor and his ego huge. His dispatches and
sworn testimony are unreliable. Before the Morgan Committee, Stevens mixed up
dates and even lied. He testified that Wiltse landed troops only upon his request,
but Stevens himself testified that Wiltse had the landing order ready when the
minister came aboard the *Boston*. Backtracking, Stevens claimed Wiltse took
direction from previous discussions. They had "talked over the situation" during
the *Boston*'s voyage, but there was no "situation" then. Stevens testified that aboard
the cruiser on January 16, discussion of the landing took two minutes, but he was
aboard the ship an hour and ten minutes, according to the deck log. He said he
had no aide de camp, but his later testimony (and that of many others) identified
Cadet Pringle as his aide. Stevens swore he acted only because there was no func-
tioning government—his "interregnum"—and that he would have recognized any
group, including one led by Marshal Wilson, that formed a government. This was
a complete lie. Stevens' intense hatred of Wilson—the marshal returned it in full
measure—poisoned his relations with the monarchy.[82]

Did Stevens exceed his instructions? He claimed conformity with Secretary
of State Bayard's instructions to Minister George Merrill during the Bayonet
Constitution controversy in the summer of 1887, when it looked as if the
United States might have to land troops. The original copy of Bayard's message,
which Stevens consulted, lay in the legation files in January 1893. Bayard wrote,
"Obstruction to the channels of legitimate commerce under existing law must
not be allowed, and American citizens in Hawai`i must be protected in their
persons and property, by the representatives of their country's law and power, and
no internal discord must be suffered to impair them. Your own aid and counsel, as
well as the assistance of the offices of Government vessels, if found necessary, will
therefore be promptly afforded to promote the reign of law and respect for orderly
government in Hawai`i."[83] In 1893 no disorder threatened the life and property
of Americans. Stevens' actions, both his premature recognition and, worse, his
improper contacts with the queen's enemies, went far beyond his policy guidelines.

Was Captain Wiltse's landing proper? According the 1893 naval regulations,
when injury to the United States or to its citizens is "committed or threatened,"
the naval commander shall consult with the diplomatic representative and "take
such steps as the gravity of the case demands," including "the protection of the
state, its honor, and its possessions, and the lives and property of its citizens against

arbitrary violence, actual or impending, whereby the state or its citizens may suffer irreparable injury." Force "must be used only as a last resort, and then only to the extent which is absolutely necessary to accomplish the end required." Though he should consult with the diplomatic representative, "a commanding officer is solely and entirely responsible to his own superior for all official acts in the administration of his command."[84]

Wiltse's landing—a display of force if not "use"—was improper under the regulations. It was premature and certainly not a last resort. Diplomatic measures could have been tried, beginning with mediation. There was no threat to U.S. lives and property during January 14–17. Wiltse's actions exceeded what was necessary and prudent, though they were far closer to traditional practice than Stevens' actions. Unlike Stevens, Wiltse did not give the rebels comfort; he strove for neutrality. Alas, he did not consider that the royalists might perceive his actions as unneutral.

A final question is whether the monarchy's fall can be attributed chiefly and predominantly to the acts of Stevens and Wiltse. The queen triggered the revolt by attempting to proclaim a new constitution, but it can be argued that she sought to redress what Hawaiians saw as the wrongs of the 1887 constitution. Indeed she was, though others might plausibly argue that the maladministration of Cesar Moreno, Gibson, and King Kalākaua brought on the 1887 constitutional crisis. Ultimately this cause-and-effect chain can be carried back to the so-called European discovery of Hawai`i and to later white and Asian immigration. From this point of view, it is possible to argue persuasively that white and Asian immigrants, for more than a hundred years after Cook, deserved no rights and privileges in Hawai`i and that, consequently, any moves by the queen to preserve and enhance the monarchy and the political power of Native Hawaiians were by definition legitimate and those of her opponents illegitimate. This is less an exercise in determining causation than it is a moral judgment about the superior rights of the descendents of original inhabitants versus those of latecomers.

Because the queen had long planned to promulgate the new constitution as soon as she dissolved the legislature, and because that step would certainly arouse opposition, the revolution would have occurred even if Stevens had remained in Hilo or if he had left Honolulu right after Cleveland's election.

Was royal paralysis in 1893 due to U.S. intimidation, or was a timid royalist leadership more fearful than the facts warranted? The queen confidently took initial steps that she knew would be disliked by much of the white community and by Stevens. She drafted a new constitution she knew would arouse opposition. She orchestrated the fall of the Wilcox cabinet. Even when the *Boston* returned on the morning of January 14, she simply reminded Wilson to have security forces ready to handle any opposition and proceeded to promulgate her new constitution. If she thought Stevens and her opponents were colluding to overthrow her, why proceed? If the presence of the *Boston* was intimidating, why proceed?

At least through January 14, the royalists were confident. The *Boston* returned three hours before the queen attempted to promulgate the new constitution, so the warship's return, and therefore the presence in Honolulu of American troops, did not deter her. If there was intimidation, it must have derived from events after promulgation. What, then, were those events? First, the royalists underestimated the rapid rebel rearmament. Second, they were dismayed by the lack of support from the United States and by Stevens' partiality to the rebels. Perhaps the royalists had expected intervention on their behalf.

Although admittedly facing heavy odds, royalist leaders could have made an attempt to defend the Crown but chose not to. The presence of the *Boston* was not indispensable to the revolt, nor did it rule out a vigorous military-police response by a determined monarchy. The outcome of the 1893 revolution emerged from the personality, will, and character of the leaders of the two sides, and by the asymmetry in the fighting spirit of military forces. The role of the U.S. officials and forces was a very important influence, but not the main one, and did not chiefly determine the outcome of the revolution.

And so the Hawaiian Kingdom, proud symbol of sixteen hundred years of Polynesian predominance, passed away. But the Native Hawaiian people remained, in Tom Coffman's words, "a nation within" the white-ruled government and state.[85] The royalist Theo Davies, Princess Kaʻiulani's British guardian, penned an epitaph: "One of the saddest features of this matter is that it has been presented as a plot and a conspiracy of bad men. It is not that. It is the blunder of good men, men to many of whom I would entrust my dearest of interests. They have been goaded on by misrule into injustice, forgetting that injustice is no remedy for misrule."[86]

CHAPTER 8

❦

The Rise and Fall of the Annexation Treaty

C hauncey Depew once called John Watson Foster the "handyman of the Department of State."[1] The label fit; few men have handled so many diplomatic tasks over such a long period. Born in Indiana in 1836, Foster was a strong opponent of slavery and worked hard for Lincoln in 1860. He served in the 25th Indiana Regiment, leaving the army as a brigadier general. In 1873, in part because he had come to Grant's attention during the war, he went to Mexico as minister. Later he was minister to Russia and minister to Spain. When the Democrats won the White House in 1884, the Republican Foster established an international law practice in Washington. Under Benjamin Harrison, Foster successfully negotiated reciprocity treaties with Brazil, Germany, the British West Indies, and several Central American states.[2]

Foster was a slim, regal man with a high, domed forehead and bushy, white muttonchop sideburns. Always calm, logical, and soft-spoken, he was easy to underestimate because he had no ego and never sought the limelight. When ill health forced Secretary of State Blaine's resignation in June 1892, Foster was an obvious successor. The chief issue facing the State Department was the Bering Sea Arbitration, a fur seal dispute with Britain and Canada that threatened to evolve into a shooting war in the frigid northern waters. As the principal government lawyer, Foster had been working on the American case for months. His withdrawal would have greatly hindered the U.S. position, so President Harrison took the unusual step of leaving him as the lead arbitration agent even as he took over the State Department. The arbitration was his chief concern during late 1892 and early 1893. His mastery of the issue was so great that even after Harrison's defeat, Grover Cleveland retained Foster in the American delegation that left for arbitration hearings in Paris two weeks before the inauguration.

A team headed by Lorrin Thurston arrived in Washington on February 3 to negotiate an annexation treaty. Although consumed with Bering Sea preparations, Secretary Foster met the commissioners seven times by February 9. The commissioners predictably suggested treaty terms favorable to white interests. Besides the obvious—a territorial government—the Hawaiians said public and Crown lands should be under control of the territorial, not federal, government. The Hawaiians called for laying a telegraph cable and building a base at Pearl Harbor. They wished an explicit statement that Hawaiian planters would receive the sugar bounties paid to mainland planters. No federal laws should hinder the immigration of Japanese and other laborers.

Knowing that such details would hamper swift ratification, Foster nixed them. Get Hawai`i into the Union, he said, and the rest would take care of itself. Pushed by Thurston, the commissioners signed Foster's draft on February 14.[3] In a silly burst of optimism, Thurston cabled: "Treaty annexation signed today. Goes to Senate tomorrow. Every reason to expect early favorable action."[4] In fact, there was no sign of swift Senate approval.

Back in Honolulu, stories circulated that royalists offered Japanese laborers full citizenship if they helped restore the monarchy. Instigators apparently told laborers on one plantation that annexation would permanently extend their contracts. Armed with their long cane knives, four hundred Japanese marched on Honolulu to protest. Consul-General Fujii Saburo rushed to the city's outskirts and dispersed the mob.[5]

The arrival of the armored corvette *Kongo* on January 28 gave Fujii more leverage.[6] Stevens worried that Japan would try to extract political concessions, perhaps even the vote for Japanese, while the white rebels cobbled together a government.[7] He expected a British warship soon. He distrusted Wodehouse and worried that the commissioner hoped for a royalist countercoup. Wodehouse inadvertently fed Stevens' fears by asking Dole three times when American troops would return to the *Boston* and by meeting privately with the queen.[8]

Stevens used this meager evidence of foreign intrigues as a pretext to declare a protectorate on February 1, 1893. Dole supplied the excuse, surely at Stevens' request, asking for protection against a *Kongo* landing party.[9] The *Boston*'s men promptly raised the U.S. flag over Honolulu. Stevens claimed he prevented the "hoodlum foreigners and more vicious natives" from attacking, but there was no evidence of a counterrevolt or a Japanese landing.[10]

In Stevens' mind, the good guys had won, and he would make sure they stayed in power. The protectorate would stiffen the government's spine if Japan pressured for the vote or Britain pushed for a shared protectorate as in Samoa. Even granting Stevens' (unfounded) distrust of Japanese and British motives, the protectorate was unnecessary. There was little chance that Japan or Britain would land troops with the *Boston* in the harbor. Nor did a countercoup seem possible. The same revolutionaries that had cowed the royalists controlled the streets.[11]

Stevens also wanted to relieve the stress that continual military service placed on the white community. Colonel John Soper kept three hundred volunteers on active duty. The Guard ran street patrols, did police work, and posted details at key points.[12] They could leave their normal jobs for short periods but not forever.

Stevens' protectorate shifted the defense burden to the *Boston*'s men. Volunteers returned to their normal jobs. Government expenses dropped from more than $50,000 for the final 12 days of January to less than $9,000 per month in February and March.[13] U.S. troops did not patrol streets or do policing, so Soper sought a 103-man company of regulars, including 70 politically reliable men from the queen's disbanded regulars, to handle daily tasks, with three companies of on-call volunteers for a surge capacity of more than 400 troops.[14]

Although his protectorate made the provisional government impregnable, Stevens still questioned Japanese and British motives. Stevens truly believed that there was some foreign threat. Washington was not so worried, though the Navy rushed Admiral Joseph Skerrett to the islands with the *Mohican*.[15] The Navy also sent out the *Alliance* and readied *Adams* and *Ranger*.[16] Stevens and Skerrett were to help maintain order until the Senate acted on the annexation treaty.[17] Although Secretary of State Foster "disavowed" the protectorate, the ruling made no practical difference because Stevens was not giving orders to the provisional government anyway.[18] U.S. troops remained ashore.

The Navy did wonder about Japan's Pacific policy. George Belknap, the crusty former commander of naval forces in Asia, believed Japan intended to expand into the Pacific. He carefully monitored Japan's surging naval capabilities. The Imperial Fleet's 1890 war games off Kobe showed the young navy was "well disciplined and thoroughly drilled." He detailed Japanese ship construction and armor, gunnery techniques, and torpedoes. He warned that recent murders of American and British missionaries in Tokyo suggested an antipathy toward foreigners that might complicate Japanese–American relations. Secretary of the Navy Benjamin Tracy referred these reports to the Office of Naval Intelligence for evaluation, sent copies to the State Department, and discussed Japan's growing naval strength with other officials.[19]

On February 23, the Japanese cruiser *Naniwa* appeared off the reef. Commanded by Togo Heihachiro, who would become a legend when he defeated the Russian fleet at Tsushima in 1905, the British-built *Naniwa* far outclassed any U.S. vessel, including the *Boston*.[20] The *Naniwa* carried instructions for Fujii to press the suffrage issue. British commissioner Wodehouse attached "considerable importance" to the added leverage provided by the two Japanese warships.[21] The senior British naval officer reported that "the Japanese interest is being pushed forward and will have to be seriously considered."[22]

Although it should not have been a surprise that a few laborers would have served in the military, the press exaggerated the issue, trumpeting that these veterans would serve Japan's interests again. The press badgered Fujii, finally extracting an "admission" that a few laborers were veterans, and speculated that the *Naniwa* carried arms for them to seize the island of Hawai`i.[23] Stevens queried Fujii, who merely said Japanese residents should have the same suffrage rights of Europeans. Stevens, like nearly all whites, could not accept equality. In a typical overreaction, Stevens warned that a Japanese landing, even to keep order, would be an invasion of the United States.[24]

On March 1, the *Kongo* suddenly left Honolulu. Stevens feared the ship carried arms for other islands. The American consular agent at Hilo reported that the resident Japanese labor agent encouraged his charges to fight American political dominance.[25] The *Alliance* went to "check the pulse of the people" at Hilo and found the *Kongo* there. Captain Tashiro of the *Kongo* was not happy to see the American warship, which he indelicately labeled a "wooden tub." Tashiro admitted his mission was to find out whether Japanese supported the royalists or the whites. There was no sign of trouble or munitions.[26]

Washington also worried about British reactions. Foster thought Britain would not intervene if the United States took a strong stand. He told his London embassy to watch for any suspicious actions.[27] Foster reviewed the attitudes of foreign representatives toward annexation. He found them generally favorable. The Russian minister claimed that Britain had a secret plan to subvert annexation. British minister Sir Julian Pauncefote, as yet without instructions, could not define his government's position.[28] Mistrust of Britain was so widespread—these were still the days of twisting the lion's tail—that the *Chicago Tribune* charged that Pauncefote's silence lulled the United States into inactivity while the British rushed warships to the islands.[29] Most British press clips showed London resigned to annexation, but hostile comments there were, and Assistant Secretary of State

Alvey Adee marked them with double red lines and sent them on to Foster.[30] By extending de facto rather than formal recognition, and by directing Wodehouse to maintain a "reserved attitude" toward the new government, London gave little comfort to the white rebels and did not calm Washington's worries about British policy.[31]

Stevens saw Wodehouse's hand behind royalist intrigues and labor unrest.[32] The cruiser HMS *Garnet*'s February 13 arrival renewed worries about British intervention. When the captain called on the governor of O`ahu, the brother-in-law of the ex-queen, but did not call on the new president—because he did not know whether Britain recognized the Dole government—royalist hopes soared. In the swirl of rumors about British machinations, Admiral Skerrett received an informant's report that the *Garnet* would land troops during the night, not to reinstall the queen but to hoist the Union Jack and demand that the United States agree to a joint protectorate, similar to the arrangement in Samoa. Skerrett overreacted, readying reinforcements for American troops already ashore. The Hawaiian Guard sandbagged the Government Building and the nearby barracks, emplaced cannon and Gatling guns, and stepped up waterfront patrols. HMS *Hyacinth*'s arrival in late February further fanned the embers of suspicion.[33]

Britain had no intention of intervening in Hawai`i in 1893. When the French ambassador asked if Britain would protest annexation, the Foreign Office said, "we had no intention of sending ships of war, for we considered that the lives and property of British residents were safe under American protection." The Admiralty noted that warships transiting the Pacific routinely stopped in Honolulu, so *Garnet*'s and *Hyacinth*'s port calls were unexceptional.[34] The Foreign Office instructed Pauncefote not to protest annexation.[35] In April London told Wodehouse that Britain would let events take their course. He should maintain friendly relations with the provisional government.[36]

Neither Britain nor Japan had any thought of challenging American preeminence in 1893. Both nations simply played the big power game of deploying warships to gain influence over events and reassure their citizens in Hawai`i. Both accurately sensed that annexation would likely fail. Nevertheless, their naval deployments and Britain's slowness in formally recognizing the provisional government inadvertently raised fears of foreign intervention.

Back in Washington, the annexation treaty was going nowhere. The annexation drive lacked the urgency it would have in 1897–98. Although Foster strongly supported annexation, he was greatly distracted by the impending arbitration and had only a few days left in Washington before heading for Europe. A February poll showed only twenty senators favored annexation, thirty-five preferred a protectorate, and twenty-five did not like either course. President Harrison seemed indifferent about rapid action on the treaty. On February 9, 1893, the *New York Herald* reported that the administration, though drafting an annexation treaty, doubted it would pass the Senate.[37] It seemed perfectly possible—it *was* perfectly possible—to check out the nasty rumors of a Stevens-inspired overthrow and then decide what to do. The treaty commissioners informed Honolulu that most senators "regard the question as one that will keep without difficulty." There seemed little chance of immediate ratification; partly because of a vigorous anti-treaty lobbying effort by the queen's supporters.[38]

British commissioner Wodehouse believed Stevens tried to use the protectorate to shove Washington toward annexation.[39] A protectorate signaled Hawaiian vulnerability, which annexation would cure. If that was Stevens' reasoning, it back-fired. By making Hawai`i safe, the protectorate and the U.S. naval buildup elimi-nated any reason for swift annexation. Without an imminent threat to American predominance, there was simply no need to rush the treaty through the Senate. President-elect Cleveland put out the word that he wanted more time to examine the annexation question. The Senate took no action on the treaty.

Grover Cleveland took his first oath of office in 1885 before large crowds on a bright sunny March day with a temperature of 54 degrees. Eight years later, at his second inaugural, attendees shivered in the falling snow and a biting wind that made the 25-degree temperature feel even colder. Champ Clark said it was so "windy, stormy, snowy, sleety, icy" that several onlookers perished.[40] Had she been present, Fraulein Wolf, Queen Lili`uokalani's mystic, might have said that the turn in the weather foretold trouble. Cleveland's second term would indeed be much more difficult than his first. He underwent a painful operation for cancer. He confronted the worst economic downturn in American history, the Depression of 1893, and foreign policy crises with Britain and with Spain over Cuba. As Chief Justice Melvin Fuller administered the oath of office, Cleveland faced his first problem, what to do about the Hawaiian annexation treaty.

That evening's Inaugural Ball took place in the magnificent new Pension Building, its great central atrium strung with colored electric lights; draped with red, white, and blue bunting; and decorated with thousands of cut flowers, remark-able in an age when cut flowers were a rare luxury in the winter. The several thou-sand guests gazed down from three levels of parapets around the atrium at the main floor, where the U.S. Marine Corps Band offered the first performance of the "The Great Republic," which band leader Francisco Fanciulli composed for the event. President Cleveland and the first lady greeted supporters and foreign dignitaries. The beautiful Frances Cleveland, twenty-eight years old and pregnant with her second child, stood arm in arm with a special guest, a lovely teenage girl named after the British queen by her father, Archibald Cleghorn, a Scottish resident of Hawai`i. Victoria Cleghorn was royalty herself: Ka`iulani, Crown Princess of Hawai`i.

Born in 1875, Ka`iulani grew up near Waikīkī with her father and her mother, Princess Likelike, sister of Lili`uokalani and Kalākaua. Her mother, never in good health and troubled by depression, died in 1887. It is said her last words to her daughter were "you will never be queen." Ka`iulani loved riding her pony, Fairy, enjoying lū`aus with friends, surfing—a replica of her surfboard is still in the British Surfing Museum—and even appearing at royal functions with her uncle, the king. Like many others in her extended family, she loved music. She sang and played the `ukulele. The Cleghorn estate was near the beach resort Sans Souci, where Robert Louis Stevenson resided in 1889 on his doctor's advice that Pacific weather would improve his health. The thirteen-year-old Ka`iulani's beauty and good nature entranced the writer, and he spent hours at her favorite place—under a giant banyan tree surrounded by her hordes of roaming peacocks—telling the child stories of the lands beyond the ocean. He had some musical talent himself, and she often wrote to remind him to bring his flute when he visited. Stevenson penned the most famous of his Hawai`i verses to console her about leaving Hawai`i for boarding school in Scotland, where Stevenson grew up. Below the verse, he inscribed this note: "When she comes to my land and her father's, and the rain beats upon the window (as I fear it will), let her look at this page; it will be like a weed gathered and pressed at home; and she will remember her own islands, and the shadow of the mighty tree; and she will hear the peacocks screaming in the dusk and the wind blowing in the palms; and she will think of her father sitting there alone."[41]

She spent almost four years studying at Great Harrowden Hall, not in Scotland but in England, watched over by Theo Davies, a politically well-connected friend of her father. Still in Britain when Queen Lili`uokalani was overthrown, Princess Ka`iulani rushed to the United States to lobby against the annexation treaty, accompanied by Davies. She spoke at Wellesley College, granted many press interviews, and issued a ghostwritten "Appeal to the American People," which was printed widely during the final days of the Harrison administration.

Ka`iulani was seventeen and in difficult straits. She was next in line for a throne that suddenly no longer existed. The Clevelands received her with great warmth. Frances Folsom Cleveland sympathized with a distressed young girl; her own father had died when she was eleven. Frances had coped partly with the aid of her guardian, Grover Cleveland, a longtime friend of her parents. Cleveland had given

Emma and Oscar Folsom a baby carriage when "Frankie" was born. Her father's will had named Cleveland executor and Frankie's guardian. Cleveland had taken this task seriously. His own father's death when Grover was sixteen had forced the boy to abandon college. No one knows when sympathy and concern for his ward turned to something more romantic, but when Frances had entered Wells College, the proper Cleveland had asked Emma Folsom if he might write to her daughter. Later, Frankie and her mother had visited Cleveland in the White House. Love blossomed, and in 1886, twenty-one-year-old Frances and forty-eight-year-old Grover had married in the first White House wedding of a president. The young princess in trouble surely aroused the president's chivalrous and protective spirit.[42]

Born in New Jersey, young Grover soon went to Buffalo. He had worked as a law clerk and entered the New York bar. He had held minor posts in the local Democratic Party. He was county sheriff from 1871–73. Never one to take the easy way out, Cleveland had personally dropped the gallows trapdoors on two murderers. In 1881, friends persuaded him to run for mayor. Elected on a reform plank, he distressed some in his own party by vetoing padded city contracts, including those intended for Democrats. He swiftly gained a statewide reputation for honesty and became governor in 1883, applying, again to the dismay of some Democrats, the same honest government in Albany that he enforced in Buffalo.

Cleveland was the only Democratic president elected during the fifty-six years between James Buchanan's election in 1856 and Wilson's victory in 1912. He is the only president to serve nonconsecutive terms. He beat James Blaine in 1884, lost to Benjamin Harrison in 1888, and defeated Harrison in an 1892 rematch. He regarded his victory as a vindication of his principles, but his second term was unhappy. In 1894, the Democrats lost control of both houses of Congress, and in 1896 lost the presidency as well. Cleveland left office bitterly disappointed and feeling unappreciated. But he was always proud of his scruples. When he died in 1908, his last words were, "I have tried so hard to do right."[43]

On March 9, 1893, Major Octavius L. Pruden, Civil War veteran and White House correspondence secretary, marched to Capitol Hill. Under his arm was a big manila envelope containing a message withdrawing the annexation treaty from the Senate.[44] An immense shift in policy, this sudden withdrawal stunned political circles. Taking more time to consider the treaty was understandable. Discarding it entirely before debate was another matter. Despite the treaty's lukewarm support in either party, John Hay sputtered that "I can see no reason, except the fact that Blaine and Harrison favored it, to account for this stupid and senseless opposition of Cleveland and Gresham."[45] But Cleveland simply sought to do the right thing.

Cleveland opposed territorial acquisition on principle, but he wrote Carl Schurz that "I do not . . . hold annexation in all circumstances and at any time unwise, but I am sure we ought to stop and look and think." He believed that annexation should not even be discussed unless endorsed by Native Hawaiians, free of manipulation and influence by American diplomats.[46] He suspected inappropriate behavior by Minister Stevens, as did the new secretary of state. Walter Quintin Gresham, a proud, self-proclaimed moralist, was not about to follow a path of unrighteousness. At Gresham's urging, the president ordered an investigation.

To this thankless mission was consigned James Blount of Macon, Georgia.[47] Just retired from twenty years in the House of Representatives, Blount chaired the Committee on Foreign Affairs during 1890–92. At the inauguration, Blount mentioned to Gresham that he wanted to be a delegate to a European monetary conference.[48] This yearning for a cushy appointive position soon turned him into Cleveland's investigator. On March 10, 1893, Cleveland messaged Blount to "come here immediately, prepared for [a] confidential trip of great importance to the Pacific Ocean." On Sunday, March 12, Blount visited Cleveland, who betrayed no sign of either favoring or opposing annexation. But Blount's talk with Gresham showed that the secretary strongly doubted the legality of Stevens' actions, questioned the provisional government's legitimacy, and distrusted the information inherited from the Harrison administration. Gresham instructed Blount to determine the "true facts" of the revolution.[49]

To head off partisan criticism, the secretary allowed no scrutiny of the birth of what would become the most divisive foreign policy episode of Cleveland's presidency. Gresham dissembled about Blount's mission. After he penned Blount's instructions, Gresham informed President Dole, Minister Stevens, and Consul-General Severance of Blount's appointment, but in none of the three missives did he mention his doubts about the revolution, or how Blount's investigation would help determine the legitimacy of the Dole regime. Instead, Gresham said the Georgian would simply report on the "present state of affairs." Blount would "advance the interest and prosperity of both Governments."[50] If not an outright lie, this was an intentional glossing-over of Blount's real mission.

At the White House on Monday, Gresham displayed Blount to the cabinet so quickly that the Georgian did not even sit down, much less discuss his assignment. Blount recalled that "the subject of the islands was not mentioned at all. I only stayed a minute or two; in fact, I could not see why I was taken in there." As the commissioner was whisked out of the room, Cleveland was heard to say: "Blount, you will let us hear from you."[51] There was no thought of exposing Blount to the press. The following morning he was on the train west.

Blount arrived in Hawai`i on March 29, 1893. Fifty-six years old, he was a slight, handsome man with a clean-shaven, unlined face and carefully combed white hair. He was given to white linen suits, vests and watch chains, shiny black shoes, and a big white hat to block the sun, a Southern habit useful in Honolulu. After graduating from the University of Georgia, Blount had barely begun to practice law when the Civil War began. Enlisting in the Army of Northern Virginia, Blount was wounded in the Peninsular Campaign in early 1862. In 1865 he was elected to the state constitutional convention. When Georgia rejoined the Union in 1872, he won a House seat, retiring twenty years later as the chairman of the Foreign Affairs Committee.[52]

It seems a little odd that such a quiet, unassuming man as Blount—he prided himself on holding his tongue, leading the *New York Times* to say that the Sphinx was a chatterbox next to him—was festooned with so many nicknames. Because he never said anything, he earned himself the title "Minister Reticent." The *Chronicle* called him an "oyster-like" diplomat because he was always "clammed up." Some mistakenly called him "Senator," though he served in the House. Others gave him the traditional Southern honorary title of "colonel."

But the nickname that stuck—"Paramount Blount"—grew from the paramount powers Cleveland bestowed, powers that even subordinated the naval commander, Admiral Skerrett, to his authority.[53] Blount saw his job as "dissipating all the mists" surrounding the revolution.[54] He strove to act impartially. Debarking at Brewer's wharf, he declined offers of a carriage from both royalists and revolutionists. He took a public hack to the Hawaiian Hotel's Snow Cottage. He told Dole that the protectorate must end and American troops returned to their ships. He readily assented to a twenty-four-hour delay to allow the call-up of volunteer Guard companies. Unperturbed, Dole told the San Francisco *Chronicle* that the lowering of the flag was not unexpected. The government was in no hurry to sign a new treaty of annexation. Perhaps it would happen by Christmas, perhaps not. William R. Castle thought that, despite the end of the protectorate, Blount did not favor the royalists.[55]

Back in Washington, Thurston was confused about the Blount mission because Gresham still did not speak the whole truth. Thurston saw Gresham twice on the very day that the secretary wrote Blount's instructions. Gresham did not even mention the investigation, saying Cleveland withdrew the treaty because of insufficient knowledge of the situation. His dissembling somehow fooled Thurston, a man who easily sniffed out an opponent, sometimes where one did not exist. Thurston reported that Gresham was "heartily in sympathy with the annexation proposal and will do all he can to forward it."[56] Gresham tricked others as well.

He told Admiral George Brown that the president would maintain the advantage gained by the United States in the islands but had not made up his mind about the treaty and therefore was withdrawing it to give himself more time. When the Hawaiian minister declared that "native government" could never be restored, Gresham stated that "it is not our business or purpose to restore anybody or impose any new forms."[57]

It was ignoble for Gresham, so proud of his devotion to truth and honor, to have knowingly let people walk away with the wrong impression. Thurston wised up quickly. On March 16, he advised Dole that in four interviews Gresham had "declined utterly to give any expression of indicating what the policy of the government was going to be." Thurston's sources reported that Cleveland suspected that revolution was "part of a Republican plot, and that Mr. Blount's investigation will be largely directed toward that point."[58]

Gresham was a political rarity, switching parties without damaging his political career. He had only been a Democrat for a few months. An Indiana Republican, Gresham distinguished himself at Vicksburg and Atlanta, and finished the war as a brigadier general. In 1865 he returned to his law practice and, after serving briefly as Chester Arthur's secretary of the treasury, became a circuit judge. Gresham loved the bench so much that, after he left it, he preferred to be called "Judge," rather than "General." On the bench, his high-mindedness and independence attracted attention. In a celebrated case, he courageously ordered one of Jay Gould's friends tossed from the receivership of the Wabash railroad. At the 1884 Republican convention he received mention but no votes; in 1888 he got 107 first ballot votes, second only to John Sherman's 229 votes. (Benjamin Harrison won on the seventh ballot, after finishing fourth in the first round.)

No doubt some of Gresham's hostility toward Harrison emerged from the nomination battle, but it was Gresham's gradual conversion to low tariff ideas that led him to the Democratic Party. He was known as a friend of the workingman and as an opponent of the hated railroads. In 1892, he spurned a feeler about becoming the presidential nominee of the Populist Party, but he no longer felt at home in the GOP. He declared himself a strong supporter of Grover Cleveland, a risky move that he understandably thought meant his political death. Gresham told a friend: "I have committed political suicide. Some people are unable to understand that a man can deliberately do that."[59] Cleveland, for his own obscure reasons, offered him the State Department. A stunned Champ Clark said Cleveland "slapped every Democrat betwixt the two seas squarely in the face" by appointing a brand-new Democrat to such a senior position.[60]

It was an odd choice. Gresham lacked diplomatic experience or expertise. He struggled to adapt his work habits to his new position. As a judge, he worked alone, pondering evidence and perusing law books. Distractions were few. But as secretary of state, office seekers, reporters, members of Congress, and foreign diplomats besieged him. He was unorganized. He could have deflected less urgent problems to his staff, such as the skillful Alvey Adee, but he did not. He allowed visitor interruptions throughout the day. He often invited callers to return to receive personally an answer to routine questions, when he might have sent a short note by messenger. With those he liked, he was warm and talkative, and such conversations went on longer than necessary, delaying Gresham's work and forcing him to remain at his desk in the evenings. He often felt overworked and tired. His many enemies thought him aloof and arrogant. Champ Clark said the duties of the State Department were "not to his taste and he found no pleasure in them."[61] It is probably too harsh to say Gresham tended to see the worst in people, but he judged them harshly by his own stern rules. He tolerated no shades of gray. People, ideas, and events were either correct and proper, or incorrect and improper. Benjamin Harrison claimed he had never known a man so given to suspecting the motives of other people.[62]

That Cleveland included Gresham among his poker-playing cronies showed their cordial bond. Much of Gresham's clout grew from his ability to persuade the president. He knew Cleveland liked praise and disliked forceful advice. The best way to reach the president was "to watch for an opportunity when he seemed to be inclining to views similar to your own, and then to support them, not as your own, but as his."[63] Both men aimed to do what was right, so Gresham rarely perceived the need to manipulate the president. But far more than Gresham, Cleveland blended his moral sense with dose of practicality, a trait that ultimately saved his Hawaiian policy from total disaster. Gresham suffered from ill health, took long sick leaves several times, and died in office in May 1895.

Gresham disliked expansion on principle, particularly of territory "not a part of our continent." This anti-imperialist view colored his opposition to annexation, but moral and legal factors clearly were the chief influence: "Should we acquire the Hawaiian Islands with their population, we will have a hot bed of corruption."[64] He told Carl Schurz that "the immorality of the situation" precluded annexation.[65]

In Hawai`i, Blount interviewed participants in the revolution, with secretary Ellis Mills taking shorthand notes. Mills then summarized the interview or asked the person interviewed to write a summary. Besides some of the main actors, such as John Colburn, Samuel Damon, Joseph O. Carter, and Fred Wundenberg,

Blount spoke with all manner of people, including Native Hawaiian leaders and foreign businessmen. He spoke with none of the *Boston*'s officers, but he did ask Lieutenant Commander Swinburne and Lieutenant Draper to submit short statements about the timing of Stevens' recognition of the provisional government.

There was no truth in the revolutionists' charge that Blount was overly close to the British minister, but it is true that he interviewed more royalists than revolutionists. Among the thirteen members of the Committee of Safety, he interviewed only Henry Waterhouse. William O. Smith declined to be interviewed but left a copy of a discussion among himself, Henry Cooper, and James B. Castle about the revolution. Henry Cooper came to Snow Cottage for his interview but Blount was busy and asked him to submit a statement. Cooper never did. Blount believed he had made it clear that he wanted to talk to the revolutionists. On a visit to the Government Building, "President Dole and his cabinet were sitting around, and I said to them, 'Gentlemen, I would like to examine any of you with regard to the revolution; I can conceive that you might not care to submit to it.' There was no response."[66] They saw little to gain from talking to Blount, whose real focus, they knew, was not on the context and background that the former rebels believed justified their revolt. They expected Blount would confine himself to examining whether Stevens' actions were improper, whether they intimidated the queen, and whether the majority of Hawaiians supported the white government. None of the answers to these questions would make the revolutionaries look good.

By early May, more than thirty interviews into his work, Blount made up his mind on his key questions. Stevens recognized the provisional government too early, while it was not yet in possession of the "chief points of defense of the Queen, to wit: the station house and the barracks." These strongpoints, Blount argued, would not have surrendered if Stevens' early recognition had not convinced the defenders that they would soon confront the *Boston*'s landing party. "Unquestionably," wrote Blount, the queen surrendered only because she thought that the United States was a party to the revolution, that her troops could not resist the combined forces of the *Boston* and the revolutionists, and that, via an appeal to Washington, she might regain her throne.[67] In his main report, written in July, Blount declared that the revolution lacked majority support: "The undoubted sentiment of the people is for the Queen, against the Provisional Government, and against annexation." He condemned Stevens' role throughout the revolution, particularly in the landing of troops, and charged that Stevens both precipitated the revolt and guaranteed its success. Because the revolution would not have occurred without Stevens' meddling and because it did not have the majority support, Blount concluded that it was unjustified.

Why did Blount decide what he did? Living through federal efforts to remake his state during Reconstruction may have created in Blount a dislike of Yankees imposing their own brand of civilization on another people.[68] Blount tried to be objective. As Richard Olney declared, "Whatever irresponsible penny-a-liners may say, no one in Washington pretends that his report is not the result of his honest convictions after as thorough and impartial an investigation of the facts as he could make."[69]

But the results of an investigation flow from the questions posed. Blount's instructions and his preconceptions determined what he chose to investigate, thereby influencing what topics he made conclusions about. Blount did not explore whether the queen bore some responsibility for the revolution by trying to proclaim a new constitution. His unshakable conviction that the queen surrendered only because she feared U.S. forces prevented him from imagining that the rebels were militarily stronger than the royalists, a failure that would painfully distort policy formulation over the next few months.

Just before departing, Blount predicted that if annexation were rejected, political instability would increase and the provisional government would eventually collapse or be overthrown. The power of the government, he wrote Gresham, rested on military forces drawn from the white community. Because the whites were only a tiny fraction of the total Hawaiian population, the white government must ultimately fall. "It may preserve its existence for a year or two, but no longer."[70] As the next five years would show, this assessment reflected no understanding of the provisional government's substantial capacity to exert military and political control, at least in the short term. The letter highlighted Blount's preconceptions, from which flowed his conclusions. Confronted by the success of the revolution and the military inaction of the royalists, and believing the small white community incapable of military dominance, he had to believe that the landing of American troops was the key factor in the queen's overthrow.

The Blount mission eliminated any chance of annexation. It was clear that Stevens egregiously exceeded his instructions, that Captain Wiltse mishandled the landing of troops, and that Native Hawaiians opposed annexation. Given the lack of a compelling reason for annexation, such as a foreign threat to Hawaiʻi's independence, the treaty was dead. But what would Cleveland do about Hawaiʻi? That looming decision would shape the most contentious foreign policy episode of Cleveland's presidency.

CHAPTER 9

❧

The Restoration Fiasco

B ack in Washington, Gresham pondered Blount's messages. Until the fall
of 1893, Gresham determined the direction of Hawaiian policy. The president dedicated himself to the business downturn, which worsened into
the Depression of 1893. He confided to a friend: "I am in the midst of much
turmoil and perplexity."[1] More than 15,000 businesses failed. The unemployment
rate soared. Restoring confidence was the key to escaping the depression. So long
as people believed the Treasury would always pay out gold, not silver, for paper
money, paper money would circulate freely and gold would stay in the Treasury's
vaults. For two years Cleveland struggled to maintain the nation's gold reserves.
Only help from the House of Morgan in 1895 finally ended the gold crisis.

Tariff reduction was another Cleveland priority. The 1890 McKinley tariff
applied record high duties—they averaged 49.5 percent—to finished and semi-
finished imports that competed with products of the domestic industrial sector.
Raw materials were subject to considerable duties as well. Cleveland thought high
tariffs hurt the average American. He succeeded in cutting rates slightly with the
1894 Wilson-Gorman tariff, though he let it become law without his signature
because its 39.9 percent average rate schedule did not lower rates enough.

While wrestling with gold reserve and tariff problems, Cleveland suffered
through difficult cancer surgery in the summer of 1893. He complained of mouth
soreness, common in men who smoked as many cigars as the president. The

White House doctor discovered a festering area the size of a quarter on the roof of the president's mouth. Lab tests confirmed cancer; the growth would have to be removed. Cleveland feared his illness might add to the country's difficulties, so he hid his condition with a complicated subterfuge. Cleveland left Washington, supposedly to visit his wife, Frances, at Buzzards Bay, and ended up in the yacht *Oneida* in New York harbor. On July 1, five doctors, one a dentist with experience in nitrous oxide anesthesia, spent two hours cutting out the growth—they were afraid to probe too deeply for fear of slicing into Cleveland's left optic nerve—and cauterizing the large hole. Cleveland spent the next month isolated at Buzzards Bay, enduring more cutting by one of the medical team. For the rest of his life, Cleveland wore a rubber plug in the roof of his mouth. The ordeal took its toll. In mid-July, when Richard Olney visited, he found the beefy Cleveland thinner because he could not eat with his mouth stuffed with bandages, nor could he speak clearly. His first muffled words were, "My God, Olney, they nearly killed me!"[2]

Gresham had full control of Hawaiian policy while the president, recovering from surgery and managing repeal of the Sherman Silver Purchase Act, was "thinking the matter over," as Blount put it.[3] By early September 1893, but probably much earlier, Gresham decided to restore the queen to power. He told Schurz that Stevens' actions and the landing of American troops "overawed the Queen— put her in fear—and induced her to surrender to the so-called Provisional government, with the understanding, however, that her case would be fairly considered by the President. . . . Should not this great wrong be undone? 'Yes,' I say decidedly."[4]

Gresham did not recognize the many difficulties inherent in restoration. His personality and his training as a lawyer and judge led him to view the issue in legal and moral terms. He thought of the royalists and the provisional government as two contesting parties before his bench. He expected them to abide by his judgment. His juristic approach prevented him from entertaining the possibility— indeed, the likelihood—that his policy would fail. Gresham ignored Schurz's gentle warning that it would be a "very delicate task to undo the mischief that has been done."[5]

Gresham thought restoration required a new minister—Blount's departure left the post vacant—as well as a naval commander who would follow orders to the letter. With dependable men in Honolulu, restoration could be swiftly executed. On September 19, Cleveland appointed Albert Willis as minister. Willis was a five-term Democratic member of Congress and a friend of Treasury Secretary John Carlisle.[6]

Next Gresham secretly maneuvered to replace Admiral Skerrett, who Gresham thought unreliable. The admiral had been sailing in hot water for months because he supposedly dragged his feet about ending the protectorate on April 1. In late July Skerrett imprudently told Secretary of the Navy Hilary Herbert that he hoped several royalist plotters would be convicted and punished. Herbert quickly warned: "Do not give aid physical or moral to either party contesting for the government."[7] There was no contest, in most people's minds at least, for the government in Honolulu. The provisional government had firm control. Herbert's unrealistic orders directed Skerrett to treat a government recognized by the United States and other powers the same as the ex-queen and her supporters. (Ironically, former Minister John Stevens had erred by treating future rebels equally with the royal government to which he was accredited. Now Herbert repeated the error from the other direction, further evidence that the Cleveland administration believed the provisional government illegitimate.)

Skerrett continued to blunder. He reported that the government's leaders still showed "the same courageous disposition to control and to display their power to direct these peoples in the right way."[8] Herbert counseled the admiral against "an unconscious leaning on your part towards the new government." Skerrett should occupy a position of "complete neutrality" because the administration "does not intend to be the partisan either of the Queen or of the present government, and you are not to favor the one or the other by act, word, or deed."[9] Skerrett could not know that treating the provisional government gently would leave the administration looking two-faced when attempting to put the queen back on her throne.

On October 9 the administration relieved Skerrett and sent Admiral John Irwin to Honolulu.[10] This day Gresham committed irrevocably to restoration. Whether American troops would restore the queen by force or by bluffing and intimidating the white government, Gresham would need an obedient officer who did not have friendly relations with those he would coerce and intimidate.[11] So that the new minister and commander could brandish ample force, Herbert kept both the *Philadelphia* and the *Adams* at Honolulu.[12] On October 6 Gresham described to the cabinet his restoration plan. Cleveland's vigor had returned and he was ready to listen.

At this juncture Attorney General Richard Olney played the key role in amending Gresham's planning. Olney was fifty-eight, a stolid, industrious man. Although not born to money—his father was a bank cashier—he attended Leicester Academy and Brown University. In 1856, he entered Harvard Law, an unusual course when most lawyers trained by apprenticeships. Olney applied himself and passed the bar exam in 1859. He partnered with Benjamin Thomas, a well-known Boston judge, initially specializing in wills and trusts for the aristocrats controlling business and social life. Olney soon mastered corporate law as well and spent the next decades as lawyer to the elite. His big break came in 1879. After brilliantly handling a difficult reorganization for Eastern Railway Company, he became a recognized expert on railroad law. Soon he became chief legal counsel for Eastern and a member of its board of directors.[13] He had little interest in politics; Cleveland had to persuade him to become attorney general.[14]

Olney's short, steel-gray hair topped a head that a *New York World* reporter described as a square block of wood with two huge lumps of coal for eyes. A thick-shouldered six-footer, Olney played sports for exercise, not for fun, and was famous for walking to work so rapidly that companions dropped from exhaustion. Olney was not a gregarious man. He was always "Richard"; no one dared call him "Dick." He was a loner—despite more than three decades rubbing shoulders with Brahmins, he made no true friends among them—and relied on his family, which he dominated if not domineered, for companionship. His life was work, a principle he respected from his first days as attorney general and, after Gresham's 1895 death, as secretary of state.[15]

The Friday, October 6, cabinet meeting reached no consensus, so Cleveland postponed a final decision. No one knows exactly what Gresham proposed, but Olney became sufficiently alarmed that, for the only time in his tenure as attorney general, he intervened in foreign policy. Working over the weekend—and with great delicacy, for he was trespassing on Gresham's turf—Olney crafted a private letter to Gresham that brilliantly analyzed the policy options. The letter was so gracious and apparently helpful that Matilda Gresham printed it in her hagiography of her husband.[16] She missed the point that Olney wrote to remedy grave flaws in her husband's plan. Olney urged restoration solely by diplomatic pressure. What is remarkable is that Olney felt obliged to devote so much of his letter to the problems of using force.

Had Gresham suggested forcible restoration? In addition to Olney's reaction, circumstantial evidence suggests that he did. In letters to Cleveland on October 18 and Schurz on September 14, Gresham's vehemence in demanding restoration betrayed little sense of self-restraint or practicality. In May 1894 Gresham hinted that he put forward a firmer course than the one adopted.[17] Olney later declared that his October 9 letter kept the administration from a serious mistake.[18] Restoration could not have been the mistake because the administration pursued that course, and Olney supported it. Quite likely, the potential mistake was forcible restoration.

Olney's reservations were purely tactical. He wrote his cautionary letter only because Gresham did not see the "practical difficulties" of forcible restoration. He agreed that the queen had been wronged. When Olney's daughter, Agnes, asked him about Hawaiian affairs for a debate club presentation, Olney said the queen was deposed by "a mixture of fraud and force to which the United States Minister Stevens was a party and brought the aid of the naval and military forces of the United States. A greater outrage upon a weak nation by a strong one could hardly be imagined."[19] Force per se did not bother Olney. This was the man who in 1894 wanted to send the Army to squash the Pullman strike and who prosecuted and convicted Gene Debs for leading it. Rather, Olney saw the main problem as the provisional government's firm hold on power. It might fight if challenged. And because the Harrison regime accepted Stevens' actions, the Cleveland administration could not permit "the men who were Stevens' instruments . . . to be hung or banished, or despoiled of their estates, or otherwise punished for the connection with the Stevens government."[20]

Olney asserted that forcible restoration would be an unconstitutional act of war. Restoration must be attempted only by diplomatic pressure and only if the queen accepted conditions. The queen must grant the United States wide authority to negotiate on her behalf, and she must renounce vindictive measures against the provisional government and its supporters. It is not clear whether Olney expected that restoration under these conditions would succeed or whether he was simply trying to head off the worst features of a bad plan. Olney's scheme was no more likely to succeed than Gresham's, but it would not involve bloodshed.[21]

When Cleveland blessed Olney's suggestions, Gresham reluctantly modified his plan. Rather than use force, he would intimidate and coerce the provisional government. This change fit perfectly with Gresham's mistaken belief that the white revolutionists were weak and succeeded in overthrowing the queen only because of support from American forces. This time American forces would be on the other side. Therefore, Gresham reasoned, the weak provisional government would surely surrender.

On October 18 Gresham summarized a revised plan. As Charles Calhoun showed, Gresham intended the summary as a public relations device in anticipation of later publication of the relevant correspondence about restoration.[22] In the document, he strongly supported restoration. "Can the United States insist that other nations shall respect the independence of Hawai`i while not respecting it themselves?" he asked.[23]

The first act of the drama played out as Gresham hoped. In Honolulu, a dumbfounded Skerrett received orders to San Francisco.[24] Captain Barker of the *Philadelphia* called it "a bolt out of a clear sky!"[25] Admiral Irwin left Yokohama on the *China*, scheduled for Honolulu on November 6. Albert Willis arrived November 4 but, waiting for Irwin, did not present his credentials and secluded himself in the legation. Soon the *China* arrived, flying Irwin's flag as commander of the Pacific Station. A surprised Irwin spotted Skerrett's own flag still flying and lowered his own.[26] The two admirals conferred that night. Skerrett departed on the *China* the next morning "a broken-hearted man," Barker recalled, "for he felt his immediate replacement was virtually a disgrace."[27]

The administration had been lucky so far. It kept its restoration policy secret and successfully installed obedient men in the two key jobs. But that was the easy part, and from then on, Gresham's restoration policy went quickly off-course. Tuesday morning, November 7, Willis prepared to present his credentials. If he suspected how difficult his task would be, he gave no sign. The new minister—who struck Captain Barker as "an earnest man of the Presbyterian type"—did not look strong enough for much hard work.[28] He was fifty years old—though he looked seventy—an odd-looking fellow, bald dome surrounded by sparse white fringes and a round face with a thick gray beard. Large jutting ears seemed to stretch outward as far as his narrow, bony shoulders. But his soft brown eyes and gentle manner signaled his kindly nature, and, after the restoration crisis passed, his popularity grew among all parties while his health, never good, steadily deteriorated. He died at his post in early 1897.

At eleven o'clock in the morning, Companies E and F of the Hawaiian Guard lined the driveway of the Executive Building and snapped to attention as Willis passed. Dole and Willis exchanged brief remarks. Willis said nothing about restoration as he had not yet talked with Queen Lili`uokalani. The November 11 steamer to San Francisco carried Willis' report that he would interview Lili`uokalani on the thirteenth. He advised Gresham to release the Blount Report on November 19 to prepare the public for what was to come. (A dispatch sent by ship on November 11 would be telegraphed from San Francisco and probably arrive in Washington on November 18 or 19.) Willis promised early news of the queen's restoration. Why Willis took so long to meet with Lili`uokalani—nine days, despite Gresham's order to have an early meeting with the queen—is not clear. It might have taken time to arrange what he mistakenly thought was a secret meeting. He deceived himself that "neither side has the vaguest idea . . . of the attitude of our Government, and consequently no outbreak has occurred, although every night is filled with rumors."[29]

Willis met the queen on November 13. He transmitted Cleveland's regrets about American actions during the revolution and assured her that he intended to rectify the injustice. Beyond that simple fact, nothing is clear. The queen and Willis sat alone in the parlor. Ellis Mills, vice consul, and John Robertson, the Royal Chamberlain, were either out of earshot in another room or, as Lili`uokalani later claimed, listening from behind a large Japanese screen.

The queen had been waiting almost a year for the United States to right its wrong. Although the queen spoke English well, Willis spoke slowly and precisely to be sure his meaning was clear. Should you be restored to the throne, he asked, will you grant amnesty to the members and supporters of the provisional government? According to Willis, Lili`uokalani replied that the law required that persons connected with the provisional government "should be beheaded and their property confiscated," though she was inclined to substitute banishment for beheading. Amnesty was out of the question. There could be no peace while the revolutionists remained in the islands.

Why did she not agree? Most likely she thought she was back in the driver's seat, that the United States would soon put her back on the throne, and that she need not tie her hands. The *Advertiser* carried a story, sourced to Washington Place, that November 13 would be "Restoration Day," and that provisional government officials would be asked to vacate their offices.[30] Albertine Loomis described how hard it would have been for the queen to forgive those who, in her view, had tormented and weakened the monarchy and deposed and humiliated her.[31]

Willis asked again: "It is your feeling that these people should be beheaded and their property confiscated?" She replied: "It is." Willis tried once more. "Do you fully understand the meaning of every word which you have said to me, and if so, do you still have the same opinion?" Lili`uokalani replied that she both understood what she said and meant it all, but that she might let her ministers make the ultimate decision. Willis sensed an opening. What if she had to make a declaration of amnesty before she appointed any ministers? Would she do it? The queen correctly declared that she lacked the right to pardon wrongdoers without the cabinet's concurrence. There would never be peace while the troublemakers of 1887 and 1893 remained. If they were not killed, they must be banished and their property confiscated. The queen later claimed that she never used the word beheaded, and that she could not have done so because beheading had never been used in Hawai`i. Willis was equally certain that she had. It did not matter. Anything short of an amnesty did not meet the preconditions.[32]

A surprised Willis pondered his next move. Gresham told him to ask for further instructions if the queen would not pardon the revolutionists. He informed the queen this process might take three or four weeks. The two stared at each other. Strangely, neither Willis nor Lili`uokalani asked what the other's preconditions were, or made any attempt to see what they could agree on and move forward from there. The queen had never been much for explaining herself or imagining alternatives; this had been clear during the January revolution. Willis was a neophyte diplomat, unskilled in getting past obstacles. Willis cabled Gresham: "Hold back

[Blount] report until further advised." He said: "Views of first party so extreme as to require further instructions."[33] Willis had expected the queen to agree to amnesty, allowing him to demand that the provisional government dissolve in favor of a restored monarchy.

To soften up the provisional government, American forces adopted an overtly threatening posture from the moment of Willis' and Irwin's arrival. On November 7, the day Willis presented his credentials, the *Adams* had seventy sailors practice with both pistols and rifles. On November 9 the *Philadelphia* went to general quarters, exercising all companies and at eight o'clock that evening "made preparations to land battalion if necessary." The Navy held target practice, landing drills, and other highly visible and noisy exercises thirty-five times from November 7 until December 26. One of the warships exercised daily between Willis' arrival and his unsatisfactory meeting with the queen.[34] The extraordinary frequency and scale of drills and landing practices aimed to intimidate the provisional government into agreeing to Willis' demands.[35] Because the queen did not meet the preconditions, Willis made no demands, so naval intimidation continued.

The constant drills and exercises excited royalists. Willis fretted that they might revolt out of false confidence that he would aid them. The Honolulu press published Gresham's October 18 letter to Cleveland, in which the secretary did not rule out forcible restoration. Given "active military preparations" by all factions, Willis tried to dampen the rumors. He told the *Hawaiian Star* that unforeseen contingencies prevented action until new instructions reached him. Meanwhile, "no change will take place in the current situation, nor will any be allowed."[36] Willis' "plain talk" failed to defuse the situation. Lili`uokalani feared for her safety and asked Willis for protection. He told her to ask the provisional government, which sent the six Hawaiian police officers she requested by name.[37]

On November 24 executive council members read an *Advertiser* story, datelined in Washington on November 11, that Admiral Irwin would land troops to restore the queen.[38] Dole and William O. Smith immediately queried Willis. He said the "whole matter was hung up" because of unforeseen issues, and that he awaited a reply to his dispatches. The executive council therefore assumed forcible restoration was still on the table. The government rescinded permission for U.S. naval forces to exercise ashore, and ordered sixty more rifles and five thousand rounds of ammunition for the Hawaiian National Guard.[39] The British cruiser *Champion* and the Japanese cruiser *Naniwa* now lay in the harbor with the American warships. The British and Japanese expected trouble when the United States attempted restoration and wanted to be able to protect its citizens. Both foreign ships received permission from the executive council to land troops to protect their legations.[40]

The council discussed how obstructionist to be with American landing parties. Samuel Damon and Sanford Dole preferred resistance but not to the extent of firing on U.S. troops whereas most whites wanted to fight. The Hawaiian Guard recommended the government not yield, even if it meant killing American troops. The guard placed sandbags and gun positions around the palace.[41] The council ordered Colonel Soper to resist forcibly an American landing. Admiral Irwin noted that the provisional government built fortified positions and claimed a thousand armed men were on call. Willis pleaded for instructions.[42]

Back in Washington, the situation was deteriorating almost as fast as in Honolulu. The press savaged Gresham's restoration plan, saying restoration was a wrong to correct a wrong. On November 21, to a similar chorus of boos, the administration released the Blount Report in a doomed effort to convince doubters.[43] The Democratic *Atlanta Constitution* remarked sarcastically, "The Democratic Party has not been in the habit of restoring monarchies anywhere, and as Mr. Gresham is not a Democrat he may have made a mistake in this regard."[44]

In Chicago, closing his world's fair volcano panorama, Thurston read a story that predicted Gresham would restore the queen. The Hawaiian legation sought clarification. Gresham stated that when the administration decided its Hawaiian policy, Hawai`i's diplomats would be the first to know. Dissatisfied with Gresham's lie—for such it was; the Cleveland administration settled on restoration weeks before—Thurston rushed to Washington and saw Gresham on November 14. Gresham would not rule out the use of force. Gresham later claimed that by promising that Willis would undertake no action to harm revolutionists' lives or property, he had been clear enough. But he dared not rule out force, for his restoration plan rested on Hawaiian uncertainty about the use of force.[45]

On December 7, the cabinet reexamined his plan and, for the first time, found it wanting. The practical Cleveland now doubted success. He asked Gresham to prepare a message that would lay out the issues and ask for a congressional solution. Gresham's draft proposed that the queen and the provisional government share power, a plan even more impractical than outright restoration.[46] Cleveland now regretted the whole restoration notion. He gave Gresham's draft to Richard Olney, asking him to see "what he could do with it." Olney's revisions formed "by far the larger part of the message" Cleveland sent to Congress on December 18, declaring an inability to solve the Hawaiian problem and referring the matter to the legislature.[47]

Unaware that his political bosses had thrown in the towel, Willis strove mightily to get the restoration policy back on track. The denouement—popularly called Black Week—began at dawn on December 14. The *Corwin*, with Gresham's revised instructions aboard, arrived flying the American flag, instead of the revenue flag, which caused a great crowd of Hawaiians to gather at the landing. Everyone expected a message to order Willis to restore the queen immediately, by force if necessary. After all, Cleveland's December 4 message to Congress, carried in the *Corwin* and published in extra editions within four hours, stated that the administration's only honorable course was "undo the wrong done by those representing us, and to restore as far as practicable the status existing at the time of our forcible intervention. Our present Minister has received appropriate instructions to that end."[48] While the legation staff decrypted the short cipher, thousands of people thronged the wharves hoping to see the Americans land. The captains of the British warship *Champion*, the Japanese cruiser *Naniwa*, and USS *Adams* came aboard the *Philadelphia* to decide who would guard which portions of the city. Captain Evan Rooke of the *Champion* expected forcible restoration and promised one hundred British tars for patrol after he secured the British legation and the Anglican church, where Her Majesty's citizens might take refuge. Captain Barker readied the *Philadelphia*'s landing parties, boats in the water beside the cruiser and guns and supplies stacked on deck. Barker grew so frustrated with Admiral Irwin's refusal to let him plan the tactical disposition of troops ashore that the captain gave the admiral a letter of complaint with a copy in the ship's log. This is another strong indication that Irwin's drills and exercises were intimidation, not preparation for a real landing, or the admiral would have permitted proper tactical planning.

Sanford Dole called this tense situation "warfare without the incidence of actual combat." Willis intentionally prolonged the psychological offensive. He knew that only the threat of force might induce the provisional government to resign.[49] On December 16 Willis reinterviewed the queen. Joseph Carter accompanied Lili`uokalani because Willis suggested she bring a trusted advisor. As Albertine Loomis points out, the queen had a month since her first meeting with Willis to consult with others and prepare for subsequent negotiations. She (and her advisors) should have surmised that her answers of mid-November had not satisfied Cleveland's preconditions. Why else would Willis be back? She might have changed her own position. She might have asked what commitments were required. But when Willis asked about amnesty, the queen again demurred. There was no need for a death penalty, but supporters of the provisional government must be expelled and their property confiscated. Twice the queen refused to offer amnesty, so the second interview ended.[50]

As Willis prepared a report to go out on the *Corwin* that evening, Carter called to say that yet another meeting with the queen might produce the desired result. Willis hurried to Washington Place. Lili`uokalani seems not to have understood or at least not cared that, unless she agreed to Cleveland's amnesty precondition, she would never get back on the throne. She may have been heeding bad advice from hotheads, or perhaps she believed Willis would restore her no matter what her attitude. This feeling, if she had it, must have been daily strengthened by the all-so-public and intimidating "readiness" posture of American forces. If so, the intimidation posture backfired on Gresham, making the queen more stubborn. Or perhaps the queen suspected that there would be no forcible restoration. Compromising would simply weaken her position with her supporters.

Carter tried to help, giving a little speech about forgiveness, but for the third time, the monarch refused to accede. Lili`uokalani read and approved the notes of the meeting. That evening, as the *Corwin* prepared to sail, Carter telephoned that the queen now accepted the amnesty precondition and would deliver a written promise, which she did. Willis postponed the cutter's departure and gathered himself for what was sure to be a tense meeting with Dole the next day.[51]

Dole met Willis in `Iolani Palace with the other council members: Frank Hatch, William O. Smith, Samuel Damon, and James King, a Scot who ran the Wilder Steamship Company. Speaking carefully from prepared remarks, Willis said it was his duty to acquaint the council with the conclusions that President Cleveland reached from Blount's report. It was clear that the revolution did not emerge from the will of a majority of the Hawaiian people, nor had the provisional government subsequently won the people's hearts. Willis described Lili`uokalani's guarantees of amnesty for the rebels and displayed her signed promise. The executive council should therefore "promptly relinquish to her, her constitutional authority." Willis asked, "Are you willing to abide by the decision of the President?"[52] They were not, but to gain time, they replied that the matter would be carefully considered. The *Alameda* was due, and they hoped for favorable news from Washington. On December 22, the steamer arrived not only with better news but also with Lorrin Thurston aboard, who outlined the antirestoration atmosphere in Washington. Now certain that force would not be used, Dole told Willis the provisional government would not yield.[53] The crisis was over.

In a December 18 message, Cleveland reviewed the Hawaiian revolution, condemned Stevens and the revolutionists, defended the Blount Report, and asserted that the lawful government of Hawai`i was improperly overthrown by "a process every step of which ... is directly traceable to, and dependent for its success upon, the agency of the United States acting through its diplomatic and naval representatives." Therefore, supposing that "right and justice should determine the path to be followed," he attempted to restore the situation as it existed before the "lawless landing" of American forces. Various difficulties prevented a presidential solution, so he was referring the matter to Congress.[54]

Passing the buck was the only way out. Cleveland would not forcibly restore the queen, nor would he endorse the white government that toppled her. Cleveland and Gresham passed between the horns of this dilemma by having no active Hawaiian policy at all. They would let Congress take the lead. Unfortunately, the Congress led not by making policy but by raking the administration over the coals in months of nasty debate.

From the outset, the administration's policy was doomed. Gresham never understood the impossibility of restoring the status quo antebellum. He complained that Willis' dillydallying lost the day, claiming that a better man "would have carried out the plans ... promptly, before they ... became known. The revelation of the plans was followed by an outcry in the U.S. and the Provisional Government consequently assumed an attitude of resistance which they would not have ... ventured to do otherwise."[55] Gresham was completely wrong. The provisional government did not quail before the threat of force, yet achieving restoration through force or the threat of force was the foundation of Gresham's plan.

His belief that the provisional government was purely Stevens' creature blinded him to his plan's impracticality, just as Blount's belief that white rebels could never have overturned the queen by themselves led to his faulty assumption that rebel forces were militarily weak. The provisional government would have fought if attacked. Even if American forces had successfully put the monarch back on her throne, she could only have remained there by force of American arms. Throughout his entire time in the State Department, Gresham underestimated the strength and determination of the rebels.

The restoration fiasco polarized Hawaiian policy. Previously, Hawaiian affairs, like naval expansion and coastal defense modernization and even reciprocity, had been largely bipartisan. Because of Gresham's restoration debacle, Hawaiian policy became bitterly contested between the parties. These differences were both tactical—Hawaiian policy was an easy target for the Republican opposition—and ideological, as many Republicans began to consider the idea that the United States might have to annex the islands should American control be threatened.

A noble attempt to right a wrong, restoration was politically impractical. Few Americans liked the idea of restoring monarchs, especially one overthrown by whites who, in the minds of most Americans, represented progress and modernization. Restoration was also impractical in the literal sense in that it was based on a total misunderstanding of the power balance in the islands. Restoration's failure made Hawai`i into a hardy perennial, a significant foreign policy issue that commanded constant attention from politicians, opinion makers, and the public.

❧

CHAPTER 10

Cleveland's Informal Protectorate

T he Hawaiian Revolution of January 1893 lasted four days, far less time than it would take to scrutinize the voluminous congressional debates and reports about it. When Gresham's restoration policy leaked, Republican minorities in both houses seized on the tremendous unpopularity of restoration to force the Democratic majority to defend the administration. As soon as Cleveland dumped the Hawaiian problem in Congress' lap, the two houses pounced on the president. The Senate directed an investigation of irregularities in Hawaiian–American relations.[1] From December 1893 through May 1894, both houses reviewed diplomatic and naval correspondence, heard all manner of testimony, including that of John Stevens and James Blount, and reported conclusions that satisfied no one.

Chief among these accounts was the Morgan Report, an 809-page tome of the Senate Foreign Relations Committee, chaired by the redoubtable John Tyler Morgan of Alabama. "Old Morgan," as deferential colleagues called him, was a wiry man, slightly stooped, with a carefully clipped mustache and snow-white hair. In his younger days, his features had seemed dignified, but in old age, his mussed hair, grim lips turned down at the corners, and fierce eyes gave him a savage look. He could usually be found in heavily starched wing collars, snug vests, and dark, shapeless coats. In his late sixties in 1894, Morgan lawyered in Selma before entering the Confederate Army. He led a cavalry charge at Chickamauga, emerged unscathed, and later became a general. After the war, he entered politics after the lifting of restrictions on former rebel officers. He served in the Senate from 1877 until his death in 1907.[2] From 1894 to 1898, Morgan played a huge role in Hawaiian annexation, first as the supportive chair of the Foreign Relations Committee and then, from 1895, as its ranking Democrat.

Morgan was an unreconstructed racist; his views on race relations were scandalously behind the times. Work and a good fight were his two greatest pleasures. Few dared to cross him. He was well known as industrious and irascible. These twin traits may explain why no one publicly doubted his claim that he worked eighteen-hour days. Morgan may have been more famous for speechmaking than for hard work or crankiness. He spoke so long on the floor that a Philadelphia inventor once asked—tongue in cheek, one hopes—to examine the senator's vocal cords, wherein he confidently expected to find the secret of perpetual motion.[3] After one address of many hours, somebody asked Morgan how long he could talk. Morgan offered one of his rare jokes: "It depends upon the subject. If it were a matter that I thoroughly understood, I could talk for two or three days. If it were upon a matter I know nothing about, I could talk for two or three weeks."[4] He may have spoken long, but he did not speak well. Morgan's robotic delivery did not impress a reporter: "He stands like a pillar, without motion of hands or movement of body. His voice never varies in tone. There is not the slightest attempt at elocution or modulation."[5]

Commercial factors dominated Morgan's views on foreign affairs, especially his tireless efforts to build a Nicaraguan canal. Although a canal had huge security benefits, allowing the Navy to rapidly move ships from coast to coast, the commercial benefits would be even more important. A canal would hugely shorten the route to Asia, where China was increasing imports of cotton, Alabama's major export. His canal advocacy was popular beyond the South.[6] For westerners, a canal would be a great boon to trade with the East Coast and Europe.[7]

Morgan possessed a linear, workman-like mind that preferred to focus on one or two pet projects. Senator Shelby Cullom said he was an "extraordinary man. . . . He had a wonderful fund of information on every subject. . . . He was one of the most delightful and agreeable of men if you agreed with him . . . but he was so intense on any subject in which he took an interest, particularly anything pertaining to the inter-oceanic canal, that he became almost vicious toward anyone who opposed him."[8] Morgan's practice was to study carefully, offer closely reasoned arguments, then expect others to follow his advice while he carped at deviations. Not a good habit for a legislator seeking consensus.[9]

It was not a surprise, therefore, when only Morgan, of the five Democrats and four Republicans on the Senate Foreign Relations Committee, signed the committee's "majority" report on February 24, 1894. The remaining members

produced minority reports. Morgan—and the Republicans, who submitted a
separate list of findings—blamed the queen for triggering the revolt, exonerated
Stevens, justified the troop landing, and judged Blount's appointment unconstitutional. The four Democrats simply chastised Stevens for improper behavior before
and during the revolution.

The House did no better than the Senate at reaching consensus but embar-
rassed itself more. Republicans saw political opportunity in assaulting Gresham and
Blount. Some attacks were silly. The attempt to restore the queen, some said, was
an abomination contrary to international law and the U.S. Constitution. Stevens
had done no wrong. Gresham had done no right. The queen was a bloodthirsty
monster with no morals and fewer scruples.[10] On February 7, 1894, the majority
Democrats succeeded in passing a resolution condemning Stevens' "illegal" use of
American troops to overthrow the queen, and warning against foreign meddling
in the islands.[11] By not vindicating Gresham's restoration attempt, the measure
was a defeat for the administration.

Despite the Morgan Report, Senate debate continued sporadically as some
sort of consensus formed. On May 31 the Senate passed the Turpie Resolution
55–0, with 30 abstentions. The resolution announced that "any intervention in the
political affairs of these islands by any other government will be regarded as an act
unfriendly to the United States."[12] Before the vote, propaganda essays from Frank
Hatch and W. D. Alexander about the potentially dangerous Japanese suffrage
helped mobilize pro-Hawaiian support: "The representations . . . in regard to the
attitude of the Japanese Govt. were of the greatest importance. Our friends in the
Senate now say that since the resolution has passed declaring foreign intervention
an act unfriendly to the U.S. that the Japs will keep hands off."[13]

During the rest of Cleveland's term, the administration pursued a policy of
benign neglect. The president moved on to other problems, but Gresham could
not let bygones be bygones. As Charles Calhoun concluded, he treated the provisional government as a "miscreant who had escaped punishment and was hardly
worthy of the barest diplomatic civility."[14]

Nevertheless, Cleveland did not want Hawai`i to fall into foreign hands, espe-
cially Japanese hands, hence the significance of the so-called secret mission of
Admiral John G. Walker in the spring of 1894. Given Admiral Skerrett's 1893
recall for annexationist sympathies, Walker's appointment seems odd. Skerrett
had been replaced by Admiral John Irwin, who did what he was told during the
restoration effort. But with Irwin retiring, the Cleveland administration turned to
Walker. He was a tough, crusty, iron-willed man of independent mind who, unlike
Minister Willis, would not toady to his Washington chiefs. As head of the powerful

Bureau of Navigation, Walker backed the creation of the Naval War College. He had much support in Congress among those who favored naval modernization. He endorsed the immediate development of Pearl Harbor. Captain Barker said Walker was "one of the strongest officers in our Navy mentally, and he also had strong political and social influence."[15] His social habits and attitudes made it likely that he too would be captured by the white annexationist circle. He was precisely the kind of naval officer the Cleveland administration should *not* have wanted in Hawai`i. Why, then, was he sent?

The Honolulu rumor mills said that the admiral had secret orders to prevent, by force if necessary, foreign intervention during the establishment of the new government. Walker promoted this story, saying that he and Cleveland met privately to discuss the mission. Walker claimed he wrote his own orders, wording them so that Willis could not command him as he had Irwin, or as Blount commanded Skerrett. The admiral read the orders to the president, who approved, or so went Walker's story. Willis complained that the admiral "often referred to these private talks with the President."[16] There is not a shred of documentary evidence for the secret mission theory. Rather the Walker mission was just what it appeared. Besieged by the congressional investigations of its policy, the administration knew both parties demanded that no foreign meddling should threaten Hawai`i as it set up a permanent government.[17] Secretary of the Navy Herbert instructed Walker to report "any effort or attempt on the part of any foreign power to interfere."[18]

From his first day, Walker operated differently than Blount and Willis. Walker immediately pressed the flesh, though mostly with provisional government supporters. Within hours of his sunrise arrival, he arranged a change of command with Irwin, conferred with Willis, and walked to the Hawaiian Hotel to meet with Lili`uokalani's lawyer, Paul Neumann, whom Walker described as "a royalist and a very bright, agreeable man." Later, he chatted with Chief Justice Judd and accepted Judd's loan of a horse. He wrote his wife, Betty, that everything seemed quiet and peaceful but "there are various things that may bring about trouble at any time." Perhaps sensitive to his wife's fears, he told her he doubted there would be bloodshed.[19] He attended a dinner party hosted by Lizzie Judd Wilder, whom he had met during his Hawaiian visit forty years earlier. He rode the O`ahu Railway out to Pearl Harbor, though he admitted to Betty that the trip would surely "set a crop of rumors going large enough to fill a newspaper." So many people called that he complained they interfered with his letter writing.

Walker's popularity grew from Willis' isolation. As the local agent for Gresham's restoration debacle, the minister was on bad terms with the provisional government. Walker observed, "Our minister . . . goes nowhere, knows very few people, has cut himself off from the society, and is heartily disliked by the better class of residents.... Instead of going to the minister, people now come to me for advice." The "better class" Walker referred to was clearly the group that overthrew the queen. "I mean to know all parties and judge for myself as far as possible," he claimed. But, like most naval officers before him, he was soon captivated by the white clique epitomized by the "well-appearing" Sanford Ballard Dole. The admiral attended services at the First Union Church and came away marveling that it had been like services back home. He lunched with Foreign Minister Frank Hatch. At the literary society, he met prominent whites and heard a lecture about the World Columbian Exposition in Chicago, where Thurston had managed the wildly popular Kīlauea volcano panorama. He "met lots of people" at a spiffy lawn party. "The whole tone of the place," he wrote revealingly, "is much like New England."[20]

Even in his dealings with royalists, Walker preferred whites. He judged the partly white Samuel Parker "typical Hawaiian in all his mental qualities—amiable, generous, heedless, and irresponsible, more like a boy of twelve than a grown-up man." Walker lunched with the royalist Hermann Widemann, Queen Lili'uokalani's minister of the interior, who was married to a Native Hawaiian. The admiral called Widemann honest and upright but a man of narrow views, bitter prejudices, and strong dislikes of revolutionists. Walker met the queen's advisor, Joseph Carter.[21] But nowhere in his letters or reports did he mention meeting Native Hawaiians, or even observing them. Surely he had, but it reveals much that Walker recorded only meetings with influential whites and, less often, with people of mixed race.[22]

Walker's behavior contrasted markedly with that of his second in command, Captain Albert S. Barker. Barker's memoirs record frequent interactions with Native Hawaiians. While on a vacation trip to the Big Island, Barker was extraordinarily impressed with the efficiency of the Native Hawaiians crewing his small vessel. The sailing master bragged that his 20-man crew once ferried 475 tons of sugar in 7,600 bags from shore to ship in a little more than 9 hours. Even had they carried the sugar on their shoulders, it would have been an impressive feat. But the work was even more difficult, for the crew had to load the sugar from the dock into 4 small boats, row 400 yards to the ship, offload the sugar, and return to the wharf for the next load. Barker marveled at the seamanship and work habits. Barker attended an exhibition at the Kawaiahao Seminary and recorded that "the young Hawaiian girls and women did excellently well." He heard a visiting American preacher, T. De Witt Talmage, speak in Central Union Church to an audience of Native Hawaiian preachers. Barker noted gleefully that the pompous Talmage made two crucial mistakes. First, he wrongly assumed the Hawaiians did not speak English. Second, he therefore employed as an interpreter a Hawaiian preacher so mesmerizing that the interpreter got the applause and not the unwitting Talmage. When this same group of preachers toured the *Philadelphia*, Barker noted that Admiral Walker insisted on wearing white gloves—for "sanitary purposes"— before he would shake hands with the Hawaiians.[23]

In the spring of 1894 the white oligarchy moved to solidify its rule. The provisional government had been intended as a caretaker until annexation, but it was still in place more than a year after Cleveland withdrew the treaty. There was no legislature. The small executive council, headed by Dole, and the fourteen-person advisory council made the big decisions, but the queen's bureaucracy still administered the country under the monarchy's laws. The ruling clique had to put the government on a permanent footing. But elections held under the 1887 Bayonet Constitution might produce a legislature dominated by Native Hawaiians.[24] Most rebels thought the whites had made a mistake in 1887 by not boosting voter qualifications, with the result that Native Hawaiians could vote in a government with their votes alone. To preserve white power, Thurston said, "we should fix the qualifications high."[25] Other contentious issues needed attention. Should royalist bureaucrats be ousted? Who would replace them? What government structure could best preserve the power of the current ruling elite against the more numerous royalists?

In particular, Japanese immigration, once seen as an economic lifeline for the labor-starved sugar industry, now began to seem threatening.[26] The ruling whites began to fret two months after the 1893 revolution when Japan's foreign ministry insisted that Japanese receive the same voting rights enjoyed by Americans and Europeans.[27] Japan had complained before. After 1842, 731 Chinese and 3 Japanese were naturalized.[28] A few even became voters. But the 1887 Bayonet Constitution limited the franchise to Hawaiians and whites, stripping Asians of any possibility of voting.

President Dole stalled. He said annexation was still pending, and that if it were consummated, the United States would set voter qualifications. He denied depriving Japanese of entitlements. He asked Consul-General Fujii which clause of the Hawai`i–Japanese 1886 labor convention conferred voting rights.[29] Instead, Fujii quoted Article 11 of the 1871 Hawai`i–Japan treaty, whose most-favored-nation clause stipulated that Japanese traders receive the same privileges as subjects of other nations. Fujii asserted that these privileges—he called them rights— applied to all Japanese residents, even those on short-term labor contracts.[30]

In Tokyo, Robert W. Irwin met with his friend of twenty years, Foreign Minister Mutsu Munemitsu, already in early negotiations with Britain to renounce its unequal treaty with Japan. If Hawai`i set up a permanent government, Mutsu expected that Japanese would have the same voting rights as German, American, and British subjects. The same property, citizenship, and education qualifications used for whites should be applied to Japanese.[31] Irwin warned of a Liberal Party plan to push the Imperial Government to demand Japanese suffrage.[32] Hoshi Toru, the speaker of the Diet, gave a fiery speech urging the Imperial Government to take a stronger stand. The Japanese press carried inflammatory articles every day.[33] Irwin told Mutsu that he advised Dole to grant the franchise to Japanese.[34] This inappropriate behavior showed that Irwin worried more about pleasing Mutsu and preserving his lucrative business as immigration agent than vigorously representing his own government.

Perhaps Irwin realized he appeared self-serving, for he asked to inform Mutsu simply that Hawai`i would give serious consideration to Japan's request. "Such an answer will be acceptable to the Imperial Cabinet," he wrote.[35] Dole replied that contract laborers had a special status because they arrived under a binational convention and were supervised by the Japanese government through its inspectors in the islands. Their status was akin to contractors on an overseas mission, under the "control" of their government. Japanese should not be allowed the vote because "no government can ask for an opportunity of exercising an influence in the local affairs of another government."[36]

In July 1893 the worried provisional government enlisted Commissioner Blount's support. After reading the correspondence, Blount declared his opposition to Japanese suffrage.[37] Blount gave Dole, to use as he wished, an intemperate letter declaring that giving political power to "inferior classes of Japanese subjects" would endanger American preeminence.[38] The administration remained watchful. In January 1894, during one of their periodic arguments masquerading as meetings, Gresham asked Thurston if Hawai`i wanted a protectorate to stave off Japanese military intervention.[39] Strangely, Thurston said no.

In April 1894 Admiral Walker fretted over "the possible disaffection of the Japanese." The *Philadelphia* was the only U.S. warship in port. "We ought to have the controlling force here," Walker said, but "we are equaled in strength by the English and exceeded by the Japanese."[40] He reported that the white clique did not dare grant to "a horde of Asiatics a privilege, the exercise of which might become . . . dangerous to the state." If Japanese did not get the vote, Japan might stop sending laborers or recall all of them entirely: either course would ruin the sugar industry.[41]

The executive council decided to write a new constitution for a permanent government. The council discussed key provisions between April 27 and May 28.[42] Regarding citizenship and voting, Thurston proposed that all persons who were citizens of Hawai`i at the time of the revolution should automatically be citizens of the Republic of Hawai`i. Noncitizen residents who helped overthrow the queen should also be made citizens, or denizens, if they did not want to renounce their current citizenship.

Thurston's proposal triggered a discussion of what to do about the Japanese. The council invited Robert W. Irwin to speak. He said the Japanese government did not want its immigrants to take Hawaiian citizenship. Making citizenship a requirement for voting would satisfy the desire for equal treatment, even if the lack of a bilateral naturalization treaty prevented Japanese from becoming citizens. Samuel Damon and others urged finding a way to give Japanese a mechanism for being heard. Others warned that the radical whites were absolutely against Asian participation. Hatch said the Asians must be shut out. No one felt strongly enough to challenge that view.[43]

The executive council carefully rigged the vote for delegates to a constitutional convention. All nineteen members of the executive and advisory councils were automatically delegates, joined by eighteen popularly elected delegates. Right from the start, the white revolutionaries had a guaranteed majority in the convention, even if royalists won the other eighteen seats. But there was no chance of that. A loyalty oath was required to vote for convention delegates. Most Native Hawaiians refused to swear allegiance to a government they thought illegal. The loyalty oath also discomfited white foreigners who voted as denizens. Denization did not require renunciation of former allegiances. Thus denizens voted in previous elections and even held office while still claiming protection from their birth country. Now the fear of losing consular protection stopped some American denizens from reregistering. The largest group of white voters, the Portuguese, obtained a pledge that the loyalty oath did not make them citizens, so many made the pledge.

In the May 2 election of convention delegates, the property and income requirements and the hated oath of allegiance cut the Native Hawaiian vote dramatically. About twenty-five hundred Native Hawaiians voted in Honolulu in 1890 and 1892, but less than 10 percent of that number cast ballots in 1894.[44] The white vote also declined, but not by nearly as much. About 75 percent of whites who voted in 1890–92 voted in 1894. Probably the whites who did not vote were royalists or foreigners afraid to take the loyalty oath. Overall, in this highly unrepresentative election, with many Native Hawaiian and white royalists abstaining and the Asians ineligible, the whites elected whom they pleased. There were six Native Hawaiians among the thirty-seven convention delegates—nineteen unelected and eighteen elected—but the rest were whites, half island-born.[45]

This homogeneous group—baldly put forward as representative of one of the world's most ethnically diverse populations—met May 31 to draft a new constitution. The constitution presented to the convention was largely the work of Thurston, Dole, and Hatch. Almost unchanged, this "insider" draft formed the final document. The government never intended a vote on the pact. Instead, on July 2 a mass meeting endorsed it by acclamation. At eight o'clock in the morning on July 4, from the steps of the Executive Building (the name the government now applied to `Iolani Palace), Dole proclaimed the Republic of Hawai`i. A band played, a salute was fired, and Dole and other officials were sworn in. The whole thing was quickly done, and everyone celebrated the American Fourth of July, for which the *Philadelphia* and the American legation arranged a day of boat races, rallies, and fireworks.

The Constitution of 1894 contained undemocratic provisions created by undemocratic, nontransparent procedures, with undemocratic effects. The constitution intentionally entrenched white rule, chiefly by denying the franchise to Asians and cutting the Native Hawaiian vote by property and education requirements and especially by the hated oath of allegiance. In truth, property requirements were not a 1890s white invention; Hawaiian practice flip-flopped in the nineteenth century, depending on who was in power and whether they thought a property or literacy requirement was helpful to keep them there. The Constitution of 1852, largely written by the American jurist William Lee, provided for an upper house of nobles appointed by the king and a lower house of representatives elected by the American principle of universal manhood suffrage. However, both Kamehameha IV and Kamehameha V disliked universal manhood suffrage and sought constitutional changes. When Kamehameha V could not reach a compromise with the legislature, he abrogated the 1852 constitution.

His words were the exact opposite of the royalist position in the 1890s. Kamehameha V asserted that suffrage was not a right of the people: "In all other monarchical countries suffrage is limited, and it is thought that the possession of property is proof of industry and thrift, therefore in those enlightened countries it is said that the class who possess property are the proper persons to advise their Representatives in regard to the necessities of the Government, and the poor, lazy, and ignorant are debarred from this privilege. It is clear to me that if universal suffrage is permitted, this Government will soon lose its monarchical character."[46] The king proclaimed, on his own authority, the Constitution of 1864, which created both property and literacy requirements, ending twelve years of universal male suffrage. Many people criticized the new property requirement and other clauses. In 1873, King Lunalilo, rather than decreeing changes, offered thirty constitutional amendments that the legislature approved at the beginning of Kalākaua's reign in 1874. One amendment reintroduced universal male suffrage in the voting for the lower house; the king still appointed upper house members, called "nobles." (Both houses convened and voted as a unified legislature.)

Thirteen years later, the Bayonet Constitution of 1887 both widened and limited the vote. Males over twenty years old of Hawaiian, American, or European birth could now vote. Voters must swear support for the 1887 constitution. They must be literate in Hawaiian or a European language and must have resided in the islands for a year. There was no income or property requirement to vote for the lower house. To vote for nobles, who were now elected, three years residency was necessary as well as three thousand dollars in property or six hundred dollars in income. Persons who had voted in previous elections were "grandfathered" into the vote. The Bayonet Constitution imposed age, residence, and property requirements for office holding as well.

Although tinkering with voter qualifications was an old practice, there is no question that in 1894 the provisional government shaped the voting and citizenship requirements for immediate political reasons, primarily to exclude Asians from the franchise and secondarily to shrink the Native Hawaiian vote. The 1894 constitution further increased the property and income requirements for both officeholders and voters. Voters had to pledge not to support restoration of the monarchy and had to be literate in either Hawaiian or English.

In their franchise restrictions in 1887 and 1894, the American-led rebels had moved a long way indeed from universal suffrage that their countryman Judge Lee put into the Constitution of 1852. On the other hand, in the 1890s the royalists saw universal suffrage as their route back to power and opposed the property requirements preferred by the last two Kamehamehas. Political expediency governed the positions of both camps, but the white minority, in 1894, was able to impose its system on the majority of island residents.

The 1894 constitution finessed Asian suffrage. Only citizens could vote. Only persons from countries with a naturalization treaty with Hawai`i might be granted citizenship. This excluded all Asian countries.[47] Admiral Walker reported on July 12, "All apprehension of trouble with the Japanese here has subsided."[48] This was due less to constitutional finagling, though that was important, than to the Sino-Japanese War, which temporarily distracted Japan from Hawaiian affairs. On June 19, during the middle of the convention, the heavy cruiser *Takachiho* was suddenly recalled to Japan. On July 4 a mail steamer brought orders for the *Kongo*, which took on coal all night for an early morning departure.[49] With no warships and a home government preoccupied with war, Consul-General Fujii shelved the franchise issue for the moment.

Satisfied with the political edifice built by his friends, Admiral Walker requested recall.[50] Before his mission, the Navy promised to make him superintendent of the Naval Academy in September 1894.[51] But Gresham, irked that Walker included political observations in communications, grumbled to Willis that "Walker had no written or verbal instructions to act in any diplomatic capacity."[52] Gresham believed a permanent naval presence intimidated internal political activity. He must have meant antigovernment activities by royalists because the white government was a dynamo of activity. He decided to remove both the *Philadelphia* and the troublesome admiral.[53] The Navy ordered Walker to take the warship home. Just before leaving, Walker rose even higher on the long list of people Gresham disliked. The admiral left behind a memorandum for the next U.S. warship commander at Honolulu, taking potshots at Willis.[54] In a blunt final report written en route to Mare Island, Walker declared that if, by removing the *Philadelphia*, "we are not at hand to perform the duties of our virtual protectorate," another power would surely play that role.[55]

These two missives enraged Gresham, who correctly inferred criticism. He had the Navy cancel Walker's Naval Academy orders and assign him to the dead-end Lighthouse Board.[56] He had served his purpose. He made the administration appear vigilant, as indeed it was, and now he could be pushed aside. His prowhite behavior only increased Gresham's desire to punish him. Gresham lambasted Willis too, writing a nasty note accusing him of concurring with Walker's opinions. Willis quickly produced a suitably groveling explanation.[57]

Cleveland and Gresham's dispatch of the Walker mission showed they would not accept any risk that Japan could pressure Hawai`i to grant voting rights during the delicate establishment of the Republic of Hawai`i. Cleveland maintained an informal protectorate that meshed perfectly with the Turpie Resolution's "hands off" tone and indeed with traditional American policy of keeping Hawai`i independent. Hawai`i would not be annexed, but it would be watched over carefully.

CHAPTER 11

❦

Mahan, the New Navy, and Hawaiʻi's Strategic Value

A t the time of his death in 1914, Admiral Alfred Thayer Mahan was the preeminent naval strategist of his age.[1] Lionized by the British, Japanese, and German navies, he authored some twenty books and more than one hundred published essays. But Mahan was a late bloomer, reaching middle age before anyone outside the U.S. Navy knew his name. He was fifty years old in 1890 when he published one of the most famous American books of all time: *The Influence of Sea Power upon History, 1660–1783*.[2] His principal idea—that control of the seas was indispensable to national greatness—was hardly fresh; indeed, it too was middle-aged. Other officers and civilians had previously recognized the relationship between national power and security, the Navy, and the safety of American commerce.[3]

But Mahan had the propagandist's skill for weaving seemingly disparate threads into a persuasive tapestry. Mahan claimed he coined the term "sea power" because it was catchy.[4] Mahan's principal biographer, Robert Seager II, asserts that with the possible exception of *Uncle Tom's Cabin*, "no book written in nineteenth century America had greater immediate impact" on national policy as *Influence*.[5] Even more than his books, during the 1890s his magazine articles presented his ideas to the opinion leaders, policy makers, and politicians who controlled national policy. Before long, hardly a speech given in the Congress on naval expansion failed to invoke his name as "proving" an argument.

Born in 1840 at West Point, where his father, Dennis, was a renowned professor, Mahan grew up entranced not in the maneuvering of ground troops but in the romance of a seafaring life. He loved sea tales—Seager calls them "Boarders Away!" stories—such as the adventures penned by the retired Royal Navy captain Frederick Marryat and James Fenimore Cooper. Bored at Columbia College, Mahan met Secretary of War Jefferson Davis, his father's former student, and wangled an appointment to Annapolis. There Alfred's romance with the sea continued. During the academy's 1857 summer cruise to the Azores he proclaimed seafaring "the most happy and entrancing life that there is. In a stiff breeze, when the ship is heeling well over, there is a wild sort of delight that I never experienced before. . . . I long for next summer when I will again be on the ship."[6]

Once in the fleet, his romance foundered and he served without joy, laboring anonymously aboard Union blockade ships. He served two years as the moody executive officer of the *Iroquois* during 1867–69. Mahan spent the next quarter century like other peacetime officers, commanding larger ships as he rose in rank and laboring at unchallenging shore jobs between sea assignments.

Mahan's career bridged the transition from sailing vessels to steel-hulled steam warships, and from the outdated, cruiser-based "commerce preying" strategy to one of controlling broad zones off the coasts and in the Caribbean with battleship fleets. His descriptions of Hawai`i's growing strategic worth exemplified the conviction, widespread by the late 1890s, that the islands were too valuable to national security to leave independent and hence vulnerable. By 1898, many Americans saw Hawaiian annexation as a security concern, intertwined with expanding and modernizing the Navy, improving coastal defenses, acquiring overseas bases, and building an isthmian canal.

The proud fleet that strangled the Confederacy was gone. From 700 ships—including 65 ironclads—the Navy shrank so fast that by 1880 only a couple dozen ships could make an overseas cruise. Only 4 had iron hulls. Mahan complained "we have not six ships" that a foreign Navy would think worthy.[7] In 1885 he bitterly compared his dismal *Wachusett* to the impressive Chilean, Italian, and German armored warships in Callao. The "tremendous" German cruiser could turn 14.5 knots, almost twice that of the *Wachusett*, whose guns, "respectable twenty years ago—are absolutely obsolete. . . . The worst of it is that it cannot be said that she is an unfair specimen of the U.S. Navy."[8]

As Mahan and other officers railed about patched-together tubs, they still embraced an increasingly outmoded view of naval war. The traditional American concept of ignoring enemy fleets while attacking commerce with swift cruisers and privateers may have worked for a fledgling nation, but it was startlingly inadequate for an economic giant with long settled coastlines and valuable ports. In war, a strong enemy fleet would sweep up American coastwise and overseas trade, destroy ports with long-range guns, and raid the thousands of miles of vulnerable coast.

From the 1600s to the Civil War, neither strategy nor technology changed much. The ship of the line—the battleship of the Age of Sail—changed little over the centuries.[9] The 1850 version was still built of wood, moved by the wind, attacked with guns mounted along broad sides, and fought by the same tactics.[10] In the old days, successful naval warfare depended on leadership, judgment, and seamanship. The weather significantly affected sailing ships. Wind patterns channeled ships into zones of steady breezes. Wind shaped the ship's direction and speed.

Commanding a ship of the line in battle was not book learning. It was long experience, good judgment, and deep knowledge of ships and the sea. The crucial tactical principle was holding the weather gauge. As Bernard Brodie observed, (1) the wind usually determined the character of a battle (fight or flee), (2) maintaining the wind gauge—a big part of which was a function of seamanship and judgment—imparted immense advantages, and (3) whether one had the wind gauge was usually an accident.[11] The best way to acquire fighting skill was to spend a lot of time at sea.

This was an effective technique in the Age of Sail, but not in the Age of Steam, when sweeping technological changes rapidly revolutionized hardware and strategy. Overnight, ships became much more sophisticated. In 1862 the Union's most advanced ironclad had one machine, a steam engine. Everything else ran by muscle. The ship steered, signaled, took on cargo, ran out the guns, set its sails, and raised its anchor by human hands, as ships had done for centuries. But the battleship *Iowa*, built only 30 years later, had more than 150 machines! Steam propelled the ship and machines performed "all work of steering, communications, lighting, ventilation, and gunnery."[12]

Steam propulsion was the most important development since tacking into the wind emerged in the fifteenth century. Steam propulsion "completely revised the conditions governing naval tactics; it modified the whole geography of position and distance, thus profoundly affecting strategy; it enhanced the potential military power of industrialized states; and it injected the all-important factor of fuel into naval supplies, thus affecting the range of fleets and the strategic importance of stations abroad."[13] Steam changed all the old rules.

But many officers resisted change. First, the line officers hated that, by mastering the mysterious steam engines, engineering specialists increased their numbers, prestige, and influence. Second, many old-school officers simply found steamships offensive. Compared to creamy white canvas and clean, sanded decks, who could prefer belching smokestacks and coal dust permeating every deck and compartment? John D. Alden aptly described the 1880s Navy as "a fleet of sailing ships into which had been dropped the incongruous and ill-tolerated engines and boilers of the uncouth engineers. Rakish bowsprits and full sail rigs dominated the squat, telescopic stacks as completely as sail dominated steam in the thinking of the officers of the line."[14]

Technological advances demanded that the United States transform strategy and build the proper warships to execute it. Slowly new thinking spread. In 1883, following the recommendation of Robert Shufeldt's Naval Board, Congress authorized the famous "ABCD" steel ships—the cruisers *Atlanta*, *Boston*, and *Chicago*, and the dispatch boat *Dolphin*. The cruisers were a hybrid design with rifled guns, fairly substantial sailing rigs, and coal bunkers girdling the steam engines. Because the filled bunkers gave some protection to vital innards, as did an internal, horizontal armor deck across the hull at the waterline, the ship was called a "protected" cruiser. Undergunned and underarmored compared to European equivalents, the ABC cruisers were still a giant step toward modern ships.[15] Admiral Bradley Fiske, then a lieutenant, said, "The *Atlanta* was the first United States ship to have modern ordnance, search-lights, and protective deck, and to conform in general to the changes in naval construction and ordnance that had come about in the foreign navies during the preceding twenty years."[16]

Subsequent administrations added more steel ships. In 1885 Congress authorized two small cruisers, the *Charleston* and the *Newark*, and the gunboats *Petrel* and *Yorktown*.[17] The first Cleveland administration ordered thirty vessels, with the second-class battleships *Texas* and *Maine*, the excellent armored cruiser *New York*, and six more protected cruisers, including the *Olympia*, Dewey's flagship at Manila Bay. The *Texas* and *Maine* had old-fashioned aspects—they were small for battleships, retained sailing rigs, and their main batteries could fire only to one side—but they incorporated modern features. *Texas* carried two 12-inch rifled guns and 12 inches of armor. The heavily armored *Maine* mounted four 10-inch rifled guns in two turrets.[18] *Texas* and *Maine* were useless for preying on commerce. As Walter Herrick noted, the building program represented technological advances outrunning a revised vision of how the ships should be fought.[19] Even Mahan wrote Sam Ashe in March 1885 that an enemy attack on the United States was unlikely but that "the surest deterrent will be a fleet of swift cruisers to prey on the enemy's commerce."[20]

But this was Mahan's final articulation of "old-think." His metamorphosis into naval prophet began four months earlier. Reading Theodore Mommsen's *The History of Rome*, he realized Rome's control of the sea-lanes forced Hannibal to lose a quarter of his forces making a roundabout land march to Italy.[21] From this quiet moment, Mahan traced the emergence of his sea power theory.

Mahan was but one of a group of talented officers questioning conventional wisdom. In 1873 they organized the Naval Institute to exchange ideas about the Navy's future. Members included the men who could imagine new fighting strategies: Stephen B. Luce, Mahan (vice president in 1878), Caspar Goodrich, and George Belknap.[22] Even the Naval Institute initially did little to promote new strategic thinking, spending much time on technical issues such as engines and ordnance.[23] Only gradually did most officers see that naval strategy must be modernized along with the warships.[24]

But how to study strategy and tactics? Commodore Luce, the Navy's reigning intellectual, took the lead in training officers in strategic thinking. Luce could have been a foot-dragger. He had grown up professionally in the Age of Sail and authored the Navy's best-known guide to the handling of sailing ships. But he embraced new ideas, and he was a fanatic on the subject of training and education.[25]

In 1884 Luce and Commodore John G. Walker persuaded Navy Secretary William Chandler to establish a naval war college, with Luce as its first president, to improve officers' ability to fight the new ships.[26] Many of Luce's peers thought it a silly idea to go from the prestigious command of the North Atlantic Squadron to skippering a school with one building and no students or faculty. (Bradley Fiske wrote of "covert sneers and loud guffaws.")[27] Nor did the college start with a bang. Only nine officers received orders to the inaugural monthlong September 1885 session.

Luce invited Mahan to join the faculty. Mahan was then the complaining and unhappy commander of the *Wachusett*, zigzagging between crises in Central America and Ecuador. Such an independent command would have delighted most officers, but Mahan's personality was not well suited to command. At sea as a midshipman, without much responsibility, the sea had been fun. Captaining the *Wachusett*, with total responsibility, he fretted constantly, judging by his letters.[28]

Luce wanted not Mahan, the frazzled, mediocre ship driver, but Professor Mahan, the teacher of naval history and strategy, the Mahan who would become famous. The two men had worked together at the Naval Academy early in the Civil War, and Mahan served as Luce's executive officer on the *Macedonian* on an 1862 summer cruise. Mahan's essay "Naval Education" placed third in an 1878 competition sponsored by the Naval Institute. In 1883 he published a solid history of Civil War littoral operations called *The Gulf and Inland Waters*.[29] He had cruised the Caribbean and Brazilian coast in the *Congress*, surveyed the waters off Uruguay and Argentina, patrolled China, taught at the Naval Academy, showed the flag in messy revolutions in Ecuador and Central America, decked out the *Macedonian* in Fourth of July bunting in Plymouth harbor, sighted Cape Town's majestic Table Mountain while transiting the Cape of Good Hope, steamed the Persian Gulf, mingled with multiethnic street crowds in Aden, watched the final convulsions of the Meiji Restoration in Kobe, sailed through Suez in the month that it opened, wandered through Rome's opulence, and toured Southern France and wrote an essay about the region. His exceptionally varied experiences, his formal education and diligent self-study, and his first book prepared him for serious academic work.

Mahan buried himself in New York libraries and completed hundreds of pages of lecture notes. In the summer of 1886 the Navy assigned Luce, now an admiral, back to the North Atlantic Squadron. Captain Mahan assumed the War College presidency.[30] Luce's ally, Commodore John G. Walker, chief of the Bureau of Navigation, assigned twenty-one students to the fall term and told Luce: "I shall hope to tide over the college until it has more friends."[31] Because the North Atlantic Squadron was still in port, Luce ordered junior officers to join the "regular" students. Bradley Fiske, one of the draftees, said they went petulantly to class but soon learned that ships and guns were but tools for the naval strategist, "just as a hammer and a chisel are tools in the hands of a sculptor."[32]

Mahan extended the term to ten weeks. Each major course consisted of several lectures; in 1887 lectures totaled 147.[33] Students reported by nine o'clock in the morning and remained until one thirty in the afternoon. The point was not to simply sit in lectures but to think, to study, to learn on one's own time. This kind of learning was anathema to "old-think" officers such as Commodore Francis Ramsay, who succeeded Walker as chief of the Bureau of Navigation. Ramsay may be most remembered for saying of Mahan, "it is not the business of naval officers to write books."[34]

The small teaching staff possessed real talent, including James Russell Soley, a professor whom Mahan met while teaching at Annapolis during 1877–80. Soley, assistant secretary of the Navy in the Harrison administration, taught international law. A brilliant army lieutenant, Tasker Bliss, taught military history, strategy, and tactics.[35] Bliss would become chief of staff of the U.S. Army in 1917–18. The analytical Caspar F. Goodrich, a future president of the War College, taught coast defense. The 1888 courses included the War of 1812, taught by the noted historian-politician-rancher Theodore Roosevelt, who at age thirty had already written *The*

Naval War of 1812, biographies of Thomas Hart Benton and Gouverneur Morris, and who was just finishing the first two volumes of his *The Winning of the West*.

Mahan focused the curriculum on big-picture courses, such as "The Proposed Isthmian Canal and the Caribbean," the "Strategic Features of the Pacific Coast," "Naval Logistics," and "War Games," the latter taught by William McCarty Little, who would become the most famous war-gamer in the United States. Though he helped in Naval Tactics and the "strategic features" courses, Mahan's teaching centered on naval history and strategy. It surprised the cool, aloof Mahan that his lectures were instantly popular, even among Fiske and the draftees.[36] *The Influence of Sea Power upon History, 1660–1783* emerged from Mahan's course. When *Influence* appeared in 1890, Roosevelt wrote Mahan that he went "straight through" the book, high praise from a man who alternated between several books at once: "It is a very good book—admirable; and I am greatly in error if it does not become a naval classic."[37]

The turning point in the building of battleships, the heart of the New Navy, also came in 1890. Benjamin Tracy, Harrison's secretary of the Navy, formally abandoned the outmoded cruiser-based, commerce-preying idea, saying, "These vessels cannot be counted on as an element of force."[38] Tracy authorized three cutting-edge battleships, the *Indiana*, *Oregon*, and *Massachusetts*, equal to the best European warships. The *Indiana* class had 18-inch armor, 13-inch primary batteries, and 16-knot speed. They were an order of magnitude better than the *Maine* and *Texas*, authorized just five years before. The *Indiana*s sat low on the sea, oozing lethality, and their front and rear center-line turrets allowed all four big guns to fire to either side. To appease monitor supporters, the Navy limited range to 5,000 miles—hence their contradictory title of "sea-going, coastline battleships." (As late as 1900, "coastline" appeared in battleship authorizations to mollify the traditionalists.) In 1892 Tracy funded the battleship *Iowa* and the armored heavy cruiser *Brooklyn*, three times larger than the ABC cruisers of only nine years before.[39]

Hilary Herbert, naval secretary during Cleveland's second term, also converted to capital ship thinking.[40] In August 1893 Herbert took the *Dolphin*, the D of ABCD fame, to Newport to inspect the Naval War College. During the trip, he read *The Influence of Sea Power upon the French Revolution and Empire*, Mahan's second book.[41] Herbert wrote Mahan that "you deserve all the encomiums of the British and American press for this great work . . . by far the ablest history of the epoch from 1792 to 1812. . . . I have also run over your first volume, and am particularly impressed with your citations from history of the comparatively little effect of commerce destroyers in bringing the war to a successful conclusion."[42]

Herbert funded five battleships: *Kentucky, Kearsarge* (the only battleship in U.S. history not named for a state), *Alabama, Illinois,* and *Wisconsin.*[43]

The New Navy—both ships and strategy—was a product of continual experimentation and adjustment from the 1870s until after the Spanish-American War. Fits and starts characterized the development of ships, weapons, and propulsion systems.[44] Good things were done: better engines and armor, rifled guns, screw propellers. Some changes occurred very slowly. The conversion to pure steam power was sluggish. Even in 1905 some ships entered service with sail rigging. Monitors appeared in authorizations as late as 1898, though the design was dangerously unseaworthy. The Navy experimented with rams, submarines, and the strange "dynamite ships" whose 15-inch air-powered mortars threw giant "gun cotton" shells. The engineers dithered whether turrets should turn by hydraulic, electric, or pneumatic power. The Navy procrastinated at installing new range finders and aiming systems. In 1898 accuracy was so bad that at Manila Bay only about 2 percent of shots struck home, and off Santiago, only 1.8 percent.[45]

The first ten years of steel ship construction created the fleet that fought Spain, for Herbert's battleships funded in 1895 and 1896 did not enter service until after the war. In 1898, the Navy had six battleships, two armored heavy cruisers, and thirteen protected cruisers. The Navy had moved from twelfth in the world to sixth, still second rate.[46] Nevertheless, at last a majority of navalists and members of Congress realized that new technologies necessitated high-tech fleets built around battleships and fought by new rules. They also realized that the new technologies and strategies hugely increased the importance of commanding locations like Hawaiʻi.

Mahan probably did more than any other person to explain Hawaiʻi's immense strategic value to the United States. It seems odd, therefore, that he never visited Hawaiʻi, never surveyed Pearl Harbor, never examined Honolulu port. Aboard the *Wachusett,* he did not sail north of Central America. He steamed to Japan via the Suez Canal and the Straits of Malacca. He "explained" Hawaiʻi's strategic value not from personal observation but by applying his theories to Hawaiʻi's particular circumstances, especially its geographical location, its ports and potential naval stations, and its people and resources.

His theories evolved slowly for years, then crystallized suddenly. He initially took a historical approach. His two sea power books examined the Age of Sail from 1660 to 1812, concluding that naval supremacy ensured national greatness. Rather than tactics, which he thought fluid, grand strategy never changed. One needed to study the big picture, not transitory fighting techniques. He proudly told Admiral Luce that *Influence* did not contain a single, blow-by-blow "ship action."[47] *Influence* laid out Mahan's principles: a strong Navy built around capital ships and used as a fleet operating from key locations and geographic choke points. As historians have documented, *Influence* contained few original thoughts, but it was a highly innovative, compelling achievement of packaging and presentation. William Livezey put it well: "Mahan is best seen as a catalyst offering justification for policies already adopted or contemplated. He clarified strategic concepts ... though offering little that was essentially new."[48] The timing of *Influence* was crucial. It appeared when "ideas were in the air."

Many publishers rejected the manuscript, thinking it too academic. James Soley suggested adding an opening chapter, "The Elements of Sea Power," as an easily digestible summary for layman readers. That chapter was so good that some later joked that reviewers needed to read only "Elements" to capture the book's essence. Little, Brown, and Company presented the book to the world in May 1890. Mahan boasted: "I have remembered the public."[49] He would not forget again. With *Influence* garnering favorable reviews, Mahan reached out to a broader audience. Roosevelt wrote a glowing review for the *Atlantic Monthly*, which promptly published, in December 1890, Mahan's article "The United States Looking Outward," summarizing his key strategic arguments.[50] After his second big book—*The Influence of Sea Power upon the French Revolution and Empire*— appeared in 1892, Mahan thought constantly about his reputation outside the academy. He turned to the direct, topical arguments of a policy advocate or even a propagandist, writing often for magazines and newspapers.

When Mahan learned of the Hawaiian revolution in January 1893, he dashed off a letter to the *New York Times*. "The Sandwich Islands," he wrote, had a "geographical and military importance unrivaled by any other position in the North Pacific." Their proximity to the West Coast made the United States the "proper guardian of this most important position." To hold the islands in wartime would require "great extension of our naval power." "Are we ready to undertake this?" he asked.[51] The letter impressed the *Forum*'s editor, Walter Hines Page. He ordered a long article for the March 1893 issue. In "Hawai`i and Our Future Sea Power," Mahan elaborated on the strategic rationale for annexation.[52] From 1893–98, as Hawai`i remained a hot policy topic, Mahan expanded his arguments in influential magazine articles.[53]

Navalists kicked off a decade of powerful writing in 1890. Essays and books and letters to editors—by Mahan, Luce, Roosevelt, George Melville, and many others with a common view about security and defense issues—steadily reached the foreign policy public. What were the implications for Hawaiian annexation of these theories, particularly Mahan's, as they existed between 1890–98?

Mahan deemed the principle of concentration of force essential to modern naval warfare. Survival in an imperialist world depended on mustering "menacing and efficient" military forces.[54] A vigorous and successful nation, Mahan declared in 1896, required not only strength but also "strength *organized*."[55] Military effort should be concentrated rather than dispersed ineffectively around the area of operations. A massed force could deliver a more powerful blow and impel the enemy to concentrate his own forces to withstand the blow, thereby preventing the enemy from scattering and falling upon the unprotected American coasts. A Mahanian massed force was a fleet built around battleships and heavy cruisers. Naval war would be fought between fleets maneuvering as units. Gone for good was the practice used at, say, Trafalgar, where warships sailed as fleets to the scene and, after the battle commenced, operated largely on their own. Hawaiʻi was the only place in the vast North Pacific where a battleship fleet could be massed and efficiently based and supplied.[56]

A second principle was that strategic positions, such as Hawaiʻi, produced naval superiority. Mahan passionately endorsed Napoleon's dictum that "war is the business of positions."[57] A position's strategic value depended upon location, military strength or ease of defense, and logistical resources. Two of these were changeable. Military strength could be improved by building fortifications, installing better guns, or deploying a garrison. Logistical resources could be augmented by stockpiling food, fuel, and ammunition and ensuring a water supply. In Hawaiʻi's case, Pearl Harbor could easily be defended, it had abundant food and water, coal could be stockpiled, and skilled labor was available for ship repairs. An ideal fleet base was one that could defend itself without the fleet. Regarding defensibility and resources, Hawaiʻi was nearly perfect.[58]

Location, being unalterable, was the most important component of strategic value. Hawaiʻi's location was unmatched. A valuable strategic position must be situated in an important geographical area, close enough to strategic lines as to be worth occupying. The best strategic positions bestrode strategic lines and stood between a nation and possible enemy avenues of attack. The best positions facilitated the rapid concentration of military forces and allowed their easy tactical use. The fewer the strategic positions in a given area, the greater the military value of each one. If there was but one strategic position, Mahan wrote, its worth depended on the size and importance of the area over which its "unshared influence" extended.[59]

By this measurement, Hawaiʻi's strategic value was unequalled. The only strategic position in the North Pacific, Hawaiʻi commanded a huge and vital area of growing importance. Melville, the Navy's chief of engineering and expert on maritime propulsion and coaling issues, explained: "On our globe there are no islands whose strategic position, with respect to the area commanded, equals that of Hawai`i."[60] Mahan concluded that "it is rarely that so important a factor in the attack and defense of a coast-line—of a sea frontier—is concentrated in a single position, and the circumstance renders it doubly imperative upon us to secure it."[61] Melville also noted Hawai`i's peculiar remoteness. Between the United States and the Hawaiian Islands "lie no further islands to bridge a passage or give shelter or support to friend or foe. Alone, with neither peer nor rival, they watch, as nature's fortress of these seas."[62]

Hawai`i's remoteness gave an unparalleled geostrategic significance, particularly in the days of coal-fired armored warships. A fleet based at Hawai`i could control a huge expanse of the earth. The Pacific Ocean is the largest geographical feature on the globe, covering nearly 64.2 million square miles, more than all the land area of the earth combined. Consider a circle centered on Honolulu with a radius of 2,200 miles—roughly the distance from Hawai`i to the U.S. naval bases at San Francisco. This imaginary circle contains 15.2 million square miles, representing—amazingly—one twelfth or 7.5 percent of the earth's entire surface and almost a quarter of the vast Pacific Ocean.[63] Its isolated geographical position made Hawai`i unique: no other position on earth dominates so absolutely such a vast area. Other great bases—Gibraltar, Halifax, Singapore, Hong Kong, Scapa Flow, Norfolk, Yokosuka—do not extend control in all directions due to constrictions of nearby land or, like Bermuda and Malta, they dominate smaller areas. Commodore Melville's words look prescient: "If Hawai`i shall be annexed by the United States, the conclusion is inevitable that, in case of maritime war being waged against us, the island group will be the scene of the earliest, perhaps the only, conflict on Pacific waters."[64] He was right about Pearl Harbor being the first battle, if not the only one.

The enormous speed increase, intensified by the ability to steam directly without tacking, had an equally enormous effect on naval strategy. In 1895 Mahan observed that the sea had always been a means of communications between nations, though now traversed with a "rapidity and certainty that have minimized distances." Technology shrank the world, increasing the frequency of nations bumping shoulders. "Events which under former conditions would have been of small concern," Mahan wrote, "now happen at our doors and closely affect us. Proximity . . . is a fruitful source of political friction, but proximity is the characteristic of the age. The world has grown smaller."[65]

Positions formerly distant, such as Hawai`i, now seemed closer—in military terms they *were* closer—and therefore played a larger role in coastal defense.

Commodore Melville echoed the dictum of the famous British strategist, Admiral Philip Colomb, who likened the sea to "territory over which military forces march." Melville recalled that Napoleon marched 25 miles a day. In 6 days, the time needed to steam from Honolulu to San Francisco, the emperor would have gone 150 miles. If one thought of the sea as a great plain, Hawai`i should be imagined as 150 miles from San Francisco. From this point of view, Hawai`i was on America's doorstep.[66] Neither Melville nor other navalists saw a contradiction in finding Hawai`i valuable for its isolation and control of a vast North Pacific region while simultaneously arguing that technology had made it seem less remote. In their minds, both arguments were true, especially given what might be called the "fuel factor."

The new steam warships had one weakness: coal. Mahan called it "the life of modern naval war; it is the food of the ship." Much of Hawai`i's importance to coastal defense grew out the insatiable coal hunger of battleships. Battleships lacked the coal capacity to cross the Pacific and successfully attack the West Coast unless they recoaled en route. Mahan and other strategists believed that "it should be an inviolable resolution of our national policy" to prevent any naval power from acquiring a coaling station within 3,000 miles of San Francisco," a distance that included the Hawaiian Islands and the Central American and Canadian coasts.[67]

The Navy determined that the "actual practical steaming radius" of American, British, and Japanese battleships was about 4,000 miles; that of French, German, and Russian capital ships about 3,000 miles.[68] Range was not fixed, though coal bunker capacity was the major determinant. Range varied with the amount of deck coal (extra coal carried on deck in burlap bags), coal quality, the number of boilers fired, boiler efficiency, and speed.[69] In the *Oregon*'s dramatic 66-day redeployment from California to Cuba in 1898—it arrived just in time to participate in the fight—the battleship steamed 14,700 miles, averaging 13.4 miles per hour and burning 4,100 tons of coal, roughly 3.75 tons per hour.

Coal consumption rose dramatically as speed increased. At 18.4 miles per hour (flank speed for the *Indiana* class), the *Oregon* burned about 10 tons of coal per hour, 338 pounds per minute.[70] Thus speed alone significantly affected range. At flank speed, maximum range was 3,054 miles. At any speed, combat range was far less than maximum range. The increased coal consumption incident to maneuvering a fleet prior to and during combat might well reduce the combat radius of battleships to 2,000 miles or less. No captain wanted to enter combat without considerable fuel, so that full or flank speeds could be used in fighting (or fleeing) with a hefty reserve to get to a safe recoaling port.

An enemy fleet bound for the West Coast must recoal at Hawai`i. Enemy battleships recoaling at Hawai`i—roughly 2,200 miles from San Francisco—could raid the poorly defended cities of the Pacific coast, sweep up the coasting trade, return to Hawai`i, recoal, and maintain these operations indefinitely. If the Navy could somehow increase its forces on the West Coast sufficiently to control or at least contest for control of American coastal waters, the fighting would occur along the mainland, thus the West Coast, instead of Hawai`i, would bear "the loss and suffering of naval war." However, if the United States held Hawai`i, an enemy fleet desiring to attack the coast must first attack the islands and secure coaling facilities. And the attacking enemy fleet would reach Hawai`i with only enough coal for a short operation against concentrated, well-coaled U.S. warships ranging from a fortified base at Pearl Harbor.[71]

Bypassing Hawai`i and striking the West Coast directly was completely impractical. The distance from any foreign naval station in the Pacific (except Esquimalt on Vancouver Island, which will be discussed later) to the American coast exceeded the practical combat radius of battleships.[72] From a couple of the nearer foreign bases—Tahiti, for example—battleships could reach the West Coast but would arrive with almost no coal left for combat maneuvering, let alone enough to make it back to a safe port. Nor could an enemy fleet directly attack the West Coast via the northern Great Circle route. The Great Circle route from Yokohama, headquarters of the Japanese Navy, to San Francisco is 4,536 miles, at least 500 miles more than the most generous estimate of steaming radius, and perhaps twice the real-world combat radius. A fleet departing the British base at Hong Kong or the Russian base at Vladivostok would have to steam even farther.[73] Thus the Pacific coast could not be attacked, no matter what the route, without recoaling. Only Hawai`i was near enough to the Pacific coast—within a battleship's practical combat radius—and suitable for recoaling a fleet.

Other potential bases had major flaws. Midway Island, claimed by the United States in 1867, was 1,153 miles northwest of Pearl Harbor. Composed of two coral atolls totaling two square miles, Midway had no freshwater. A reef of 12–18 feet obstructed the channel, and given the heavy sea breaking on the reefs and shoals, "it is difficult for vessels to gain the anchorage" and only whaleboats could be used to land stores, the Navy reported in 1905.[74] Necker Island, 430 miles northwest of O`ahu, was worse: tiny and rocky with no anchorage and no water.[75]

Antiannexationists sometimes claimed that an Aleutian island would be a good coaling alternative. Because the Aleutians lay near the Great Circle route to Asia, recoaling at Unalaska or Kiska instead of Honolulu cut hundreds of miles off a transpacific voyage. Commercial captains happily forwent this mileage savings of 16 percent against the much better weather (and more restful crew stopover) of the Honolulu route.[76] Naval commanders were particularly concerned with the weather. When the *Petrel*, a modern steel gunboat commissioned in 1889, went to San Francisco from Yokohama in December 1895, her captain worried about icing. When he passed through Unalaska on previous cruises in the late spring and summer, the shipping agents there said that "during the winter, though the Road itself was only frozen over during an abnormal winter, the pockets forming the harbor where the two wharves are situated were frozen over and not accessible for coaling purposes" until mid-April at the earliest. The captain preferred to go via Honolulu, the "most agreeable route to San Francisco."[77] Bradley Fiske recalled a remote 1890s Unalaska from his days on the gunboat *Yorktown*: "Communication with the outside world lasted from May until October, and then ceased until the following May." Fiske recalled the "exceedingly rough" and "exceedingly irregular" seas that marred the *Yorktown*'s transit from the Bering Sea through the Aleutian chain into the Pacific.[78] The terrible winter weather made the Aleutian route impractical, even if an enemy could build a surreptitious base there.

Most important, even if the Navy could recoal at Unalaska on some transpacific missions, as Senator Stephen White claimed in his 1898 argument against annexation, it did not address the key point that only possession of Honolulu prevented an enemy from basing there.[79] Finally, regarding surreptitious bases, the United States would surely detect a coal depot large enough for a fleet in the American Aleutians, or on the Mexican or Central American coasts. As for British Esquimalt, strategists expected the Army to seize it quickly.

Theoretically, a fleet could dispense with a base, bring colliers, and recoal en route. But a fleet's coal consumption was enormous. Many colliers would be needed. Slow, they hindered fleet mobility. Heavy swells common in the North Pacific would hamper the transfer. Squalls, fog, or winds would have the same effect. The recoaling process left warships and colliers so vulnerable that no sane captain would have taken the risk if the enemy were near. Alone, the unarmed and unarmored colliers would be defenseless. The peacetime practice of deck coaling would be dangerous in wartime, interfering with use of the guns and making the warships top-heavy.

Coaling at sea from colliers was a delicate, unreliable operation. A captain preferred to coal from barges in protected anchorages. The crew employed a small crane to lift the burlap-bagged coal to the main deck and used wheelbarrow-like contraptions to dump it into chutes leading directly to the bunkers. This was quite similar to recoaling alongside a wharf. Recoaling on the open sea was much more risky. In calm seas, the collier—festooned with cotton-bales to protect the hulls in case of collision—would steam a slow straight course alongside the warship as seamen winched the coal bags across. In any seas whatsoever, if either ship rolled more than three or four degrees or rose more than one or two feet, coaling was considered too dangerous to attempt. Even when recoaling could be done, it was very slow at best, and weather made the recoaling rate very unpredictable. During the Spanish-American War, the *Brooklyn* recoaled at the rate of 18 tons per hour on May 31 and on June 7 at the rate of 57 tons per hour. Only rarely could more than a few hundred tons be loaded before the weather forced a halt. Recoaling at Guantánamo, seized by the Marines on June 10, and Key West was crucial to station-keeping off Santiago for the U.S. fleet. The sea was too rough off Santiago for colliers, so the battleships *Oregon* and *Massachusetts* took turns coaling in Guantánamo.[80] Coaling difficulties significantly complicated movements of both U.S. and Spanish squadrons in the Caribbean during the war.[81] If it was so difficult to recoal at sea in the Caribbean in early summer, one can imagine the problem in the stormy North Pacific or the Aleutians in winter.

Coal chained fleets inescapably to coaling stations. Mahan pointed out that steam power increased the interdependence between base and fleet: "The renewal of coal is a want more frequent, more urgent, more preemptory, than any known to the sailing-ship. It is vain to look for energetic naval operations distant from coaling stations."[82] Arguing for annexation in 1893, Mahan declared: "to recoal, a base must be had."[83] Quite simply, in the North Pacific, it all boiled down to Hawai`i.

An American-controlled Hawai`i would also enhance national security by helping to guard the northwestern approaches to an isthmian canal, which once built would itself be a major enhancement of naval power. An enemy fleet making the eight-thousand-mile journey across the central or north Pacific to the isthmus must recoal en route, and Hawai`i was a most convenient place. Even if an enemy fleet recoaled at sea, it would subject itself to attack from American forces based in Hawai`i. The canal protection role of Hawai`i was far less important than its role in coastal defense or as a concentration point for the fleet. California bases, closer to the isthmus than Hawai`i, were much more important to canal defense.[84] And in the early 1890s, it was not certain that the French would finish their canal, much less that America would have its own.

Hawai`i's potential role in protecting the Pacific coast was for a great many people the most compelling reason for acquiring the islands, especially given the sad state of American coast defenses. Naval expansion was closely linked to the major effort to modernize coastal fortifications, and both were related to the coastal defense aspects of Hawaiian annexation. These topics should be studied together, but no studies of Hawaiian annexation or American expansion discuss in detail the interconnection between coastal security and the drive to improve seaboard defenses. It is all too easy to view fortifications separately, as an anachronism that, until finally abandoned after World War II, drained money for over half a century from more worthy military endeavors. But an examination of the strength and duration of the effort to improve coastal fortifications casts much light on naval rebuilding and the acquisition of certain strategic places among which Hawai`i was far and away the most important. More than anything else, the huge fortification effort illuminates American fears for coastal defense.

The same circumstances that underlay naval expansion—the need to cope with advances in technology coupled with post–Civil War neglect—underlay the movement to improve coastal fortifications. Advances in naval technology complicated harbor defense. Civil War–era fortifications were as obsolete as wooden ships. Modern naval guns could destroy these casemated forts (masonry fortifications with smoothbore guns firing from casemates, or alcoves within the outer walls). Nor could smoothbores seriously damage armored ships. Steam power made it easier to penetrate harbor defenses because the warships could ignore the wind, make swift course changes to disrupt the aim of shore gunners, and cut their transit time past the defensive batteries. Once into unprotected inner waters, such as the Chesapeake or San Francisco bays, hostile warships could wreak havoc. If an enemy laid off the coast and bombarded the shore, speed made the steam warships harder to hit. More powerful munitions made bombardment more destructive. Longer range guns allowed longer stand-off distances and, if enemy warships closed the coast, significantly increased the amount of valuable (nonmilitary) real estate under threat, particularly in older seaports built near open water. Another advantage of naval gunfire was the ship's ability to position itself for maximum advantage, whereas shore-based guns were nearly always immobile.

Naval gunnery had some inherent disadvantages. Gunners had to compensate for forward movement of the ship and, especially, the ship's roll, aiming the guns and then waiting for the ship to roll back to the same point before firing. By World War I rangefinders and gunnery sights improved dramatically, but in the 1890s accuracy was still low, particularly as range increased.

Turret and gun design limited the range of naval gunfire. Naval architects preferred to mount the heavy guns in the center of the turret because rotating the turret was easier the closer the gun's center of gravity lay to the turret's. When the gun elevated, the barrel rose through an opening in the turret roof. Because this opening represented an unarmored weak spot, designers limited the gun's potential angle of elevation to minimize the opening. But the less the gun could elevate, the shorter the range. Therefore, naval gunfire tended to be line-of-sight, direct fire with a customary range of two to three miles. The same gun mounted ashore could elevate to 45 degrees, allowing much greater range. Hence, shore-based guns were more accurate and longer ranged. Complaints about coastal vulnerability to foreign warships emerged not from the superiority of naval gunfire to shore gunfire but from a dearth of modern shore fortifications, a flaw magnified by inadequate naval forces to clear coastal waters.

After the Civil War, Congress paid scant attention to the implications of technological change for coastal defense. With no obvious threat of a foreign invasion and occupation, few sought a costly makeover of coastal fortifications. Congress failed to appropriate enough money even to maintain the old system. By 1885 the decay of defenses coupled with the modernization of foreign navies set enough alarm bells ringing in Washington and in the country at large that the politicians knew something had to be done. In older American ports like New York, there was simply too much valuable property close to the water. Even in newer ports, a warship could do great damage if it entered the inner harbor. A tremendous amount of developed real estate lay within the range (10,000–12,000 meters) of modern naval guns. The Senate Committee on Coastal Defenses estimated that a fleet penetrating New York harbor would endanger $4 billion of property. More than $10 billion of property lay exposed at the 27 principal American ports.[85]

During his first term, Cleveland, who, like Tilden, hailed from the state with the port—New York City—with the most to lose from naval attack, named Secretary of War William Endicott to lead an examination of coast defense modernization. The Endicott Board recommended a huge construction program. Some thirteen hundred weapons should be installed in new style forts at twenty-nine ports. To entice American steelmakers and gunsmiths to modernize rapidly, the board suggested spending $8 million on procurement immediately—more than twenty times the current, miniscule fortification budget. The plan called for $21 million the first year and $9 million annually until the system was complete.

The Endicott plan was so sweeping, and so expensive—more than $100 million over its life—that the scheme took not ten but twenty years to complete. And improvement came slowly in the beginning. Congress allocated only an average of $1.5 million a year until 1894 and about $4 million in 1895.[86] Politics sometimes interfered. Most Americans were willing to spend money to defend against invasion and conquest, but outside the seaboard states, some politicians felt little urgency about protecting what they saw as the seafront property of the wealthy. When states petitioned Congress to fund the Endicott system, nearly all the appeals came from coastal states.[87]

Congress also worried that the new technology was immature. Why spend money until the United States had the capability to design and fabricate the weapons? Continued advances in gun technology, permitting fewer guns to achieve the desired effect, delayed implementation as engineers revised their plans. Industrialists slowly mastered the manufacture of high-quality steel, learned to machine breech-loading rifled guns, and invented proper gun carriages. These tasks were more difficult than many outsiders appreciated. The Army's ordnance chief, summoned to testify on the development of "disappearing" gun carriages, newly invented mechanisms that allowed crews to load a gun below a berm, out of sight from the sea, and then briefly raise the gun to fire, tried to make a Senate committee understand his difficulties:

> To us sitting here, it sounds very simple to say that we will make a disappearing carriage for a 12-inch gun, but when you remember that it means to put sixty or seventy tons up on arms [as high as] where this ceiling is; that when the gun is fired there is a crash somewhat equivalent to the ram of a big ship; that it all has to be so delicately balanced as to meet this pressure; that the gun must then come down and lie on this table and let you load it; and that by turning a lever it must go back and be in a position to be fired, you see that it is not a simple problem.[88]

Some legislators simply could not grasp the implications of new technology. At an 1896 hearing, Army chief Nelson Miles testified: "While there are guns . . . in the harbor of San Francisco, they are mostly obsolete guns mounted on old and rotten carriages, I doubt if they would make any impression whatsoever on the armor of ships, as men now fight from behind 10 to 15 inches of steel plate. . . . Smooth-bore, short range guns would be useless." Senator Joseph Hawley, evidently not having believed Miles' testimony, listened to Senator Stephen White tell a later witness that old smoothbores "are of no account." Hawley retorted that they "could do considerable damage to a ship." Another senator reminded him Miles considered the guns worthless. Senator Hawley: "If they could be fired at proper range they would be effective enough."[89]

Why did such skepticism persist in 1896, years after reams of technical studies showed smoothbores could not hurt armored vessels? Perhaps it was politics, perhaps parsimony. Most likely people such as Hawley simply could not grasp that the smoothbores so useful earlier in their own lifetimes were now not worth salvaging the metal. A few members of Congress, if not stupid, had their heads in the sand. If an invasion fleet appeared off the coast, trumpeted Missouri's Francis

Cockrell, "the people of this great country . . . would rise en masse, men, women, and children to defend the honor of this great country, and all the nations of the earth know it."[90] One wonders what tactics the children would use against battleships.

Part of the reason that seaboard fortification proceeded slowly lay in the distinction between *port* defense and *seaboard* defense. Seaboard defense was simultaneously impossible and not worth worrying about. Army Chief of Engineers John Wilson: "When it is considered that the aggregate length of the coast of the United States . . . is 5,715 miles, and that more than 700 towns and villages on this extensive line can be attacked by ships drawing 10 feet of water, the practical impossibility of immediately and adequately defending every vulnerable point becomes readily apparent."[91] Defending every mile would have been impossibly expensive. And unnecessary. No power except Britain could land sizable forces and resupply them. Therefore, *port* defense was more important and more achievable than defense of the entire seaboard. America need only defend points "important by reason of their wealth and population or of their strategical situation."[92] Port cities contained the valuable real estate that naval raids put at risk. Through those ports American exports flowed and imports arrived. Port defenses allowed the Navy to range freely, protect the coast indirectly by destroying the enemy at sea, and ensure that the Navy could rely on the ports' shipyards, dry docks, gun factories, and coal supplies. The Endicott plan aimed to guard vital ports but not the whole coast.

Alas, nearly all vital ports, including Washington, D.C., Baltimore, Philadelphia, New Orleans, Puget Sound, San Diego, and Norfolk, remained unprotected. Not a single modern gun protected those ports, testified General Miles in 1896.[93] Just two months earlier, Miles wrote that the British could burn Washington in 1895 as easily as they did in 1812.[94] As war with Spain approached in spring 1898, coastal security fears surged when Admiral Pascual Cervera's flotilla prepared to transit from Spain. The public outcry compelled the Navy to order a "Flying Squadron" under Admiral William Schley to the Chesapeake Bay to engage Cervera if he descended on the helpless East Coast.[95] The Flying Squadron consisted of the battleships *Massachusetts* and *Texas*, the armored cruiser *Brooklyn*, and the protected cruisers *Minneapolis* and *Columbia*. These ships represented a lot of combat power needlessly detached from the main war effort in the Caribbean. The Navy had to create another special unit, the Northern Patrol Squadron, built around unarmored cruisers, to patrol from Maine to Delaware. Continued fears of coastal attack forced the Navy to mold a useless collection of ancient monitors, gun-toting tugboats, and yachts-turned-privateer into a New

York Auxiliary Force. On April 29 Cervera sortied from the Cape Verde Islands and promptly disappeared. Panic gripped the East Coast until his flotilla appeared off Martinique on May 14. Schley's muscular Flying Squadron finally could be shifted south to Cuban waters.[96]

During the run-up to war, these coastal fears led Congress to dramatically increase fortification funding. From just under $8 million in 1896 and roughly $10 million in 1897, the appropriation zoomed to $35 million in 1898. Appropriations in these three years constituted 53 percent of the Endicott funding. Congress completed the Endicott system at the end of Teddy Roosevelt's presidency. Fortification engineers built low, thick concrete bunkers and installed behind them some three hundred rifled 8-, 10-, and 12-inch guns on the "disappearing" carriages. About four hundred 12-inch mortars backed up the heavy guns. Floating harbor defense batteries and minefields augmented the forts, with swift torpedo boats and rapid-fire guns to keep the enemy from sweeping the minefields or landing troops nearby. To improve command and control, the Army formed the seacoast defense units into the Coastal Defense Artillery. The Army added enhancements such as rangefinders, sophisticated aiming systems, telephone communications, and powered ammunition handlers. A scholar of the fortification drive concluded that by World War I, the United States possessed "a system of harbor defenses unexcelled by those of any other nation."[97]

This was still not enough safety margin for many Americans, so the improvement drive continued, albeit more slowly. After 1910 technology once again began to make the existing fortifications obsolete. Improvements in the design of guns, turrets, ammunition, and aiming devices greatly increased the range at which warships could deliver highly accurate fire. Instead of the relatively short-range "line-of-sight" fire of the 1890s, long-range fire was "plunging fire." High arcing shells fell at steep angles onto coast artillery no longer safe behind thick concrete walls. Engineers turned to mobile artillery on rails or towed by tractors. Another tactic—"protective dispersal"—quit the forts entirely and widely spaced the guns so the enemy could not concentrate fire.

The high-water mark for defensive forts may have been reached in Hawai`i. In the 1920s, engineers fabricated the most powerful cannon ever built in the United States. The Army installed at Pearl Harbor two Model M-1919 16-inch cannon, so gigantic that each barrel weighed two hundred tons. Firing one-ton projectiles twenty-eight miles, these monsters could reach enemy ships far off the south coast of O`ahu and nearby waters around the entire island.[98] The Japanese attack on Hawai`i on December 7, 1941, briefly spurred another building program, but tacticians soon realized that air power sounded the death knell of fixed harbor fortifications.

Those who argued the vulnerability of the coasts never spoke about invasion and occupation by any power except Britain. They talked about attacks, bombardments, and raids but not the landing of troops for extended operations ashore. Only Britain possessed that capability: a strong navy and army and bases and coaling stations in Bermuda, Halifax, Jamaica, Esquimalt, and other locales. When the Spanish-American War began, the U.S. Navy had but 6 battleships afloat. The British Navy was ten times bigger, with 54 battleships and 104 cruisers. Thus, asked what would happen if the U.S. Navy engaged the British fleet, Admiral Walker's words represented the collective wisdom of his peers: "They would probably capture or destroy our whole Navy."[99] Britain's naval power was so great that Americans hoped Britain would be deterred from war by the probability of losing Canada to a ground assault.

Regarding raids off the coast as well as operations ashore, a look at German war planning shows the difficulty of mounting a major operation against the United States without access to a midocean recoaling base. After the Samoan incident of 1889, the Anglo-American war scare over the Venezuelan boundary, and the increasing American involvement in what the Germans considered a fellow European power's proper business with its rebellious Cuban colony, Germany began to watch American policy more closely.

An incident in Manila six weeks after Dewey's victory heightened Admiralty dislike of the American upstart. Several European nations sent warships to the Philippines to observe the war, but the Germans hoped to take a naval base or two by working the margins of the eventual peace settlement. In an eight-day period in mid-June 1898, Vice Admiral Otto von Diederichs gathered at Manila five armored cruisers. For what purpose, wondered Admiral George Dewey, would Germany assemble a force equal to his own blockading squadron? Dewey's rigorous inspections of ships entering blockaded waters led to petty incidents and, finally, a blow-up over an inspection of the German cruiser *Irene*. Von Diederichs sent his flag lieutenant to the *Olympia* to complain to the unmannerly Americans. One thing led to another, and Dewey's famously explosive temper . . . exploded: "Why, I shall stop each vessel whatever may be her colors! And if she does not stop, I shall fire at her! And that means war, do you know, sir? And I tell you, if Germany wants war, all right, we are ready."[100] This sort of rancor in German–American relations stimulated the first serious war planning against the United States.

During 1897–1902, German officers wrote war plans outlining an attack on the East Coast. In his detailed study of German planning, Holger Herwig concludes, "the possibility of war was very much in the minds of some of Germany's leading naval officers." Contingency plans "formed the basis for, and reflected the direction of, official Admiralty planning."[101] Before Manila Bay, the Supreme Command ordered Lieutenant Eberhard von Mantey to write a war plan against the United States. The Mantey plan and its subsequent revisions revealed the difficulties of invading the United States that foreign war planners throughout the 1890s would have recognized. The same von Diederichs who provoked Dewey became Mantey's boss in late 1898. With von Diederichs' prodding, Mantey sketched an attack on New York that assumed a 1900 time frame, though his seniors soon shifted the invasion site to the less risky Cape Cod region. He estimated that the United States would have seven battleships, fourteen armored cruisers, and fourteen unarmored cruisers. The German fleet would need at least one-third superiority to defeat the American fleet, and at least a two to one ship advantage to land an army corps while simultaneously coping with the U.S. Navy. A fleet that size—seventeen battleships and thirty-three cruisers—would consume three thousand tons of coal per day, requiring a resupply chain of forty to sixty freighters just for the coal. (Mantey ignored what surely would have been an even more immense logistical tail to maintain the army corps in Massachusetts, apparently assuming that the troops could live off the land or coerce supplies from the inhabitants.) Lacking an Atlantic coaling station, the German fleet would transit to New England via the neutral Azores, where, in another risky assumption, coal would be available. Even refueling in the Azores meant shorter-range ships would have to be towed part of the way.

A review by General Alfred von Schlieffen, chief of the General Staff, infused reality into the war planning. Walking a tightrope between Admiral von Diederichs' desire to get approval for Mantey's revised plan for a 100,000-soldier invasion and the Kaiser's nutty suggestion that the best way to do it was send 50,000 Germans to seize Cuba as a staging area, von Schlieffen cautioned that an army corps was barely enough to control eastern Massachusetts, much less undertake inland operations. He worried too that the Cubans might resist the Germans. (He had the grace not to call to the Kaiser's attention that 190,000 Spanish troops under "The Butcher" Valeriano Weyler failed to beat the Cuban rebels.) Although the American Army was much smaller than the proposed German landing force, von Schlieffen gently hinted that invasion might provoke the angered Americans to mobilize far greater numbers.[102] Even for a strong military power such as Germany, conquest of the United States was impossible in the 1890s. German war planning demonstrated that a midocean recoaling station was essential, and that the larger the U.S. Navy, the smaller the chances for German success. This was precisely the argument by American advocates of naval expansion and Hawaiian annexation.

If invasion were ruled out for all but Britain, raids were not. In the Atlantic, much smaller than the Pacific, even a midrate sea power could inflict damage, bombarding ports, cutting off foreign commerce, and ravaging coastwise trade until the Navy could concentrate against the raiders. Such a raid might be a card to play in a diplomatic dispute. Even the threat of a raid might influence American policy or naval deployments, as in the Cervera incident.[103] Numerous newspaper scare stories—two of the most vivid had the Chilean armored warship *Prat* bombarding San Francisco during an 1891 bilateral dispute, or British battleships destroying New York City during the Anglo-American dispute over the Venezuelan boundary—focused on raids, not on conquest.[104] Senator Joseph Dolph of Oregon declared that in a future war with Britain, the Pacific coast would be quickly raided because of its defenseless condition and the dearth of American warships in the Pacific. He put into the *Congressional Record* a bit of lurid war fiction about the destruction of San Francisco by British armored warships.[105] Senator John Wilson of Washington asserted that in less than twelve hours an enemy, obviously Britain in this case, could devastate $100 million of property on Puget Sound.[106] Senator Watson Squire of Washington, Senator Stephen White of California, and Representative Marion de Vries of California joined other westerners in decrying the defenseless condition of their coast and demanding that the Congress beef up coastal defenses.[107] Squire chaired the Senate Committee on Coastal Defenses; White served on and later headed the same committee. For westerners, the bulk of the New Navy was two months away in the North Atlantic. Admiral Walker testified that without the battleship *Oregon*, then nearing completion in San Francisco, the United States possessed less Pacific naval power than Chile.[108] Even in 1898 the Navy had in the Pacific less than half Britain's tonnage and only a quarter of Japan's.[109]

Two important points emerge from an analysis of the coastal fortification drive. First, although naval expansionists sometimes saw modernization of fortifications as siphoning off scarce funds from ship construction, they also realized that strong port defenses unleashed the Navy to seek out an enemy fleet. The Cervera scare and the consequent diversion of significant naval assets away from the main point of attack in the Caribbean was dramatic proof to Mahan that the human and emotional elements of national defense made port fortifications essential. In his 1899 collection of essays, *Lessons of the Naval War with Spain*, he advocated strong port fortifications to keep hysteria from compromising naval strategy.[110]

Second, and most important, the continued attention, stretching over more than a half century after the 1886 Endicott report, to modernize coastal fortifications shows the strength and depth of fears of raids on the coasts. Against this rich context of real, deeply rooted concern for coastal security, the claims that expanding the New Navy and annexing Hawai`i would enhance coastal defense look quite reasonable. Indeed the slowness with which these fears dissipated—not until 1950 did the Defense Department merge the last harbor defense commands into the Artillery Branch—explains much about persistence of the modernization movement. Surely there was exaggeration in the speeches about foreign warships ravaging defenseless ports. But exaggeration and unfounded political argument could not have impelled several decades of expensive modernization. Coastal defense concerns were not just talked about. They were genuine—the coast could indeed have been raided by a determined enemy—and spurred concrete policy actions for many years. In this atmosphere, the nation considered the annexation of Hawai`i, which Mahan and others asserted would greatly augment American security and make the West Coast safe from attack.

Many people besides Mahan understood Hawai`i's strategic value. Their collective judgment was that Hawai`i was the single-most important strategic feature in the Pacific. From Hawai`i the Navy could protect the West Coast. It could intercept enemy fleets far from American shores. If the islands had not existed, an enemy fleet with 1890s coal-fired technology would not have posed a serious threat to the coast, but since they did exist, they must be controlled by the United States. In 1893–94, this belief was already so widespread that the antiannexationist Cleveland administration deployed naval forces to prevent any foreign meddling after the revolution and during the creation of the Republic of Hawai`i. This heightened sensitivity to Hawai`i's role in coastal security made it certain that if a threat to Hawaiian independence emerged, the United States would react strongly.

Mahan's writings contributed to another strong reaction, one that affected him personally. His March 1893 *Forum* article trumpeting the strategic rationale for annexation hit newsstands in Washington just as Cleveland withdrew the annexation treaty from the Senate and sent James Blount to investigate the genesis of the tainted pact. Unwittingly—stupidly—Mahan placed himself squarely athwart the new administration's policy. He was on the wrong side of the line separating what serving naval officers might say—in his case, should *not* have said—about current policy. Mahan's nemesis, Commodore Francis Ramsay, chief of the Bureau of Navigation, sent him back to the sea duty he abhorred.[111]

His final command led to unpleasantness but also a good deal of satisfaction. By this time, Mahan had lost all interest in the running of a ship. He distanced himself from his duties, turning over as much as possible to his executive officer and doing less than the recommended amount of handholding of the salty old Admiral Henry Erben, the squadron commander whose flagship (the ABC cruiser *Chicago*) Mahan commanded on their cruise to Europe. Mahan attempted to configure his quarters as a study and arrange his day to allow reading and writing from morning to early afternoon, but the demands of the ship intruded. Writing from the mid-Atlantic, he told his wife, Elly: "I have tried to do some reading since we left, but the interruptions are numerous."[112] The petty details of managing the flagship were worth less of his time than the details of, say, Trafalgar, from which one might infer a practical lesson or even a principle. Accordingly, how could Mahan, one of the Navy's most senior captains, commanding one of the Navy's newest warships, *not* have problems with Admiral Erben, whose easy, confident command style and devotion to duties contrasted so sharply with Mahan's? Erben wrote two damning fitness reports, which Mahan buried by calling in political favors from men such as Roosevelt and Lodge.

At last, Mahan's ego had its reward. His books were even more popular in Europe than at home. He was lionized by the European media and high society. He sniffed in a letter to Luce that his *Chicago* tour had turned out to be "one of the luckiest things . . . a boomerang for all that wished me ill."[113] By the time he retired in 1896 Mahan had become the symbol of a strategic rationale for naval modernization and expansion, and for the acquisition of key points necessary for coastal defense in the Age of Steam. He and the other navalists had discovered Hawai`i's immense strategic value in modern warfare. In this rich strategic context, the United States considered Hawaiian annexation in 1897–98.

❧

CHAPTER 12

The Republican Party Embraces Annexation

D uring the final years of Cleveland's presidency, Congress supplanted the executive as the prime mover in Hawaiian policy. Republicans used a strong Hawaiian policy to differentiate their foreign policy from that of the Democrats. Until 1893 party stances on Hawaiian affairs had not been so different. It had been Grover Cleveland, after all, who extended reciprocity in 1887 by incorporating the Pearl Harbor clause. But Cleveland's inept restoration attempt, and the Democratic Congress' fumbling defense of it, dramatized party differences. During 1894–96, Republicans embraced annexation or a strong protectorate as they became the majority party. In 1894 Republicans won both houses and added the presidency in 1896.

Three themes characterized the congressional debates.[1] The first was the maturing appreciation for Hawai`i's immense strategic value. The second was Japan's emergence as an imperialist power in the Sino-Japanese War of 1894–95. Even Democrats worried about Japan. John Pendleton asserted that Japan was preparing for future wars and urged the United States to do the same.[2] Amos Cummings concluded: "The Yalu [River battle] will live in history at the side of Trafalgar. Let us heed well the lesson."[3] Henry Cabot Lodge, close to Mahan, Roosevelt, and other strategic thinkers, sought to "expose the Japanese threat." He asserted that Japan endangered American control of Hawai`i. The great Japanese victory at the Yalu River showed they were a "great fighting race at sea." They ordered from British shipyards two 14,000-ton battleships, bigger than any American warship. Lodge continued: "Remember . . . they have just whipped somebody, and . . . they think they can whip anybody."[4] A threatening Japan seemed intent on destroying the Asian and Pacific balance of power. Many Republican speakers thought Hawai`i must be annexed and the Navy enlarged to meet the Japanese head-on.[5]

The apprehensions about Japan fed into the third theme: continued bipartisan support for naval expansion. In 1895 Congress authorized two battleships, six gunboats, and three torpedo boats; in 1896 three more battleships, and twenty torpedo boats.[6] Politicians named coastal security as the chief reason for naval expansion, followed by protection of the proposed isthmian canal and commercial interests abroad.[7]

Most members, regardless of party, desired a bigger navy. Opponents did not question the need for a strong navy but objected to what Senator George Gray called "breathless haste."[8] Gray wanted two rather than three battleships in 1896. Senator William Chandler, who as Arthur's naval secretary presided over the beginnings of naval expansion and modernization, expressed the views of most senators: "We all agree . . . in naval construction. Both parties are patriotically inclined in that direction. . . . It is a mere practical question as to whether we shall construct three battleships at this time, or two, or none at all."[9]

By now, Mahanian doctrines were widely accepted in both parties. John Pendleton declared that "sea power gives empire and victory." He announced that he recently read Mahan's first sea power book.[10] Hernando Money supported "the old salts of the Naval Committee" instead of the dissents of "landlubbers and fresh-water sailors" like "Sockless" Jerry Simpson, a Populist representative from Kansas. Money said the Yalu River engagement proved Mahan's dictum that battleships were a navy's fighting heart. He lectured on naval strategy, the naval lessons of the Sino-Japanese War, and the value of armor-piercing shells.[11] Navalists saw the fleet as a vital part of a grand strategy to build national security, strength, and prestige. History's lessons, they believed, taught that national greatness came only to nations possessed of strong navies, vigorous people, and strategic redoubts, such as Gibraltar, Malta, and Hawai`i.[12]

Despite a strong appreciation for Hawai`i's military value, a shared desire for naval expansion, and a common regard for Japanese power, the parties disagreed whether Cleveland was adequately safeguarding the islands. Late in 1894 Congress learned the administration had withdrawn the *Philadelphia*. Despite the Republican sweep of the midterm elections, the Democratically controlled Congress' third session would continue until March 1895. Feisty Republicans raised a great outcry about the *Philadelphia*'s withdrawal. Lodge charged that "Cleveland and Gresham may at any moment make some fatal concession which we can never recover."[13] By removing the cruiser, Cleveland subverted the Turpie "hands off" resolution of the previous spring. The islands were invaluable both "commercially, and still more from a military point of view," Lodge said, and no one will "interfere with us there."[14]

A Lodge demand for the administration's correspondence with Admiral Walker passed the Senate on January 7, 1895, 33–12 with 40 not voting. Many Democrats abstained because their belief in Hawai`i's strategic importance made them unwilling to block the resolution. They knew that they would pay a price should something happen to Hawai`i while no U.S. warship was present. The publication of Walker's recommendation that strong forces be permanently stationed in Honolulu made the *Philadelphia*'s withdrawal look rash.[15]

Precisely in the midst of this uproar came the news of an attempted royalist counterrevolution. Despite restoration's failure, royalists had still nurtured hopes for a return of the monarchy. In late 1894 royalist emissaries failed to get the United States and Europe to push for the queen's return. With no peaceful way out, some royalists plotted an uprising and imported arms. Despite heavy surveillance and police questioning, they kept their plans mostly secret. Perhaps 400–500 men affiliated themselves with the revolt of January 6, 1895. The police and military forces of the republic outnumbered the royalists and were better trained and motivated. Over several days, the government crushed the rebellion, killing a few and capturing a couple of hundred, including Robert Wilcox and Samuel Nowlein. Police found rifles, pistols, and some small bombs buried in the queen's garden. A military court tried 191 persons and convicted roughly a third. Most received suspended sentences, but the queen, Wilcox, Nowlein and others were confined until Dole pardoned them six months later.[16]

Senator James Kyle crafted a bill requiring that the administration send at least one warship to Honolulu. Debate produced the same old strategic arguments and familiar Democratic claims that the Republicans sought only to embarrass the administration.[17] The Democrats stifled the Kyle resolution but could not snuff out the larger Hawaiian debate.[18]

The climax came on March 2, 1895. On that final day of Democratic control, Lodge delivered a great address illustrating the close connection between annexation and U.S. security. After six years in the House and two in the Senate, the forty-four-year-old Lodge had forged a reputation as an aggressive expansionist and snobby intellectual. Born to wealth in a blue-blooded Massachusetts family, he had both a law degree and PhD from Harvard. He mixed his whole life with true intellectuals, like his teacher Henry Adams, and with brainy men of action, like his soul mate Theodore Roosevelt. Cabot Lodge—never Henry—had vivid blue eyes, a stylish Vandyke beard, and a jarring soprano voice. Ostensibly pushing a bill for an undersea cable to Hawai`i, Lodge delivered "by far the most successful speech I ever made in Congress."[19] Symbolic of the direction of the incoming Republican majority, Lodge's speech attracted great interest. Senators and representatives came in from the cloakrooms. Even messengers, pages, and doorkeepers entered the chamber to listen.[20]

As he began to speak, assistants propped up a huge world map marked with bold red Maltese crosses to show the locations of British naval bases and coaling stations. Standing before the great map, with dramatic flourishes of a wooden pointer, Lodge outlined Hawai`i's incalculable military value. He echoed Mahan: "Without the sea power no nation has been really great. Sea power consists ... of a proper navy and a proper fleet but ... to sustain a navy we must have suitable posts for naval stations, strong places where a navy can be protected and refurbished." The British Navy had such bases, and the dancing pointer touched Halifax, Bermuda, Jamaica, the Falkland Islands, all British bases in the Atlantic. In the Pacific, the pointer touched Fiji, Vancouver, and many others. Tapping the map, Lodge said: "There in the center ... in the heart of the Pacific, ... lie the Sandwich Islands. They are the key to the Pacific."[21]

Senator Richard Pettigrew interrupted, asking how the Navy could prevent British warships from seizing Hawai`i. The atmosphere was tense and charged with emotion: senators and gallery watchers shifted in their seats. Lodge began to speak but Senator Marion Butler loudly complained that he could not hear. The Senate floor was in an uproar; the chair admonished Pettigrew for interrupting and ordered all senators to stop talking and resume their seats. Lodge continued: "It is on account of the military and strategic importance of the Sandwich Islands that I so greatly desire their control." Hawai`i lay astride the trade routes to the Far East as well as the approaches to the canal. "The control of these great points in the highways of commerce is the control of the sea power." Lodge concluded with a patriotic, nationalist call: "We are a great people; we control this continent; we are dominant in this hemisphere ... We do not want too great a rival posted too near our coasts." It would be madness to "throw away" those islands. As Lodge sat down, senators thronged around him, cheering and trying to shake his hand.[22]

Lodge's speech demonstrated that annexation had become a party matter. When the 54th Congress convened in December 1895, Republicans controlled each chamber. Second, Lodge's speech showed strategic factors now dominated the annexation debate. Most legislators viewed Japan as a potential threat to

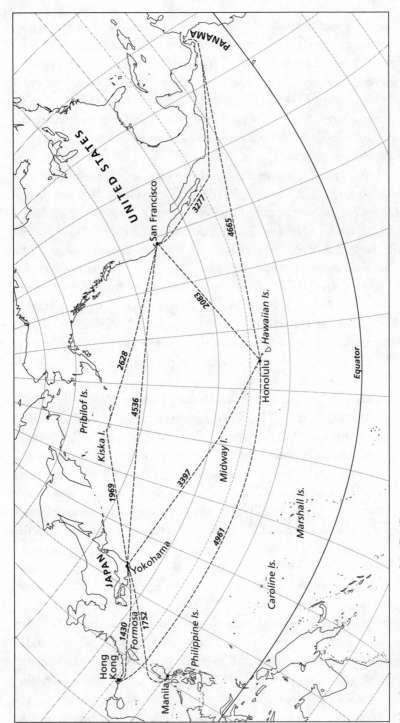

Map 2. Lodge's strategic map of the Pacific

Hawai`i and, therefore, to U.S. security. If that threat ever became more concrete, the Republican Congress would surely react.

In the presidential election of 1896 Republicans embraced an assertive foreign policy: Hawai`i, isthmian canal, Caribbean bases, strong Navy, and coastal defenses. These were the interlocking strategic building blocks advocated for years by the navalists. These themes were ends in themselves, not steps toward further overseas expansion. The 1896 platform stated: "The Hawaiian Islands should be controlled by the United States, and no foreign Power should be permitted to interfere with them." The platform endorsed "control," which could mean a strong protectorate as well as annexation because the party was not yet of one mind whether annexation was necessary to preserve American preeminence.[23]

Along with the strategic rationale for annexation, commercial factors played a key role as well.[24] Like strategic factors, commercial factors were deeply rooted in the past. After the United States expanded to the Pacific, Secretary of State William Marcy imagined in 1853 that the "intercourse between our Pacific ports and the ports of the distant East is destined perhaps to be upon as large a scale as that we now enjoy with all the world, and the vessels engaged in that trade must ever resort to the ports of the Sandwich Islands."[25]

Tremendous economic growth in the late nineteenth century and restrictive trade policies in old markets suggested a need for new markets. Hawai`i, astride transpacific routes, was a logical stopping point for ships bound for the Orient. Some expansionists argued Hawai`i would be a naval base guarding trade routes, thereby pointing to the strategic significance of commerce protection. In fact, annexation was not required to permit merchant ships to stop at Hawai`i on the way to Asia, nor required to deploy warships to cruise the sea-lanes in peacetime. However, many people missed this distinction and lumped the two arguments— strategic and commercial—together. If they believed Hawai`i would help trade, the argument influenced them, true or not. It was claimed that the economy produced so many more goods than the country could absorb that the excess drove prices down and caused depressions. Increased exports were the answer. Some thought China's multitudes were potential buyers. That the 1890s China market was miniscule, mainly because the Chinese were too poor to consume, made little difference. Until after the Spanish-American War, the China market was more myth than reality, but the myth helped drive behavior.[26]

Ideological developments reinforced the annexation drive. Foremost among these was social Darwinism, the name given to ideas of Herbert Spencer and other thinkers who applied to human society Darwin's theory of the evolution of biological species. Social Darwinism had many vociferous U.S. adherents who misapplied Darwinian ideas to the international scene. They reasoned that nations, like biological organisms, were subject to the laws of natural selection. A nation either progressed or decayed; there was no middle ground. To survive, a nation must compete vigorously with other nations or be swallowed up. The lesson? National power and security depended upon a vigorous, expansive foreign policy.[27] A nation could not stand still; it must grow or die.[28] European imperialism illustrated social Darwinism's prescription for growth. In the last third of the nineteenth century, Africa had been divided by European imperialists; much of Asia met a similar fate. Strife and growth seemed everywhere in the real world, not just in Spencer's theories. In his famous 1899 call to arms, *The Strenuous Life*, Theodore Roosevelt declared: "If we stand idly by, if we seek merely swollen, slothful ease and ignoble peace, if we shrink from the hard contests where men must win at hazard of their lives and at the risk of all they hold dear, then the bolder and stronger peoples will pass us by, and will win for themselves the dominion of the world."[29] Captain Mahan declared that annexation of Hawai`i should be a "first fruit," a "token" in the battle for Pacific supremacy.[30]

Because social Darwinism encouraged the view that some races were stronger than others, it was related to Anglo-Saxonism, a race patriotism that lauded the supposed inherent superiority of Anglo-Saxons. Charles Darwin himself had written that there was "much truth in the belief that the wonderful progress of the United States, as well as the character of her people, are the results of natural selection."[31] Similarly, the Reverend Josiah Strong, in his enormously popular 1885 book *Our Country*, spoke of "the final competition of races for which the Anglo-Saxon is being schooled." Strong predicted "this powerful race will move down upon Mexico, down upon Central and South America, out upon the islands of the sea, over upon Africa and beyond. And can anyone doubt that the result of this competition of races will be the 'survival of the fittest'?"[32] Cushman K. Davis, chairman of the Senate Foreign Relations Committee, wrote that "Slavonic, Teutonic, Latin, and that composite people known as the Anglo-Saxon" were beginning a fierce competition after which England and the United States—"the old mother and her big boy"—would dominate the world "as Gibraltar dominates the straits."[33] While many expansionists still regarded Britain as a potential enemy, Anglo-Saxonism led them to see the mother country as a model.[34] Thus Alfred Thayer Mahan wrote that Britain had become the world's greatest power by a "step-by-step" acquisition of strategic spots such as Hawai`i. Annexation would give the United States a leg up in the struggle for supremacy.[35]

Social Darwinism and Anglo-Saxonism contributed to the enlarged sense of American destiny so common among expansionists.[36] If Anglo-Saxons were superior, was it not their duty to serve as teachers of the less-endowed races, such as Native Hawaiians? One expansionist asked, "Are the borders of liberty to be circumscribed" by a failure to take Hawai`i?[37] A friend of Henry Cabot Lodge told him that annexation not only set the United States "on an immovable rook of prestige among nations" but was "uplifting and purifying our own national consciousness, and ensuring the permanence and universal spread of the principles of popular government."[38]

Gender beliefs added to the imperialist impulse, with respect to broader U.S. policy as well as Hawaiian annexation. The condescension with which John Stevens treated Queen Lili`uokalani is just one example. Native Hawaiians were often imagined as childlike, unformed and immature. Opponents of assertive policies could be characterized as effeminate. Some men's beliefs about what constituted manliness disposed them in their personal life to "the strenuous life," as Roosevelt put it, which prized muscular physicality like boxing, pursued by Roosevelt as well as his close friend, Henry Cabot Lodge, and to a foreign policy of activism and strong stands. Manliness infused Roosevelt's thinking: "The nation that has trained itself to a career of unwarlike and isolated ease is bound, in the end, to go down before other nations which have not lost the manly and adventurous qualities."[39] That a combat veteran like William McKinley could ever be successfully characterized as a timid old woman or a little fat man who lacked "backbone"— two famous political cartoon images—shows the importance of gender in foreign policy analysis.[40]

The election of 1896 gave McKinley the White House and solidified Republican majorities in Congress. Republicans won 204 House seats to 113 for the Democrats. In the 88-seat Senate, Republicans held a 47 to 34 margin over the Democrats; minor parties took 7 seats.[41] Crucially important was Republican control of committees that would deal with an annexation treaty or joint resolution.

Cushman Kellogg Davis chaired the Senate Foreign Relations Committee. Fifty-nine years old in 1897, Davis was a Civil War veteran. He was the law partner and relative of young Frank B. Kellogg, destined to become secretary of state for Calvin Coolidge. Davis served as governor of Minnesota in the 1870s and in 1886 entered the Senate. His biographer said Davis preferred to work behind the scenes and mainly spoke privately to other senators. Like a number of men who commanded troops, he appreciated military strategy. Napoleon fascinated Davis, whose study held a vast collection of books, coins, and other artifacts from Napoleon's time.[42] Despite his veneration for Britain's great enemy, he was a devout Anglo-Saxonist. In the hostile, imperialist world of the 1890s, England and the United States must "recognize common interest." He expected the two

Anglo-Saxon nations to dominate the world as Gibraltar dominated the straits, by virtue of "latent power" and acquisition of "commanding position." He saw the Pacific Basin as a great potential market, but he paid as much attention to intercoastal trade and to trade between the West Coast and Europe.[43] Security needs were paramount. Ownership of Hawaiʻi was "indispensable to the defense of our Pacific coasts."[44]

Davis' counterpart in the House was sixty-three-year-old Robert Hitt of Illinois. Hitt had a first-rate mind and a remarkable appearance, with a thick, droopy Fu Manchu mustache that completely dominated his face. As a young reporter Hitt covered the 1858 Lincoln–Douglas debates. Because Hitt took short-hand, he recorded the debates accurately, which Lincoln noticed. Once, when Hitt arrived late, Lincoln refused to speak until the young Illinoisan appeared, saying only Hitt could correctly record the remarks. Hitt became Lincoln's White House stenographer. After the war, Hitt served as assistant to Senator Oliver Morton. In 1872 Morton arranged for Hitt's appointment as chief clerk of the Senate Committee on Privileges and Elections, an important position in Reconstruction days. Two years later Hitt went to Paris as the number two official in the embassy. In 1881 he became James G. Blaine's assistant secretary of state, then the number two position in the department. Hitt idolized Blaine. After Blaine's death, Hitt's study took on the look of a Blaine portrait gallery, containing more than a dozen paintings.[45]

After Garfield's assassination, Hitt won election to the House of Represent-atives, where he remained until his death in 1906. His closest friend in Washington was Speaker Tom Reed. Hitt was a tireless worker despite poor health, he made no enemies, and he had the reputation of a man whose word was his bond. Like Cushman Davis, he preferred to work behind the scenes. Like Davis, he was not a great orator—he was called the "Gentle Mr. Ah! Ah!" for always begin-ning his remarks with "Ah! Ah!"—but in his quiet way Hitt was very effective in forging Republican solidarity on diplomatic issues. His speeches combined tightly constructed arguments with blatant appeals to all camps and emotional, patriotic flag-waving. One auditor of Hitt's 1896 speech for recognition of Cuban belliger-ency evaluated his rhetoric well: "There are parts of it that cannot be parsed but it goes all the same."[46]

Hitt was an ardent annexationist. Shortly after McKinley's election, Hitt said that Republicans favored annexation to give the United States "a great naval port" for the defense of the West Coast and of American interests in the Pacific.[47] Hitt was not primarily concerned with economic or financial questions. When he learned in the spring of 1897 that the draft tariff bill contained provisions that, by violating the reciprocity treaty, might cost the United States the right to develop Pearl Harbor, he declared that mere "revenue" questions should not have priority over security needs.[48] "National defense is paramount," he asserted.[49]

A third important committee relating to annexation was the Senate's Select Committee on the Construction of the Nicaragua Canal, chaired by John Tyler Morgan. This is not as odd as it might seem at first glance, for expansionists linked annexation and canal construction. "These two matters are so closely related that the consideration of the canal proposition would at once suggest the other," a Hawaiian emissary noted.[50] A strong annexationist, Morgan served as a rallying point for annexationist Democrats and Populists.[51]

Pleas from relatives and friends buttressed Morgan's pro-annexation views. His cousin, Thomie Morgan, lived in Honolulu and often wrote to plead for annexation. During the 1897 Hawaiian–Japanese immigration confrontation, Thomie thanked the senator for "the good fight for annexation. . . . This is the burning question with us in Hawai`i at the present moment." She asked him to meet with Hawaiian diplomats and come to the islands to view the situation first-hand.[52] Morgan met the diplomats and led a delegation to Honolulu, returning with the entirely predictable conclusion that only annexation could save Hawai`i from Japan's clutches.[53] Close friends—including Zephaniah S. Spaulding, whose 1870 letter provoked the first American interest in Pearl Harbor—had long urged annexation.[54]

Finally, annexationists filled congressional leadership posts. The president pro tem of the Senate, William Frye, was a strong annexationist. So was Charles Grosvenor of Ohio, who led the House Republican Conference (caucus) and who was very close to McKinley. Grosvenor's deputy, Representative James Tawney, shared the annexationist views of fellow Minnesotan Cushman Davis.

While the Republican majorities and annexationist control of key leadership positions suggested fertile ground in Congress, two dark clouds loomed. First, Speaker Tom Reed opposed annexation. He might use his vast powers to block annexation by joint resolution. Reed's opposition suggested that a treaty, which would need only Senate approval, would be easier than a joint resolution.

Here was the second dark cloud: the Republicans could not approve a treaty by straight party vote. Ratification required sixty of ninety senators, and only forty-three of forty-seven Republicans were reliable party voters.[55] A treaty needed seventeen votes from among thirty-four Democrats and seven third-party sena-tors. Though almost two-thirds of the Senate supported annexation, a few more votes were needed. At a dinner for annexation supporters sponsored by Frank Hatch, including William Chandler, Mark Hanna, Cushman Davis, William

Frye, Redfield Proctor, Robert Hitt, John Watson Foster, and Admiral John G. Walker, most thought a joint resolution easier, despite Reed's opposition.[56]

Even with strong congressional support, the administration would have to initiate and lobby for a treaty or joint resolution. McKinley's intentions were therefore paramount. At fifty-four years of age, he was thick-bodied, thick-necked (his collars always appeared too tight), and, some wrongly said, thick-headed. He looked like a well-to-do, middle-aged banker: a handsome fellow with regal, intelligent features and flashing hazel eyes under bushy, graying eyebrows. But while McKinley's outer self was distinct and impressive, his inner self has never been satisfactorily explained. He left no body of evidence for historians to mine. He almost never wrote letters; neither his voluminous papers in the Library of Congress nor those of friends such as Mark Hanna or John Davis Long contain much written by McKinley. He kept no diary and wrote few memoranda. He relied on verbal orders, yet he was close-mouthed and often refused to take a position. His reply to a question about Cuba was vintage McKinley: "I must politely decline to go on record. At this time I do not care to speak about it. In my position it is better that I say nothing now. Perhaps later I may have something to say."[57]

McKinley's character was above reproach. He never cursed and occasionally rebuked those who did. He reserved Sunday for church and family obligations. When meeting citizens in the Oval Office, the childless McKinley invariably found a shy youngster in the group, pulled a flower from his button-hole, and presented it to the little one.[58] A charitable, sensitive man, he anonymously donated five thousand dollars for Cuban relief. He lavished attention on his semi-invalid wife and sometimes left cabinet meetings to see personally to her needs.[59]

McKinley's career was distinguished. He came from a poor family and dropped out of Allegeny College for lack of money as well as a lengthy illness. In 1861, at age eighteen, he enlisted as a private in the 23rd Ohio Infantry, later commanded by Rutherford B. Hayes. Resupplying frontline troops, he saw considerable action and soon made lieutenant. Commended for bravery under fire, he came out of the war a major at age twenty-two. Hayes called McKinley "one of the bravest and finest officers in the Army."[60] He gave up his Canton, Ohio, law practice in 1876 to win a House seat. Consistently spurning offers of under-the-table money, he lived off his federal salary. A master of tariff legislation, he authored the highly protectionist McKinley Tariff of 1890 that, by removing Hawaiian sugar's equality with domestic sugar, inflicted, to his regret, considerable damage on the Hawaiian economy. When Ohio's Democratic legislature gerrymandered his district, McKinley failed reelection in 1890 by three hundred votes. This turned out to be a blessing, for sympathetic Ohioans made him governor, the start of a steady rise to the White House. At the 1892 Republican convention, McKinley received a fifth of the first-round votes against the incumbent Harrison. Four years later he defeated William Jennings Bryan for the presidency. He was the last Civil War veteran to become president.

Close friends, such as his clever private secretary, George B. Cortelyou, and the capable Charles G. Dawes, comptroller of the Currency, thought him an excellent president. Even when McKinley was under fire, Dawes recorded: "The President, as always, remains the firm, cool, able leader of men.... In the greatness of McKinley the safety of the situation lies."[61] Henry Adams, who, as Walter LaFeber noted, said few nice things about anybody in power after 1828, believed that McKinley's "judgment of men was finer than common in Presidents," and thought he was a "marvelous manager of men."[62] Champ Clark said McKinley was one of the most gentle, modest, and gracious men in public life, a man who persuaded men to comply instead of compelling them, as Reed or Roosevelt might do.[63] These favorable views contrast sharply with Roosevelt's alleged statement that McKinley had no more backbone than a chocolate eclair, or a biographer's more judicious opinion that the president was a follower, not a leader.[64]

The truth lies somewhere between. McKinley was a reasonably good leader. He was not a charismatic, vocal, or inspirational leader, but McKinley possessed good leadership qualities. He did not allow events to stampede him into rash decisions. He was honest, moral, and fair in his dealings. He had a sense of priorities and thus concentrated on the most important problems, such as tariff reform, Cuban affairs, and Hawaiian annexation. McKinley's best leadership quality was his ability to work with talented subordinates and with senior congressional Republicans.

McKinley's top-level appointments were generally good, especially three closely connected with Hawaiian affairs. Secretary of the Navy John Davis Long was one of McKinley's first appointments. After graduating from Harvard Law School in 1861, Long spent many years as a lawyer. Elected to the Massachusetts legislature in 1874, his people skills were so obvious that he soon became speaker. In 1880 he served a term as governor and then three terms in the U.S. House of Representatives, where he became close to McKinley before returning to the Massachusetts bar. Fifty-eight years old, short and stocky, with a pudgy round face and graying blonde hair, he worried his weak health might force an early departure from office. Instead of seeking permanent quarters in Washington, he lived in a hotel. Little did he know that he would remain in the cabinet until 1902 and live until 1915. His exercise was walking to work, toting a little leather bag so overstuffed with his night reading that he kept it from popping open by wrapping it with twine. At the Navy Department, he was highly efficient, ably delegating authority, not meddling in minor matters, and watching key issues carefully. He had no ego, respected expertise, and his judgment was finer than most. Perhaps his greatest strength was the skillful management of people, which allowed him to cope with Roosevelt's impetuosity while reaping the rewards of Roosevelt's zeal. McKinley and Long were quite close, partly because they had identical personalities, preferring collegiality and courtesy even in tense moments.[65]

Assistant Secretary of the Navy Theodore Roosevelt soon had the president's ear as well. His unquestioned mastery of naval and military issues and his incredible energy were just what was needed in the spring of 1897, when Japan and the United States squared off over Hawai`i. Long and Roosevelt meshed much better than most observers expected. Long favored annexation, but, unlike Roosevelt, he did not trumpet his position publicly. The outspoken Roosevelt repeatedly clamored for annexation; if his views had been abhorrent to Long, the secretary would have chosen another lieutenant. Roosevelt's ardor amused Long, who observed that Roosevelt's "typewriters knew no rest."[66] Long considered Roosevelt the "most fitting man for the place."[67] While riding with the president, Long discussed Roosevelt and then met with Roosevelt's close friend, Senator Lodge. Roosevelt was soon appointed, giving Hawai`i another powerful voice within McKinley's inner circle.[68]

Assistant Secretary of State William Day, a native Ohioan, came to McKinley's hometown, Canton, fresh out of college. He practiced criminal and corporate law while participating in local politics as a Republican. He became a close friend of McKinley's, and his political and legal confidant during the 1880s and 1890s. In 1893 McKinley faced lawsuits for his unwise cosigning of loans to a friend who went bankrupt. Day got McKinley out of that mess unscathed, raising money from McKinley's friends and serving as trustee for his estate. Day was forty-eight when McKinley appointed him as John Sherman's deputy at the State Department. A reed-thin and frail man who nevertheless loved the deep woods—to the end of his life he summered at Michigan's remote Mackinac Island—the low-key, self-effacing Day had an almost fanatic love of baseball. Parsing the box scores brought a rare smile to his lips. In 1898 McKinley entrusted him with Cuban affairs, wartime diplomacy, and then the peace negotiations in Paris. McKinley later made him an appeals judge, and in 1903 Roosevelt appointed him to the Supreme Court, where he served for nineteen years. But his first crucial task was Hawaiian affairs, dropped in his lap as soon as he joined the administration in May 1897.[69]

Among McKinley's senior appointees, only John Sherman opposed annexation. Seventy-three years old when he became secretary of state, Sherman was at the end of a long and distinguished career as a U.S. representative, senator, and secretary of the treasury. Tall and lean like his brother, General William T. Sherman, he had the same piercing eyes and sharp-boned face. Although Sherman was a devoted family man and affectionate husband, he publicly seemed so cold and aloof that he was dubbed "the Ohio icicle." He was a facts and figures man; his speeches were jammed with numbers, his remarks sounded like scientific reports. Poor at pressing the flesh and chatting with voters, probity and competence kept him in office. He authored the 1890 Sherman Antitrust Act, the first federal attempt to curb bloated monopolies. Sherman opposed Hawaiian reciprocity in the 1880s, claiming the treaty cost the United States thirty million dollars of lost tariff revenue, "more than all the islands are worth." He opposed acquisition of "Hawai`i or Cuba or any of those Islands," but said if the cabinet supported annexation he would go along.[70] However, if a foreign power threatened the islands, he told the Hawaiians, "we might have to make an exception to our rule and take you in."[71]

Although Sherman was one of the most illustrious Republicans when McKinley asked him to join the cabinet, the president was less interested in his fame or diplomatic skills than in freeing up Sherman's Ohio Senate seat for McKinley's intimate advisor, Mark Hanna. Once in office, it quickly became apparent that Sherman's health was failing. His memory had been weakening for a couple of years, forcing him to abandon extemporaneous remarks for reading prepared texts. His once incredible concentration disappeared, and his once remarkable grasp of statistics and apt examples faded away. To manage the State Department, McKinley turned increasingly to Sherman's deputy, William Day.[72]

After the election, Lodge went to Canton and persuaded McKinley to meet with Foreign Minister Henry Cooper, visiting to explore chances for annexation.[73] Cooper warned the president-elect of the long-term implications of Japanese immigration. When McKinley asked what Hawai`i desired, Cooper said immediate annexation by treaty or joint resolution. Not convinced that Japan was pressing so hard, and conscious that he was not yet president, McKinley offered a typically noncommittal reply: "Of course I have my own ideas about Hawai`i; but consider that it is best at the present time not to make known what my policy is."[74] McKinley saw no urgent, overriding need for immediate annexation.

Cooper and Hawaiian Minister Frank Hatch realized McKinley had no timetable for his Hawaiian policy. They recommended not sending negotiators until McKinley decided to take the islands.[75] Nevertheless, an overly eager Honolulu dispatched three treaty commissioners. They broke their trip in Chicago to consult *Tribune* editor Herman Kohlsaat, known to speak informally for McKinley.[76] Kohlsaat cautioned that McKinley would focus exclusively on economic recovery and enlargement of government revenues through tariff revision. He advised patience.[77] Hatch lamented: "We must not deceive ourselves with the idea that annexation is of the same momentous importance to the people of the U.S. as the deficit in their treasury."[78] Sobered, the commissioners went on to Washington but withheld their credentials. That Hawai`i had been carried away can be seen in the silly establishment of twenty-two code words for the legation's telegrams to Honolulu. "White," for example, meant that the secretary of state would negotiate with the commissioners.[79]

To pass his tariff bill, McKinley convened a special congressional session on March 15, well ahead of the regular December session.[80] Only committees necessary to process the tariff bill were organized. McKinley's priority to tariff reform was unshakeable, as Senator William P. Frye and John Watson Foster discovered when the president-elect rejected their plea for immediate annexation. Frye bluntly told Hatch that annexation must wait for the tariff bill. Hatch warned Honolulu: "We ought not to take any chance of antagonizing Pres. McKinley, or giving him any idea that we are arranging a programme for him."[81]

On March 24, Hatch and William O. Smith met privately with McKinley, facilitated by Mrs. McKinley. Several days earlier, Hatch's wife paid a call on the First Lady, and while the ladies talked, the president joined them. Very shortly, Mark Hanna dropped by Hatch's residence and spent a half hour "talking about Hawai`i in a general way." He told Hatch to visit after talking to the president.[82] Hatch had no idea that a presidential invite was in the works, but sure enough, Hatch and Smith were soon in the White House.

Hatch came directly to the point, requesting that McKinley commit to annexation. In the long meeting, McKinley talked much more than usual and without notes. His many detailed questions and comments demonstrated deep knowledge. He had "great interest" in the annexation issue and had discussed it with Foster and Frye. Domestic matters such as the tariff needed urgent attention, he said, "but as soon as some of the pressure is off, I hope to have an opportunity to take this matter up." He went over the revenues and expenses of the Hawaiian government and asked whether it favored a treaty or a joint resolution. Hatch replied that either course was fine. McKinley explained how a joint resolution easily brought Texas into the Union without the need for Senate confirmation. Knowing that Sherman might be an obstacle, McKinley queried them about the secretary's attitude. Having met Sherman earlier that very morning, they said he opposed annexation but promised to follow McKinley's wishes. At end of the meeting, McKinley returned to the method of annexation, again asking if the Hawaiians were agreeable to either a treaty or a joint resolution. Again they replied that either was fine, but they hoped he would move soon. McKinley replied, "I don't know but what I may come to that." He wanted to think about the issue further but assured them that he realized the necessity of early action.[83]

Hatch promptly visited Hanna at the Arlington Hotel. Hanna "declared plainly that he was in favor of annexation and took up at once the details of the problem in a business way." Hanna "was going to be a worker when the time comes," Hatch reported, but "unfortunately, he is going to be the judge of that point. He said squarely that annexation could not be allowed to interfere with the tariff bill." When the tariff bill was further along they could see if another measure could be taken up. Hatch was greatly encouraged. Hanna's declaration was highly significant. "There was no reason to anticipate any special interest in us on Mr. Hanna's part," Hatch wrote Cooper, "and we would not find it now if it did not proceed directly from the President."[84]

In his first weeks in office, McKinley had moved Hawaiian policy higher on the priority list. But an immediate push for annexation was not in the cards. There was no reason for swift action. McKinley wanted the congressional session focused solely on tariff reform. He did not want to challenge Speaker Reed's opposition to annexation when he needed the Speaker's help with the tariff. Unless Hawai`i somehow became an urgent issue, several months—even years—might pass before annexation.

Nevertheless, the basics were in place: a Republican Congress, a helpful Republican president, true believers among senior administration advisors and congressional leaders, and committed supporters among the political elite. Hatch reported: "everything is coming along very nicely here."[85] Smith too was happy: "The difference between the attitude of the present administration and the last one is like that of the difference between daylight and darkness. The present is the friendly one, waiting for the best opportunity and most favorable means of presenting the matter."[86] The question was not whether annexation would eventually occur—the stars seemed aligned for that—but how soon and by what method. As Hatch put it, "we may have a long wait ahead of us, but we can be easy in our minds, I think."[87]

❦

CHAPTER 13

Japanese Immigration:
From Lifeline to Threat

Japanese immigration had immense consequences for eventual annexation. Along with the immigration of other groups, it reversed the declining population, it recast the ethnic makeup of the inhabitants, and it allowed the stupendous growth in the sugar industry. But only Japanese immigration was the product of a bilateral diplomatic agreement, the Convention of 1886. The persistent official nature of the Japanese inflow complicated island politics much more than the entry of other groups. The Japanese government was deeply involved in the recruitment and transport of immigrants as well as in their welfare in the islands. According to the convention, the immigrants were not immigrants at all but temporary workers expected to return home after three years on the sugar plantations. With the Imperial Government's strong encouragement, worker remissions quickly became a major source of foreign revenue. Returnees infused sizable sums into their communities. When the Hawaiian government sought to slow down the Japanese inflow during 1894–97, the Japanese government pushed back strongly.

As Western imperialists gobbled up territory around the world and pushed into Asia, Japan too became more assertive and aggressive. It brought Hokkaido firmly under central government control. In 1875 it gained the Kuriles from

Russia by renouncing claims to Sakhalin. It invaded Taiwan to enforce claims to the Ryukyu chain and then formally annexed the islands in 1879 as Okinawa prefecture. In 1890 Prime Minister Yamagata Aritomo said Japan, to grow and prosper, must not only defend its current territory but defend a "line of advantage," which included Korea. The belief took hold that Western imperialism and racism threatened Japan's future and must be met by resolute action. The intellectual Tokutomi Soho argued that imperial expansion was the way to ensure security and earn the respect of western powers.[1]

For years, Japan's chief foreign policy goal was eliminating the unequal treaties signed with the United States, Britain, France, Russia, and the Netherlands in 1854 and 1858.[2] Japan felt insulted by the extraterritoriality, loss of control over tariffs, and other condescending privileges of the Western powers.

Mutsu Munemitsu, foreign minister from 1892–96, made treaty renegotiation his top priority. Painfully thin from tuberculosis, sporting a spade-like Vandyke beard, the towering Mutsu had an ego, and a talent, to match his height. Born in 1844, Mutsu, like most 1890s Japanese leaders, grew to adulthood in the tumultuous end of the shogunate and the birth of the new Meiji government. He went to Edo (Tokyo) at age fourteen, the year the shogunate signed the first unequal treaty with the United States. He worked as a janitor in a monastery in order to eat. After the Meiji revolution, he held several posts due to recognition by seniors of his immense talent. He befriended another talent, Hoshi Toru, who encouraged his English study. But in 1878 Mutsu got tangled up in with Saigo Takamori's plotting for rebellion against the government. After Saigo's rebellion collapsed, the government confined Mutsu for almost five years while he read voraciously and improved his English skills, translating Jeremy Bentham's *Principles of Moral Ethics and Legislation* with some editing help from Hoshi. After release he studied in Europe before reentering government service with the help of friends. During 1888–90, he was minister to Washington. He became agriculture minister in 1890 and foreign minister in 1892. Long working hours and stress worsened his tuberculosis, forced his resignation in 1896, and killed him the following year.

Although previous foreign ministers had been forced from office by their failure to obtain treaty revision, Mutsu's tactical brilliance and doggedness produced a diplomatic coup that resonated across Japanese society. On April 4, 1894, Hawai`i renounced any claim to special privileges originating in the "most favored nation" clause of the 1871 Hawai`i–Japan treaty. But the masterstroke, in July 1894, was persuading the world's greatest power, Britain, to strike unequal provisions from its 1854 bilateral pact. It is said that Mutsu was so overcome by emotion when carrying the news to the Emperor Meiji that he not only bowed deeply but fell to his knees, with tears streaming down his face. Japan had taken a giant step toward equality with the West. In short order, the United States and many European powers equalized their own treaties with Japan.[3]

Japan's drive for equality and suffrage for its nationals in Hawai`i during 1893–94 paralleled its drive for equality with all powers. Mutsu's triumph with Britain occurred just days before Japan went to war with China. Even the expansionist Mutsu was surprised by the popular support for imperialism. The swift victories against China on sea and land created an unrealistic jingoism. Mutsu fretted that the people, "agog with vain ambitions," cared only when "the Japanese flag would be carried through the gates of Peking." "Their ambitions for the future knew no bounds," he complained.[4] Japan reaped many war spoils: the annexation of Taiwan, Chinese withdrawal from Korea, the right to send trading vessels up Chinese rivers to the interior, and the acquisition of the strategic Liaotung Peninsula. The spoils were forgotten when the Triple Intervention of Russia, France, and Germany forced Japan to return the Shantung Peninsula to China. When Russia occupied the territory itself and fortified Port Arthur, public outrage drove out the Ito government. Given the belligerent public temper, any new government had to prevent another insulting national humiliation. Japan poured money into the military so it would never be pushed around again. The Army's budget doubled, and the naval building program was so large that British minister Ernest Satow warned the foreign ministry that other powers would be alarmed.[5]

In this jingo context, the Hawai`i–Japan immigration arrangement began to fray. For years, the Convention of 1886 satisfied both nations. It met Hawai`i's desire for sugar workers who would work hard and supposedly go home after the contract ended. It allowed Hawai`i to stop the politically unpopular Chinese immigration. It produced significant remittances for Japan's economy and a better life for thousands of its people. Both countries addressed, if not always solved, problems such as the lack of enough interpreters or doctors, or the mistreatment of laborers on the plantations. Above all, the convention made the inflow predictable and controllable. This was acutely important for Hawai`i. Immigrants arrived only in the numbers requested. Because the Japanese government controlled passport issuance, virtually no Japanese went to Hawai`i except as contract laborers.

By 1894, however, both countries soured on their immigration arrangements. The ever-growing number of Japanese and their government's consistent and assertive push for suffrage seemed to threaten white rule, especially as Japan's power and aggressiveness increased.

The suffrage issue was an old one. Although the discriminatory 1894 constitution barred Asian suffrage, Hawaiian leaders knew the issue would reemerge.

Given Tokyo's determination to eliminate unequal treatment of Japanese by foreign countries, Tokyo would again demand voting rights. The Japanese suffrage question was much more significant than that of the Chinese, though the two populations were of roughly equivalent size. Chinese sought voting rights as individuals or as a local community. The Chinese government did not advocate on their behalf, had no representation in Hawai`i, and sent no warships to show the flag. The Chinese suffrage quest could be safely ignored.

But Japanese suffrage meant dealing with a proud government aware of its growing power and strongly determined to obtain equal rights for its nationals. Japan had aggressive diplomatic representation in Honolulu and in 1893–94 deployed warships to demonstrate its strong interest. By mid-1894, the Hawaiian government viewed Japanese immigration as a long-term threat. Even the usually unflappable Dole worried that "the increasing number of Japanese is a menace."[6]

The privatization of the immigration flow scared the Hawaiian government. Until 1894 the Imperial Government's control had been absolute. But in 1894, without abrogating the convention, Tokyo let private emigration companies assume tasks previously handled by Japanese officials. The reasons for this change are unclear. First, allowing companies to take over a project once the government had gotten it started matched other privatization efforts. Second, other countries wished to import Japanese labor. It seemed easier to privatize the process than to create a series of bilateral conventions. Third, the China crisis may have prompted busy officials to outsource bothersome tasks, such as arranging transportation, passports, and working with Robert W. Irwin to get prior approval for contracts. Finally, and perhaps most important, politically influential Japanese discovered that a lot of money could be made in the immigration business. Many profit-seeking emigration companies started operations.[7] The potential for profit was so great that Nakayama Joji, the chief of the Japanese section of the Board of Immigration, whose six-thousand-dollar annual salary exceeded that of any Hawaiian government employee except members of the cabinet, resigned in 1895 to return to Japan and join the profiteering.[8] Tateno Gozo, former Japanese minister to Washington, headed the Japan Emigration Company, one of the largest emigration firms.[9]

An April 1894 Emigrant Protection Ordinance preserved the Imperial Government's ultimate authority over immigration but gave companies free rein to recruit and transport contract laborers and other travelers.[10] Under the new ordinance, fifteen government-approved companies sent laborers during 1894–98.[11] The Japanese government sponsored no immigrants. Hence, by definition, no Japanese immigration after June 1894 took place under the Convention of 1886. Freed from the convention restraints, the newly empowered emigration companies sold transport tickets directly to individuals and advanced the cost of tickets at high interest rates. These advances were repaid once the immigrant started work. They charged fees to arrange passports, for transportation to Yokohama and on to Honolulu, for temporary lodging in boardinghouses both in Japan and in Honolulu, and for predeparture medical exams. They took commissions from shipping companies and boardinghouses for throwing business their way. The companies sold life insurance. They set up a Honolulu bank and required immigrants to deposit $2.50 a month to cover the loan advances and return passage to Japan.[12] And the more immigrants they sent, the higher their profits.

The two countries did not abrogate the convention but simply ignored it.[13] Alas, dealing with immigration outside the convention proved quite troublesome.

The emigration companies brought in a new type of contract laborer. These immigrants did not sign, with Irwin in Japan, contracts preapproved by Honolulu, as the convention required, but signed agreements with the emigration companies. The companies took the position that, because the Japanese government no longer sent immigrants, the convention's preapproval requirement could be ignored. The companies worked with plantation agents to place arriving workers. Planters cooperated because the new system was easier. They no longer had to predict their labor needs in advance and get the Board of Immigration to preapprove contracts. Nor did the planters have to cover the transportation charge or guarantee a wage rate. Planters hired quickly from a local pool of laborers contracted to the emigration companies.

In addition to transporting laborers with company contracts, the companies brought free immigrants without contracts. When Hawai`i insisted that these free immigrants carry fifty dollars in "show money" to prove they would not become public charges, the companies loaned them the money. Those who satisfied the free immigration procedures lodged in boardinghouses known to plantation recruiters. Free immigrants usually found work quickly. Not bound by contracts, some moved directly into town jobs. Nor were they pressured to go home after three years by withholding return transportation charges from their salaries. As we have seen, white opposition to Chinese free immigrants drove Hawai`i toward the convention's strictly controlled, preapproved flow of laborers. Now the same problem—uncontrolled immigration—arose with Japanese.[14]

Hawai`i reacted swiftly. New laws of March 1, 1894, and February 1, 1895, forbade any person or company to encourage and assist immigration without preapproval of the Board of Immigration. The laws made illegal many emigration company activities, such as loaning money for transportation, loaning show money, and signing prospective laborers to contracts that were not preapproved.

The new Hawaiian laws applied convention procedures to the company-driven immigration flow. The laws directed customs officials to extend the show money requirement to immigrants with contracts signed with the companies but not preapproved.[15]

The companies exploited a gray area. What constituted "possession" of fifty dollars? Customs inspectors determined if the fifty dollars truly belonged to the free immigrant. One rumor was that immigrants would line up before the inspectors, display their fifty dollars and be admitted, then hand the cash to the next person in line. This surely never happened; the violations were not that blatant. Rather, the companies loaned fifty dollars in Japan for repayment after the immigrant entered Hawai`i and started work. Strict inspectors saw this practice as evasion of the "possession" rule. They scorned the display of exactly fifty dollars (or its equivalent, about one hundred yen) in new crisp bills. They cast a wary eye on bank statements showing an account of fifty dollars. The cranky chief inspector James Castle refused in 1895 to admit seventy-one passengers who possessed bank drafts issued by the Yokohama Specie Bank, saying "as far as [bank] drafts are concerned, I do not consider that any promise to pay money, is, in the words of the law, money."[16] Even cash wasn't always welcome, as Soga Yasutaro complained: "When I showed my 100 yen [about $50] in a bundle of 100 one-yen bills . . . , a mean-looking Japanese interpreter yelled at me furiously, saying, 'Who in the world has time to count them in the middle of busy inspections' and threw the money at me."[17]

Those who failed to qualify as free immigrants were supposed to be sent back to Japan at emigration company expense. In practice, the government waffled and did not consistently enforce its new laws. The executive council sought to control immigration while not angering Japan and while fully meeting the labor demands of the planters. J. B. Atherton summarized the dilemma: "It is against public policy to admit more Japanese. . . . Portuguese cost so much that . . . planters cannot take any more . . . and there is no other source of supply but Chinese."[18] Moriyama said the white oligarchy "faced the dilemma that confronted many 'colonizers.' . . . They could ensure economic success by importing non-white workers, or they could guarantee their own political domination of Hawai`i by keeping out immigrants of color. It was impossible to do both."[19]

Nevertheless, the Hawaiian government attempted this unworkable straddle, bouncing between stern and conciliatory stances. The admission standards were governed as much by the council's changeable moods as by the quality of immigrant documentation. Japanese sometimes entered with a letter of credit from a Japanese bank—presumably these entrants did not pass by James Castle—or with fifty dollars provided by the emigration company with paperwork good enough to convince the inspectors. Even individuals without any show money might be allowed entry if they had a commitment letter from a well-known employer.

The council considered a total ban on Japanese, but when the Japanese minister heard about it, he charged that the Treaty of 1871 guaranteed the unimpeded entry of Japanese. Article 2 of the treaty stated that subjects of each country should enjoy the same privileges as the subjects of any other nation. In Hawai`i's view, Article 2 referred only to traders, not to all persons, but the internal correspondence shows that Hawaiian officials did not think their interpretation was impregnable.[20] They considered asking Japan to revise the treaty. For Japan's part, now that the convention no longer applied, the 1871 treaty was the only possible document on which to rely. Whichever treaty interpretation was correct, as a practical matter an angry Japan might withdraw laborers already in Hawai`i, devastating the sugar industry.

The council backed off, deciding for the moment not to challenge the contention that Hawai`i could not restrict Japanese immigration. The council next attempted to decrease Japanese immigrants by limiting the number on any single ship and by bringing in two Chinese for every Japanese. The planters did not cooperate and more Japanese entered than the council wanted. Foreign Minister Henry Cooper partly blamed Irwin, "as he is connected to one of the shipping firms here, and through his instigation a large majority of the applications for plantation laborers are made out for Japanese."[21] Alarmed by the increasing numbers of Japanese and the demand for suffrage, the Republic of Hawai`i was uninterested in solving the show money issue by accepting bond from the companies. Hawai`i wanted complete control of newcomers, whereas a bond would allow the companies to increase the flow.[22]

The council vainly tried to recruit other nationalities. Lorrin Thurston went to Portugal to restart Portuguese immigration. Zephaniah S. Spaulding went to recruit Belgians. The council discussed importing Koreans and Germans. None of these efforts succeeded.[23] The sole success was restarting Chinese immigration, although that was quite significant; 8,758 arrived during 1894–97.[24] However, even that number paled beside the 21,880 Japanese who received passports for Hawai`i during the same period.[25] With few viable options left, in early 1896, the Hawaiian government decided to tighten the screws on immigration by Japanese.

A necessary step was confirming American backing if Japan reacted badly. In March 1896 Frank Hatch asked Secretary of State Olney if Hawai`i could count on America in a confrontation with Tokyo. Olney expected no trouble: "Japan surely cannot intend to run against us out there." He hinted that help would be forthcoming if Japan pressed too hard. Hatch reported the United States would prevent Japanese interference in Hawaiian affairs.[26] With American support ensured, Foreign Minister Cooper told Hatch, "We have concluded to take a firm stand."[27]

This tough line came many months before the 1896 presidential election and long before the candidates were chosen. The Democratic administration was supportive enough that the clampdown could proceed. But after the election, Hawai`i quickly assessed Republican intentions. Informal contacts suggested eventual annexation. Typical was the feedback from a private dinner in November 1896, hosted by John W. Foster to introduce the visiting Henry Cooper to eight senators, editors of the *Washington Post* and the *Washington Star*, John Hay, and McKinley's right-hand man, Mark Hanna. When Cooper fretted about uncontrolled immigration, Senator William Chandler declared that the United States would look out for Hawai`i: "Don't you be afraid of that Japanese treaty. If any hostile demonstration should occur by either England or Japan, we would annex you in fifteen minutes." John Sherman reminded the group that the Turpie Resolution was "tantamount to a protectorate."[28] Hawai`i drew the obvious conclusion that America would prevent military action against Hawai`i.

At the beginning of 1897 Japanese immigration was still increasing. The emigration companies had not been deterred by government warnings or by stricter immigration inspections, such as the rejection in late 1896 of forty-one of sixty-six Japanese on the *Toyo Maru* who received fifty dollars to gain entry but returned it to the emigration company once ashore. The refused immigrants were sent back to Japan.[29] Dole complained about "considerable activity in the bringing in of free Japanese immigrants. The several immigration companies are working the business for profits and are preparing to run it for all it is worth." In early 1897 Dole told Hatch that "the Japanese are still piling in."[30] William O. Smith grumbled: "The Japanese question is steadily assuming more importance. Not so much that the Japanese Govt has any definite designs on these islands. But Japanese interests here are growing stronger all the time. And designs will inevitably follow."[31] W. D. Alexander believed that "the crisis . . . must be met without delay" to avoid Hawai`i becoming "virtually a Japanese colony."[32]

Dole asked Robert Irwin if Japan would amend the 1871 treaty to clarify that Hawai`i controlled immigration.[33] Irwin responded with a flat "no." After years of unequal treaties, Japan would not weaken any treaty rights of its own.[34] Foreign Minister Cooper recommended informing Japan that "Japanese are being introduced into the country contrary to our laws." Hawai`i should stop the inflow regardless of complications for the labor supply. A recent steamer brought 350 Japanese, only 41 of whom were preapproved contract laborers. The emigration companies intentionally sought to "circumvent our policy; and . . . should be called to terms at once."[35]

The 1896 Hawaiian census raised eyebrows in Washington and Honolulu. The census counted 109,020 persons. Fewer than 40,000 were Native Hawaiian or part-Hawaiian. The 24,407 Japanese were now the largest ethnic group in the islands, followed closely by the Chinese with 21,616. Asians comprised 42 percent of the population, up from 33 percent in 1890 and 22 percent in 1884.[36]

The suffrage question intertwined with the number of males of voting age, twenty years old. The census listed 72,517 males of all ages and ethnicities. Deducting younger males and breaking out the data by ethnic group shows the following numbers of voting age males:

Japanese: 18,156
Chinese: 17,663
Hawaiian: 13,148
White: 8,275

Because China was not pushing suffrage for Chinese, it was Japanese males, the single largest group of men, who made the suffrage issue explosive. Enfranchising Japanese would significantly alter voting patterns. Enfranchising all Asians would create a bloc almost twice the size of the rest of the voters.[37]

That Japanese formed the majority of sugar laborers was causative. Had immigration been composed of many nationalities whose governments did not concern themselves with the status of their nationals, Hawai`i might have been less worried about preserving white rule. But Japanese immigration appeared much more threatening. Only Japanese immigration had an official, binational character. Japanese immigration, uniquely, was inseparable from Japan's official concerns, even after the emigration companies assumed recruitment tasks. The Japanese government stood behind the companies when they ran afoul of Hawai`i's immigration laws.

Japanese immigration was created entirely by diplomatic negotiation, governed by a bilateral convention, and adjusted by bilateral talks. Japanese immigration required constant dialogue between the two governments. Even after the emigration companies took charge of the immigration flow, the Japanese legation in Honolulu tracked immigration matters carefully and complained against unreasonable procedures, such as the short-lived idea of cutting off all Japanese immigration. The Imperial Government even deployed warships—though less frequently than the United States and Britain—to support its interests, conspicuously during the franchise debate just after the 1893 overthrow and again during the 1894 constitutional convention. Only Japanese immigration brought unwanted attention from a powerful foreign government.

Thus, for the white oligarchy, Japanese immigration went from a very welcome economic lifeline in 1885 to a political menace by early 1897. The transfer of immigration to profit-seeking companies both accelerated the inflow and made it uncontrollable. Yet Tokyo refused to accept Hawai`i's right to regulate arrivals and even pushed strongly for suffrage as the Japanese population soared. The white-run Republic of Hawai`i now regarded immigration as a mortal threat that had to be addressed, no matter how painful the short-term consequences.

CHAPTER 14

The U.S.–Japan Crisis of 1897

Fifty-eight years old when he became foreign minister for the second time in late 1896, Count Ōkuma Shigenobu was a rare breed among Meiji politicians in that he never went abroad and he disliked many traditional Japanese arts. He hated calligraphy and wrote virtually nothing after age sixteen. In all the archives of Japan, there is not a scrap of paper in his own hand. Though bright, he was not an intellectual, and organizing and recording his thoughts on paper was tedious. He learned through conversation, and his nearly photographic memory let him strew facts throughout his conversations, giving at least the appearance of learning. His judgment was the problem. A friend criticized him for "feeling that you know everything after hearing only one tenth of it." One biographer assessed him as insensitive and shallow, imperious, and gruff. Nearly every photo shows him unsmiling, jaw pugnaciously thrust forward, mouth bending down at the corners in a kind of scowl. Even his dog got little tenderness. The story goes that Ōkuma never gave the canine a name, summoning him simply by calling out, "Dog! Dog!" Ōkuma loved the Japanese strategy game "Go," but he was a bad player. A friend said Ōkuma's tendency in "Go," as in life, was "moving carelessly through the first plays and beginning to think only when he ran into trouble."[1] He had the same impetuous trait as foreign minister. Reflection was not in his nature.

Ōkuma had known Inoue Kaoru, who jump-started Japanese immigration to Hawai`i in 1885, for more than twenty years when he replaced him as foreign minister in 1888. Inoue resigned because of his failure to renegotiate the hugely unpopular unequal treaties giving the U.S. and European powers special privileges, such as extraterritoriality and preferential tariffs. In his first term as foreign minister, Ōkuma also failed to eliminate the treaties and was soon viewed as soft. An outraged right-wing fanatic blew off Ōkuma's right leg with a bomblet in 1889 and committed suicide on the spot with a short sword. More than most Meiji leaders, Ōkuma was a bit of a democrat, opposing rule by the genro, the nine retired senior leaders—among them Inoue—whose stature and connections gave them tremendous influence even when out of office. Ōkuma was honest, disliking the corruption and backroom dealings typified by younger men like Hoshi Toru, who in 1896 became minister to Washington.

In late 1896 Ōkuma returned to the foreign ministry amid vociferous public dissatisfaction with Foreign Minister Mutsu Munemitsu's supposedly weak foreign policy. It says much about the jingo environment that the country had already forgotten Mutsu's brilliant success in eliminating the unequal treaties, his careful stewardship during the aggressive war against China, and the plentiful war spoils, only partially reduced by the Triple Intervention. The two men hated each other. Mutsu believed that Ōkuma was deficient in "thorough and detailed planning." Ōkuma thought Mutsu an overrated egghead. In his second stint in the ministry, Ōkuma paid much more attention to public opinion. He knew the people despised Japanese passivity toward Western resistance to an equal international role for Japan. He surely recalled similar public perceptions that previously cost his leg. This time, Ōkuma determined, no one would ever accuse him of softness. With this tough attitude, immersed in a jingoistic popular fervor, Ōkuma would manage a serious 1897 crisis with Hawai`i and the United States.

The crisis was definitely not of McKinley's seeking. The new president wanted no diplomatic distractions from economic recovery through tariff reform, his paramount issue in the 1896 elections. In March 1897, rather than wait for the regular congressional session in December, the Republicans convened a special session for tariff reform. Speaker Tom Reed appointed only those committees needed to pass the Dingley tariff bill. After more than eight hundred Senate amendments, the House passed the bill on July 24. Congress immediately adjourned until December.[2]

Nor did Hawai`i create a crisis with Japan to push the United States to annex. First, that was too risky, because Japan might react militarily. Second, McKinley had made it clear to the Hawaiians that he would address annexation after tariff revision, and they had accepted his decision. There was no need to foment an incident. Third, an angry McKinley would surely scuttle his long-range plans for annexation if he discovered any manipulation. Fourth, the 1897 clampdown on ballooning Japanese immigration was not a sudden initiative to spur annexation but the logical result of three years of failure to control the inflow.

Most Hawaiian officials saw the inflow chiefly as a by-product of the money-grubbing immigration companies and sugar planters seeking cheaper laborers. But even if there was no Japanese intent to take political power, uncontrolled immigration would eventually produce the same result. Stronger measures were needed to preserve white rule. Frank Hatch foresaw a crisis "rapidly approaching in Japanese matters. It is certainly not of our seeking. A stand must be taken somewhere or abandon the country to Japan."[3] It was not just firebrands such as Hatch who sensed a threat. The British minister reported that immigration "has assumed proportions which have become alarming and the Government have seized on this opportunity to check it. There are already thirty to forty thousand Japanese in these islands and it is conceivable enough that the continued growth of such a large colony should suggest disquieting contingencies."[4]

In January 1897 the Japanese consulate announced the probable stationing of a warship at Honolulu. Hawai`i believed the vessel was retaliation for the late-1896 rejection of the *Toyo Maru*'s illegal immigrants. The State Department prudently kept the Navy apprised, although neither department suspected that the immigration spat would soon become a major confrontation.[5]

In February 1897 the Kobe Immigration Company admitted that laborers on the *Shinshu Maru*, expected shortly at Honolulu, lacked the preapproved contracts required by Hawaiian law. The company asked that they be admitted anyway. "Our answer to them was 'no,'" Foreign Minister Cooper recorded, "we had talked the matter over carefully and came to the conclusion that we should make a stand against this whole and illegal immigration now."[6] Hawai`i denied entry to 480 of the 671 passengers on the *Shinshu Maru*.[7] This second rejection incident was followed by a third on March 19, when the authorities denied entry to 163 of 361 passengers aboard the *Sakura Maru*.[8] Outraged Japanese residents met to protest and produced a resolution stating that they would report the facts to Tokyo officials and abide by their decision.[9] Besides implying that Japanese might not obey Hawaiian law, the resolution offered an ideal excuse for the Japanese government to involve itself, possibly by demanding redress. Consul General Shimamura Hisashi requested a warship "to exhibit our power and protect 26,000 Japanese, almost one-fourth of the total population of Hawai`i."[10]

A nervous McKinley administration quickly took precautions. Secretary of the Navy Long assigned Admiral Montgomery Sicard to rewrite the Navy's current war plan to reflect the growing possibility of a clash with Japan over Hawai`i.

Within three months a Sicard board produced the first war plan aimed at Japan.[11] To guard against troublemaking by Japanese residents (the administration especially feared riots against the minority regime), Long sent Admiral Lester Beardslee to Honolulu with the cruiser *Philadelphia* and two smaller warships, the *Marion* and *Petrel*.[12]

The immigrant rejections created "a good deal of excitement" in Tokyo. Ōkuma confided to British Minister Ernest Satow, a fluent Japanese speaker with more than twenty years in Japan, that Hawai`i sought trouble to compel the United States to annex. Assuming that Britain opposed annexation, Ōkuma spoke frankly. Japan had "large interests in the group, both commercially and through the fact that some 30,000 Japanese inhabit the islands." Japan opposed annexation by any power. Instructions had been sent to Minister Hoshi Toru to represent that view to the McKinley administration and ask for a "disavowal of any intention to annex." Ōkuma denied that Japan wanted the islands, which should be left independent for the benefit of all nations. He charged that Japanese residents were being egged on by royalists to overthrow the government. Japan would send warships to "preserve order and not in any way as a menace." He clearly hoped Satow would advise London to join in opposing the Americans. Suspicious of Japanese motives, Satow gently warned that the United States "would not remain indifferent to any attempt at annexation by another power."[13] The following day Japan ordered the protected cruiser *Hiyei* to Honolulu but soon substituted the larger *Naniwa* as well as the armored corvette *Kongo*. Satow telegraphed, "Nominally the object is to preserve order among the Japanese . . . but the real object is to support the demands of the Japanese Government."[14]

Count Ōkuma tried to use the crisis to hinder any American move toward annexation. He asked London and Berlin to join in opposing annexation. The Germans did not immediately reply. The British opposed annexation but would remain passive because overt opposition would simply convince the Americans that annexation was necessary to preserve U.S. interests.[15] As instructed, Minister Hoshi delivered Ōkuma's note assailing the "flagrant denial of justice and protection" for immigrants supposedly guaranteed in Japan's 1871 treaty with Hawai`i.[16] Ōkuma also had Hoshi to inform Sherman that Japan opposed annexation, even before McKinley committed to it, because of Japan's now extensive interests in the islands.[17] This was earthshaking news, but it appears that Sherman did not realize its significance, and so did not inform McKinley, or misplaced or even forgot Hoshi's note. There is no sign that anyone else in the American government understood that Japan officially opposed annexation as early as April 1897. McKinley did notice Sherman's weakened mental powers. To manage the State

Department, in late April McKinley gave Sherman a deputy, the president's old Canton friend, William Day. Day gave full attention to the Hawaiian issue.[18]

When the Convention of 1886 opened the door to immigration, Japan had no interests in Hawai`i. Now, in 1897, its interests had grown so much that they could only be maintained by blocking U.S. annexation and pressuring Hawai`i not to interfere with the immigration flow that would, coupled with suffrage, bring the islands into the Japanese orbit.[19] The rejections also hit the influential Japanese who owned the immigration companies right in the pocketbook. The companies had to return the immigrants' ticket fees and transport them home. Ōkuma complained that "a good deal of money had been lost."[20] But instead of confining the matter to compensation, Ōkuma enlarged it to define Japanese interests as much more extensive than anyone else previously thought while simultaneously blocking American annexation. This was a startlingly new development.

The seriousness of the crisis, coupled with pressure from relatives and friends, impelled Secretary of the Navy Long to proactively support annexation. This was significant, for Long was closer to the president than any other cabinet member, and McKinley often heeded his advice. Long's friend Major Nathan Appleton, a respected authority on the isthmian canal, warned that inaction would lead to Japanese control of the Pearl River lagoon's immense strategic benefits.[21] Just after he ordered the Beardslee flotilla to Hawai`i, Long wrote Appleton that "the administration is alive to the Hawaiian question, and giving it consideration along the lines you suggest."[22]

Long's niece, Julia Castle, also influenced him toward annexation. Married to James Castle, the strict Honolulu customs inspector, Julia sent letters expressing her fears of a Japanese takeover. Long reassured her that the administration would take care of Hawai`i: "What makes you worry about my deciding against the Hawaiian Islands? . . . You know my personal sympathies are with you, and that I shall take great pleasure in giving the subject, if it ever comes before me, the most liberal and generous consideration. I have already had some very interesting conversations with Hartwell, the [Hawaiian] Attorney General, [William O.] Smith, and others."[23] Friends urged Long to support annexation.[24] Convinced, he offered to arrange private interviews with McKinley for annexationist spokesmen such as Appleton.[25] Hawaiian Minister Hatch reported that "the *Philadelphia* was sent out in consequence of hints given Sec. Long. He is very friendly."[26]

John Watson Foster, influential in Republican foreign policy circles, tirelessly pushed annexation. Returning from a visit to Hawai`i, Foster told reporters that the "ultimate fate" of the islands was rule by a great power. The United States must act or some other nation would snatch up the islands.[27] Before what the

New York Times called the "most prominent men in Washington" at the National Geographic Society, he declared that the quickening inflow of Japanese would make them dominant. Annexation would apply U.S. laws to Hawai`i, a sure way to prevent Japanese control.[28] Foster knew Japan well. He spent December 1895 to July 1896 in Japan and China helping the Chinese negotiate the Treaty of Shimonoseki, which ended the Sino-Japanese War. Foster believed annexation was a "political and military necessity" to preserve American dominance.[29] His address, replicated four times in New York City and in other cities, was widely replayed in newspapers, printed in the *Congressional Record*, and distributed by the tens of thousands by Hawai`i's propaganda organ, the Hawaiian Committee on Annexation.[30]

By early April the administration's Hawaiian policy moved forward on two fronts. Militarily, the goal was protecting Hawai`i from Japanese retaliation for the immigrant rejections. Politically, the dispute accelerated thinking about annexation, as revealed by Long's pro-annexation stance and remarks by leading Republicans. Robert Hitt endorsed annexation and warned that voting rights for the Japanese would radically alter the Hawaiian government, preventing American acquisition of a most desirable military outpost.[31] Informal gatherings of Hitt's Committee on Foreign Affairs produced the consensus, according to the *Chicago Tribune*, that the "invasion of the Asiatics can be stopped only by immediate annexation."[32]

Washington carefully watched for evidence of military intervention by Japan. The American minister to Japan, Edwin Dun, reported that the rejections had been "most unfavorably received." The Japanese press was quarrelsome and the popular mood warlike, but Dun doubted that Japan would intervene militarily or attempt a show of force. Nevertheless, he predicted that two warships of the Imperial Navy would soon be sent to Honolulu to satisfy popular demands for retaliation. Dun's reluctance to call a spade a spade did not alter the fact that sending two warships in the midst of the immigration crisis to tiny Hawai`i, which had no army or navy, would be a formidable show of force.[33] Hatch concluded that deep distrust of Japan was driving the United States toward a stronger stand.[34]

The administration was further alarmed when Hawai`i rejected 548 of 668 passengers on the *Kinai Maru*.[35] This fourth episode promised to inflame an already hot situation, for if the earlier incidents provoked Ōkuma's strong protest and threat to send a warship to Honolulu, what retaliation might now result? Sherman anxiously instructed Consul General Mills: "Keep the Department thoroughly advised in regard to the Japanese labor question."[36] On April 21, the Navy warned that the *Naniwa* departed for Honolulu with a special representative of the Imperial government aboard. Long sounded the alarm. Unsure if the

Navy had enough force on hand, McKinley had Roosevelt list numbers and types of warships available for swift deployment. Roosevelt told Admiral Beardslee, now in Honolulu with the *Philadelphia, Marion, Petrel*, and *Mariposa*, to keep all of his warships in Hawai`i.[37]

During this furious naval activity, Harold Sewall's appointment as minister to Hawai`i confirmed the administration's favorable attitude toward annexation. Sewall had been Cleveland's consul in Samoa but claimed he broke with the Democrats because of Cleveland's spineless policy toward Hawai`i and the Pacific.[38] Sewall asserted he received the crucial Hawaiian post only after "a full avowal to the President of my belief that annexation was the only course for the United States to pursue."[39] Hatch said Sewall was "an avowed annexationist."[40]

Neither Sewall's appointment nor the naval deployments satisfied the combative Roosevelt, who complained: "I wish to heaven we were more jingo about Cuba and Hawai`i!"[41] Mahan griped: "Are we going to allow her [Japan] to dominate the future of those most important islands because of our lethargy?" Roosevelt wanted immediate annexation because the two Japanese battleships nearing completion in British yards might appear in Hawai`i.[42] Roosevelt wished to "annex those islands tomorrow." He was "fully alive to the danger from Japan."[43] This jingoist letter suggests the kind of advice reaching McKinley. Roosevelt said Secretary Long "shared our views."[44] McKinley's inner circle—Mark Hanna, Foster, Long, Roosevelt, Day, Lodge, Hitt—advocated annexation. No one with significant access to the president vigorously opposed it, except Speaker Reed. With McKinley digesting a steady diet of annexationist views, Roosevelt hoped for quick action: "With Hawai`i once in our hands, most of the danger of friction with Japan would disappear."[45]

Throughout May the administration grew steadily more suspicious of Japanese ambitions. On May 4, the cabinet discussed Hawai`i; Long presented annexationist memoranda prepared by Roosevelt.[46] Quite likely Mahan's letters to Roosevelt were read to the cabinet. On May 5 the *Naniwa* moored at Honolulu, sparking a Republican attempt to fund a naval base at Pearl Harbor.[47] Robert Hitt charged that the *Naniwa*'s visit was part of a plan to overthrow the Hawaiian government.[48] Japan would back down before a show of forcefulness, of which the Pearl Harbor bill was to be a part. Though the United States had the right to develop Pearl Harbor, nothing had been done. Speculators had bought much land. Many legislators opposed development until all surrounding land had been obtained and until it was clear that Hawai`i would not be lost to a foreign power.[49] The episode revealed that the House recognized both the seriousness of the Japanese threat and Hawai`i's value to coastal defense. Using Hitt as a source, the *Washington*

Star announced that the president favored annexation and waited only for passage of the tariff bill.[50] An *Omaha Bee* poll showed most representatives supported annexation.[51]

Meanwhile, the situation in Hawai`i grew more tense. On May 18 the administration learned that special emissary Akiyama Masanosuke, sent aboard the *Naniwa*, thought that the immigrant rejections violated the 1871 Hawaiian–Japanese treaty. If Akiyama's final investigation bore out this preliminary conclusion, Japan would demand an indemnity for the expense of repatriating the disappointed immigrants.[52]

An indemnity demand was the last thing the McKinley administration wanted, for Hawai`i surely would refuse, which might provoke Japan to use force. Egged on by the Hawaiian legation, predictions that this scenario would occur preoccupied Washington. On May 22 Hatch told Day that "relations with Japan are becoming critical to a grave degree." Self-preservation compelled enforcement of the immigration laws, and "yielding to Japan means the complete and final establishment of their power, through the machinery of our own Constitution." If Hawai`i granted political equality, Japanese voters would surely end white minority rule, which had for many years deprived Asians of important civil rights. Japanese coercion might result if Hawai`i continued to resist suffrage demands, or did not settle the immigration dispute.[53]

The administration was acutely aware of the possibility of coercion, as demonstrated by a special assignment given to the Naval War College in late May. Captain Caspar Goodrich, president of the school, asked Secretary Long to think up a special problem in naval strategy for the student officers. Long bucked the request to Roosevelt, who sent a tasking "of interest and importance in certain contingencies." It read: "Special Confidential Problem for War College: Japan makes demands on Haw. Islands. This country intervenes. What force will be necessary to uphold the intervention and how shall it be employed? Keeping in mind possible complications with another Power on the Atlantic Coast (Cuba)."[54] Thus, by the end of May 1897, two groups—Admiral Sicard's war plans board and the War College—were working on war plans against Japan. Significantly, the administration initiated both planning efforts during the immigration crisis. Before 1897 the Navy possessed war plans for only Britain and Spain. Both were old adversaries. War planning against Japan demonstrated how seriously the Navy viewed the Japanese threat.[55]

Amid intense concern over the Japanese danger, the administration asked John Watson Foster to draft an annexation treaty. Foster reworked his 1893 treaty that Cleveland scuttled.[56] When Foster handed over his new draft, rolled up and secured with a rubber band, William Day held it up and said: "And that little roll can change the destiny of a nation."[57] The cautious McKinley kept the treaty a secret. He was not completely convinced that Japan intended to coerce Hawai`i.[58] When Harold Sewall departed for Hawai`i in late May, the president asked for a quick report on the "Japanese question."[59]

The drafting of the treaty concurrent with war planning against Japan and naval deployments shows that the treaty was part of American contingency plans. If suddenly announced, the treaty would be a diplomatic show of force, a clear, strong, "hands off" warning to Tokyo, much stronger than the Turpie "hands off" resolution of May 1894. The treaty "deterrent" would be used only if the Navy's buildup failed to moderate Japanese policy.[60]

If deterrence failed, Roosevelt was ready to fight. When the captain of the *Naniwa*, on its 1893 trip to Honolulu, refused to surrender to police an escaped prisoner of Japanese descent, Roosevelt asked Thurston if "the Japanese really intend to fight in Honolulu? If they do, I hope they will do so now, and we certainly will give them a bellyful."[61] In 1897 Roosevelt was still feisty. On June 2 he addressed the Naval War College on the topic: "To be prepared for war is the most effectual means to promote peace." National greatness came through strife, or the readiness for strife. A strong navy was necessary to protect islands that guarded the strategic approaches to the hemisphere.[62] Written during hurried contingency planning against Japan, the address exemplified the belligerent, jingoist spirit that infested Roosevelt, Mahan, Lodge, and other powerful annexationists.[63] Captain Goodrich praised the speech as "about the best address ever made here."[64] Even the peaceable McKinley showered Roosevelt with compliments and declared that he read it carefully.[65]

In this tense situation, three alarming dispatches received June 7 from Honolulu caused the administration to bring forth the secret treaty.[66] The dispatches had a tremendous impact. They confirmed suspicions that Japan was using the immigration dispute to push for greater power. According to the dispatches, Japan demanded that Hawai`i both indemnify the rejected immigrants and guarantee that future immigrants would never face "arbitrary and capricious" treatment. The guarantee against future disruptions of the continuing inflow (463 Japanese had entered during the first three weeks of May) attested to Japan's intent to keep sending immigrants despite Hawai`i's insistence on preapproved arrivals.[67]

Japan's demands also included the right for Japanese to travel, trade, and reside anywhere in Hawai`i and to join any profession or industry. Japan insisted that Hawai`i provide Japanese with complete protection for their persons, property, and civil rights. These civil rights were expressly to include voting, although that question supposedly had been settled by the discriminatory Constitution of 1894 that excluded Asians from the franchise. Although there was considerable justice in Tokyo's position, the United States saw only that Japan had enlarged a local immigration dispute into a major conflict over the political privileges of twenty-five thousand Japanese in the islands.[68]

The dispatches confirmed fears that Tokyo, and not merely an impetuous diplomat in Honolulu, ran the Japanese side of the confrontation. Japan's demands appeared in a letter from Count Ōkuma to the Republic of Hawai`i delivered by Akiyama, the special emissary. Ōkuma's letter and Akiyama's investigatory mission demonstrated that the confrontation was more than a local show. Akiyama had come to Hawai`i on Japan's most powerful warship instead of a civilian vessel. And recently Tokyo had promoted Shimamura to the same rank—minister—that senior U.S. diplomat Sewall would have. All this suggested that the Hawaiian–Japanese confrontation was now a deadly serious and potentially violent crisis.[69]

Finally, the dispatches suggested that Tokyo's demands amounted to an ultimatum. On May 22 Minister Shimamura appeared at the Foreign Office for a reply to the demands for an indemnity and a guarantee against future disruptions. The minister ominously stated that on instructions from Tokyo no more time would be permitted. After this meeting, Shimamura committed a huge tactical error by making incendiary remarks to the press: "Japan wants nothing unreasonable. . . . If she cannot get it—well, I do not know what will follow . . . the honor of Japan is at stake. . . . If I cannot get a reasonable answer to my request I may go home, and perhaps someone else will have better success. If I withdraw, you know what follows. I hope it will not reach that point."[70] Because Shimamura made these provocative statements while being advised by special emissary Akiyama and pressing Count Ōkuma's messages, the United States assumed that the minister represented Tokyo's official view. Refusal of the ultimatum might trigger armed intervention from the *Naniwa*.[71] Yet it was certain that Hawai`i would refuse. Hawaiian officials told the United States that a stand must be made to preserve Hawaiian independence. The American flotilla in the harbor made it much easier to stand tall.[72]

On the morning of June 8 Sherman forwarded the dispatches with a terse note: "Respectfully submitted to the President. This paper and the two enclosed are of extreme importance."[73] No dispatch from Hawai`i after the revolution of 1893 had received such swift attention and such an alarming endorsement. Judged by policy impact, the three missives of June 1897 were probably the most important ever received from Hawai`i.

McKinley, who evidently believed that Japanese intervention was at hand, promptly summoned Roosevelt. It was at this meeting, on the same day that the three dispatches were received, that the president "heartily endorsed" Roosevelt's belligerent June 2 address at the War College. McKinley's policy to date fitted in with the brief held by Roosevelt and Mahan that preparedness and a show of force would help a nation out of a tight spot. Roosevelt advised moving quickly toward annexation to avoid conflict with Japan. A treaty would be a powerful "hands off" warning. Surely the Japanese would back off once they knew how strongly America felt about the matter. McKinley agreed, saying he would "very shortly" submit an annexation treaty.[74]

The Japanese threat was the primary cause of McKinley's submission of the secret treaty. He later told Senator George Frisbie Hoar that the Japanese menace impelled strong measures for the islands: "Japan has her eye on them. Her people are crowding in there ... Japan is pressing them in there ... to get possession before anybody can interfere. If something is not done, there will be before long another Revolution, and Japan will get control." The president cited reports that recent immigrants marched ashore in a military step, indicating that they were former soldiers. (There is no evidence that Japan sent soldiers disguised as immigrants.) When Hawai`i prohibited further immigration, McKinley told Hoar, Japan claimed a violation of treaty rights and sent the *Naniwa* as a show of force. The president had notified Japan that the United States would not tolerate coercion.[75] Two days after McKinley received the three dispatches, the Hawaiian legation reported that "the Japanese question is helping us tremendously."[76] Hatch was pleased that Japan made a quiet settlement "next to impossible by coming on butt end first with an ultimatum."[77]

The extraordinary speed surrounding the treaty's submission came from the urgent need for a diplomatic weapon. After deciding on June 8 to reveal the treaty, McKinley tied up the loose ends in the draft so rapidly that, on June 11, Day asked three very surprised Hawaiian commissioners if they were ready to sign.[78] They were, but Sherman, whose signature was necessary, was with the president in Nashville until June 15. At nine thirty on the morning of June 16, the principals signed the treaty in the State Department's Diplomatic Room, decorated with portraits of Blaine, Foster, Jefferson, and Seward. The former two portraits had, in a strangely fitting coincidence, just replaced a massive portrait of Gresham, a fierce opponent of annexation.[79]

There was no domestic political reason for such swift action. The tariff bill, still wending its way through Congress, promised to prevent action on the treaty for weeks. Even if the Senate immediately took up the treaty, the customary debate probably would prevent ratification in the current session, which would end July 24. Moreover, the administration was not sure of sixty protreaty votes, although a big majority of the Senate favored the pact. Nor had McKinley informed Senate Republican leaders such as Cushman Davis, chairman of the foreign relations committee, that he would submit a treaty. McKinley undoubtedly realized that ratification would take a long time. Why did he conclude a treaty so quickly? The best explanation is that he saw the treaty as a means to deter Japan from rash action against Hawai`i.

American fears of Japanese military intervention were powerful and genuine. This was conclusively demonstrated on June 10, when Long secretly cabled Admiral Beardslee: "Watch carefully the situation. If Japanese openly resort to force, such as military occupation or the seizure of public buildings, confer with Minister and authorities, land a suitable force, and announce officially provisional assumption of protectorate pending ratification of treaty of annexation."[80] Long's telegram, sent even before the administration informed the Hawaiian legation of the existence of the treaty, allowed American forces to ready themselves before news of the signing reached the islands. The telegram shows the administration was not completely convinced that the treaty's public announcement would defuse the situation. Military precautions seemed prudent. Beardslee was not to act unless "force is actually resorted to by Japan."[81] Although the forcible repulsion by American troops of a Japanese landing would mean war, the administration believed that Hawai`i was worth it.

The treaty text shows that the administration intended to prevent a Japanese takeover, even if limited to "Japanization" through immigration. The treaty would abrogate all existing Hawai`i–Japan agreements. The State Department noted that "the operation of our immigration and contract labor acts would at once stop Japanese coolie immigration to Hawai`i."[82] On June 16 Sherman informed Minister Hoshi that the United States would not assume treaty obligations from Japan's past agreements with Hawai`i.[83]

The whole tenor of American policy during 1897 indicates that the so-called Japanese menace triggered the annexation treaty. Although the administration planned to obtain tariff reform before dealing with Hawaiian matters, provocative Japanese actions necessitated vigorous responses. The important American actions in Hawaiian policy—the urgent dispatch of the Beardslee flotilla, the drawing of the first war plans against Japan, the swift and secret preparation of the Foster draft treaty, and the sudden submission of the treaty—were reactions and not initiatives. Japan's demand for an indemnity and voting rights for Japanese, the Ōkuma ultimatum, and McKinley's decision to bring forth the treaty as a warning to Tokyo demonstrated the cause-and-effect relationship between Japanese and American policy: Japan moved and America jumped.

But would Japan heed the hands-off warning? If Japan attempted coercion, Beardslee's June 10 orders made a military clash, even war, a certainty. Despite the precautionary orders, U.S. officials somewhat naively assumed that Japan would quickly back down. Naval precautions and diplomatic warnings worked in 1893 and 1894, so they assumed the same tactics would work again, even though Japan's claimed interests, and willingness to support them, had grown enormously. Like other senior officials, Sherman was initially unconcerned with Japan's reaction. At the treaty signing ceremony, Sherman asked Hatch: "I suppose you know that Japan protests against this?" Hatch shook his head no. Sherman said, "Yes, Mr. Hoshi . . . protested against annexation." When Hatch asked upon what grounds, Sherman muttered: "Well, Mr. Hoshi does not talk very good English and I knew it would not amount to anything anyway, so I did not pay very much attention to what he said."[84] Hoshi sensed the inattention, following up with a diplomatic note that Japan "could not view without concern . . . a sudden and complete change in the status of Hawai`i whereby the rights of Japan and of Japanese subjects may be imperiled."[85] Sherman urged Hatch to settle differences with the Japanese. Hatch called on Hoshi the following day.

Minister Hoshi Toru was one of Japan's most powerful party politicians. A biographer of Ōkuma described Hoshi as a man of "genius and energy, with great force of character, of iron will and independent mind, imperious and haughty, more feared than loved."[86] Born the son of a plasterer in 1850, Hoshi was adopted as a child by a physician. He quickly learned to speak English—his English was surely better than Sherman's description—and his language skills helped make him chief of the Yokohama Customs Office in the 1870s. He studied law in Britain. In 1877 he became the first Japanese to qualify as a barrister, another indication of his language and intellectual skills. Even on the busiest days, he read for a couple of hours. Hoshi liked getting his way. He bragged that he manipulated people with gold and a big stick. If they could not be bribed, he coerced them. Persuasion and principle were not in his arsenal. In 1892 Hoshi entered the Diet's lower house and soon became speaker. He was often accused of financial impropriety. While speaker, it was discovered that he was concurrently serving—illegally—as a salaried official of the Osaka Stock Exchange. A motion removing Hoshi as speaker passed 166–119. The Diet was therefore stunned when, the following day, Hoshi occupied the speaker's chair, declaring he had done nothing wrong and would not obey the resolution. After a week of disorder, the Diet expelled him. In 1896 Hoshi decided he wanted to be minister to Washington. A short, stocky man with a lot of energy, Hoshi was excitable and, according to the *New York Times*, "greatly imbued with a sense of his own importance."[87] When challenged, one Japanese observer noted, Hoshi was "always for war to the death."[88] As a representative of the new generation of politicians as well as the cantankerous Japanese public mood, his attitude would be a good predictor of Japan's reaction to the annexation treaty.

Hatch said he regretted that Japan sensed its national honor at stake. Hawai`i did not intend an insult and would gladly make an "explanation or statement of regret" to assuage Japanese feelings. Hoshi asked if Hawai`i would pay an indemnity. Hatch said if the national honor question were put aside, an indemnity could be discussed. Hatch asked what Tokyo thought of annexation. Hoshi hesitated, then said Japan would be opposed to annexation. He himself disliked the new treaty.

Hoshi's admission shocked Hatch. For months, Hoshi ridiculed assertions that Japan had designs on the islands. He dismissed fears of Japanese coercion.[89] Hoshi portrayed Japan as a victim of arbitrary Hawaiian immigration procedures. He charged that Hawai`i provoked the crisis to "stir up public opinion . . . in favor of annexation." Hatch complained that the Japanese story was "gaining credence in some quarters."[90] He counseled against intemperate actions by "our hot headed supporters" that could be touted as evidence that Hawai`i sought to provoke Japan. Hatch himself did not believe that Japan intended coercion because he too had bought into Hoshi's public deception.[91] In fact, the whole Hawaiian government doubted until June that Japan would use force, which partly explains Hawai`i's willingness to take a strong immigration stance earlier in the year.[92]

Hoshi achieved a nice public deception, hiding the fact that Japan opposed annexation. Personally, he wanted Japanese dominance. With the annexation treaty threatening to end that possibility, he urged seizure of the islands. He cabled Ōkuma: "This is strictly confidential. I desire to submit to your consideration what I believe is the only possible means by which the proposed annexation could be prevented. It is this: that taking advantage of the present strained relations between Japan and Hawai`i a strong naval armament should be at once dispatched for the purpose of occupying the islands by force."[93]

If the McKinley administration could have monitored Japanese diplomatic traffic, it would have trumpeted Hoshi's message as proof of subterfuge. Those who had not previously believed in Japanese designs would have joined the annexation drive. Almost certainly the treaty would have been brought to a vote and passed in the special session. No senator, no administration official would permit Japanese occupation of the islands.

Ignorant of Hoshi's proposal to use force, the Americans relaxed, confident the treaty's "hands off" warning would deter Japan. On June 17, Roosevelt lunched with his friend Day, then wrote Goodrich that "there doesn't seem any immediate likelihood of trouble with Japan at present."[94] He told the vacationing Long that the Japanese "are feeling decidedly ugly about Hawai`i, but I am very sure that their feelings will not take any tangible form."[95] The relaxation period lasted less than two weeks.

Foreign Minister Ōkuma ruled out Hoshi's rash suggestion to attack. To calm the excitable Hoshi, Ōkuma worded a temperate reply: "It is too late." With the United States formally committed to annexation, seizure would mean war. The best option was "to protest in as strong a language as is permissible . . . without running the risk of war."[96] Ōkuma was far less temperate speaking to the British chargé d'affaires, Gerald Lowther. He greatly resented Sherman's failure to inform Hoshi that a treaty was in the works. He insisted annexation would damage Japan's "very material interests." Lowther told London that one newspaper close to the government demanded a very strong protest and if Japanese demands were not met, Japan must "appeal to the ultimate resort."[97]

Japan three times asked Britain to join in blocking annexation, and Britain three times replied that although it opposed annexation, open protests would make the United States more determined.[98] Ōkuma ignored this wise advice. He had Hoshi deliver a second protest listing three reasons why Japan opposed annexation: (1) maintenance of the status quo in Hawai`i was essential to the good understanding among the Pacific powers, (2) annexation would endanger the rights of Japanese subjects, and (3) annexation might delay settlement of the immigration dispute. Just a day after privately urging an attack, in a note to Sherman conveying Ōkuma's points, Hoshi went to great lengths to stress that Japan had no designs on Hawai`i.[99]

Japan's second protest mightily surprised American policy makers. Like Hatch, they too had misread Japanese intentions. Although Japan deployed the *Naniwa* and the *Kongo* after the 1893 revolution and pushed for voting rights for Japanese, Tokyo had not protested the 1893 annexation treaty and silently accepted the May 1894 Turpie resolution, which warned all nations against meddling in Hawai`i. But now Japan declared that its interests had grown so much that the United States must take them into account. Japan's assertiveness, along with upsetting news from Minister Sewall in Honolulu, reignited American fears of military action.

Roosevelt huddled with Admiral Sicard, Commander Goodrich, and other senior officers to brainstorm how to cope with military intervention.[100] The resultant June 30 plan assumed a war with Japan during 1897. Hawai`i was the key to success: "Our principal object should be to concentrate a sufficient force at the Hawaiian Islands to hold them against the Japanese fleet." If the Imperial Navy steamed directly to the West Coast, it would have to refuel from colliers, always a risky and unreliable procedure, especially in the rough North Pacific, or arrive off the coast with insufficient coal for a successful attack. Only at Hawai`i could the Japanese fleet conveniently and safely recoal; therefore, it was the most likely place of attack.

The Sicard war plan embraced the now-standard strategic argument that possession of Hawai`i greatly enhanced coastal security.[101] Roosevelt paid attention when retired Admiral George Belknap noted that Japan's first battleships—the *Fuji* and the *Yashima*—neared completion in British yards.[102] Should the warships appear in Hawai`i, America would be outgunned. Roosevelt requested that American consuls throughout the world report movements of the *Fuji*, about to depart the Thames Iron Works.[103]

On June 25 Sherman replied to Japan's second protest, denying that annexation would disadvantage Japan or affect the status quo, which he asserted was American predominance. For more than a half century, America exercised predominant influence in Hawai`i and twice negotiated annexation treaties—in 1854 and 1893—without Japanese objection. He ignored the fact that the replacement of Hawaiian laws with tougher American rules would extinguish Japan's claims that the Treaty of 1871 allowed Japanese residents full civil rights, including suffrage.[104]

When Long returned from vacation on July 3, he recorded that "the horizon seems peaceful."[105] Yet within a week Long was directing military preparations against Japan, triggered by news that arrived between July 3 and 10. Long and Sherman were bothered by Sewall's report that "after three months of discussion and correspondence the two governments are at their widest divergence in their views, with no probability of reconciliation. Irritation and strong feeling has developed." A Japanese "rupture with the Government of Hawai`i is possible, which will lead to a demand made on it and enforced." On the heels of this dispatch—sent to the president—came another, asserting that Japan had "more serious intentions in its actions here than has been apparent or seemed probable."[106]

The final straw was a third, even stronger Japanese protest on July 10. Hoshi noted—with some justification—that moving beyond predominant influence to actual annexation disrupted the status quo because Japanese interests were greater than when annexation was previously considered. Japan could not accept annexation's disadvantages "in a spirit of acquiescence."[107]

On the same day of this third protest, a worried Sherman sent Sewall an alert order similar to Long's June 10 message: "If Japanese should openly resort to force, such as a military occupation or seizure of public property, you will confer with local authorities and Admiral, land suitable force, and announce provisional assumption of protectorate."[108] Long renewed his own alert order to Admiral Beardslee. The messages of June 10 and July 10 were unique; no similar orders had ever been sent to Hawai`i. Washington emphasized that the warning orders were precautionary. Of course they were precautionary. That they were sent at all is the important point.[109] Day and Adee may also have reflected on how far beyond his instructions John Stevens had gone in 1893. By stressing that the orders were precautionary, Sewall would know that Washington was not hinting that he should preemptively land troops.

Reports from Japan portrayed a feisty atmosphere. The *Japan Times*, often a government mouthpiece, called the rejection of the immigrants "an affront which ought not to be passed over."[110] The *Mainichi Shimbun* editorialized: "Japan cannot ignore this. . . . If Japan submits tamely to such wrongs, it will be generally understood that her people cannot count on her protection outside her own dominions. . . . Japan has made her entry on the world's stage in the Chinese war, and she may not shrink from asserting her rights."[111] The U.S. consulate in Yokohama said Japanese were "intensely wrought up . . . over the recent refusal of Hawai`i to accept their emigrants and our supposed endorsement of the action."[112] Anti-American feeling in Kobe may have caused the violent incidents in July involving crew of the *Yorktown* and *Boston*, and the apparent murders of *Olympia* and *Yorktown* men in Nagasaki later in the year.[113]

As the Japanese and Hawaiians remained at loggerheads, the Navy took further precautions. Long ordered the *Oregon*, the sole American battleship in the Pacific, to be "coaled and prepared in all respects to proceed on short notice to the Hawaiian Islands. The Department especially desires that this should be done in a manner as not to attract attention."[114] Admiral Frederick McNair in Yokohama watched for additional Japanese warships going to Hawai`i.[115] Long gave Admiral Beardslee only a week to analyze the strategic points in Hawai`i that the Navy would need to occupy in case of war.[116] He permitted no U.S. ships to rotate home and added *Bennington* to the flotilla.[117] The department ordered intelligence analyses of Imperial Navy facilities at Yokohama, Nagasaki, Yokosuka, and Kobe.[118] The department received secret reports on the capabilities of the new battleships *Fuji* and *Yashima*, and the cruiser *Naniwa*, probably from the British, who built all three ships.[119]

A final flurry of activity demonstrated how carefully the Navy watched the islands. Roosevelt learned on September 20 that the *Naniwa* departed for a six-week trip home for maintenance. He seized the opportunity to rotate his overstretched naval forces. He ordered *Philadelphia* home for a long-overdue overhaul: "Secret and confidential. I have informed the President that *Baltimore* will be . . . en route to Honolulu within five days of arrival of *Philadelphia* at Mare Island. This is a case of emergency."[120] The *Philadelphia*'s crew should transfer immediately to *Baltimore*, without a crew during overhaul, and return swiftly to Honolulu. *Wheeling*, then at Mare Island, should also go to Hawai`i, and *Yorktown*, en route home from China, should hold at Honolulu. Finally, he instructed the Navy yard: "Enlist servants [for] *Baltimore*. No Japanese. This point not to be mentioned."[121]

McKinley personally approved Roosevelt and Long's naval preparations. Between September 14 and 21, the president conferred with Roosevelt four times. McKinley told Roosevelt that he had been "quite right" in saying in a recent speech that Hawai`i should be annexed without regard to Japan's protests.[122] As late as September 22, McKinley still fretted about war with Japan and heartily endorsed Roosevelt's furious shifting of warships in the wake of the *Naniwa*'s departure.[123]

Sherman, with Day and Adee looking over his shoulder, took his time in responding to Japan's July 10 protest. His August 14 reply gave no ground. He criticized Japan's (correct) contention that annexation did not command a majority of the Hawaiian people, saying the will of a country is expressed by its government policy, and the Hawaiian government supported annexation. Sherman pointed out that before Japan had an elected Diet, no one inquired whether the government was popularly accepted. (The Diet was first elected in 1889.) He strongly disputed the notion that annexation would restrict Japan's influence in the Pacific.[124] To make sure Japan got the message, Sherman leaked the existence of the three military alert orders. On August 19 the *Philadelphia Press*, in an article based on an interview with Sherman, said that Sewall undoubtedly had orders to seize Hawai`i if Japan took offensive action. An attack on Hawai`i would be considered an assault on the United States itself.[125]

The annexation treaty forced other powers to formulate a policy. All disliked annexation but did not want to follow Japan's lead. Germany asked Britain to join in demanding that American rights in Samoa should be forfeited. Britain told Germany that the best method to prevent annexation was remain quiet. Britain remained passive when Russia suggested joining the Japanese protest. New Zealand's prime minister R. J. Seddon twice urged opposition to annexation so that America should not control the best potential naval base in the Pacific. The Foreign Office demurred, drafting a reply that said the United States would regard interference as a casus belli.[126] The Colonial Office added: "No doubt it would be advantageous to have a naval base in the center of the Pacific, but we cannot have everything, and as things are we have got a very fair share of the Pacific."[127] Britain would lead no charge against the United States.

Japan began to shift course itself. Strong protests and naval deployments had
not scared the United States. Japan floated an idea of welding Germany, Russia,
Britain, and France along with the Americans into a six-party conference to discuss
Hawai`i's status as well as plans for transpacific cables. Britain's passivity made the
conference completely impractical.[128] By late summer, Japan's confrontational spirit
began to ebb in the face of the unyielding American attitude as well as by political
distractions at home. By fall, British minister Satow no longer saw a danger of
Japan using force in Hawai`i. The Matsukata-Ōkuma government, weakened by
internal strife, slowly lost its grip on power. Ito Hirobumi became prime minister.
Baron Nishi Tokujiro replaced Ōkuma as foreign minister on November 6. Nishi
steered toward compromise, counseled by Satow, who reminded him that if Japan
wanted the United States to annex Hawai`i, it would be "very easy to provoke
them to it." At the end of the year, Satow reported that Japan no longer sought to
block the treaty, simply hoping for its defeat in the Senate.[129]

Foreign Minister Nishi did not send the *Naniwa* back to Honolulu. The
atmosphere seemed right for a settlement. The United States urged Hawai`i
to avoid provoking Japan further. Hawai`i relaxed its get-tough immigration
measures.[130] On December 22, 1897, Japan withdrew its protest, citing assurances
that the United States would assume well-founded indemnity claims. Robert
Irwin reported that the new cabinet would "absolutely" accept annexation.[131] In
the summer of 1898 Japan accepted a Hawaiian indemnity offer of $75,000, made
under significant American pressure.[132]

The U.S.–Japan crisis of 1897 was not a phony confrontation invented by
Honolulu to provoke annexation. Japan's actions drove the crisis. Japan could
have handled the immigrant rejections as a simple quarrel over unfair admittance
procedures and focused on rule changes or compensation. Instead, in April 1897,
Foreign Minister Ōkuma dramatically enlarged the dispute by opposing annexation, even before McKinley committed to it. Japan officially informed the United
States that it opposed annexation, deployed warships to Honolulu, reiterated and
fleshed out its opposition in strong protests over the next five months, tried to
enlist Britain and other powers to join in blocking annexation, and finally sought
a multiparty conference to preempt annexation through a multilateral guarantee
of Hawaiian independence. Japan's opposition to annexation and assertion of
competing interests alarmed the United States. Tokyo officials, not Hawaiian officials, created Japan's stance. Although both Hawaiian and American officials knew
Japan's tough policy helped annexation, there is no basis for occasional claims that
Hawai`i created the immigration dispute to trigger annexation.[133]

The Japanese–American clash produced the 1897 annexation treaty. The confrontation dramatized Hawai`i's vulnerability and its strategic value in case of war in the Pacific. Japan's assertion of significant national interests in Hawai`i and its attempt to block annexation surprised everyone. American worries about Japanese subversion or even coercion of Hawai`i mounted substantially, hardening annexationist sentiment in the administration and the Congress. The confrontation gave the Hawaiian issue an urgency and credibility that made annexation in 1898 a near certainty.

British ambassador to the United States Julian Pauncefote knew that the treaty marked a great watershed in American policy. He told London, "The most important act of the present administration, involving a change of policy as regards the acquisition of territory outside the Union, has just been consummated by President McKinley."[134] The American commitment to acquire its first overseas territory was triggered by the necessity to cope with Japanese pressure.

CHAPTER 15

❦

Annexation Consummated:
The Spanish-American War and Hawai`i

S peaker of the House Tom Reed was a giant, physically and politically. Fifty-eight years old, Reed was a burly, moon-faced man who was "as graceful in his manner as an elephant," and like an elephant, he had big ears that jutted from his head. Six foot three and perhaps three hundred pounds, his thick hands were as wide as dinner plates. He had thin flaxen hair, a scant blond mustache, and lily-white, soft skin. His ponderous, rolling gait ebbed and flowed, a tidal movement that, in a crowd, made him seem "like a great three-decker in a surging sea." He was so big that one fellow pedestrian blurted: "How narrow he makes the street look!" A House colleague said Reed had the largest human face he had ever seen.[1]

Reed came from tough stock. An ancestor was aboard the *Mayflower*, and his family settled in Maine in the early seventeenth century. Not that the Reeds were rich bluebloods. Reed's father put up his small coastal freighter as collateral to pay for his boy's tuition at Bowdoin. Reed offset expenses himself by part-time teaching. He served in the Union Navy as a commissary officer, never under fire, and, unlike some 1890s contemporaries such as his friends Roosevelt and Lodge, too young to serve, he never described the war as a glorious test of manhood.

"Czar" Reed earned his nickname by forging rules that greatly increased the Speaker's power as chair of the Rules Committee to bring up or delay legislation.

Champ Clark called him the "greatest parliamentary leader of his time ... far and away the most brilliant figure in American politics." Republicans were afraid to cross him, even when they were the minority party and he wasn't Speaker. Charles Crisp, the Democratic speaker during 1891–95, lamented: "When Reed says do it, they all step up and do it."[2] His friends were carefully chosen. Only those of superior intellect qualified, but to them he was good-natured. That may explain his friendship with Hitt, Lodge, and Roosevelt, with whom he disagreed on expansion.

Reed opposed any and all territorial acquisitions. He coined the phrase "Empire Can Wait" as the title of his December 1897 article in the *Illustrated American*. Reed's study of empires convinced him that they always collapsed from within as the people ceased to think the same thoughts and promote the common good. It would cause problems to take in people from ethnic and religious groups not already present in the United States, he warned.[3]

The big man was a big obstacle to Hawaiian annexation. Only two days were normally allotted for debate and voting on a bill or resolution. If action was not completed within two days, the House moved on to other business. If the Rules Committee—meaning the speaker—did not rule that a vote must take place, anti-annexationists could easily kill the measure by filibustering for two days, allowing Reed to drop the measure without a vote.

In opposing annexation, Reed positioned himself against his friends but particularly against President McKinley. There had always been some bad blood between the two. Some went so far as to call it hate, at least on Reed's part. This was partly politics. When the Republicans won the lower house in 1888, Reed beat McKinley for the post of speaker. However he felt about the loss, McKinley kept his mouth shut and, as majority leader and chair of the Ways and Means Committee, focused on his work, including crafting the McKinley tariff of 1890, highly unpopular with Democrats. This effort cost McKinley his seat when the Democratic Ohio legislature gerrymandered his district, but Ohioans soon elected him governor. By 1896 he was the leader for the Republican presidential nomination that Reed lusted after. Reed thought he deserved it, an attitude that was glaringly, even obnoxiously, obvious. An unworried Mark Hanna knew that Reed's inability to compromise and his insistence on straightening people out would limit his appeal. McKinley easily won at the convention, 661 delegates to 84.

Personality, more than politics, underlay the rivalry. Two more dissimilar politicians could hardly be imagined. McKinley was smart, but Reed was an intellectual and flaunted it. McKinley moved men through persuasion and subtle manipulation; Reed used pressure and compulsion. McKinley was so pragmatic that he could appear without principles; Reed followed his own star relentlessly. McKinley was quiet, unassuming, and seldom said a harsh word about anyone. Reed spoke loudly, dominated every gathering, and had a rapier wit. When a pompous House member solemnly declared that, like Henry Clay, he, the member, would rather be right than president. "The gentleman from Illinois need not be disturbed," interjected Reed from the chair, "he will never be either." Another time, Reed was in the full swing of a speech when interrupted by a trivial question. Turning, he answered the query with a few sarcastic words, then added: "And now, having embalmed that fly in the amber of my remarks, I will proceed."[4] Reed's sarcasm did not endear him to colleagues: "Sometimes he cut the skin off, sometimes he cut to the bone, and sometimes he crushed in a skull as though it were an eggshell."[5]

Reed's opposition greatly complicated the strategy for getting annexation through Congress. The administration intended the treaty as a quick warning to Japan, so no spadework had been done to smooth its passage. But it seemed easier to gain the few votes needed for the two-thirds majority of sixty than to challenge Reed with a joint resolution. And some thought a joint resolution would erode the Senate's role.[6]

Friendship made some Republicans, such as his old friends Roosevelt and Lodge, slow to break with Reed. An intimate friend was Reed's arch-foe on Hawai`i, Robert Hitt. The two men met years before on Hitt's first day as a congressman when both boarded a streetcar to the Capitol. Hitt fumbled through his pockets muttering about forgetting his wallet. Reed calmly passed the conductor a nickel for Hitt's fare, sat down, waited until Hitt was comfortably settled, fixed him with a steely glare, and said "I don't think you can work that racket successfully all winter." The whole car burst into laughter and even the shy Hitt chuckled. The two men became fast friends. Their families dined together to celebrate the tenth anniversary of two men's friendship. When Hitt became severely ill during an 1895 recess, Reed came down from Maine to Hitt's Washington residence to see him. When Hitt recovered, often they could be seen strolling around the Capitol as they discussed some legislative matter, the voluble Speaker's huge right arm draped across his slight friend's skinny, sloping shoulders, and his left arm gesturing as he pressed his arguments.[7]

In the fall of 1897 senior Republicans liked the treaty's chances. The New York Herald counted sixty-one senators favoring the pact.[8] The crisis with Japan had cooled but not gone away. Annexationists kept it in the public mind with feisty comments. Foster declared "the most threatening present danger is from Japan." A Hawai`i visit by a congressional delegation returned the foreordained conclusion that only annexation could prevent Japanese dominance.[9] Annexationists knew Japan's opposition helped their cause. Hatch thought Japan's protest "must help the treaty through the Senate."[10] In September, as Roosevelt juggled naval deployments, Cushman Davis wrote Lodge: "I see that Japan is apparently menacing Hawai`i. Dole ought to have requested us six months ago to land troops. I am afraid that we shall have trouble there: though perhaps I express myself more accurately by writing 'I am afraid we shall not have trouble.'"[11]

When all senators arrived for the December session, the treaty lacked sixty votes. Davis claimed the antitreaty sugar interests turned a couple of senatorial heads. Nor did four Populist senators support the treaty, as hoped.[12] McKinley met several times with senior Republicans to plan policy toward Cuba and Hawai`i.[13] Davis and Roosevelt worked furiously on doubtful senators. Roosevelt courted another senator "wrong on the Hawaiian treaty" and arranged for Mahan to write the undecided Senator George Frisbie Hoar.[14] He offered to review Mahan's new book, *The Interest of America in Sea Power*, for the *New York Sun*, to "say something on behalf of Hawai`i."[15]

Roosevelt's belief in the strategic desirability of annexation had grown even stronger. "For military reasons Hawai`i is almost more important to us" than Cuba, where he wished to intervene immediately. He lamented that "in the Pacific we are now inferior to Japan." If annexation failed, the United States would have to fight when Japan or some other power took the islands.[16] Predictable views from a man who just spent six months orchestrating naval deployments to deter Japanese intervention.

McKinley was "turning heaven and earth" for ratification.[17] Senator Hoar returned from a White House talk convinced McKinley genuinely feared Japan would seize Hawai`i if the opportunity presented itself.[18] McKinley pressed other wavering senators about "the growing power of Japan."[19] Japan's withdrawal of its protest of annexation passed unnoticed in late December because no one believed it ended the long-term threat. The "Hawaiian matter looks better than it did three weeks ago," Cushman Davis told his law partners, and "we shall eventually obtain the necessary two-thirds vote."[20] When President Dole made a goodwill visit, McKinley assigned a military escort, hosted a state dinner, and arranged a congressional resolution of welcome.[21] Annexationists staged so many dinners that the *Post* quipped that "Dole may have to annex a new digestive apparatus before he completes his mission!"[22]

The Senate discussed the treaty behind closed doors seven times in January 1898.[23] Leaked immediately, these sessions ventilated arguments for and against annexation. Davis' opening remarks gave "especial attention" to Hawai`i's strategic importance. He displayed a map (similar to Lodge's 1895 map) of strategic positions in the Pacific. He trotted out the familiar arguments that annexation would guarantee the safety of the West Coast, provide an invaluable naval base in the event of a Pacific war, and aid in the defense of an isthmian canal. Davis believed annexation would stimulate trade with Asia, but his concern about "the opening of a new condition of affairs in the Far East" was only partly commercial. The threatened partition of China enhanced Hawai`i's military value, he declared, for if hostile European powers held large segments of the Asian coast, and based warships there, the American navy needed Pearl Harbor to protect the American coast.[24] This strategic argument is what Cushman Davis had in mind when he claimed that "the intervention of European powers in the affairs of China and Corea is having a beneficial effect on the prospects of the treaty."[25]

John Tyler Morgan also linked Hawai`i's strategic value to European imperialism in Asia. Some power would grab Hawai`i if the United States pulled out. And from Hawai`i, a power could easily attack.[26] Hitt agreed that European intervention in Asia strengthened the strategic argument, for "national defense is paramount."[27] Admiral George Belknap, the former commander of the Asiatic squadron, told the Commercial Club of Boston that economic competition caused imperialism. European powers were ready to divide up the Chinese empire. Hawai`i was more a potential foreign target than an American stepping-stone. Belknap wondered: "Fancy a German squadron steaming into the harbor of Honolulu, and proceeding as a [German] squadron did the other day at Kiau Chau bay in China." Only annexation would put Hawai`i "off limits."[28]

On January 15 a *New York Times* poll revealed fifty-five to fifty-eight protreaty votes; the *Tribune* counted fifty-seven. Annexation remained a strongly partisan issue. Of the forty-seven Republicans, all but Justin Morrill, and perhaps George Hoar, would vote for the treaty. Most of the thirty-four Democrats hesitated to approve what they saw as a Republican measure. The administration hoped for sixty votes within a week.[29] The British embassy judged prospects for ratification "brighter than some few days ago," but Hatch estimated four to six weeks to line up a favorable vote.[30] Protest petitions signed by thousands of members of the Native Hawaiian societies Hui Kalai`aina and Hui Aloha `Aina changed no minds.[31]

Cuba now took up so much time and attention that it was hard to complete the horse trading for the final few votes. For a time in 1897, it looked as if the Cuban matter might settle down. The Spanish government relieved the hated General Weyler, architect of the brutal *reconcentrado* policy. But things flared up again during the treaty debate. McKinley sent the *Maine* to Havana in January 1898 to demonstrate American concern.

Impatient annexationists wanted to abandon the treaty for the joint resolution.[32] At a Hatch dinner for senators William Chandler, Mark Hanna, Cushman Davis, William Frye, and Redfield Proctor, Rep. Robert Hitt, former secretary of state

John Watson Foster, and Admiral John Walker, all agreed a joint resolution was easier.[33] A big annexationist majority existed in the House. Republicans outnumbered Democrats 206 to 124—with 27 Populists and pro-silver Republicans—but the huge majority did not matter if Reed blocked a vote.

So, barely short of 60, the administration stuck with the treaty. On February 2 the Senate resumed debate.[34] The latest canvass counted 58 protreaty votes; Senator Stewart of Nevada tallied 57.[35]

Precisely at that moment, Cuba permanently scuttled the treaty. On February 9, the *Herald* published an indiscreet private letter from Spanish minister Enrique Dupuy de Lôme. The Cuban rebels intercepted the letter at the Havana post office and gave it to Hearst's paper. De Lôme's slanders enraged Americans: McKinley was "weak and catering to the rabble . . . a low politician, who desires to leave a door open to me and to stand well with the jingoes of his party." De Lôme swiftly resigned, but Americans reconfirmed their jingo view of Spain as devious and backstabbing. In this poisonous atmosphere, the *Maine* blew up in Havana on February 15. Most Americans instantly assumed the Spanish destroyed the ship. Cuban affairs filled every nook and cranny of national politics. With no time for further lobbying, the administration reluctantly turned to a joint resolution.[36]

After the *Maine* disaster, Hatch said the shocked capital "centered on Cuba" with "very little heart" for anything else.[37] Foster judged that "the Spanish imbroglio was uppermost in the minds of Senators, and it was difficult to secure attention to any other question."[38] The administration erred in sticking with the treaty so long, but without the huge distraction of Cuba, the administration probably would have secured sixty votes in January or February 1898. The treaty's failure was hardly a triumph of antiannexationist views that represented barely more than a third of the Senate and less than a third of the House. Nevertheless, treaty advocates failed to overcome the anti-imperialists' strongly held beliefs, of which, as Thomas J. Osborne concludes, the most powerful was "the hallowed American doctrines decrying territorial expansion overseas."[39]

The administration introduced a joint resolution in the Senate, thinking upper house passage might induce Reed to allow a House vote, for the speaker often proclaimed he would not stand against a majority, and majority support for annexation was glaringly evident.[40] On March 16 the Senate Foreign Relations Committee approved the resolution and issued a report named after the chair, Cushman Davis.[41]

The Davis Report was a compendium of annexationist arguments and a good guide to their relative priority. It is worth remembering that the report appeared six weeks before the emergence of the "war measure" argument that the United

States needed Hawai`i to prosecute the war with Spain. The report's five reasons for annexation paralleled those in Lorrin Thurston's propaganda masterpiece, the *Handbook on the Annexation of Hawai`i*. Annexation would, first, give America strategic control of the North Pacific, thereby "protecting its Pacific coast and commerce from attack." Second, annexation would prevent Japanese dominance. Third, annexation would increase Hawaiian–American commerce and, fourth, secure the shipping business of the islands. Finally, annexation would remove Hawai`i as a "certain source of international friction."[42]

The Davis Report's main theme was Hawai`i's great military value. The "chief reason" for annexation was to protect "what the United States already owns. It is not primarily to secure new territory, promote shipping, and increase commerce, but is a measure of precaution to prevent the acquisition by a foreign, and, perhaps in the future hostile, power of an acknowledged military stronghold."[43] An important appendix titled "The Strategic Position of Hawai`i" reiterated the crucial recoaling argument. Because there was "no place to recoal except Hawai`i," annexation would "protect the Pacific coast from trans-Pacific attack."[44]

The Davis Report highlighted the Japanese threat represented by the immigration and suffrage matters discussed so extensively during the confrontation of 1897. During late 1896 and early 1897, Japanese arrived in the islands at the rate of more than two thousand per month. In a year, Japanese would constitute half the population. Hawai`i's curtailment of the massive inflow met vigorous protests. Although Japanese were currently ineligible for citizenship, such an "energetic, ambitious, warlike, and progressive people" could not long be denied political equality. The "ultimate supremacy of the Japanese" would constitute "a grave military danger" to the Pacific coast.[45]

Recent events in Asia "added strength to the strategic reasons favoring annexation." "The Europeanizing of China" and the rapid growth of Japanese power could mean that the United States would face "relatively large fleets . . . , not only in the Far East but in some of the Pacific islands." The commercial advantages of annexation were American trade with the Hawaiian islands themselves and protecting and enhancing trade among the Pacific coast states.[46] Transpacific trade was a growing but not yet a top priority, as demonstrated by U.S. dismissal of British worries in March 1898 that European powers or Japan would restrict free commerce with China by establishing leaseholds. Britain asked the United States to jointly oppose any restrictions on commerce. Day declined, as the United States did not believe that "open trade in China" was endangered.[47]

Like the treaty, the Davis Report and the Senate joint resolution quickly disappeared in the maelstrom of the war crisis. A day after the March 16 Davis Report,

Senator Redfield Proctor, just returned from Cuba, delivered an enormously influential indictment of Spain that many senators thought made war inevitable.[48] Roosevelt could not see "how we can avoid intervening in Cuba."[49] On March 21 the *Maine* investigators reported that a submarine mine, set by unknown persons, destroyed the warship. Most Americans thought the report confirmed Spanish treachery. Who else had reason to destroy the ship?

War fever surged even higher. After the *Maine* report, the Cuban crisis kept Hawai`i sidelined for seven weeks, until the fighting of early May. Congress spent those weeks debating war or making war preparations. The State Department was consumed with Cuba, so Hatch stayed away.[50] Cushman Davis spent every moment on Cuba.[51] Secretary of State Sherman, old and forgetful, could not help. His deputy, William Day, missed most of April and early May because of his wife's illness. Robert Hitt too was home sick all of April.[52] With war fever peaking and the government consumed with war preparations, there was no chance to press annexation.

The war crisis dramatized the Navy's defensive role and, indirectly, the necessity for offshore naval stations such as Hawai`i, both key annexationist arguments. Anticipating war, Congress unanimously voted $50 million for the largest peacetime military appropriations bill in history, followed by a huge naval appropriations bill.[53] Coastal security was the chief argument for the naval increase, although the 38 warships authorized would not enter the fleet for years. But the bill funded leases that soon brought 128 civilian vessels into the Navy for coastal defense patrols.[54] Coastal security fears surged when Admiral Cervera's flotilla sailed from Spain. Public pressure forced the Navy to divert considerable combat power to protecting the East Coast. The Navy sent the powerful Flying Squadron to the Chesapeake and created two other coastal patrol squadrons.

On May 2 came early reports of Dewey's Manila Bay victory.[55] Francis Newlands soon introduced an annexation bill transferring sovereignty, terminating Hawaiian treaties, banning further Chinese immigration, and deferring other details.[56] For reasons discussed in the following, this House resolution replaced the Senate resolution.

Dewey's victory did not revive the dying annexation issue—as William A. Russ argues—for the issue was not dying before the battle.[57] The administration and senior Republicans in Congress worked hard on the treaty for months. They wanted to push the Davis resolution too but had to deal first with the much more urgent war preparations. They never lost their focus. Nor did any annexationist supporters in the Congress jump ship. Annexation had at least the same support in May 1898 as in December 1897. Said another way, annexationist support solidified before the Cuban crisis derailed the treaty and did not shrink thereafter.

The so-called war measure argument—that Hawai`i must be annexed to successfully prosecute the war—was bogus. All three Manila resupply fleets stopped at Honolulu, the only viable recoaling port in May and June. (Any alternative would have taken months to develop.) Hawai`i waived port charges and provided a troop rest area. Hawaiian ladies, including Mrs. Dole and Princess Ka`iulani, staffed a soldiers' aid society. Thousands of tons of coal and provisions went onto the Navy ships.[58] Foreign Minister Cooper told American officers: "Hawai`i has cast its lot with your country in the pending conflict."[59] Hawai`i built much goodwill by its unneutral behavior. This probably helped the annexationist cause a little.

But because Dewey destroyed Spanish naval forces in the Pacific, Hawai`i was safe from reprisal. With no military reason for immediate annexation, a few opportunists claimed that honor required it. This argument changed no minds because Hawai`i did not believe it acted ignobly. The *Hawaiian Star* expressed the attitude of the white government and Native Hawaiians as well, few of whom sympathized with colonial Spain: "We have thrown in our lot with the United States . . . [and] the position is one in which we all acquiesce heartily."[60]

The lack of military necessity or a debt of honor made it easy to ignore a few silly warnings by extreme annexationists that McKinley would occupy Hawai`i as a war measure using executive powers. Frank Hatch was a rabid, irrational, advocate of occupation. He thought it would make annexation certain. But neither the McKinley administration nor the Hawaiian government found the occupation idea persuasive or necessary, so nothing was done. Although Hawai`i was indeed needed to resupply Dewey, it was obvious that the Navy could use Hawai`i as it wished, whether or not the islands were immediately annexed. No harm would have resulted from annexation later in 1898 or even in 1899. The war measure argument had no force. What then was the war's impact?

The war had two effects on the annexation drive. First, the war reconfirmed a key annexationist tenet that modern war meant fighting far from the American coast, making midocean bastions invaluable. Second, the battle offered a golden opportunity to push a joint resolution to a vote quickly. Hatch noted that "the situation in the Philippines is bringing home to the minds of many, who had hitherto been doubtful, the necessity of closing up the annexation business at once."[61] There was no need to wait. Key arguments had been ventilated for years. By summer 1898, minds were made up. Discussion was now the ritual presentation of points of view rather than the give-and-take leading to persuasion. For most, the war "proved" (again) the strategic and security arguments for annexation. Hawai`i was not a war spoil. It was a special case unlike Guam, the Philippines, Cuba, and

Puerto Rico, none considered as possible acquisitions before the war. Therefore, most in Congress and the administration believed Hawai`i should be acquired separately and immediately. Francis Newlands explained: "Hawaiian annexation does not rest at all on colonial expansion and should be considered entirely apart from it. . . . The Philippines question is new; the Hawaiian question is old. . . . The distinction should be kept in mind. The Philippines means conquest; Hawai`i means defense."[62] The war had no true causative effect; it created few annexation-ists. Rather, it was a validation and a trigger.

The Republican leadership was now determined to deal with Reed. Hatch said the speaker would "not be moved by anything short of a caucus, and possibly not by that." McKinley could not permit further delay and directed "a supreme effort" for annexation. "There have been consultations with the President, consultations in the Senate," Hatch reported.[63] Hitt's foreign affairs committee approved the Newlands resolution ten to four. The Hitt Report duplicated the Davis Report with a fresh introduction and new testimony by General Schofield and Admiral Walker.[64]

In the two months between the prewar Davis Report and the Hitt Report, no new arguments appeared. The fresh material reemphasized Hawai`i's strategic importance in light of the lessons provided by the war, particularly coastal secu-rity. Manila Bay demonstrated "the inestimable importance . . . of possessing the Hawaiian Islands in case of war with any strong naval powers" instead of weak Spain. General Schofield testified: "if we do not annex . . . we cannot control the political population of the islands. Japan would dominate through immigration."[65]

German meddling may also have influenced the administration, particularly in the context of Dewey's concerns about the German flotilla hovering outside Manila. Britain suggested Germany might demand part of Samoa if the United States annexed Hawai`i. The British knew but did not say that Germany already secretly asked Britain to join in demanding that the United States surrender its rights in Samoa as compensation for annexation. Britain declined the German proposal for fear of antagonizing America.[66] Now the British alerted the Americans to the German plan. The British advised: it is "vitally important if Hawai`i is to be annexed without compensation, that you annex it now. . . . Germany would not dare object."[67]

Helping Robert Hitt move the Speaker were Charles Grosvenor of Ohio, friend of McKinley and the chairman of the House Republican Conference (Caucus), and James Tawney, the Republican majority whip. During May 17–23, these powerful leaders pressured Reed to move the Newlands bill. Hitt stayed behind the scenes, but he prepared to break openly with Reed if necessary. He hoped to take advantage of Reed's declarations that he would not oppose the majority wishes.[68] To save face for his friend, Hitt proposed a petition calling for a special rule to fix a day for a vote. Reed could appear to be bowing to majority sentiment rather than compromising his principles.[69]

Reed refused. Hitt warned that the growing rebellion against the speaker's anti-annexationist stance would soon threaten Reed's position as speaker. Reed would have to concede in the end, so why not do so immediately and avoid grievous political wounds? Perhaps Reed seemed to agree, for on May 20 Hitt predicted a favorable rule on the Newlands resolution.[70] Day and Hitt tried to make annexation appear inevitable by telling reporters that McKinley would occupy Hawai`i should the joint resolution not be brought to a vote.[71] Portraying annexation as a war measure—despite the fact that America already enjoyed Hawai`i's unneutral behavior—might create a patriotic façade behind which Reed might concede. This phony argument carried no weight with the Speaker, nor with anyone else. When Charles Grosvenor demanded a vote on the Newlands resolution, Reed again stalled, arguing that a war revenue bill had priority and claiming that most Republicans opposed a vote in the current session. This was false, as numerous canvasses showed.

Hitt and Grosvenor turned to coercion. Tawney circulated the petition demanding a rule requiring a vote. Virtually all Republicans signed. Confronted with this document on the House floor on June 10, Reed finally gave way. Further resistance would have been futile. The Republicans would oust him from the speakership. McKinley's "quiet and telling work in the national legislature" to undermine Reed removed the last obstacle to annexation.[72] On June 11 debate began on the Newlands resolution, and Reed fixed June 15 for the vote. The Senate would then take up the bill immediately. A friend of both Reed and Lodge concluded: "McKinley has done wonders!"[73] Hatch gloated: "The Speaker has been routed!"[74]

Reed's capitulation made the final result certain, given strong support for annexation in both houses. Attitudes were fixed. Nearly all members had made up their minds about annexation long before. Over twenty-five days, from June 11 through the Senate vote on July 6, they spoke to explain their positions for the record, attack the positions of the other party, and, in the Senate, obstruct the resolution by filibustering. Rather than a debate, there was a series of presentations. Which arguments appeared, and even their relative frequency and length, can be misleading. Speakers offered miscellaneous arguments that might be appealing and acceptable to constituents—that is, arguments they passionately supported and others they cared less about. In the Senate, annexationists spoke less, trying to let the filibuster talk itself out.

Therefore, the debates must be analyzed with caution. In the several hundred dense pages of the *Congressional Record* that record the debates, every reason to acquire or reject the islands is repeated many times, as speakers jammed their remarks with all possible arguments. One can all too easily tease out a strand of argument and make a case for its impact. This means all analyses, including this one, are inescapably subjective. With this caveat, let us look briefly at the debates. Deserving the most attention are arguments matured over many years, consistent with previous positions, and grounded in recent events.

The debates of the Newlands resolution revealed that, among the several reasons for annexation, the strategic argument was most important.[75] As the first speaker in the debates, Robert Hitt emphasized security benefits. A big globe and a large strategic map of the Pacific that showed Hawai`i's unique position as a naval and coaling station were placed before the speaker's rostrum, frequently consulted by members studying the geography of the Pacific.[76] Hitt asserted that "with the great change in the construction of fighting ships, all of which are now moved by steam, coal has become an essential of maritime war, as much so as powder or guns, and across that wide ocean any vessel of war coming to attack the United States must stop for coal and supplies at the Hawaiian Islands before it can attack us. . . . No battleship exists . . . which can make the trip from the other side of that wide sea to our shores, conduct any operation of hostility against us, and ever get back unless it has its supply of coal renewed."[77] The "teaching of recent events," Hitt said, proved that "for a war of defense the Hawaiian Islands are to us inestimably important, most essential, and in this light they have been most often discussed." He stressed "the military necessity of possessing those islands."[78]

The influential Senator Hoar took this strategic line in his famous speech of July 5. Reading it more than a hundred years later gives the feeling of listening to Hoar speaking from the heart. He declared that he would resist annexation to the death if it was to be the first step in the acquisition of a foreign empire or the commercial exploitation of Asian peoples. But Hawai`i was essential to the defense of the West Coast in any future war. The lessons of the war with Spain proved possession of Hawai`i was a great military advantage. Conversely, possession by any foreign power would be a "great military and naval danger to our Western coast." If not annexed, the islands would fall "prey" to Japan.[79]

The conversion of Representative Freeman Knowles perfectly illustrates the war's role as a validating lesson. Knowles, a Populist from South Dakota, was one of the few who claimed the war made him an annexationist. He described his conversion as follows:

Previous to the war with Spain I was opposed to the annexation of Hawai`i. I had conceived reasons and arguments sufficient to form such a conclusion. I had made up my mind that its acquisition, instead of being a source of strength, would be an element of weakness, necessitating large expenditures in fortifying and defending it, and dividing our Navy between its defense and that of our coast. How completely arguments and conclusions drawn from a preconceived theory are knocked out by actual experience has been well-illustrated in this case. It is true that our war with Spain has been entirely a one-sided affair. But let us for a moment suppose our country at war with England, Germany, France, Russia, or even Japan, all of whom have powerful fleets in the Orient. Then Hawai`i would become an element of strength [not] weakness to the nation which possessed it. No fleet can sail from the Orient and attack our coast without recoaling. Hawai`i offers the only practical point for a coaling station in the Pacific Ocean. It is the outpost of our coast, and is as necessary to our defense as the picket line of an army.[80]

Like Knowles, virtually all annexationists believed the war validated the strategic argument for annexation, although, unlike him, they learned their strategic lesson long before 1898. For De Alva Alexander, Dewey's victory proved Hawai`i was as important as the strategists had claimed: "the reasons for annexation are no stronger or truer today than they were almost a year ago."[81] A year earlier, almost to the day, McKinley brought forth the annexation treaty as a strategic response to the Japanese threat. William Sulzer and others agreed "we should have those islands without reference to the present war with Spain."[82] Nineteen representatives, a large fraction of those who spoke, cited strategists like Mahan, admirals Walker and Belknap, Commodore Melville, and General Schofield.[83] Many speakers linked annexation, coastal defense, and preventing Japanese control, on the one hand, and a broader policy of acquiring an isthmian canal, Caribbean bases, and a bigger navy, on the other.[84]

Not surprisingly, the annexationists pounded away at Japan. If, through another show of force, as in 1897, Japan obtained the vote for its 19,000 males in Hawai`i, the result would be a Japanese colony detrimental to American coastal security.[85] Francis Newlands asked: "Can we permit them, through the action of existing internal forces, to drift under the control of Japan, that rising power of the Orient, possessing today a navy superior to our own—a nation strong, self-assertive, aggressive, reaching out for power?"[86]

Marion De Vries of California said the precarious American title to Pearl Harbor did not justify development of a base. The lease option was, like the reciprocity treaty of which it was part, subject to termination on a year's notice. No one would risk building a major base on such shaky grounds. Pearl Harbor could be an unconquerable redoubt, an American Gibraltar, but only if the United States controlled the hinterland. With Hawai`i fortified, the Navy could sweep the Pacific in a future war.[87] He concluded: "annexation alone will provide against all menacing contingencies upon our western coasts."[88]

Commercial arguments for annexation were important, as they had been for years, and appeared often. Most annexationists, such as John Barham of California, favored annexation for both commercial and strategic reasons. "We cannot too highly estimate Hawai`i from a commercial view," he said, while citing Hawai`i's "great strategic importance ... demonstrated by ... the pending war with Spain."[89] Enhancing Hawaiian–American trade was probably the key commercial argument, though bilateral trade would likely grow even if annexation failed. Lorenzo Danford predicted bilateral trade would quadruple under American ownership, but more important than "mere trade relations" was "the great strategic importance of these islands in time of war."[90] Horace Packer said the most important question was "the necessity of annexation from a strategic standpoint," while noting the likely growth of Pacific commerce.[91]

Many speakers mentioned Hawai`i in connection with expanding trade with the Far East. This was the so-called stepping-stone argument. Charles Grosvenor advocated acquiring "this half-way house" to Asian markets.[92] To Samuel Hilborn of California, assuming the United States would keep the Philippines, annexation would provide "one of the steppingstones in the ford . . . crossing the Pacific to reach our distant possessions in the Orient."[93]

To antiannexationist claims that the great circle route through the Aleutians was a shorter route to Asia, Galusha Grow, a former Speaker of the House, said this was contradicted by the flow of commerce, which largely went through Hawai`i. He told a story about the New York financier who claimed he knew a railroad route to Chicago 250 miles shorter than the present one. When he produced the map, a heavy red line ran straight between the two cities over the Alleganies' highest summit, a route that would have cost a fortune to build. Grow concluded that the route that most ships actually followed was more important than lines on a map.[94] Charles Pearce knew the great circle route was shorter, having traveled from Vancouver to Yokohama aboard the British Empress Line. But the shorter northern route was irrelevant. Hawai`i was still "necessary to the proper defense of the Pacific coast."[95] Jonathan Dolliver quipped: "My friend says you can go to China and the East by a shorter route than if Hawai`i were annexed. If that were true, it would not touch this question. This is a question of national defense, not a problem for passenger agents."[96] Speakers therefore often intertwined strategic and commercial arguments, sometimes inadvertently and sometimes intentionally lumping them together to add force to the annexationist appeal.

In fact, fostering trade with Asia did not require annexation of the Hawaiian stepping-stone. In peacetime, barring pirate activity, there was no need for commerce protection or proprietary coaling stations. The sea-lanes were unhindered. Vessels easily purchased coal at public ports. No obstacle had slowed the increase in American transpacific commerce during the late nineteenth century. Commerce protection in wartime—escorting merchant ships and patrolling sea-lanes to clear them of enemy warships—was a military function, like the protection of lives and port facilities and coastal private property, that would be greatly enhanced by a base at Pearl Harbor.

The lure of the Asian market was still more talk than action. That not much had been done to operationalize enhanced future trade via the stepping-stone is suggested by the inquiries received by the American consulate in Honolulu during 18 months preceding annexation. Of the 149 letters received, 83 were routine inquiries about lost relatives, deaths, births, wills, etc. Of 66 letters touching commercial matters, 30 asked about markets in Hawai`i itself for American products. Among the senders of these letters were a pool chalk manufacturer, an exporter of horses, a hat maker, and banking and insurance companies. Another 31 letters asked about broader business conditions in Hawai`i, such as the availability and price of land and, especially, employment opportunities. Only 5 letters—among them missives from Pitt and Scall's shipping agency, a bicycle maker, and a whiskey producer—inquired about using Honolulu as an onward route to other markets. If the idea of Hawai`i as a peacetime stepping-stone to Asia was powerful, one might expect that the consulate files would contain many more inquiries about port facilities, the availability of coal, cargo handling, and other services that ships touching at Hawai`i might need.[97] Probably this information was so well known—because Hawai`i was already being used by transiting cargo vessels—that no inquiries were needed. If so, one wonders why annexation was needed to acquire a way station already so familiar and well used. A more extensive survey of consulate records in Hawai`i and key Asian ports, though beyond the scope of this book, might increase our understanding of whether businessmen thought American ownership of Hawai`i contributed anything new and necessary to accelerating trade with Asia, at least in early 1898.

The lure of Asian markets grew rapidly after the acquisition of the Philippines, which made the United States an Asian power, and the Open Door Policy, which involved the United States in the maintenance of unhindered access to the China market. It grew even more rapidly after the United States acquired the Panama

Canal route in 1903. But during 1897–98, there was a weaker linkage between Hawaiian annexation and opening Asian markets than between annexation and enhanced security.

This led many members of Congress to rank commercial arguments behind the strategic ones, though they valued both and often argued for both. Robert Hitt argued that commercial considerations "should not be allowed to overweight questions of foreign policy which in a few years may have much greater importance than a mere question of dollars and cents."[98] Francis Newlands repeatedly stressed that his bill aimed to defend territory and trade that the United States already possessed; Hawai`i was not to be a "steppingstone to a policy of imperial aggrandizement" in the Far East. Senator Eugene Hale stated: "I vote for the acquisition of Hawai`i now not in any way as a war measure, not associated with the progress of the war, not marked in any way as a steppingstone to anything else, but because of reasons that had matured and become convincing long before the war was agreed upon."[99] The military or strategic advantages primarily explain why annexation was necessary. Hawai`i was already a stopping point, a steppingstone, to Asian markets, but it was not yet an American naval bastion.

Opponents repeated eight arguments against annexation made three weeks before by the four Democrats on the House Foreign Relations Committee:

1. The Hawaiian people had not approved annexation; most opposed annexation.
2. The American people had not approved annexation.
3. Annexation by joint resolution was unconstitutional and annexation of noncontiguous territory would start the United States down a mistaken path.
4. The islands were too far from the United States to be adequately defended; they were a defensive liability that would require a larger navy.
5. The Hawaiian population was not racially or otherwise homogeneous with the existing American population and would not make good citizens.
6. There was no commercial necessity for ownership of the islands; recoaling at an Aleutian island was a shorter route to Asia.
7. The islands were not necessary for defense of the West Coast.
8. Should their ownership ever become necessary for defense, they could be acquired at that time; their independence was not threatened internally or externally.[100]

Good analyses of the antiannexationist resistance have been done elsewhere and are unnecessary here. The best, by Thomas J. Osborne, shows that the anti-annexationist movement was chiefly though not exclusively "based upon a reverence for America's republican tradition and an inveterate hostility to colonialism."[101] Annexationists rebutted the eight arguments. They maintained that the two governments represented their peoples, so popular approval was unnecessary. Acquisition by other than treaty was constitutional and had been done before, as with Texas. The islands were a defensive asset. While the Hawaiian and American populations were indeed not homogeneous, these lesser peoples would not become citizens and Hawai`i would remain a territory. The shorter great circle route to Asia had disadvantages, thus few ships stopped in the Aleutians. Recent technological and diplomatic developments made Hawai`i indispensable to defense of the Pacific coast. Annexation must occur now because the islands were vulnerable to foreign pressure, especially from Japan.

In the end, big majorities in both houses found the annexationist case persuasive or—better said—found no reason to change the attitudes they already held. On June 15 the House overwhelmingly passed the Newlands resolution, 209 to 91.[102] Voting was highly partisan. Of 182 Republicans, 179 voted for the resolution along with 18 Democrats, 8 Populists, and 4 minor party members. Opposing the bill were 77 Democrats, 7 Populists, 4 minor party members, and 3 Republicans.[103] The Senate took up the measure on June 20.

A filibuster, principally by Stephen White of California, James Berry of Arkansas, and Richard Pettigrew of South Dakota, dashed hopes of immediate action. Perhaps they hoped that delaying the vote would entice an exasperated Senate, sweltering in the Washington summer, to defer Hawai`i to the December session.[104]

The appeal of strategic and defense arguments explains why the United States annexed the islands instead of dealing with them in some other fashion. The annexationists killed by large margins six amendments proposing protectorates vice outright acquisition. The strongest protectorate proposal stated the United States would view as "an act of hostility any attempt upon the part of any Government of Europe or Asia to take or hold possession of the Hawaiian Islands, or to exercise upon any pretext or under any conditions sovereign authority therein. That the United States hereby announces . . . their guarantee of the independence of the people of the Hawaiian Islands and their firm determination to maintain the same."[105]

This would have resulted in a strong Hawaiian–American relationship. Foreign interference would mean war. The references to Asian as well as European powers and to exercising authority under any pretext or condition were intended to prevent a takeover under the pretext of securing political rights for Japanese subjects. Significantly, these references to Japan were added by antiannexationists. Even they saw the necessity to address the potential Japanese threat. The protectorate proposal seemingly met American requirements. It preserved Hawai`i as coaling and supply station for transpacific trade. It ensured the continued availability of Dewey's most important resupply base.

Nevertheless, the annexationists rejected the proposal. Only annexation would ensure the construction of a major naval base. Many congressmen hesitated to develop Pearl Harbor until the United States acquired the necessary land and until Congress was certain Hawai`i would not be lost to a foreign power.[106] Thus the train of annexationist thought ran like this: American security required a Hawaiian naval base. Only annexation could guarantee that the base would be built, that no foreign power would gain the right to build a naval base in the islands, and that the island government would not be subverted by a foreign power. Therefore, Hawai`i must be annexed.

The Senate did not truly debate the resolution. The annexationists largely remained silent, allowing the filibuster to talk itself out. Senator Teller, like Senator Hale, made no remarks because he was "anxious to get to a vote." Cushman Davis declared that his views had been formed years before, were well known, and needed no further elaboration.[107] By "sweating and struggling," Davis kept a quorum available. Lodge thought "we have the Hawaiian matter very much in hand." The filibuster was a futile attempt to postpone the inevitable.[108]

The filibuster collapsed on Saturday, July 2, when the Democrats sought to stay adjourned on Monday, July 4, as well as Sunday, July 3. Davis insisted that the Senate convene on the holiday and when his party supported that view, it doomed the filibuster. The Senate would "stay in session until a vote is had."[109] The Democrats conceded to vote on July 6, allowing themselves a few more days of speechifying. On July 6 the bill carried 42 to 21 with 26 paired and not voting. Counting the paired and absent senators' statements of how they would have voted, 56 favored the measure and 32 opposed it. The 56 annexationist supporters included 44 Republicans, 10 Democrats, and 2 Populists. The 32 nays consisted of 28 Democrats, 2 Populists, and 2 Republicans.[110]

In American politics, an issue's priority is constantly adjusted by such factors as relative urgency, changes in support among elite advocates as well as the public, and unforeseen events. Annexation had broad support when McKinley took office, but it did not seem urgent. The 1897 clash with Japan increased the urgency of annexation, so it was accelerated. However, the Cuban crisis, which took the

United States into its first foreign war in fifty years, naturally assumed paramount importance in late 1897 and early 1898. Cuban policy and associated issues such as the national defense and naval appropriations bills became highly urgent, immediate concerns, bumping annexation down the priority list, but not very far. If annexationist support had truly weakened, it would have been very easy to let Reed's opposition stand, and take up Hawai`i after the war, with the Philippines, Puerto Rico, and Guam.

The triumph of the joint resolution was the outcome of a yearlong process begun in the spring of 1897 when the U.S.–Japan confrontation made Hawai`i a high priority and triggered the June 1897 annexation treaty. The confrontation welded the McKinley administration and much of the Congress into a united front determined to annex the strategic isles. Through all the ups and downs, the annexationists maintained a strong, cohesive majority in the Congress and the government. Events subsequent to the June 1897 treaty converted only a handful of members of Congress. Neither the threatened partition of China, nor Dewey's great victory at Manila Bay, nor Hawai`i's unneutral support for the war effort added much to core annexationist beliefs. These events were not causes in themselves. Instead, they were validations of the traditional strategic arguments and, to a lesser degree, old economic arguments. They made it easier to move Reed out of the way. The war was a facilitating trigger but did not create new votes for annexation.

The congressional debates of the resolution were akin to the final act of a play. The curtain had gone up in 1897 and several acts—the clash with Japan, the treaty's signing, the Cuban crisis and the outbreak of war—had been played. Between June 11 and July 6, the players read their familiar lines from a script whose denouement was known.

❦

Local Power, Eclectic Imperialism, Enhanced Security

To understand why the United States, for the first time, acquired territory outside of North America, we must look not only at American but
Hawaiian politics. Had Hawai`i not sought annexation, it would not have
occurred. There was zero support for forcible acquisition. Hawai`i sought annexa-
tion because a pro-annexation white minority composed the government after the
1893 revolution. That government sat atop a population largely opposed to annexation. Certainly most Native Hawaiians (composing slightly more than a third of
the population) opposed it. The opinion of Asians, the largest ethnic group, is less
clear. Because U.S. immigration laws were harsher than Hawaiian ones, it is likely
that most Asians preferred the status quo. For Japanese in particular, annexation
would dilute the ability of Japan to influence and pressure local officials for better
working conditions and possibly even voting rights. It is a reasonable assumption
that a majority of the population opposed annexation.

Disease and sugar shaped the arena for the local power struggle. The catastrophic decline in Native Hawaiian numbers greatly weakened the monarchy. As
Polynesians became a shrinking minority in their own country, their comparative
political power shrank as well. The booming sugar industry increased the political
influence of the white community, which coerced King Kalākaua and toppled

Queen Lili`uokalani. Ironically, sugar also threatened white control. Sugar created a torrent of Asian immigrants who, before long, composed half the population. (Had there been enough Native Hawaiians to meet surging demands for sugar workers, immigration would not have been necessary, which would have had huge implications for subsequent politics.) After the 1893 revolution, the white oligarchy sought to preserve white preponderance and privilege, particularly against creeping Japanization. Hawaiians, of all ethnicities, cared little about American predilections for naval bases, the China market, trumpeting their manhood, or uplifting other races. Hawaiians struggled over local political power and wealth. American acquisition would forever enshrine the white-dominated order.

American motives for annexation were far different. Historians have identified many factors spurring 1890s U.S. imperialism. In each acquisition—including Hawai`i—security, economics and trade, ideology, race, gender, and humanitarianism were always part of the story, but depending on the case, they operated with differing strengths and timing. Humanitarian and gender factors powerfully shaped the response to Spain's brutal campaign to suppress the Cuban rebellion. The persistent drive for an isthmian canal, culminating in the Panama revolution of 1903 and the beginning of U.S. construction of the canal in 1904, was primarily driven by economic and commercial factors, though the canal would certainly bring great military benefits. The postwar establishment of Caribbean bases such as Guantánamo related to the protection of the canal's eastern approaches. Commercial and trade concerns drove the Open Door Policy of 1899 and its broader application over following decades. The acquisition of the Philippines, Puerto Rico, and Guam—not even imagined before the war—were unplanned opportunities to apply commercial and other motives. Some causal factors—the quest for an open door and new overseas markets—were newer and strengthened substantially after the war with Spain and the retention of the Philippines, which made the United States an Asian power with Asian interests to nurture and protect. Strategic factors matured before the war, which was seen as a validation of them. Racial and ideological factors were much older, operating since the birth of the American republic, and to some degree, both advanced and hindered imperialism. An example was Roosevelt's willingness to take in or tutor non–Anglo Saxon peoples that contrasted sharply with Tom Reed's fear that absorbing foreign peoples would disrupt the American social and political order.

While Hawaiian annexation nestles easily into a theory of eclectic American imperialism, noted by a number of historians, annexation was more heavily influenced by strategic factors than any other imperial acquisition or policy. Strategic factors were the most important of the several American motivations for annexation. Above all, the intertwining of security issues and rivalry with Japan were unique to the Hawaiian event. Among the many strategic waypoints were the 1873 Schofield-Alexander investigation of Pearl Harbor, the Pearl Harbor clause in the 1887 renewal of reciprocity, and the 1898 Davis and Hitt reports that asserted national security was the single most important reason for annexation. From the 1880s, strategic arguments permeated the ranks of military and opinion leaders, leading to the steady building of the New Steel Navy, the evolution of fresh methods for basing and fighting the new warships, the massive Endicott plan for coastal fortification, and the quest for control of Hawai`i, America's Gibraltar. By the mid-1890s, Republicans and many Democrats consistently agreed on naval expansion, coastal fortification, and Hawaiian independence, but not outright annexation. Most Republicans thought annexation the best long-term solution to preserve Hawaiian independence, but most Democrats disagreed. Neither party thought the question was urgent. When overly eager Hawai`i pushed McKinley to commit to early annexation, the new president said Hawai`i would have to wait until after tariff reform and economic recovery.

The U.S.–Japan crisis of 1897 destroyed this timetable and made Hawai`i a top priority. The clash was not a phony confrontation invented by Honolulu to provoke annexation. Japan could have avoided a crisis by defining the immigrant rejections as a simple quarrel over unfair admittance procedures. Instead, Foreign Minister Ōkuma enlarged the dispute by opposing annexation, even before McKinley committed to it. Japan officially informed the United States in April 1897 that it opposed annexation, deployed warships to Honolulu, reiterated and fleshed out its opposition in strong protests over the next five months, tried to enlist Britain and other powers to join in blocking annexation, and finally sought a multiparty conference to preempt annexation through a multilateral guarantee of Hawaiian independence. Japan believed that American acquisition hurt significant Japanese interests, including what Japan called the power balance in the Pacific. The United States logically assumed that Japan meant what it said. The trend was clear: growing Japanese assertiveness in Hawai`i based on interests rooted in the ever-growing Japanese population. Tokyo officials, not Hawaiian ones, forged Japan's strong opposition to annexation. That unexpected and alarming stance triggered U.S. naval deployments, contingency orders to defend Honolulu against a Japanese landing, and the first war plans aimed at Japan. The United States spent most of 1897 dealing with Hawai`i as a military issue. Although both Hawaiian and American officials knew Japan's tough policy helped annexation, there is no basis for occasional claims that Hawai`i created the immigration dispute to trigger annexation.[1]

During the crisis with Japan, Republicans, having coalesced around a stronger Hawaiian policy during 1894–1896, committed to annexation. The McKinley administration moved annexation to the front burner, well aware that roughly two-thirds of the House and the Senate supported acquisition. Hawai`i was the only potential imperialist acquisition that came to the forefront. In 1897 and early 1898, neither Republicans nor the country itself had made up its mind about other aspects of imperialism, such as war with Spain over Cuba, the retention of the Philippines and other war spoils, or the later push for a Panama canal and an open door on trade. Those episodes—what we might call new policy—had their own time line and played out in a new context formed by the victory over Spain.

Annexation succeeded because it was old policy, formed by two decades of maturing argument, and made urgent by the U.S.–Japan clash. The fight to ratify the treaty and then to pass the Newlands joint resolution involved little changing of minds. Each side had its cards in hand and now the game played out in the complex and difficult political circumstances of the impending war. The final months before annexation were marked by politics and posturing, not persuasion and conviction. The politics of the Cuban crisis explains the timing but not the causes of the annexation of Hawai`i. The determined annexationist bloc emerged in 1897.

Annexation put Hawai`i on a trajectory leading to territorial status and ultimately statehood. Hawai`i would not be a colony, nor would it be an independent nation. Could Hawai`i have remained independent, either as a monarchy or a republic? Given the islands' tiny population and enormous strategic importance, true independence very likely would have been impossible. Japan, Britain, and Germany would have sought control if the United States had been disinterested. Japan's interests had grown so much in just ten years that in 1897 it tried to kill U.S. annexation. Had the United States been disinterested, and given the increase in Japanese immigration after 1898, it is quite likely the islands would have become a Japanese possession. Britain was not eager for another Pacific colony but might well have assumed a protectorate over Hawai`i. Given Germany's strong push for control of Samoa and later scheming for bases in East Asia—including in the Philippines, had the United States not taken control of the whole archipelago—it seems quite likely that Berlin would have pushed for a Pearl Harbor base, if not a protectorate or a colony, had the United States, Britain, and Japan stepped aside.

Of course, the United States was not disinterested. If we assume a continued, strong American interest, could Hawai`i have maintained its independence? A realistic possibility was independence coupled with a strong U.S. protectorate, including the unfettered use of permanent military installations on perpetually leased or ceded land. The practicalities of establishing such a protectorate would have been formidable. But a protectorate would have preserved Hawaiian sovereignty while giving America the islands' massive strategic advantages. How Hawaiian politics might have developed under a protectorate is hard to estimate. Immigration, which soared after annexation, removing any fear of foreign control, would surely have continued at a high rate. Given the demographic trends, Native Hawaiians would have become an even smaller minority and Asians a big majority. It seems unlikely that either the monarchy or the Republic of Hawai`i could have continued without evolving into a true parliamentary democracy with majority rule. How ethnic voting blocs would have developed and interacted among themselves and their home nations is unknowable. The American protectorate would have complicated local politics, as the United States reacted to political developments—for example, voting rights for Japanese and other Asians—that might threaten use of Hawaiian bases by changing the island government.

The United States did wrong by Hawai`i during the 1893 revolution, even judged by 1890s standards and practice. To conspire is to secretly plot with others for an illegal or deceitful purpose. Strictly speaking, John L. Stevens did not conspire to cause a revolt in January 1893. He certainly did not conspire to entice the queen into a rash act by taking the *Boston* away from Honolulu. As we have seen, the cruise had no political purpose. The warship's return on January 14 was coincidental. But Stevens conspired in his heart. His self-proclaimed evenhandedness meant improperly treating potential rebels the same as the royal government to which he was accredited. By meeting with rebels, declining to help the queen's government suppress the revolt, and failing to communicate the purpose for landing U.S. troops and bivouacking them at Arion Hall, he made it much easier for the rebels to intimidate the royalists. While the intimidating effect of the Arion Hall bivouac was unintentional, Stevens purposefully treated the rebels respectfully and the royalists disdainfully. Stevens egregiously violated even the loose diplomatic norms of the 1890s and deserved severe censure. Captain Wiltse violated naval regulations that a landing be a last resort. Although Wiltse ordered his troops to remain neutral, naval officers unthinkingly carried out the landing and the initial movements ashore in a way that allowed the timid royalists, ignorant of the troops' mission, to feel intimidated. That the rebels' military superiority (by January 17) and the self-generated paralysis of royalist leadership were the most important elements in rebel success does not excuse American transgressions.

Grover Cleveland tried to correct the wrong. Alas, there was no practical way to set things right. Certainly the method he chose, restoration, was completely impractical. Restoration was doomed by Gresham's false and America-centric assumption—buttressed by the Blount Report—that only U.S. intervention allowed the weak rebels to succeed. Therefore, Cleveland and Gresham mistakenly assumed that military intimidation would force that weak rebel government to restore the queen. But the rebel government was resolute. Despite a carefully orchestrated, coercive schedule of U.S. landing practices and gunfire training, the rebel government did not blink, and even prepared to fight.

In Hawai`i, race underlay everything from voting rights and the architecture of politics to employment practices. Whites sought to reserve good town and plantation jobs for themselves. Pay scales, even for sugar field-workers, were highly discriminatory, with whites at the top and Asians at the bottom. Native Hawaiians and Asians banged into a very low ceiling when seeking managerial positions or business loans. Asians were intentionally excluded from the vote not by education or language ability or even income and property holdings but by race. White suspicion of Japanese motives related not to naval strategy but to the local competition for power. After 1893 the white government came to fear uncontrolled immigration as a long-term threat.

Crucial on the Hawaiian side, race was important on the United States side as well. A few of many possible examples: Naval officers such as John G. Walker became enamored of whites and hardly noticed Native Hawaiians, who Walker labeled child-like. Race surely played a role in American inattention to the many Native Hawaiian protests of U.S. Hawaiian policy after 1893. The white faces at the top of the Hawaiian government after the revolution made it easier for official Washington to see Hawai`i as already heading toward "modernity." And so on.

Although beyond the scope of this book, Hawai`i's story of course did not end with annexation. The Newlands resolution placed the Republic of Hawai`i under presidential authority until Congress created a new governmental structure. In 1900 the Hawai`i Organic Act provided for a popularly elected territorial government. Many preannexation players remained influential. Sanford Dole became the first territorial governor. The inveterate rebel Robert W. Wilcox became Hawai`i's delegate to the U.S. House of Representatives. Tough Charlie Wilson's son Johnny became one of Honolulu's most famous mayors. Lorrin Thurston became publisher of the *Pacific Commercial Advertiser*, run by his family for the next century. Tragically, Princess Ka`iulani died suddenly in 1899, at age twenty-three, on the Big Island. At the moment of her death, it was said, her pet peacocks back at her O`ahu home woke the neighbors with their shrieks. Samuel Parker, head of Queen Lili`uokalani's first and last cabinets, turned from politics to management of his property, the famous Parker Ranch, until his death in 1920. The queen resided at her home, Washington Place, making dignified public appearances and remaining the spiritual heart of the Native Hawaiian nation until she passed away in 1917 at age seventy-nine. Count Ōkuma served two times as prime minister and founded the famous Waseda University.

More than a century has passed since Hawai`i passed under the Stars and Stripes. Issues raised before annexation remain controversial, partly because of differing judgments on how and why annexation occurred. This is as it should be. Historians will forever examine the topic with varied interests, approaches, standards. Well-known facts will be reevaluated and new evidence mined from archives. Both will provoke new interpretations.

As strategists predicted, Hawai`i became the most important military bastion of the United States, both as territory and, after 1959, as a state. The Navy developed a great base at Pearl Harbor and the Army and Marine Corps built massive facilities. In the twentieth century, navies abandoned coal for oil-powered engines, mooting the coaling argument so crucial in the 1890s. But Hawai`i's unique, commanding location made it indispensable in the airpower age, not only in World War II, the Korean War, and the Vietnam War, but into the twenty-first century. Acquired more for strategic reasons than for any other, it seems fitting that Hawai`i became—as in the assertions of annexationists—America's Pacific Gibraltar.

Notes

Abbreviations Used in the Notes

AH	State Archives of Hawai`i
Blount Rpt	The Blount Report. House Executive Document no. 47, 53rd Cong., 2nd sess. (Washington, DC, 1893)
BROL	Blount Report online; http://libweb.Hawaii.edu/digicoll/annexation/blount.html
Cong. Rec.	*Congressional Record*
Davis Rpt	The Davis Report. Senate Report no. 681, "Annexation of Hawai`i," *Cong. Rec.*, 55th Cong., 2nd sess., March 16 (Washington, DC, 1898)
Despatches	"Despatches from United States Ministers in Hawai`i, 1843–1900," General Records of the Department of State, RG 59, NARA, microcopy T-30
FO	Foreign Office records, National Archives of the United Kingdom, Kew
FO-EX	Foreign and Executive Files, State Archives of Hawai`i
FRUS	*Foreign Relations of the United States* (followed by year)
HExDoc	House Executive Document (followed by document number)
HMW	(Hawaiian) Minister at Washington, 1893–98, State Archives of Hawai`i
LC	Library of Congress
Morgan Rpt	The Morgan Report. Senate Report no. 227, 53rd Cong., 2nd sess., (Washington, DC, 1894). This is the report of an investigation chaired by John Tyler Morgan, chair of the Senate Foreign Relations Committee, about the revolution of 1893, the Blount investigation, and the abortive restoration. (Pagination varies slightly across the various printings of the Morgan Report held at different libraries, but the quotes are easily located in the testimony.)

MROL	Morgan Report online; www.morganreport.org
NARA	U.S. National Archives and Records Administration
NHC	Naval Historical Center, Washington, DC
PCA	*Pacific Commercial Advertiser*, Honolulu
RG	Record Group (of documents in NARA)

Introduction

1. The area of a disc with a radius of 2,200 miles (3,540 km) is 39,369,182 square kilometers, 7.5 percent of the total surface area of the earth (510,066,000 square km). Because the disc in question does not lie flat but is a curved part of a globe, the calculation is not perfect but is more than adequate to prove the point.

2. This simplistic description does not address the whole problem of determining "true facts," as President Grover Cleveland called them in his instructions to James Blount to investigate the Hawaiian revolution. As we know from cognitive psychologists, what evidence seems worth our attention and what judgments flow from that attention are heavily influenced by preexisting mental schema.

3. Pub. L. 103-150, 103rd Congress Joint Resolution 19, November 23, 1993.

Chapter 1. Hawai`i on the Cusp of Revolution

1. Mabel Craft, *Hawai`i Nei* (San Francisco: William Doxey Co., 1899), 9. For the warship's arrival see: *Boston* deck log, August 1892, Log of the USS *Boston*, Logs of U.S. Naval Ships, 1801–1915, Logs of Ships and Stations, 1801–1946, Records of the Bureau of Naval Personnel, Record Group 24, NARA, hereafter cited as "deck logs," preceded by the ship's name.

2. The first pages of the three volumes of the *Boston* deck log for 1892–93 list the ship's complement and the types of boats, guns, and ordnance carried.

3. Michael Dougherty, *To Steal a Kingdom: Probing Hawaiian History* (Waimanalo, HI: Island Style Press, 1992), 5, 10–11.

4. Edward D. Beechert, *Working in Hawai`i: A Labor History* (Honolulu: University of Hawai`i Press, 1985), 5. I relied heavily on this fine work, especially chapter 1 ("Ancient Hawai`i").

5. Dougherty, *Steal a Kingdom*, 16, 18.

6. Charles C. Mann's masterful *1491: New Revelations of the Americas before Columbus* (New York: Knopf, 2005) is highly relevant to Hawai`i as well. See esp. 102–24.

7. American activity before 1842 is detailed in Harold Whitman Bradley, *The American Frontier in Hawai`i: The Pioneers 1778–1843* (Palo Alto: Stanford University Press, 1942); and Ralph S. Kuykendall, *The Hawaiian Kingdom*, vol. 1, *1778–1854: Foundation and Transformation* (Honolulu: University of Hawai`i Press, 1938). Hawaiian–American relations from the earliest contacts through 1893 are in *Foreign Relations of the United States, 1894*, Appendix II (cited hereafter as *FRUS, 1894*). The Tyler message of December 30, 1842 is in *FRUS, 1894*, 39–41.

8. Webster to George Brown, March 15, 1843, *FRUS, 1894*, Appendix II, 60.

9. Hugh Legare did not warn the British directly but instructed the American minister to inform the Foreign Office. Legare to Edward Everett, June 13, 1843, *FRUS, 1894*, Appendix II, 111.

10. Kuykendall, *Hawaiian Kingdom*, vol. 1, *1778–1854*, ch. 12 and 13.

11. William D. Alexander to James Blount, enclosed in Blount to Walter Q. Gresham, July 26, 1893, *FRUS, 1894*, 607–8; Ralph S. Kuykendall, *Hawaiian Kingdom*, vol. 3, *1874–1893: The Kalakaua Dynasty* (Honolulu: University of Hawai`i Press, 1967), 402, 400; Severance to Webster, no. 8, March 31, 1851, Despatches, T-30, roll 4, NARA; and Ralph Kuykendall and A. Grove Day, *Hawai`i: A History*, rev. ed. (Englewood Cliffs, NJ: Prentice-Hall Inc., 1961), ch. 8.

12. Kuykendall, *Hawaiian Kingdom*, vol. 1, *1778–1854*, 251; and Sylvester K. Stevens, *American Expansion in Hawai`i, 1842–1898* (Harrisburg: Archives Publishing Company of Pennsylvania, 1945), 48.

13. James D. Richardson, ed., "Annual Message of December 4, 1849," in *Compilation of the Messages and Papers of the Presidents*, vol. 17. (New York: Bureau of National Literature, 1897).

14. Marcy to William L. Gregg, July 8 and September 22, 1853, "Instructions to Hawai`i," RG 45, M-77, roll 99, NARA. See also Stevens, *American Expansion in Hawai`i*, 69–72, 79.

15. Marcy to William Lee, September 21, 1855, in Stevens, *American Expansion in Hawai`i*, 79.

16. Gregg to Marcy, March 12, 1855, Despatches, T-30, roll 6, NARA.

17. Stevens, *American Expansion in Hawai`i*, 82–83.

18. Edward D. Beechert, *Honolulu: Crossroads of the Pacific* (Columbia: University of South Carolina Press, 1991), 36–37.

19. The Music Hall burned down in early 1895 and was replaced by another theater named the Opera House. Residents used both names for the same building in the 1880s and 1890s.

20. Georges Sauvin, *A Tree in Bud: The Hawaiian Kingdom, 1889–1893* (Honolulu: University of Hawai`i Press, 1987), 56–58.

21. Ibid., 120.

22. Ibid., 119.

23. Ibid., 110–11.

24. Ibid., 111.

25. Tom Dye and Eric Komori, "A Pre-censal Population History of Hawai`i," *New Zealand Journal of Archeology* 14 (1992): 113–28; and Tom Dye, "Population Trends in Hawai`i before 1778," *The Hawaiian Journal of History* 28 (1994): 1–20.

26. David E. Stannard, *Before the Horror: The Population of Hawai`i on the Eve of Western Contact* (Honolulu: Social Science Research Institute, University of Hawai`i, 1989).

27. Oswald A. Bushnell, *The Gifts of Civilization: Germs and Genocide in Hawai`i* (Honolulu: University of Hawai`i Press, 1993), 36.

28. Ibid., 56.

29. Quoted in ibid.

30. Robert C. Schmitt, *Historical Statistics of Hawai`i* (Honolulu: University Press of Hawai`i, 1977), 9; and Franklin Odo and Kazuko Sinoto, *A Pictorial History of the Japanese in Hawai`i, 1885–1924* (Honolulu: Bishop Museum Press, 1985), 18–19.

Chapter 2. Pearl Harbor and Reciprocity

1. Willis E. Snowbarger, "The Development of Pearl Harbor" (PhD dissertation, University of California at Berkeley, 1950), 52.

2. Barry Rigby, "American Expansion in Hawai`i: The Contributions of Henry A. Peirce," *Diplomatic History* 4, no. 4 (Fall 1980): 357.

3. Merze Tate, *Reciprocity or Annexation?* (East Lansing: Michigan State University Press, 1968), 77.

4. My sketch of Anglo-American relations and the Treaty of Washington is based on the definitive account by Charles S. Campbell Jr., *The Transformation of American Foreign Relations, 1865–1900* (New York: Harper and Row, 1976), 1–49.

5. Ibid., 74. Belknap issued the order on June 24, 1872. Sending officers for surveys was not unusual for Grant, who sent General Orville E. Babcock to Santo Domingo in 1869 to explore a possible naval station. In 1873 Colonel Albert Steinberger went to Samoa on a similar mission. Grant endorsed, but could not persuade the Senate to approve, Commander Richard Meade's 1872 treaty securing exclusive rights to a coaling station at Pago Pago harbor.

6. They reported their findings in a May 8, 1873, letter titled "Report on Pearl Harbor" to Secretary of War William Belknap, printed in *American Historical Review* 20 (April 1925): 560–65. For additional detail, see Robert Wooster, "John M. Schofield and the 'Multipurpose' Army," *American Nineteenth Century History* 7, no. 2 (June 2006): 180.

7. Schofield and Alexander to Belknap, "Report on Pearl Harbor," 562, 564–65.

8. Rigby, "American Expansion in Hawai`i," 364.

9. Helena G. Allen, *Sanford Ballard Dole: Hawai`i's Only President, 1844–1926* (Glendale, CA: Arthur Clark Company, 1988), 105–6. For additional information, see Kuykendall, *Hawaiian Kingdom*, vol. 3, *1874–1893*, 23–24; and Tate, *Reciprocity or Annexation*, 108–9.

10. For a less benign view of reciprocity, see Jonathan Kay Kamakawiwo`ole Osorio, *Dismembering Lāhui: A History of the Hawaiian Nation to 1887* (Honolulu: University of Hawai`i Press, 2002), 166–73.

11. U.S. Government, "Report of the Commission to Investigate Alleged Frauds under the Hawaiian Reciprocity Treaty" (Washington, DC: Government Printing Office, 1883); and Kuykendall, *Hawaiian Kingdom*, vol. 3, *1874–1893*, 380–81.

12. Gibson said, "The policy of the Government, and the need of the country, however, is to secure an actual renewal of the Treaty for a definite term of years" (Kuykendall, *Hawaiian Kingdom*, vol. 3, *1874–1893*, 382).

13. Frederick T. Frelinghuysen to John F. Miller, June 17, 1884, Senate Document No. 231, 56th Congress, 2nd session, Part 8, 242–43, quoted in Kuykendall, *Hawaiian Kingdom*, vol. 3, *1874–1893*, 384; and *Senate Executive Journal*, XXIV, 289, 335, quoted in Kuykendall, *Hawaiian Kingdom*, vol. 3, *1874–1893*, 384–85.

14. Henry A. P. Carter to Godfrey Brown, August 16, 1887, No. 112, quoted in Kuykendall, *Hawaiian Kingdom*, vol. 3, *1874–1893*, 386.

15. Walter Murray Gibson to Carter, June 12, 1886, No. 13, quoted in Kuykendall, *Hawaiian Kingdom*, vol. 3, *1874–1893*, 391.

16. Campbell, *Transformation of American Foreign Relations*, 72–83; and Paul M. Kennedy, *The Samoan Tangle: A Study in Anglo-German-American Relations, 1878–1900* (Dublin: Irish University Press, 1974).

17. Campbell, *Transformation of American Foreign Relations*, 78–83.

18. Ibid., 71–72; and Snowbarger, "Development of Pearl Harbor," 69.

Chapter 3. The Empire of Cane

1. This sketch of Spreckels is mainly based on Jacob Adler's fine book, *Claus Spreckels: The Sugar King in Hawai`i* (Honolulu: University of Hawai`i Press, 1966), especially chapters 1 and 7. Spreckels' arrival in Hawai`i is described on page 3.

2. Merze Tate, *The United States and the Hawaiian Kingdom: A Political History* (New Haven: Yale University Press, 1965), 335–36.

3. "A Claus Spreckels Anecdote," *New York Times*, June 22, 1902.

4. James D. Schuyler and G. F. Allardt, "Culture of Sugar Cane: Report on Water Supply for

Irrigation on the Honolulu and Kahuku Ranchos," pamphlet, Oakland, California, 1889, copy in the Bishop Museum.

5. A. Grove Day, ed., *Mark Twain's Letters from Hawai`i* (Honolulu: University of Hawai`i Press, 1966). This letter was written in September 1866.

6. Noel Deerr, *The History of Sugar* (London: Chapman and Hall Ltd., 1950), 504–5.

7. The Netherlands Trading Company sent out sets of sealed clear glass bottles, each containing a different color, hence a different grade, of sugar. Traders compared the color of a batch of sugar against the Dutch samples. Guilford L. Spencer, *A Handbook for Cane-Sugar Manufacturers and Their Chemists* (New York: John Wiley and Sons, 1929), 337; Deerr, *History of Sugar*, 505; Lewis Ware, *The Sugar Beet, Including a History of the Beet Sugar Industry in Europe* (Philadelphia: Henry Carey Baird & Company, 1880), 50–51; and C. A. Browne and F. W. Zerban, *Physical and Chemical Methods of Sugar Analysis* (New York: John Wiley and Sons, 1941), 1039.

8. Kuykendall, *Hawaiian Kingdom*, vol. 3, *1874–1893*, 26. In 1878, the final year of milling sugar that was planted before reciprocity, only 43 percent of Hawai`i sugar exports was raw sugar up to grade DS 12, compared to 41 percent in grades DS 13–15 (light-brown "grocery sugars") and 15 percent in grades DS 16–20 (medium-quality white sugar) (U.S. Government, "Report of the Commission to Investigate"). The breakdown of sugar grades in this report is awkward because the percentages overlap. The report cites the following distribution for sugar in 1878: 3 percent DS 1–7; 13 percent DS 7–10; 27 percent DS 10–13; 41 percent DS 13–16; and 15 percent DS 16–20. The grades described are both inclusive and exclusive. Using the lowest grades as an example, the listing of DS 1–7 should be interpreted as sugar in grades from one up to, but not including, seven, and so forth.

9. In 1890 the forty large incorporated plantations and twenty-seven smaller, unincorporated plantations had a total value of about $33.2 million, of which American money composed 75 percent, British 18 percent, and German 7 percent. Most plantations had mixed ownership, that is, American and one or more other nationalities (Thomas G. Thrum, *Hawaiian Annual, 1891*, [Honolulu: Thomas G. Thrum, 1891]; hereafter cited as Thrum, *Hawaiian Annual*, followed by the year of publication, 59, 61; and Thrum, *Hawaiian Annual, 1894*, 44).

10. Alan Takeo Moriyama, *Imingaisha: Japanese Emigration Companies and Hawai`i, 1894–1908* (Honolulu: University of Hawai`i Press, 1985), 96; Kuykendall, *Hawaiian Kingdom*, vol. 3, *1874–1893*, 83; and Tate, *Reciprocity or Annexation*, app. I; and Reciprocity and Commercial Treaties, United States Tariff Commission, Washington, DC, 1919, 168.

11. Hawaiian Sugar Planters' Association (HSPA), *The Story of Sugar in Hawai`i: The Story of Sugar Plantations, Their History, Their Methods of Operations and Their Place in the Economy of Hawai`i* (Honolulu: Hawaiian Sugar Planters' Association, 1925), 59, 95–96.

12. Anonymous, "The Sugar Producing Capacity of the Hawaiian Islands" (Honolulu: Judd

and Detweiler, nd, copy in the Bishop Museum). It was probably published in 1882 or 1883, for annual sugar production in those years was about 57,000 tons. It was likely produced to help convince the Congress that renewal of reciprocity would not mean continued dramatic increases in Hawaiian sugar imports at the expense of mainland growers.

13. In 1892 the Ewa Plantation produced 2,849 tons of sugar on 650 acres of cane (Kuykendall, *Hawaiian Kingdom*, vol. 3, *1874–1893*, 62, 69). At Koloa Plantation, yield reached 5 tons per acres in 1900 (Arthur C. Alexander, *Koloa Plantation, 1835–1935: A History of the Oldest Hawaiian Sugar Plantation*, 2nd ed. [Lihue, HI: Kauai Historical Society, 1985], 91). By way of comparison, in 1996 an acre of the best Hawaiian sugar land yielded 12.5 tons of raw sugar.

14. John W. Vandercook, *King Cane: The Story of Sugar in Hawai`i* (New York and London: Harper and Bros., 1939), 18.

15. Kuykendall, *Hawaiian Kingdom*, vol. 3, *1874–1893*, 73. For an excellent overview of the Hawaiian sugar industry, see ibid., 46–78, and Ralph S. Kuykendall, *The Hawaiian Kingdom*, vol. 2, *1854–1874: Twenty Critical Years* (Honolulu: University of Hawai`i Press, 1953), 140–49.

16. HSPA, *The Story of Sugar in Hawai`i*, 64–65; and Alexander, *Koloa Plantation*, 93–96.

17. Alexander, *Koloa Plantation*, 93–96.

18. Vandercook, *King Cane*, 67; and HSPA, *The Story of Sugar in Hawai`i*, 48.

19. Because the government was not ready to undertake such public works projects, it determined that "no obstacle should be thrown in the way of others" (Castle to Moehonua, September 7, 1876, in Carol Wilcox, *Sugar Water: Hawai`i's Plantation Ditches* [Honolulu: University of Hawai`i Press, 1996], 163–66). Wilcox's fine book is the standard history of water projects.

20. Arthur D. Baldwin, *A Memoir of Henry Perrine Baldwin: 1842–1911* (Cleveland, OH: Privately printed, 1915), 34–35.

21. Wilcox, *Sugar Water*, 57.

22. Vandercook, *King Cane*, 69; and Adler, *Claus Spreckels*, 49. According to Adler, the Spreckels Ditch delivered 60 million gallons per day, or 50 percent more than the Baldwin-Alexander project.

23. Vandercook, *King Cane*, 68–76; Alexander, *Koloa Plantation*, 97–98. Years later, the Hawaiian Sugar Planters Association calculated that one-quarter of the total capital invested in sugar plantations went for water projects ("Sugar in Hawai`i," HSPA, 2).

24. Hugh Morrison, general manager of Spreckelsville, estimated the costs this way: (1) $200 for "irrigating, stripping, weeding, cutting, transporting, grinding, and manufacturing," ($50 per ton for four tons); (2) $45 for water lifted 100 feet from artesian wells; and (3) $13.48 for depreciation of the pumping plant. Costs were $258.40 and profit $221.60. Per acre profits, therefore, were $61.60 at 4 cents per pound; $221.60 at 6 cents a pound

(Schuyler and Allardt, "Culture of Sugar Cane"). Watered by irrigation, Spreckelsville did not depend on pumped artesian water. Probably Morrison was simply trying to be helpful by assisting Schuyler and Allardt in estimating production costs for a crop grown with pumped water.

25. Sugar earnings can only be estimated, but a rough calculation can be made using the customs house records of sugar exports and multiplying by the published New York price, though the New York price was always higher, usually 20 percent higher, than the Honolulu price (Tate, *Reciprocity or Annexation*, 126).

26. "Statistical Abstract of the United States, 1922" (Washington, DC: Department of Commerce, GPO, 1923), 351. Rather than yearly totals, for the period indicated the Statistical Abstract provides five-year totals. The estimated population of the United States in 1897, the middle of the five-year period, was 72,189,000 persons (*Historical Statistics of the United States: Colonial Times to 1970*, 2 vols. [Washington, DC: Government Printing Office, 1975], 8). Hawaiian sugar exports amounted to $17,880,171 in 1897, or about $164 per capita. See Tate, *Reciprocity or Annexation*, appendix I; Kuykendall, *Hawaiian Kingdom*, vol. 3, *1874–1893*, 83; and Moriyama, *Imingaisha*, 96. This disparity is not quite as great as it seems. The United States was a huge continental economy in which certain regions of the country—the South in cotton, the Midwest in wheat, the North in manu-factures—ran sizable surpluses in these products, but these "internal" surpluses were not reflected in international economic statistics, such as export earnings. It should not be overlooked that the U.S. internal market was vastly larger than Hawai`i's, which makes Hawai`i's higher per capita exports less startling. For example, it could be said that Eastern manufacturers "exported" to the West Coast. Lacking a large internal market, Hawaiian manufactures—sugar—went almost entirely abroad.

27. Schmitt, *Historical Statistics of Hawai`i*, table 21.1. The twenty-two years were 1878–99. Given that Hawaiian exports were almost entirely sugar, the fairest measurement of exports under reciprocity's influence should begin with the 1878 harvest, the first postreciprocity crop, through 1899, when planters began to harvest the final crop planted under reci-procity and before annexation. In 1898, the U.S. exports were $1,039,029,000 and imports, $717,925,000, a ratio of $1.45 in exports for every $1.00 of imports ("Statistical Abstract of the U.S., 1922," 351).

28. Thrum, *Hawaiian Annual, 1890*, 43; and Thrum, *Hawaiian Annual, 1897*, 25. See also Schmitt, *Historical Statistics*, 552.

29. *Hawaiian Gazette*, November 22, 1876, quoted by Kuykendall, *Hawaiian Kingdom*, vol. 3, *1874–1893*, 49.

30. "Report of the Royal Commission on the Development of Resources of the Kingdom. Island of Hawai`i" (Honolulu, April 27, 1877), 9, quoted by Kuykendall, *Hawaiian Kingdom*, vol. 3, *1874–1893*, 50.

Chapter 4. The Beginnings of Japanese Immigration

1. The sketch of Irwin and his business dealings with Masuda Takashi and Inoue Kaoru is drawn from Yukiko Irwin and Hilary Conroy, "Robert Walker Irwin and Systematic Immigration to Hawai`i," in *East Across the Pacific*, ed. Hilary Conroy and T. Scott Miyakawa, 41–55 (Santa Barbara, CA: Clio Press, 1970). See also Shinichi Yonekawa, "Are General Trading Companies Unique to Japan?" in *General Trading Companies: A Comprehensive and Historical Study*, ed. Shin'ichi Yonekawa, 8–32 (Tokyo: United Nations University Press, 1990), 8, 22–25; Odo and Sinoto, *Pictorial History of the Japanese*, 22–24; and Christine Guth, *Art, Tea, and Industry: Masuda Takashi and the Mitsui Circle* (Princeton, NJ: Princeton University Press, 1993).

2. Irwin and Conroy, "Robert Walker Irwin," 45. Philbert Ono asserts that Irwin spoke only broken Japanese and customarily used an interpreter, although Ono's biographical sketch does not cite a source. See "Robert Walker Irwin," revised November 9, 2009, http://photoguide.jp/txt/Robert_Walker_Irwin.

3. Odo and Sinoto, *Pictorial History of the Japanese*, 22–24; Kuykendall, *Hawaiian Kingdom*, vol. 3, *1874–1893*, 155; and Moriyama, *Imingaisha*, 10, 15.

4. Schmitt, *Historical Statistics of Hawai`i*, 9; and Odo and Sinoto, *Pictorial History of the Japanese*, 18–19.

5. Schmitt, *Historical Statistics of Hawai`i*, 25. Although most foreign residents were white, a few African American crewmen from traders and whalers managed to make a life for themselves ashore. Their numbers were so small that they were not separately counted in the various censuses.

6. Jacob Adler and Gwynn Barret, eds., *The Diaries of Walter Murray Gibson, 1886–1887* (Honolulu: University Press of Hawai`i, 1973), 84.

7. Kuykendall, *Hawaiian Kingdom*, vol. 3, *1874–1893*, 123.

8. Ibid., 122–126; Schmitt, *Historical Statistics*, 97, 25; and Thrum, *Hawaiian Annual, 1898*, 30. By 1896 the Portuguese population, including children born in the islands, totaled 15,191, of whom 2,268 worked on the plantations.

9. D. W. Y. Kwok, "By History Remembered," in *Sailing for the Sun: The Chinese in Hawai`i, 1789–1989*, ed. Arlene Lum (Honolulu: The East-West Center and Three Heroes Publishers, 1988), 10–11, 16.

10. Odo and Sinoto, *Pictorial History of the Japanese*, 18–19.

11. Clarence E. Glick, *Sojourners and Settlers: Chinese Migrants in Hawai`i* (Honolulu: Hawai`i Chinese History Center and University Press of Hawai`i, 1980), xi.

12. Legislative file, AH, quoted in Kuykendall, *Hawaiian Kingdom*, vol. 3, *1874–1893*, 179.

13. Schmitt, *Historical Statistics of Hawai`i*, 97–98.

14. Historians differ somewhat on the size of the Chinese population. Kuykendall states that

during 1886–94, the excess of departures over arrivals was 1,733, but he notes some individuals may have been counted two or more times (*Hawaiian Kingdom*, vol. 3, *1874–1893*, 150–53). Thrum estimates the Chinese population at 15,000 in the mid-1890s (Thrum, *Hawaiian Annual, 1896*, 119–20). Odo and Sinoto list 16,752 Chinese in the 1890 census and 21,616 in the 1896 census (*Pictorial History of the Japanese*, 18–19). The low point was somewhere between those two dates.

15. Moriyama, *Imingaisha*, 7–8.

16. Masaji Marumoto, " 'First Year' Immigrants to Hawai`i & Eugene Van Reed," in *East Across the Pacific*, eds. Conroy and Miyakawa, 5–39; Hilary Conroy, *Japanese Expansion into Hawai`i, 1868–1898* (San Francisco: R&E Associates, 1973), 68–71. Conroy provides the treaty text in appendix B, 207–9.

17. Kuykendall, *Hawaiian Kingdom*, vol. 3, *1874–1893*, 160–61.

18. Inoue to Iaukea, April 26, 1884, Immigration File, FO-EX, quoted in Irwin and Conroy, "Robert Walker Irwin," 46; and Kuykendall, *Hawaiian Kingdom*, vol. 3, *1874–1893*, 163–64.

19. Irwin and Conroy, "Robert Walker Irwin," 46.

20. "Information Regarding Emigration," December 1884, Japanese Foreign Ministry, quoted in Dorothy Ochiai Hazama and Jane Okamoto Komeiji, *Okage sama de: The Japanese in Hawai`i, 1885–1985* (Honolulu: Bess Press, 1986), 15.

21. Wakatsuki Yasuo, "Japanese Emigration to the United States, 1866–1924: A Monograph," *Perspectives in American History* 12 (1979): 429, 474–75. Wakatsuki concluded that "such lopsided concentrations can only be satisfactorily explained by the influence of local and personal ties."

22. Irwin and Conroy, "Robert Walker Irwin," 46–47; and Odo and Sinoto, *Pictorial History of the Japanese*, 39–40.

23. Quoted in Wakatsuki, "Japanese Emigration," 461; and Odo and Sinoto, *Pictorial History of the Japanese*, 39–40.

24. Nakamura report to the Foreign Ministry, March 11, 1885, quoted in Hazama and Komeiji, *Okage sama de*, 17.

25. Roland Kotani, *The Japanese in Hawai`i: A Century of Struggle* (Honolulu: The Hawai`i Hochi Ltd., 1985), 14.

26. Odo and Sinoto, *Pictorial History of the Japanese*, 21–23; and Katherine Coman, "Contract Labor in the Hawaiian Islands," *American Economic Association*, 3rd Series, 4, no. 3 (August 1903): 43.

27. The convention was signed January 28, 1886. Odo and Sinoto, *Pictorial History of the Japanese*, 22; and James H. Okahata, ed., *History of Japanese in Hawai`i* (Honolulu: United Japanese Society of Hawai`i, 1971), 110.

28. The convention is reprinted in Odo and Sinoto, *Pictorial History of the Japanese*, 24–26.

29. "Treaty with Japan, 1871," Hawaiian Kingdom Treaty, http://www.hawaiiankingdom.org/treaty_japan1871.shtml.

30. Kuykendall, *Hawaiian Kingdom*, vol. 3, *1874–1893*, 171.

31. Wakatsuki, "Japanese Emigration," 399–405.

32. Ibid., 402, 407–11; and Moriyama, *Imingaisha*, 18–19, 65–66. These figures do not include the costs charged to the immigrants for return passage and for interpreters and doctors, though those costs would not significantly affect the wage disparity.

33. Moriyama, *Imingaisha*, 68, 18–19.

34. Wakatsuki, "Japanese Immigration," 444–47; and Moriyama, *Imingaisha*, 5–6, 203n5.

35. Wakatsuki, "Japanese Immigration," 453.

36. Ibid., 448, 453.

37. Moriyama, *Imingaisha*, 25.

38. Soga Yasutaro, describing his arrival in Honolulu in February 1896, quoted in Yukiko Kimura, *Issei* (Honolulu: University of Hawai'i Press, 1988), 12.

39. In 1902 the Japanese Consulate estimated that of the workers who went to Japan during 1885–94, 46 percent returned to Japan, 44 percent remained in Hawai'i, 7 percent died, and 3 percent went on to the U.S. mainland. Another analysis, which jibes with estimates made by newspapers and with reports by the American minister, concluded that 20,430 Japanese, about two-thirds of those who came during the 10 years of government-sponsored emigration, remained in Hawai'i (Moriyama, *Imingaisha*, table 8, 29; and Hazama and Komeiji, *Okage sama de*, 22–23).

40. Photo in Odo and Sinoto, *Pictorial History of the Japanese*, 72.

Chapter 5. The Fragmentation of Hawaiian Politics

1. Osorio, *Dismembering Lahui*, 146.

2. For Kalākaua's reign, two excellent recent works are Osorio, *Dismembering Lāhui*, and Ernest Andrade Jr., *Unconquerable Rebel: Robert W. Wilcox and Hawaiian Politics, 1880–1903* (Niwot: University Press of Colorado, 1996). Still useful and highly detailed is Kuykendall, *Hawaiian Kingdom*, vol. 3, *1874–1893*. See also Helena G. Allen, *Kalakaua: Renaissance King* (Honolulu: Mutual Publishing, 1994).

3. Ethel Damon, *Sanford Ballard Dole and his Hawai'i* (Palo Alto: Pacific Books, 1957), 207.

4. Ibid., 168–69.

5. Roger Robinson, ed., *Stevenson: His Best Pacific Writings* (Honolulu: Bess Press, 2003), 70.

6. Andrade, *Unconquerable Rebel*, ch. 2. The point about the monarch's balancing role is taken from Osorio, *Dismembering Lāhui*, 180.

7. Osorio, *Dismembering Lāhui*, 147.

8. Andrew Farrell, ed., *Writings of Lorrin Thurston* (Honolulu: Advertiser Publishing, 1936); and Lorrin Thurston, *Memoirs of the Hawaiian Revolution* (Honolulu: Advertiser Publishing, 1936).

9. Thurston, *Memoirs*, 608.

10. George Merrill to Thomas Bayard, July 30, 1887, no. 135, quoted in Tate, *U.S. and the Hawaiian Kingdom*, 86.

11. Thurston, *Memoirs*, 153.

12. Tate, *U.S. and the Hawaiian Kingdom*, 93.

13. Ernest Andrade Jr. offers a detailed analysis of Wilcox's life and role in the internal political discord in *Unconquerable Rebel*.

14. Farrell, ed., *Writings of Thurston*, 20.

15. Andrade, *Unconquerable Rebel*, 74–75, 95–98.

16. George Merrill to James G. Blaine, July 26 and August 1, 1889, HExDoc-48, 16–18.

17. Quoted in Andrade, *Unconquerable Rebel*, 76–77.

18. William A. Russ Jr., *The Hawaiian Revolution, 1893–1894* (Selinsgrove, PA: Susquehanna University Press, 1959), 42.

19. Morgan Rpt, vol. 1, 524; Stevens to Blaine, August 19, 1890, HExDoc-48, 67–68.

20. Stevens to Blaine, September 25 and November 14, 1890, HExDoc-48, 70, 72.

21. Wodehouse to the Foreign Office, September 10, 1890, FO 58/253.

22. A sympathetic biography is Helena Allen, *The Betrayal of Lili`uokalani: Last Queen of Hawai`i, 1838–1917* (Honolulu: Mutual Publishing, 1982).

23. Privy Council record, January 29, 1891, quoted in Kuykendall, *Hawaiian Kingdom*, vol. 3, *1874–1893*, 474.

24. Wodehouse to the Foreign Office, no. 4, February 10, 1891, FO 58/258.

25. Lili`uokalani, *Hawai`i's Story by Hawai`i's Queen* (Boston: Lee and Shepard, 1898), 209–10.

26. Wodehouse to Foreign Office, January 14, 1892, p. 17, FO 58/263.

27. Stevens to Blaine, February 8, 1892, Despatches, T-30, roll 25, NARA.

28. Kuykendall, *Hawaiian Kingdom*, vol. 3, *1874–1893*, 526.

29. Stevens to Blaine, March 8 and March 25, 1892, Despatches, T-30, roll 25, NARA.

30. Mott Smith to Samuel Parker, December 30, 1891, quoted in Kuykendall, *Hawaiian Kingdom*, vol. 3, *1874–1893*, 526.

31. Wodehouse to the Foreign Office, March 1, March 29, and April 7, 1892, FO 58/263.

32. Andrade, *Unconquerable Rebel*, 95–98; and Kuykendall, *Hawaiian Kingdom*, vol. 3, *1874–1893*, 527–28.

33. Platform of the Liberal Party, quoted in Kuykendall, *Hawaiian Kingdom*, vol. 3, *1874–1893*, 515. As part of his longer discussion of the queen's dilemma, Tom Coffman writes:

"The Queen and her National Reform Party were caught in the middle, with the Americans on one side and the rising popularity of Wilcox and Bush on the other" (Coffman, *The Nation Within: The Story of American's Annexation of the Nation of Hawai`i* [Honolulu: Epicenter, 1998], 115).

34. Kuykendall, *Hawaiian Kingdom*, vol. 3, *1874–1893*, 582. The queen told Blount that she worked with two members of the legislature to write the new document (Queen Lili`uokalani statement, *FRUS, 1894*, App II, 863–64).

35. Stevens to John Watson Foster, November 1, 1892, HExDoc-48.

36. See in particular, Wodehouse to the Foreign Office, June 2, June 21, July 29, and October 20, 1892, FO 58/263.

37. Wodehouse to the Foreign Office, no. 20, November 9, 1892, p. 87, FO 58/263.

38. Stevens to Foster, November 8, 1892, *FRUS, 1894*, App. II, 376.

39. Wiltse to the Secretary of the Navy, November 8, 1892, *FRUS, 1894*, App. II, 188.

40. Wodehouse to Lord Rosebery, no. 22, December 7, 1892, FO 58/263.

41. Stevens to Foster, November 20, 1892, HExDoc-48.

42. Stevens to Blaine, March 8, 1892, *FRUS, 1894*, App. II, 182.

43. A judicious analysis of Stevens and other Maine actors is found in Paul T. Burlin, *Imperial Maine and Hawai`i: Interpretative Essays in the History of Nineteenth Century American Expansion* (Lanham, MD: Lexington Books, 2006).

44. Foster to Stevens, November 8, 1892, HExDoc-48.

45. Campbell, *Transformation of American Foreign Relations*, 181. Campbell continued: "Having been orally informed (one may be sure) prior to assuming his post in 1889 of Blaine's convictions regarding Hawai`i, having been told to study the Secretary's instruction of 1881, having declared his own advocacy of annexation and asked whether he and the navy should 'deviate from established rules and precedents' in the event of a revolution he anticipated, Stevens was justified in interpreting Washington's silence as approval of his implicit recommendations, and therefore in acting as he did when the revolution occurred."

46. Mott Smith to Parker, April 14, 1892, quoted in Kuykendall, *Hawaiian Kingdom*, vol. 3, *1874–1893*, 527.

47. Blaine to Comly, December 1, 1881, *FRUS, 1894*, App. II, 1158, 1159, 1160.

48. Blaine to Harrison, August 10, 1891, quoted in Albert T. Volwiler, ed., *The Correspondence between Benjamin Harrison and James G. Blaine, 1882–1893* (Philadelphia: American Philosophical Society, 1940), 174.

49. Stevens to Foster, November 20, 1892, HExDoc-48.

50. Wiltse to Benjamin Tracy, October 12, 1892, *FRUS, 1894*, App. II, 185. See also George Brown to Tracy, September 6, 1892, *FRUS, 1894*, App. II, 183.

51. Kuykendall, *Hawaiian Kingdom*, vol. 3, *1874–1893*, 507.

52. Ibid., 739n141.

53. Ibid., 539–40.

54. Wodehouse to Rosebery, December 7, 1892, no. 22, FO 58/263.

Chapter 6. The Revolution Begins

1. *Boston* deck log, January 4–14, 1893. For the unusual chill, see *PCA*, January 5, 1893.

2. Robert McElroy, *Grover Cleveland: The Man and the Statesman* (New York: Harper and Brothers, 1923), quoted in Russ, *Hawaiian Revolution*, 100.

3. Tate, *U.S. and the Hawaiian Kingdom*, 130.

4. Allen, *Betrayal of Lili`uokalani*, 281, 285.

5. Rich Budnick, *Stolen Kingdom: An American Conspiracy* (Honolulu: Aloha Press, 1992), 101.

6. *PCA*, December 27, 1892.

7. New York *Times*, April 27, 1893. Wiltse retired from the Navy shortly after returning from Honolulu in early 1893. He died suddenly in April 1893.

8. Swinburne testimony, Morgan Rpt, 463–64; and Morgan Report Online, hereafter cited as MROL, 823–24.

9. Young testimony, Morgan Rpt, 345; and MROL, 705.

10. Stevens testimony, Morgan Rpt, 525; and MROL, 785. Stevens said, "Putting all the facts together, the lottery bill dead, and the opium bill dead, we had made up our minds that the Queen and her favorite would abide by the ministry for eighteen months, or until the meeting of the new Legislature, and I did not dream of any revolution that the Queen had on foot."

11. Laird testimony, Morgan Report, 380, 374; and MROL, 740, 734.

12. Swinburne said Wiltse told him, "The Wilcox-Jones ministry can not be voted out; I am certain of that; I have looked at the situation, and I am satisfied the Queen can not get votes enough to bring in a vote of want of confidence; besides that, the minister has looked into the situation, and you do not think he would leave the island if the Wilcox-Jones ministry could be ousted?" (Morgan Rpt, 464; and MROL, 824). Swinburne said he "spoke of my reasons to Capt. Wiltse for a postponement of a trip for target practice. The captain said he was satisfied, and the minister said he was satisfied that the Wilcox-Jones ministry could not be voted out; that everything was as quiet as possible, and it was as good a time to go as could be" (Morgan Rpt, 487; and MROL, 847). He had changed his mind from two months earlier, just before the queen appointed the Wilcox cabinet to end the cabinet turmoil, when he thought the *Boston*'s presence helped deter her from unconstitutionally dissolving the legislature (Wiltse to SecNav, November 8, 1892, *FRUS, 1894*, App. II, 188).

13. Stevens to Foster, November 8, 1892, HExDoc-48.

14. *Boston* deck log, January 4–14, 1893.

15. Ibid.; Laird testimony, Morgan Rpt, 338; and MROL, 734.

16. Two interisland steamer companies, the William C. Wilder Company and the Inter-Island Steam Navigation Company, ran twice-weekly boats to Lahaina and Hilo. The *Kinau* belonged to the Wilder company.

17. Laird testimony, 374; Young testimony, 326; Swinburne testimony, 464; all in Morgan Rpt; and MROL, 734, 686, 824.

18. Allen, *Betrayal of Lili`uokalani*, 281, 285.

19. *Boston* deck log, January 14, 15, 1893; Laird testimony, Morgan Report, 374; and MROL, 734. Although the warship's engine revolutions were 10 percent lower returning to Honolulu than outbound to Hilo, this was surely due to difference in wind, wave action, and currents. The ship cruised normally on both legs. Laird called it "very leisurely, half-steam power." Although Laird thought Captain Wiltse "consumed about two hours looking for the dog," entries in the *Boston* deck log suggest that the search lasted less than an hour. Laird said Stevens' elder daughter and several men were waiting for him in a small boat as the *Boston* came into the harbor. Young left the ship about thirty minutes after Stevens. See Young testimony, 326; Laird Testimony, 374; Swinburne testimony, 464–65, all in Morgan Rpt; and MROL, 686, 734, 824–26; and Lucien Young, *The Real Hawai`i: Its History and Present Condition, Including the True Story of the Revolution* (New York: Doubleday and McClure Company, 1899), 159.

20. Tate, *U.S. and Hawaiian Kingdom*, 134–35.

21. Lili`uokalani, *Hawai`i's Story*, 230.

22. A. F. Judd statement to Blount, *FRUS, 1894*, App. II, 838.

23. Queen Lili`uokalani statement, *FRUS, 1894*, App II, 864.

24. McCandless testimony, Morgan Report, 606; and MROL, 966. William O. Smith thought that in January 1893 most Hawaiian legislators knew of the new constitution's existence but not of the queen's plans to promulgate it "until very late in the session" (*FRUS, 1894*, App. II, 956).

25. Henry Waterhouse somehow learned of this letter and visited Jones on January 11, 1893, to tell him. The actual letter, dated January 11, arrived in the mail at Jones' house on January 16. Jones read it into the record of the Morgan Report (Jones testimony, Morgan Rpt, 171–72; and MROL, 567–68).

26. Emmeluth affidavit, Morgan Rpt, 454; and MROL, 814.

27. W. D. Alexander, *History of the Later Years of the Hawaiian Monarchy and the Revolution of 1893* (Honolulu: Gazette Publishing Company, 1896), 29; and Waterhouse statement, *FRUS, 1894*, App. II, 513–14.

28. A. F. Judd statement to Blount, *FRUS, 1894*, App. II, 838.

29. Kuykendall, *Hawaiian Kingdom*, vol. 3, *1874–1893*, 586.

30. Strictly speaking, King Kalākaua promulgated the 1887 pact, not the rebels. In reality, he had no choice but to follow their wishes.

31. *PCA*, December 28, 1892.

32. A. F. Judd interview with Blount, *FRUS, 1894*, App. II, 838–39.

33. *PCA*, January 5, 1893.

34. *PCA*, January 8, 1893. Lorrin Thurston proposed January 11, Robert Wilcox January 12, and G. P. Kamauoha January 13. By a vote of 23–13, January 12 was chosen.

35. *PCA*, January 5 and 13, 1893.

36. Ibid.

37. *FRUS, 1894*, App. II, 863. Judd later testified that "Wilson told me in great emotion that he had been fighting the battle alone all the morning and that the Queen was determined to proclaim a new constitution. He said the constitution was her own compilation. The members of the Hui Kalai`aina said that the constitution came from the Queen to them. Parker told me later that he stayed by the Queen, for he was afraid if left alone she would sign the constitution, take it out to the people, proclaim it from the palace balcony, and say that her cabinet and judges would not approve of it and tell her people to look out for them."

38. Parker told Blount that he arrived first and, while waiting for his colleagues, the queen told him about the constitution. The other three ministers arrived just before the beginning of the final legislative session, so they aborted the meeting and rushed to the Government Building. Parker says he told the others about the constitution while they were walking across the street (*FRUS, 1894*, App. II, 907). John Colburn later said that about ten o'clock in the morning on January 14, Arthur Peterson told him the queen intended to proclaim a new constitution. It is not clear whether the queen informed all four ministers as a group or told Peterson what she intended and he passed the word along.

39. Lili`uokalani, *Hawai`i's Story*, 384–85.

40. William O. Smith stated that when Colburn came to his office on Saturday morning upset about the impending announcement of a new constitution, it was clear from Colburn's remarks that he had known of the existence of the constitution for several days but did not believe the queen would promulgate it (*FRUS, 1894*, App. II, 955).

41. Queen Lili`uokalani statement to Blount, *FRUS, 1894*, App II, 864; and Colburn statement to Blount, *FRUS, 1894*, App. II, 498.

42. There is no evidence that a Stevens note reached the ship midday Saturday. In any event, the *Boston* never formed a landing party, nor did the crew load guns and ammunition into boats.

43. Kuykendall, *Hawaiian Kingdom*, vol. 3, *1874–1893*, 584.

44. Colburn statement to Blount, *FRUS, 1894*, App. II, 498.

45. Davies to Lord Rosebery, January 31, 1893, p. 39, FO 58/279.

46. Lili`uokalani, *Hawai`i's Story*, 384–85; Stevens to Foster, January 18, 1893, HExDoc-48; Young testimony, Morgan Rpt, 327–32; and MROL, 689–94.

47. Henry Cooper said he visited Wiltse about 11:30 AM to inform him that the queen might promulgate a constitution. Cooper said Wiltse had not yet heard of the matter but stated that he was ready to protect the life and property of Americans. Cooper said Wiltse had Swinburne make preparations. Wiltse made none, but he confined the crew to the ship so they would not get caught up in trouble ashore. Swinburne testified that he saw Cooper on the *Boston* in the late morning of Saturday, January 14. The deck log makes no mention of Cooper's visit; this was not unusual because only VIP visits were normally logged (Cooper statement, *FRUS, 1894*, App. II, 962–63; Swinburne testimony, Morgan Rpt, 467–68; and MROL, 828).

48. The *Boston*'s deck log contains routine entries, included the rigging cleaning detail on the 0400–0800 watch, until the 0800–1200 watch on Monday, January 16, when, at an unspecified time, the officer of the deck wrote, "Made preparations for landing battalion." *Boston* deck log, January 14–16, 1893. Swinburne said the crew was sanding the deck when Wiltse told him to prepare a landing party. (Even steel warships had wood-covered decks for good footing.) Regarding the precaution of keeping men on the ship, Swinburne said it occurred "Saturday afternoon, at the usual time for making out the liberty lists. It is customary while in port to make out liberty lists before 12 o'clock on Saturday; that was their best day and I was so busy I could not attend to it, but immediately after lunch, I went to the cabin to speak to the captain about the liberty list. He said: 'Don't let any men go ashore at all; everything is in a chaotic state; I do not know when we will be called upon to protect property, and I do not want the men to leave the ship. Notify all the officers to return on board ship when a gun is fired'" (Morgan Rpt, 465–66; and MROL, 824–25).

49. Morgan Rpt, 203; and MROL, 563.

50. Lili`uokalani Diary, July 1, 1892, Hawaiiana Collection, University of Hawai`i Library, Honolulu; and Kuykendall, *Hawaiian Kingdom*, vol. 3, *1874–1893*, 587.

51. Morgan Rpt, 574; and MROL, 934.

52. Morgan Rpt, 574–75; and MROL, 934–35.

53. Kuykendall, *Hawaiian Kingdom*, vol. 3, *1874–1893*, 588. William C. Wilder went in the small delegation to talk to Stevens: "Mr. Stevens replied that if we obtain possession of the Government Building and the archives and established a Government, and became in fact the Government, he should of course recognize us. The matter of landing the troops from the *Boston* was not mentioned at that meeting" (Morgan Rpt, 448; and MROL, 808).

54. Thurston claimed he told Colburn and Peterson that the Committee of Safety was not prepared to let matters rest, to sit on a "volcano" until the queen exploded it in the future. Thurston said the cabinet should declare the throne vacant and establish a government

with the support of the people, otherwise the committee of safety was going to do it (Thurston to Foster, February 21, 1893, "Notes from Hawaiian Legation," Vol. 4, RG 59, NARA).

55. Cornwell to Blount, April 24, 1893, BROL, 494.

56. Blount interview with Parker, April 6, 1893, BROL, 905.

57. Blount Rpt, 498, quoted in Kuykendall, *Hawaiian Kingdom*, vol. 3, *1874–1893*, 591. The Morgan committee asked McCandless if Stevens told Thurston and Smith on Sunday that he would recognize the provisional government. McCandless said: "I think that there was a report of that kind." This suggests that whatever encouragement Stevens gave was magnified in the retelling, encouraging the rebels. Stevens should have anticipated this reaction. Merely meeting with Thurston and Smith conveyed a sense of legitimacy to their movement. McCandless: "I think we felt this way, that without any encouragement from him, we certainly had the sympathy of the American minister" (Morgan Rpt, 618; and MROL, 978).

Chapter 7. The Landing of U.S. Troops

1. This paragraph relies entirely on Bob Krauss, *Johnny Wilson: First Hawaiian Democrat* (Honolulu: University of Hawai`i Press, 1994), 10–11, 28–29.

2. Statement of L. A. Thurston, November 21, 1893, reprinted in the Morgan Rpt, 598–99; and MROL, 958–59.

3. Committee of Safety to Stevens, January 16, 1893, enclosed in Blount to Gresham, April 26, 1893, *FRUS, 1894*, App. II, 501.

4. McCandless testimony, Morgan Rpt, 617–19, at 618; and MROL, 977–79, at 978.

5. Joint statement of Smith, Castle, and Cooper, *FRUS, 1894*, App. II, 966.

6. Boyd interview, June 13, 1893, *FRUS, 1894*, App II, 731–35. Fred Wundenberg estimated the rebel meeting at seven hundred to nine hundred men, *FRUS, 1894*, App II, 562.

7. Wilder statement, Morgan Rpt, 449; and MROL, 809.

8. Waterhouse interview, *FRUS, 1894*, App. II, 518, 521.

9. Joint statement of Smith, Castle, and Cooper, *FRUS, 1894*, App. II, 966.

10. Stevens told the Morgan committee that "Captain Wiltse called at the legation probably nearly every day after we got back" (Morgan Rpt, 575; and MROL, 925). Swinburne said Wiltse went ashore "a great deal, every afternoon." Swinburne went ashore Sunday afternoon and judged the climate tense with apprehensions among the people about rioting (Swinburne testimony, Morgan Rpt, 466–67; and MROL, 826). Stevens testified that he and Wiltse forged an agreement over the weekend that Wiltse would land troops if Stevens asked for it. Stevens also claimed that "if [Wiltse] landed at all, the request had to

come from me" (Morgan Rpt, 576; and MROL, 936). Although it is very likely that the minister and the captain discussed the possibility of landing troops over the weekend, naval regulations made Wiltse personally responsible for landing troops under his command. He was not legally bound to follow Stevens' direction. Wiltse prepared the landing order before Stevens came aboard the *Boston* on January 16. The point is not that the two did not agree on the need for the landing but rather that Wiltse moved because his analysis of the situation concurred with that of Stevens. He was not Stevens' unthinking subordinate.

11. Severance to Wiltse, January 1893, printed in Morgan Rpt, 538; and MROL, 898. Severance did not write the full date, but the contents reveal that it was January 16, 1893. W. Porter Boyd, a consular clerk, denied that Severance wanted troops to be landed (*FRUS, 1894*, App. II, 733), but Severance's note suggests that at least he thought it might be necessary.

12. Young also believed four o'clock was "the hour the two mass meetings would finish their deliberations, and should they come together in a hostile manner, we would be on the scene in time to prevent riot and bloodshed" (Young, *Real Hawai`i*, 182–84). On Monday morning, when Swinburne learned of the two mass meetings, he said, "My impression was . . . that the two meetings would probably bring the matter to a crisis" (Morgan Rpt, 468; and MROL, 828). The *Boston*'s paymaster, Goodwin Hobbs, said that at 9:30 AM on Monday, January 16, word was passed that no crew were to go ashore. His recollection was that "it was not until Monday afternoon, until 1 o'clock, after the men had their dinners, that arrangements were made in case they were to land" (Morgan Rpt, 368; and MROL, 728). Swinburne said Wiltse told him to take a Gatling gun and a 37 mm: "I had lowered the two heavy boats that took the guns; and after dinner, 1 o'clock, had the guns lowered into the boats, so as to save time, and by half past 2 I was practically ready for landing" (Morgan Rpt, 468; and MROL, 828).

13. Lieutenant De Witt Coffman said the following men were present: "Captain Wiltse, Minister Stevens, Mr. Swinburne, Lieut. Laird, Lieut. Young, Lieut. Draper of the Marine Corps, and I think those were all, unless there were some of the junior officers, whom I do not remember" (Morgan Rpt, 489; and MROL, 849).

14. Wiltse to Swinburne, January 16, 1893, printed in Morgan Rpt, 474; and MROL, 834; and *Boston* deck log, January 16.

15. Laird testimony, Morgan Rpt, 376; and MROL, 736.

16. Stevens' testimony, Morgan Rpt, 537; and MROL, 897.

17. Stevens' testimony, Morgan Rpt, 469; and MROL, 829. Just before Stevens left the ship, Naval Cadet Pringle brought in the latest note from Thurston asking for a landing. As the decision was already made, the note had no impact (Coffman testimony, Morgan Rpt, 489; and MROL, 849).

18. The *Boston* deck log for January 16 records that Stevens left the ship at 3:40 PM. See also Severance to Wiltse, January 1893, printed in Morgan Rpt, 538; and MROL, 898.

19. *Boston* deck log, January 16, 1893. Porter Boyd said Stevens stopped by the Consulate to assure the staff that a Marine guard would be deployed there. Stevens' visit would have been around the time the flag dropped to half-mast, triggering the landing (Boyd statement, June 13, 1893, *FRUS, 1894*, App II, 731–32).

20. Morgan Rpt, 335–36; MROL 696; and *FRUS, 1894*, App. II, 1034. Both Swinburne and Young described the landing force to the Morgan Committee; Swinburne also wrote an after-action report (Swinburne to Wiltse, February 27, 1893, Senate Executive Document, no. 76, 52 Cong, 2 Sess., 1893), probably the most accurate count. The *Boston's* landing party could have been easily reinforced from the *Petrel*, which had 10 officers and 122 crew.

21. *Boston* deck log, January 16, 1893. The front of the log lists a standard complement of 265 sailors upon the ship's entry into service in 1887 as well as a breakdown—248 total—on April 1, 1893, when James Blount returned all troops to the ship. Roughly two-thirds of the crew and most of the line officers formed the landing party.

22. "U.S.S. *Boston*, riot drill at Brooklyn Navy Yard," American Memory: Detroit Publishing Company, Library of Congress, LC-D4-20161 DLC (black and white glass negative). A photo of a *Boston* party in Palace Square shows the same equipment ("1893-Infantry Company, USS Boston, Palace Square, Honolulu, H.I.," Military War—Revolution of 1893, CP 103.541, Bishop Museum). This photo is labeled 1893 and probably dates in February or March of that year. A second photo of *Boston* troops in Palace Square after the revolution shows them carrying the same heavy packs ("Government Building and Marine Guards USS Boston," Military–War–Revolution of 1893, CPBM 54079, Bishop Museum). Young's quote about the troops' armament is in Morgan Rpt, 335–36; and MROL, 695–96.

23. Morgan Rpt, 346; and MROL, 706.

24. Morgan Rpt, 539; and MROL, 899. Repeatedly throughout his long testimony (sixty-two pages), Stevens asserted that from the moment the queen attempted to proclaim the new constitution, an effective government did not exist.

25. Laird testimony, Morgan Rpt, 377–78; MROL, 737–38; Swinburne testimony, Morgan Rpt, 469; MROL, 829; and Boyd statement, *FRUS, 1894*, App. II, 731.

26. McCandless testimony, Morgan Rpt, 635; and MROL, 995.

27. Lili'uokalani, *Hawai'i's Story*, 386. When the troops paused at Hopper's house, within sight of the palace, it is likely that the petty officers commanded the column to attention, to left face, and to a rest position. Therefore, the men were probably in a long line facing roughly toward the palace, though their weapons were not raised.

28. Morgan Rpt, 469; and MROL, 829. Royalist John Ross said the troops "came to a halt on the sidewalk east of the main entrance to the Royal Palace and facing the south" (Ross affidavit, June 20, 1893, *FRUS, 1894*, App. II, 640). If Ross is correct—very unlikely—the troops would have been facing away from the palace, making the queen's statement that they pointed their guns at her completely inexplicable.

29. Laird testimony, Morgan Rpt, 379; and MROL, 737. Swinburne testified: "At 9 o'clock [PM] the captain's aide came down and told me to go up to Arion Hall. I did not know the place and the aide marched on ahead. We marched down (it was late) without any drum, in order not to attract attention" (Morgan Rpt, 469; and MROL, 829).

30. Lieutenant Coffman testified that Hugh Gunn and Charles Carter may have assisted in determining that Arion Hall was available. It is possible, though not likely, that Carter and Gunn secured Arion Hall because they knew lodging the U.S. forces there would intimidate the royalists. Although Wiltse and Swinburne had no such intent, they may have been unwittingly manipulated, though I think they were not (MROL 999–1000). Stevens said he did not know Arion Hall existed until he could not rent the Music Hall and then sought other properties. He sent Naval Cadet Pringle to get permission from the owner of Arion Hall. Stevens said he had another hall in mind: "I had thought of another on my own street. If Arion Hall had not been gotten we would have tried another hall, which was nearer me, but the owner was not there" (MROL, 902–3). The legation (Stevens' residence) was on upper School Street. It is unclear whether the other hall Stevens had in mind was the same one that Coffman described.

31. Skerrett to Blount, May 20, 1893, *FRUS, 1894*, App. II, 538.

32. Morgan Rpt, 346; and MROL, 706.

33. Morgan Rpt, 486; and MROL, 846. Lucien Young noted that much American property was nearby, including the Music Hall (Morgan Rpt, 346; and MROL, 706).

34. Morgan Rpt, 485–86; and MROL, 845–46.

35. Statement by Colonel C. P. Iaukea to Blount, *FRUS, 1894*, App II, 828.

36. Waterhouse lived next door to Stevens, a fact that had led some to suspect contact between Stevens and the rebels that night. Dole and John Soper denied that they visited Stevens that evening.

37. Quoted in Kuykendall, *Hawaiian Kingdom*, vol. 3, *1874–1893*, 597.

38. McCandless testimony, Morgan Rpt, 624, 620–21; MROL, 984, 980–81; and Smith statement, *FRUS, 1894*, App. II, 968.

39. Dole's notes, quoted in Damon, *Dole and His Hawai`i*, 250.

40. *PCA*, January 19, 1893.

41. McCandless testimony, Morgan Rpt, 624–25; and MROL, 984–85.

42. Jones said, "Just as we came out of Smith's office a shot was fired up the street near E. O. Hall and Sons store and thus diverted the crowd, so that when we arrived at the Government Building there were only a few persons present." He added later, "It was a surprise to us to find that there was no force at the Government Building to protect it when we arrived there" (Morgan Rpt, 202–3, 213; and MROL 562–63, 573).

43. J. C. McCarthy to Charles B. Wilson, May 1, 1893, *FRUS, 1894*, App II, 1065–66.

44. Damon, *Dole and his Hawai`i*, 252; McCandless testimony, Morgan Rpt, 624–25; and MROL, 984–85.

45. Morgan Rpt, 470–71, 475–76; and MROL, 830–31, 835–36.

46. Lieutenant Laird said, "I do not think there was anyone in the camp but Lieutenant [Commander] Swinburne who knew what was going to take place. They may have known it, but I was officer of the day and I heard nothing about it." Morgan Rpt, 380–81; and MROL, 740–41.

47. Swinburne testified that he put the men "in the rear of the building out of sight to stack arms, and had the men kept at their company parades, so they would not lounge about or expose themselves" (Morgan Rpt, 470–71; and MROL, 830–31).

48. Morgan Rpt, 486; and MROL, 846. Blount took statements from two men claiming that the U.S. troops were ready to move, officers with swords drawn, and cannoneers ready to shift their weapons. These statements were mistaken. For example, Edmund Norrie provided a diagram that showed four heavy weapons—cannon or Gatling guns—though there definitely were only two at Arion Hall. Observing the officers forming the troops in ranks, Norrie concluded that the troops were preparing to deploy, but the officers were trying to keep the troops in order and prevent them from lining the fence rails, gawking at developments in the street. The troops' rifles were stacked. Norrie stated—likely correctly—that before Dole and his party reached the Government Building, Captain Wiltse was already at Arion Hall (Statement of J. C. Quinn, May 2, 1893; and Edmund Norrie to C. B. Wilson, undated, both in *FRUS, 1894*, App. II, 1066–68).

49. Norrie says that Charles Carter galloped up to Arion Hall and handed Wiltse, sitting on the veranda with Swinburne, a note, which the captain read and placed in his pocket. Because Swinburne mentioned meeting Carter alone, this was probably a second visit from Carter. Norrie was mistaken in telling Blount that Cooper immediately read the proclamation from the front entrance of the Government Building, whereas abundant testimony says Cooper went inside, and there was a bit of milling around before the statement was read. In the heat of the moment, Norrie may not have paid attention to how much time elapsed before the reading of the statement (Norrie to C. B. Wilson, undated, *FRUS, 1894*, App II, 1067).

50. Blount interview with Samuel Damon, April 29, 1893, *FRUS, 1894*, App II, 506. Swinburne was aware of gray areas. What if American rebels took violent action against the queen? Should their citizenship require him to protect them, or should he allow their arrest because their antigovernment, unneutral behavior meant they were disturbing the public order that Swinburne had landed to maintain? Senator Gray asked what Swinburne would have done if a crowd had "set upon" Damon, Dole, and Carter. Swinburne said it would have depended on what they were doing. Gray told him to assume they were simply walking up to the Government Building. Swinburne said he would have felt impelled to protect them as "they were entitled to the liberty of the streets." But if he had known they intended to take over the Government Building? Gray asked. "That is a difficult question to answer," came the reply. "I sympathize with you in it," Gray murmured. Swinburne

repeated: "That would be difficult to answer." "I think so," Gray consoled. Finally, Swinburne said: "I am satisfied that Mr. Carter knew exactly how I stood . . . that is, I left him to understand that I was there simply to protect American property and life" (Morgan Rpt, 483–84; and MROL, 843–44).

51. Swinburne testimony, Morgan Rpt, 471; MROL 831; and Swinburne statement to Blount, May 3, 1894, *FRUS, 1894*, App. II., 523.

52. Swinburne testimony, Morgan Rpt, 471. Swinburne's recollection was not flawless; it is likely that events occurred slightly earlier than he testified. It is very unlikely that Swinburne, a senior officer testifying under oath, lied.

53. Cornwell statement, 633; Colborn statement, 501; Hopkins statement, 523–24; Wilson affidavit, 525, all in *FRUS, 1894*, App. II. See Kuykendall, *Hawaiian Kingdom*, vol. 3, *1874–1893*, 598–600, for a good overview.

54. Quoted in Kuykendall, *Hawaiian Kingdom*, vol. 3, *1874–1893*, 601.

55. Morgan Rpt, 449–50; and MROL, 809–10.

56. Morgan Rpt, 216; and MROL, 576. When asked later when the note arrived, Jones said, "As I remember, it was dark" (Morgan Rpt, 218; and MROL, 578). Time for sunset was calculated using the U.S. Naval Observatory's Web site, which has an engine for calculating sunrise, sunset, and so on, for any location and in any year.

57. Morgan Rpt, 547; and MROL, 907.

58. Ibid.

59. Morgan Rpt, 623; and MROL, 983.

60. After meeting the queen, Damon related the story at the rebel meeting at the Thurston-Smith office. Unfortunately, Blount did not inquire into Damon's advice to the queen, and Damon did not testify before the Morgan committee. McCandless testified that he saw Damon at the law office on "Tuesday morning. We had before us the programme for the Provisional Government, and Mr. Damon had been selected as one of the members of the advisory council. That morning he was at our meeting for the first time, and he made a statement to the committee that he had just come from the palace. He stated his interview with the Queen, and he stated that he said to Her Majesty, 'On former occasions you have called on me for advice, and I now come unasked to give you some advice; you can take it or reject it just as you choose.' He said, 'Heretofore I have defended the monarchy, and thought it was possible to get along with it; but it has got to that point now, after your actions on Saturday, that I have to change my standard, and I have joined the forces who propose to annex these islands to the United States of America;' and he said, 'It would be useless for you to resist; if you do there will be bloodshed and a great many killed; you will probably be killed, and we will win in the end, because we are determined to carry this through.' She assured him that she would give up" (MROL, 984). In her diary, the queen wrote, "9 A.M. Sent for Mr. S.M. Damon to confer with him on the situation. He told me

he had been asked to join a party who called themselves the Executive Council and he had refused but asked what he should do. I told him to and join the Advisory council which he did and I attribute the leniency of the latter council to his interposition with them" (Lili`uokalani Diary, January 17, 1893). The queen later told Blount that when Damon called on her, "I told him to join the advisory council." (Satement of Queen Lili`uokalani, BROL, 866).

61. J. O. Carter statement, *FRUS, 1894*, App. II, 522.

62. Damon interview, April 29, 1893, *FRUS, 1894*, App. II, 508–9.

63. The surrender note is printed in Queen Lili`uokalani's statement to Blount, *FRUS, 1894*, App. II, 866. The note directing Wilson to surrender is in *FRUS, 1894*, App. II, 1039.

64. Macfarlane affidavit, 637–38; Neumann affidavit, 639–40; Carter to Blount, May 3, 1893, 522–23; Carter interview, May 13, 1893, 738–39; Cornwell to Blount, April 24, 1893, 495; Cornwell affidavit, 632–34; Parker interview, April 6, 1893, 903–11; Peterson statement, 935; Peterson-Colburn affidavit, 524, all in *FRUS, 1894*, App. II. See also Statement of J. O. Carter, *House Executive Document* No. 47, 53 Cong, 2 sess., December 18, 1893, 273.

65. Damon interview, April 29, 1893, *FRUS, 1894*, App. II, 508.

66. Cornwell statement, April 24, 1893, *FRUS, 1894*, App. II, 495.

67. Damon interview, April 29, 1893, *FRUS, 1894*, App. II, 508.

68. Ernest Andrade Jr. has made the strongest case that royal leadership failures were a big factor, perhaps the main factor, in the surrender of the Queen (Andrade, *Unconquerable Rebel*, 116–24).

69. Judd statement, Morgan Rpt, 410; and MROL, 806.

70. Colborn statement, *FRUS, 1894*, App. II, 501. He claimed that the government had 600 men with rifles, 30,000 rounds of ammunition, 8 Austrian field cannon, and 2 Gatling guns.

71. Nowlein affidavit, *FRUS, 1894*, App. II, 640. Of the 496 men in the two locations, 314 were volunteers and 182 Household Guards and police officers with military training.

72. Wilson affidavit, *FRUS, 1894*, App. II, 642–43.

73. Quoted in Kuykendall, *Hawaiian Kingdom*, vol. 3, *1874–1893*, 598.

74. Waterhouse interview, May 2, 1893, *FRUS*, 1894, App II, 521.

75. Fisher affidavit, Morgan Rpt, 593; and MROL, 953.

76. Morgan Rpt, 610; and MROL, 970. John Soper said most rebel arms were Springfield rifles retained by volunteers who were in the Honolulu Rifles in 1887 and 1889 (Soper interview, June 17, 1893, *FRUS, 1894*, App. II, 1777–80). Soper provided a list of rebel arms that showed substantial numbers of arms and ammunition had been in private hands and most of the remainder had been purchased from E.O. Hall and Castle & Cooke between January 14–17 (Soper to Blount, June 20, 1893, enclosing "Memorandum of arms and ammunition in hands of Provisional Government, January 17, 1893," *FRUS, 1894*, App. II, 1916).

77. Morgan Rpt, 622; and MROL, 983.

78. Morgan Rpt, 466; and MROL, 826.

79. Blount to Gresham, April 26, 1893, *FRUS, 1894*, App.II, 482–83.

80. Morgan Rpt, 642–43; and MROL, 1002–3.

81. Damon interview, April 29, 1893, *FRUS, 1894*, App. II, 508.

82. Wilson told Blount of Stevens' offenses, most petty—such as Stevens at a state dinner clapping his hands together to kill mosquitoes, which dropped inappropriately into the soup—and a few more serious, such as Stevens' basic dislike of monarchs, especially female monarchs. The most serious breach between Wilson and Stevens occurred when the police raided a gambling den and found Stevens' Chinese coachman with a wicked-looking knife. Wilson claimed Stevens insisted on his coachman's release on the extremely dubious grounds that he was an attaché at the legation. That the enmity between the minister and the marshal was two-sided can be seen in Wilson's description of the resolution of this incident: "To avoid any further fuss with the American dictator, the murderous Celestial highbinder and criminal servant over whom had been unwarrantably thrown the aegis of the American eagle, was released" (Wilson statement, *FRUS, 1894*, App. II, 1021).

83. Stevens testimony, Morgan Rpt, 532; and MROL, 892. Bayard's instruction is in *FRUS, 1894*, App. II, 1166–68.

84. In the Morgan hearings, Senator William Frye entered into the record excerpts from the naval regulations of 1893 (Morgan Rpt, 435–36; and MROL, 795–96).

85. Coffman, *Nation Within.*

86. Albertine Loomis, *For Whom Are the Stars?* (Honolulu: University of Hawai`i Press, 1976), 40.

Chapter 8. The Rise and Fall of the Annexation Treaty

1. Samuel Flagg Bemis, *The American Secretaries of State and Their Diplomacy*, vol. 8, (New York: Alfred A. Knopf, 1928), 222.

2. Foster sketch drawn from Michael J. Devine, "John W. Foster and the Struggle for Hawaiian Annexation," *Pacific Historical Review* 44 (September 1977): 29–50; Michael J. Devine, *John Watson Foster* (Athens: Ohio University Press, 1981); John Watson Foster, *American Diplomacy in the Orient* (Boston and New York: Houghton, Mifflin, 1903); and John Watson Foster, *Diplomatic Memoirs*, 2 vols. (Boston and New York: Houghton, Mifflin), 1900.

3. Thurston to Dole, February 9, 1893; Thurston memo, "Minutes of meeting held February 10 at Wormley's Hotel," both in Thurston Papers, AH; and William R. Castle to Dole, February 25, 1893, Dole Papers, AH. See also Russ, *Hawaiian Revolution*, 139–42; and Devine, *John Watson Foster*, 66–69.

4. Thurston to Dole, February 14, 1893, "Hawaiian Minister and Commissioners in Washington," FO-EX, February 1893, AH.

5. Young testimony, Morgan Rpt, 342.

6. The *Kongo*'s crew did not know of the revolution because the ship departed San Francisco before news of the revolution arrived. The *Boston* deck log, January 28, 1893, noted *Kongo*'s arrival.

7. Stevens to Gresham, no. 92, March 15, 1893, and no. 93, March 24, 1893, "Despatches from United States Ministers in Hawai`i, 1843–1900," General Records of the Department of State, RG 59, microcopy T-30, roll 25, NARA.

8. Wodehouse to Earl of Rosebery (Archibald Primrose), February 1, 1893, p. 38, FO 58/270. The queen asked Wodehouse to mediate Ka`iulani's accession to a restored throne. He told London he disapproved of her attempt to promulgate a new constitution because it was contrary to the advice she received from him and others.

9. Dole to Stevens, January 31, 1893, enclosed in Stevens to Foster, no. 84, February 1, 1893, Despatches, roll 25.

10. Stevens to Foster, telegram, February 1, 1893, and Stevens to Foster, nos. 82 and 84, February 1, 1893, Despatches, roll 25. The Hawaiian request for protection (Dole to Stevens, January 31, 1893) was enclosed.

11. James B. Castle to John H. Soper, January 28, 1893, "Military Reports," Executive and Advisory Council, FO-EX.

12. Soper to President, EAC (Executive and Advisory Council), January 22, 24, and 27, 1893, "Military Reports." On January 20, 248 men staffed these duty stations. The number was increased to 270 men on January 21 and to 295 men on January 24.

13. When Blount ordered the protectorate rescinded on April 1, the provisional government recalled some volunteers and expenses again soared (Soper to Dole, April 10, 1893, "Military Reports," FO-EX).

14. Undated but in the 1893 folder, "Military Reports," FO-EX.

15. Tracy to Skerrett, confidential telegram, January 28, 1893, "Letters to Squadrons and Ships," Entry 55, RG 24, NARA. Britain recognized the provisional government on February 10.

16. *Chicago Tribune*, January 30, 1893, and February 1, 1893.

17. Foster to Stevens, February 22, 1893, *FRUS, 1894*, Appendix II, 408.

18. Foster to Stevens, no. 71, February 11, 1893, and telegram, February 14, 1893, both in "Diplomatic Instructions," M-77, roll 100.

19. Belknap to Secretary of the Navy, April 13, 1890, Area 10 File, RG 45, NARA; Belknap to Tracy, May 26, 1890, ibid. Tracy's actions are described in notations on the face of these two dispatches.

20. Edwin A. Falk, *Togo and the Rise of Japanese Sea Power* (New York: Longmans, Green and Company, 1936), 137–39.

21. Wodehouse to Rosebery, March 1, 1893, p. 60, FO 58/270.

22. Captain H. H. Hallett's March 9 letter to the Admiralty, forwarded April 14, 1893, FO 58/279.

23. Skerrett to Secretary of the Navy, March 7, 1893, Area 9 File, RG 45, NARA. Fujii mentioned the veterans in an interview titled "The Japan Scare," *PCA*, April 3, 1893.

24. Stevens to Secretary of State, February 28, 1893, "Translations of Cipher Messages," entry 19, RG 45, NARA; and Stevens to Gresham, March 24, 1893, "Despatches," roll 25, NARA.

25. Charles Thurneaux to Severance, February 2, 1893, "Miscellaneous Letters Received, 1893," Entry 4, Consular Post Records, Honolulu, RG 84, NARA.

26. W. R. Whiting to Skerrett, March 9, 1893, enclosed in Skerrett to Secretary of the Navy, March 7, 1893, Area 9 File, RG 45, NARA. See also Skerrett to Secretary of the Navy, March 9, 1893, Area 9 File, NARA. Tashiro's purported remarks are in Stevens to Gresham, March 24, 1893, "Despatches," roll 25.

27. Foster to Lincoln, February 1, 1893, "Instructions to Great Britain," Diplomatic Instructions of the Department of State, RG 59, NARA, microcopy M-77, roll 89.

28. Foster memoranda, February 2, 1893, Harrison Papers, LC.

29. Undated clipping of the *Chicago Tribune* in the Hitt Papers, LC. The clipping is pasted next to a similar *New York Times* story of January 31, 1893.

30. Lincoln to Foster, February 4, 1893, "Despatches from United States Ministers to Great Britain, 1791–1906," RG 59, microcopy M-30, roll 164, NARA.

31. FO telegram to Wodehouse, February 10, 1893, p. 5; April 18, p. 9, FO 58/270.

32. Stevens to Foster, February 8, and 28; March 1, 15, and 24, 1893, all in "Despatches," T-30, roll 25, NARA. A good overview is Hugh B. Hammett, "The Cleveland Administration and Anglo-American Naval Friction in Hawai`i, 1893–1894," *Military Affairs* 40 (February 1976): 27–31.

33. Stevens to Foster, no. 97, February 28, 1893, "Despatches," roll 25; Stevens to Foster, telegram, February 28, 1893, "Translations of Cipher Messages," Entry 19, RG 45, NARA.

34. FO internal memo, undated but filed with papers from late January 1893, p. 27, FO 58/279.

35. FO telegram to Pauncefote, January 31, p. 29, FO 58/279.

36. FO draft reply to Wodehouse to Rosebery, April 5, 1893, p. 256, FO 58/279. This draft was marked "cancelled," with a note that Rosebery decided to send a letter rather than formally instruct Wodehouse.

37. *New York Herald*, February 5 and 9, 1893, clippings in Moore scrapbooks, Moore Papers, LC.

38. Castle to Dole, February 25, 1893, Dole Papers, AH.

39. Wodehouse to Rosebery, February 9, 1893, p. 43, FO 58/270.

40. Champ Clark observed the prophetic weather differences in *My Quarter Century of American Politics*, 2 vols. (New York: Harper and Brothers, 1920), 229.

41. Robert Louis Stevenson, *Travels in Hawai`i*, ed. A. Grove Day (Honolulu: University of Hawai`i Press 1973), xxiv–xxv, 177.

42. Harry Thurston Peck, *Twenty Years of the Republic, 1885–1905* (New York: Dodd, Mead, 1906), 327–29.

43. H. Paul Jeffers, *An Honest President: The Life and Presidencies of Grover Cleveland* (New York: Harper Perennial, 2002), 340.

44. *New York Times*, March 10, 1893.

45. Hay to Whitelaw Reid, May 16, 1893, Whitelaw Reid Papers, LC.

46. Cleveland to Schurz, March 19, 1893, Carl Schurz Papers, LC. See also discussion of this letter in Richard E. Welch, *The Presidencies of Grover Cleveland* (Lawrence: University of Kansas Press, 1988), 170; and Charles W. Calhoun, "Morality and Spite: Walter Q. Gresham and U.S. Relations with Hawai`i," *Pacific Historical Review* 52 (1983): 294.

47. The best studies of Gresham's handling of Hawaiian matters are Calhoun, "Morality and Spite," and Charles W. Calhoun, *Gilded Age Cato: The Life of Walter Q. Gresham* (Lexington: University of Kentucky Press, 1988).

48. Blount to Gresham, March 6, 1893, Gresham Papers, LC; Blount testimony, Morgan Rpt, 406.

49. Blount testimony, Morgan Rpt, 385–89, 406–8.

50. Cleveland to Dole, March 11, 1893; Gresham to Stevens, March 11, 1893; Gresham to Severance, March 11, 1893; all in *FRUS, 1894*, App. II, 469–70.

51. Blount testimony, Morgan Rpt, 406–8. See also Tennant S. McWilliams, "James H. Blount, the South, and Hawaiian Annexation," *Pacific Historical Review* 57 (1988): 30–31.

52. Sketch drawn from McWilliams, "James H. Blount," 25–46; and Carole E. Scott, "Racism and Southern Anti-imperialists: The Blounts of Georgia," *Atlanta History* (Fall 1987): 24–29.

53. Blount testimony, Morgan Rpt, 385–89, 406–8.

54. Blount to Gresham, May 4, 1893, *FRUS, 1894*, App. II, 501–3.

55. Castle to Thurston, April 8, 1893, Thurston Papers, AH; Andrade, *Unconquerable Rebel*, 129.

56. Thurston to Dole, March 10, 1893, Dole Papers, AH; and "Miscellaneous Memoranda of Conversations with the Secretary of State," March 10, 1893, Entry 872, RG 59.

57. Smith to Dole, April 6, 1893, Dole Papers, AH. Smith reported on the Gresham-Brown meeting.

58. Thurston to Dole, March 16, 1893, Dole Papers, AH.

59. Gresham to Joseph Medill, November 7, 1892, Gresham Papers, LC.

60. Clark, *My Quarter Century*, 233.

61. Ibid., 235.
62. Harrison to Foster, May 1, 1893, Box 1, Foster Papers, LC.
63. Moore memoranda, May 4–6, 1894, C-1, Moore Papers, LC.
64. Gresham to Thomas F. Bayard, December 17, 1893, C-48, Gresham Papers, LC.
65. Gresham to Schurz, November 21, 1893, C-48, Gresham Papers, LC.
66. Blount testimony, Morgan Rpt, 390, 415.
67. Blount to Gresham, May 4, 1893, *FRUS, 1894*, App. II, 502–3.
68. Scott, "Racism and Southern Anti-imperialists," 26.
69. Olney to Mrs. G. R. Minot (Olney's daughter Agnes), December 3, 1893, quoted in Henry James, *Richard Olney and His Public Service* (Boston: Houghton Mifflin, 1923), 219.
70. Blount to Gresham, July 31, 1893, *FRUS, 1894*, App. II, 630.

Chapter 9. The Restoration Fiasco

1. Cleveland to Carter H. Harrison, March 10, 1893, Cleveland Papers, LC.
2. James, *Richard Olney and His Public Service*, 31–32.
3. Blount testimony, Morgan Rpt, 395.
4. Gresham to Schurz, September 14, 1893, Schurz Papers, LC; and Blount testimony, Morgan Rpt, 395.
5. Schurz to Gresham, September 24, 1893, Gresham Papers, LC.
6. Olney to Cleveland, August 23, 1893, Cleveland Papers, LC; Memorandum of May 9, 1894, "Moore Memoranda," C-1, Moore Papers, LC; Gresham to Willis, September 19, 1893, "Instructions," RG-59, M-77, reel 100.
7. Herbert to Skerrett, August 16, 1893, "Translations of Cipher Messages," Entry 19, RG 45.
8. Hammett, "Cleveland Administration and Anglo-American Naval Friction," 29. My overview of Skerrett's troubles parallels Hammett's detailed account, but he does not link the admiral's removal and the timing of Irwin's and Willis' arrival to Gresham's restoration attempt.
9. Herbert to Skerrett, October 3, 1893, "Confidential Letters," entry 20, RG 45.
10. Herbert to Skerrett, October 9, 1893; and Herbert to Irwin, October 10, 1893, "Translations of Cipher Messages," Entry 19, RG 45. Admiral Irwin was coincidently the half-brother of Robert W. Irwin, Hawaiian minister to Japan.
11. *PCA*, November 24, 1893: "It is generally believed that Admiral Skerrett . . . was transferred to the Asiatic Station in the belief that he had identified himself in a social way with the foreign anti-Royalist element."

12. Herbert to Skerrett; Herbert to Barker, both August 18, 1893, "Translations of Cipher Messages," Entry 19, RG 45. See also Albert S. Barker, *Everyday Life in the Navy: Autobiography of Rear Admiral Albert S. Barker* (Boston: R. G. Badger, 1928), 210.

13. For Olney's role in Hawaiian policy, I have relied heavily on the standard biography, Gerald Eggert, *Richard Olney: Evolution of a Statesman* (University Park: Pennsylvania State University Press, 1974), 5–13.

14. James, *Richard Olney*, 1–7.

15. Ibid., 11, 13; and Eggert, *Richard Olney*, 173–74.

16. Olney to Gresham, October 9, 1893, C-41, Gresham Papers, LC.

17. Memorandum, May 9, 1894, a postscript to "Interview with Judge Gresham, May 5–6, 1894," Moore Papers, LC.

18. Olney to Mrs. G. R. Minot, December 3, 1893, quoted in James, *Richard Olney*, 217; and Eggert, *Richard Olney*, 183–85.

19. Olney to Mrs. G. R. Minot, December 3, 1893, quoted in James, *Olney*, 217.

20. Olney to Gresham, October 9, 1893, Gresham Papers, LC.

21. Ibid.; and Eggert, *Richard Olney*, 183–85.

22. Calhoun, "Morality and Spite," 301.

23. Gresham to Cleveland, October 18, 1893, *FRUS, 1894*, Appendix II, 459–63.

24. Herbert to Skerrett, October 9, 1893, "Translations of Cipher Messages," Entry 19, RG 45.

25. Barker, *Everyday Life in the Navy*, 215–16.

26. *PCA*, November 7, 1893.

27. Willis to Gresham, November 6, 1893, *FRUS, 1894*, App. II, 430–31; Barker, *Everyday Life in the Navy*, 217–18; *PCA*, November 7, 1893.

28. Barker, *Everyday Life in the Navy*, 217.

29. Willis to Gresham, no. 2, November 11, 1893, *FRUS, 1894*, App. II, 432–33.

30. *PCA*, November 13, 1893.

31. Loomis, *For Whom Are the Stars?* 70–72.

32. Ibid.

33. Willis to Gresham, telegram; and Willis to Gresham, No. 3, both of November 16, 1893, *FRUS, 1894*, App. II, 1241–43.

34. *Adams* and *Philadelphia* deck logs, November and December 1893.

35. Several deck log entries used the words "quarterly target practice," and the rhythm of the exercises, generally rifle training followed by pistol training, seems typical of scheduled drills. However, in such an incendiary atmosphere, why schedule so many exercises—the number was far above normal—that alarmed the provisional government? Almost certainly this was intentional. If so, only Willis and Irwin knew the master plan. Captain Barker was out of the loop: "In view of all these alarming reports [of unrest ashore], our

men were kept on board and preparations were made to land instantly should [the] occasion require it. . . . The keeping of our men in readiness perhaps encouraged the Royalists more than it did the Annexationists, as the former were positive that we were there to help them; but in truth our men were kept on board in readiness to put down *any* rioting or disturbance and thus protect American lives and property" (Barker, *Everyday Life in the Navy*, 219–20). Even if Willis and Irwin did not intend to intimidate the provisional government, in practice, they did. For weeks, the Executive Council discussed options for resisting forcible restoration (see the entries for November and December in the "Minutes of the Executive Council, June 6, 1893–March 26, 1894," Executive and Advisory Council, FO-EX).

36. Barker, *Everyday Life in the Navy*, 219–20; November 17, 1893, "Minutes of the Executive Council," FO-EX; and *PCA*, November 17, 1893.

37. Barker, *Everyday Life in the Navy*, 221–22; and November 21, 1893, "Minutes of the Executive Council," FO-EX.

38. *PCA*, November 24, 1893.

39. November 24 and 25, 1893, "Minutes of the Executive Council," FO-EX.

40. Damon, *Sanford Ballard Dole*, 272; Russ, *Hawaiian Revolution*, 260; and Fujii to Dole, December 19, 1893, AH, photocopy in author's possession.

41. November 27, 28, and 30, 1893, "Minutes of the Executive Council," FO-EX.

42. Irwin to Secretary of the Navy, December 4, 1893, "Translations of Cipher Messages," Entry 19, RG 45, NARA; and Willis to Gresham, no. 7, December 4, 1893, *FRUS, 1894*, App. II, 442.

43. *PCA*, November 29, 1893, carried a story from Washington that the Blount Report was published November 20.

44. *Literary Digest*, VIII (November 18, 1893), quoted in Russ, *Hawaiian Revolution*, 288.

45. Richardson, *Compilation of the Messages and Papers*, vol. 9, 441–42. The December 2, 1893, minutes noted that the council received Thurston's November 19 and 20 dispatches from Washington ("Minutes of the Executive Council," FO-EX). Thurston wrote that on November 14 he asked Gresham if the United States would attempt restoration by force, but Gresham said he could not answer without speaking to the president and would reply in the afternoon. Later that day Gresham said Willis had no orders to do anything that would cause injury to the life or property of anyone in the islands, and that Thurston should make the appropriate inferences from that statement Meiric K. Dutton (commentator), *A Most Extraordinary Correspondence* (Honolulu: Loomis House Press, 1958), 20.

46. Calhoun, "Morality and Spite," 304–5.

47. James, *Richard Olney*, 200. Gerald Eggert's careful study concluded that Cleveland relied heavily, though not exclusively, on Olney's draft, which is in the Olney Papers, LC (Eggert, *Richard Olney*, 187, 355n39). Cleveland's message is reprinted in *FRUS, 1894*, App. II,

443–58. Turning over the matter to Congress was surely Cleveland's idea. This was exactly what he had done with Samoan affairs at the end of his first presidential term.

48. Richardson, *Compilation of the Messages and Papers*, IX, 441–42.

49. In his revised instructions (December 3, 1893, *FRUS, 1894*, App. II, 465), Gresham directed that if the queen asked about the use of force, Willis should renounce it.

50. Loomis, *For Whom Are the Stars*, 78–80.

51. Willis to Gresham, nos. 14, 15, and 16, dated December 18–20, 1893, *FRUS, 1894*, App. II, 1236–70; and Russ, *Hawaiian Revolution*, 255–57.

52. Enclosure no. 2 in Willis to Gresham, no. 17, December 20, 1893, *FRUS*, 1894, App. II, 1274–75. See also December 19, 1893, "Minutes of the Executive Council," FO-EX.

53. Dole to Willis, December 23, 1893, in Willis to Gresham, no. 18, December 23, 1893, *FRUS, 1894*, App. II, 1276–82; and December 22, 1893, "Minutes of the Executive Council," FO-EX.

54. President's Message Relating to the Hawaiian Islands, December 18, 1893, *FRUS*, 1894, App. II, 443–58.

55. Moore diaries, quoted in Calhoun, "Morality and Spite," 304.

Chapter 10. Cleveland's Informal Protectorate

1. Morgan Rpt. On December 20, the Senate directed the Foreign Relations Committee to investigate. A subcommittee began work on December 27.

2. This sketch of Morgan draws heavily from Joseph A. Fry's excellent *John Tyler Morgan and the Search for Southern Autonomy* (Knoxville: University of Tennessee Press, 1992), especially 37–45; and the nice portrayal in David McCullough, *Path Between the Seas: The Creation of the Panama Canal, 1870–1914* (New York: Simon & Schuster, 1977), 259–61.

3. Charles O. Palmer to Morgan, undated, Morgan Papers, LC.

4. Fry, *John Tyler Morgan*, 41.

5. Ibid., 40.

6. For example, see N. D. Bon to Morgan, January 30, 1895, Morgan Papers, LC.

7. San Franciscans lauded Morgan for his canal efforts, and the Chamber of Commerce made him an honorary member. The mayor of San Diego declared that the canal bill was the most important measure before the Congress in 1895 (William Carlson to Morgan, January 28; and W. H. Dimond to Morgan, February 12, 1895, Morgan Papers, LC).

8. Shelby Moore Cullom, *Fifty Years of Public Service* (Chicago: A. C. McClurg, 1911), 348.

9. Fry, *John Tyler Morgan*, 41.

10. The best analysis of the House and Senate debates is Thomas J. Osborne, *Annexation Hawai`i: Fighting American Imperialism* (Waimanalo, HI: Island Style Press, 1998),

68–82. (This book was previously printed as *Empire Can Wait* in 1981.) See also Russ, *Hawaiian Revolution,* 281–348.

11. Osborne, *Annexation Hawai`i,* 68–75.

12. Quoted in Tate, *U.S. and the Hawaiian Kingdom,* 256. See also *Cong. Rec.,* 53rd Cong. 2nd sess. (1894), 5127, 5193–94, 5246, 5434–36, 5499.

13. Frank B. Hastings to Hatch, June 3, 1894, Hatch Papers, AH.

14. Calhoun, "Morality and Spite," 306–7.

15. Barker, *Everyday Life in the Navy,* 206.

16. Willis to Gresham, June 23, 1894, Gresham Papers, LC. See also Thurston to Hatch, March 27, 1894, HMW.

17. Herbert to Walker, March 27, 1894, Senate Executive Documents, no. 16, 53rd Cong., 2nd sess., 2. This document is hereafter cited as "Walker Report."

18. Ibid.

19. Walker to Betty Walker, April 13, 1894, printed in Frances P. Thomas, *The Career of John Grimes Walker, USN, 1835–1907* (Boston: Privately printed, 1959, copy in NHC), 81–82.

20. Walker to Betty Walker, May 10, 1894, in Thomas, *Career of John Grimes Walker,* 91.

21. Walker to Herbert, July 12, 1894, in Thomas, *Career of John Grimes Walker,* 107–8.

22. Walker to Herbert, April 28, 1894, in ibid., 87–89.

23. Barker, *Everyday Life in the Navy,* 234–41.

24. I have relied heavily on Andrade (*Unconquerable Rebel,* 137–48) and William A. Russ Jr. (*The Hawaiian Republic 1894–1898: And Its Struggle to Win Annexation* [Selinsgrove, PA: Susquehanna University Press, 1961], 1–48) to describe the new constitution and the establishment of the Republic of Hawai`i.

25. Minutes of the Advisory Council, May 15, 1894, Executive and Advisory Council, FO-EX.

26. See the handwritten notes on Willis to Gresham, personal, March 3, 1894, Gresham Papers, LC; and Irwin to Herbert, March 3, 1893, and Irwin to Herbert, March 25, 1894, both in Area 9 File, RG 45, NARA.

27. Fujii to Dole, March 23, 1893, AH.

28. Section Four of the Hawai`i Organic Act of 1900 states that between 1842 and 1892, 731 Chinese and 3 Japanese were naturalized in Hawai`i. No naturalizations occurred after 1892. The 1842 constitution was published in English in that year.

29. Dole to Fujii, April 10, 1893, AH.

30. Fujii to Dole, April 18, 1893, AH.

31. Irwin to Dole, April 27, 1893, AH.

32. Irwin to Dole, June 26, 1893, AH. The Liberal Party is commonly romanized as the "Jiyuto."

33. Irwin to Dole, July 13, 1893, AH.

34. Irwin to Mutsu, April 27, 1893, AH.

35. Irwin to Dole, June 5, 1893, AH.

36. Dole to Irwin, July 8, 1893, AH.

37. Dole to Thurston, August 1, 1893, "Hawaiian Legation at Washington," vol. 2 (1888–98), 262, AH.

38. Blount to Dole, July 28, 1893, enclosed in Blount to Gresham, no, 7, July 31, 1893, quoted in Russ, *Hawaiian Revolution*, 163.

39. Interview of January 25, 1894, "Miscellaneous Memoranda of Conversations with the Secretary of State," Entry 872, RG 59, NARA.

40. Walker to Herbert, April 28, 1894, Walker Report.

41. Walker to Herbert, personal, May 14, 1894, Walker Papers, NHC. This is not to be confused with the similar but far less detailed official dispatch of the same date. Walker knew official dispatches might be demanded by the Congress, and even published. However, in the practice of the day, personal letters were not public property. The Walker Report contains only official and not personal correspondence.

42. Russ, *Hawaiian Republic*, 18; and Alfred L. Castle, "Advice for Hawai`i: The Dole-Burgess Letters," *Hawaiian Journal of History* 15 (1981): 24–30.

43. "Minutes of the Executive Council" (Summary), May 14, 15, and 22, 1894, Executive and Advisory Council, FO-EX.

44. According to the American Legation, 10,493 persons cast ballots in the 1892 elections. Among them were 6,878 Native Hawaiians, 2,091 Portuguese, 637 Americans, 505 British subjects, and 382 Germans. Roughly two-thirds of the voters in 1892 were Native Hawaiians. A careful 1977 analysis by demographer Robert Schmitt showed 11,671 voters in 1890, though the lack of data prevented Schmitt from providing an ethnic breakdown. It appears in May 1894 there were 11,000–12,000 potential voters. Two thirds—roughly 7,000—were Native Hawaiians. About 7,000 Native Hawaiians had voted in all the islands in 1892 and probably in 1890. Normally the Honolulu vote constituted a third of the total vote in all the islands. If that pattern held true, perhaps 2,500 Native Hawaiians would have voted in Honolulu under normal conditions. However, of the 1,507 Honolulu residents registered to vote in May 1894—1,252 of whom actually voted—there were only 187 Native Hawaiians or persons of mixed blood, 101 Hawaiian-born whites, 98 persons of unknown origin, and 1,123 foreign citizens, chiefly Portuguese, Americans, Brits, and Germans (Russ, *Hawaiian Republic*, 33n147 and 22n92; and Robert C. Schmitt, *Historical Statistics of Hawai`i* [Honolulu: University of Hawai`i Press, 1977], 597–98).

45. About 3,600 whites voted in all the islands in 1892. The number of whites voting in Honolulu in 1892 is unknown, but with Honolulu generally accounting for about a third of the total vote and with whites living there in greater numbers than elsewhere, perhaps 1,500 whites could have registered. In May 1894, 1,123 whites registered, perhaps 75 percent of the potential white electorate (Russ, *Hawaiian Republic*, 27).

46. Quoted in Kuykendall, *Hawaiian Kingdom*, vol. 2, *1854–1874*, 131.
47. Summary of meeting of May 15, 1894, Executive and Advisory Council, FO-EX; and Russ, *Hawaiian Republic*, 32.
48. Walker to Herbert, July 12, 1893, Walker Papers, NHC.
49. Barker, *Everyday Life in the Navy*, 242, 247–48.
50. Walker to Herbert, July 12, 1894, Walker Report, 18.
51. Barker, *Everyday Life in the Navy*, 232–34; and Walker to Betty Walker, April 13–14, 1894, in Thomas, *Career of John Grimes Walker*, 81–82.
52. Gresham to Willis, July 22, 1894, Gresham Papers, LC.
53. Ibid.
54. Memorandum dated August 11, 1894, in Thomas, *Career of John Grimes Walker*, 113–17.
55. Walker to Secretary of the Navy, August 17, 1894, Area Files, RG 45, M-625B, reel 310, frames 0195–0202, NARA. This report was received in the Navy and State departments on August 28.
56. Thomas, *Career of John Grimes Walker*, 119, 127–28.
57. Gresham to Willis, August 31, 1894; and Willis to Gresham, September 29, 1894, both in Thomas, *Career of John Grimes Walker*, 120–22.

Chapter 11. Mahan, the New Navy, and Hawai'i's Strategic Value

1. Among the many good books on Mahan are Robert Seager II, *Alfred Thayer Mahan: The Man and His Letters* (Annapolis, MD: Naval Institute Press, 1977); Jon Tetsuro Sumida, *Inventing Grand Strategy and Teaching High Command: The Classic Works of Alfred Thayer Mahan Reconsidered* (Baltimore, MD: Johns Hopkins Press, 1997); William E. Livezey, *Mahan on Sea Power* (Norman: University of Oklahoma Press, 1947); and W. D. Puleston, *Mahan: The Life and Work of Captain Alfred Thayer Mahan* (New Haven, CT: Yale University Press, 1939). An outstanding brief overview is Robert Seager II, "Alfred Thayer Mahan: Navalist and Historian," in *Quarterdeck and Bridge: Two Centuries of American Naval Leaders*, ed. James C. Bradford, 219–50 (Annapolis, MD: Naval Institute Press, 1997).
2. Alfred T. Mahan, *The Influence of Sea Power upon History, 1660–1783* (Boston: Little, Brown, 1890).
3. Robert Seager II, "Ten Years Before Mahan: The Unofficial Case for the New Navy, 1880–1890," *Mississippi Valley Historical Review* 40 (1953): 491–512; Seager, *Alfred Thayer Mahan*, esp. 199–209; Peter Karsten, *The Naval Aristocracy: The Golden Age of Annapolis and the Emergence of Modern American Navalism* (New York: The Free Press, 1972), esp. 277–326; and Kenneth J. Hagan, *American Gunboat Diplomacy and the Old Navy, 1877–1889* (Westport, CT: Greenwood Press, 1973), esp. 13–58.

4. Robert W. Love Jr., *History of the U.S. Navy, 1775–1941* (Harrisburg, PA: Stackpole Books, 1992), 369.

5. Seager, *Alfred Thayer Mahan*, 218. My sketch of Mahan relies heavily on Seager's biography and on the collection of Mahan's letters that he and Doris Maguire edited, Alfred T. Mahan, *Letters and Papers of Alfred Thayer Mahan*, 3 vols., ed. Robert Seager II and Doris D. Maguire (Annapolis, MD: Naval Institute Press, 1975).

6. Seager, *Alfred Thayer Mahan*, 12–13.

7. Mahan to Ashe, December 21, 1882, Mahan, in *Letters and Papers*, 1:544.

8. Mahan to Ashe, March 11, 1885, in ibid., 1:592.

9. Andrew Lambert, *War at Sea in the Age of Sail: 1650–1850* (London: Cassell, Wellington House, 2000), 27.

10. Ronald Spector, *Professors of War: The Naval War College and the Development of the Naval Profession* (Newport, RI: Naval War College Press, 1977), 4.

11. Bernard Brodie, *Sea Power in the Machine Age* (Princeton, NJ: Princeton University Press, 1941), 82. Chapter 6, "War at Sea under Steam: Tactics and Strategy," is an excellent primer.

12. John D. Alden, *The American Steel Navy* (Annapolis, MD: Naval Institute Press, 1972), 86. See also Spector, *Professors of War*, 5.

13. Brodie, *Sea Power in the Machine Age*, 18.

14. Alden, *American Steel Navy*, 3.

15. Frederick C. Drake, *The Empire of the Seas: A Biography of Rear Admiral Robert Wilson Shufeldt, USN* (Honolulu: University of Hawai`i Press, 1984), 311–16.

16. Bradley A. Fiske, *From Midshipman to Rear Admiral* (New York: The Century Company, 1919), 95.

17. Harold Sprout and Margaret Sprout, *The Rise of American Naval Power, 1776–1918* (Annapolis, MD: Naval Institute Press, 1939/1966), 220.

18. B. Franklin Cooling, *Benjamin Franklin Tracy: Father of the Modern American Fighting Navy* (Hamden, CT: Archon/Shoe String Press, 1973), 56.

19. Ibid., 56–57; and Walter R. Herrick Jr., *The American Naval Revolution* (Baton Rouge: Louisiana State University Press, 1966), 36.

20. Mahan to Ashe, July March 11, 1885, in Mahan, *Letters and Papers*, 1:593.

21. Seager, *Alfred Thayer Mahan*, 144–46, and ch. 6–7; and Mahan to Luce, 16 May 1885, in Mahan, *Letters and Papers*, 1:606–7.

22. Kenneth J. Hagan, *This People's Navy: The Making of American Sea Power* (New York: Free Press, 1991), 184.

23. Spector, *Professors of War*, 38. I have relied much on this original, thorough, and superbly written book. Spector notes that the Naval Institute's journal *Proceedings*, which intended to disseminate the latest in naval learning, published not a single article on naval strategy from the inaugural issue in 1874 until 1886. During those twelve years, essays about technical issues in ordnance, armor, and steam propulsion filled its pages.

24. Lawrence C. Allin, "The Naval Institute, Mahan, and the Naval Profession," *Naval War College Review* 31 (Summer 1978): 29–48.

25. Fiske, *Midshipman to Rear Admiral*, 68.

26. Secretary of the Navy General Order No. 325, October 6, 1884, copy provided by the Naval War College library.

27. Fiske, *Midshipman to Rear Admiral*, 107.

28. Mahan to Whitney, May 15, 1885, in Mahan, *Letters and Papers*, 1:605; and Spector, *Professors of War*, 51.

29. Mahan to Ashe, July 6, 1883, in Mahan, *Letters and Papers*, 1:554–55; and Seager, *Alfred Thayer Mahan*, 134–35.

30. Spector, *Professors of War*, 30–31.

31. Walker to Luce, August 21, 1886, quoted in Spector, *Professors of War*, 52.

32. Fiske, *Midshipman to Rear Admiral*, 107–8.

33. Seager, *Alfred Thayer Mahan*, 181.

34. Jim Stavridis, "Read, Think, Write, and Publish," *Proceedings* 134 (August 2008): 18–19.

35. Ibid., 169; and Spector, *Professors of War*, 28–29.

36. Spector, *Professors of War*, 34; Mahan to Walker, October 22, 1886, in Mahan, *Letters and Papers*, 1:637; Seager, *Alfred Thayer Mahan*, 180; and Walker to Luce, October 23, 1896, quoted in Spector, *Professors of War*, 37.

37. Roosevelt to Mahan, May 12, 1890, in Richard W. Turk, *The Ambiguous Relationship: Theodore Roosevelt and Alfred Thayer Mahan* (New York: Greenwood Press, 1987), 109.

38. 1891 Annual Report, quoted in Hagan, *This People's Navy*, 197.

39. Brayton Harris, *The Age of the Battleship, 1890–1922* (New York: Watts, 1965), 20–21.

40. Herrick, *American Naval Revolution*, 150–55.

41. Alfred Thayer Mahan, *The Influence of Sea Power upon the French Revolution and Empire* (Boston: Little, Brown, 1892).

42. Herbert to Mahan, October 6, 1893, quoted in Seager, *Alfred Thayer Mahan*, 274.

43. Herrick, *Naval Revolution*, 178.

44. Brodie, *Sea Power in the Machine Age*.

45. Harris, *Age of the Battleship*, 101. Mark Hayes cites 1.29 percent hits at Santiago, in "War Plans and Operations and their Impact on U.S. Naval Operations in the Spanish-American War," Paper presented at Congreso Internacional Ejército y Armada en El 98: Cuba, Puerto Rico y Filipinas on March 23, 1998. Available at the NHC Web site, http://www.history.Navy.mil/wars/spanam.htm.

46. Cooling, *Benjamin Franklin Tracy*, 157. In numbers of ships in service in 1898, the United States lagged, at a minimum, Britain, France, Italy, Germany, and Russia. Japan was close on America's heels. Spain and China had fairly substantial navies but less naval power than the United States.

47. Mahan to Luce, October 7, 1889, in Mahan, *Letters and Papers*, 2:712.

48. Livezey, *Mahan on Sea Power*, 336.

49. Mahan to Luce, October 7, 1889, in Mahan, *Letters and Papers*, 2:712; Mahan to Roy B. Marston, February 19, 1897, in ibid, 2:494.

50. Alfred Thayer Mahan, "The United States Looking Outward," *Atlantic Monthly* (December 1890): 816–24.

51. Mahan to the Editor of the *New York Times*, January 30, 1893, in Mahan, *Letters and Papers*, 2:92–93.

52. Alfred Thayer Mahan, "Hawai`i and Our Future Sea Power," *Forum* 15 (March 1893): 1–11.

53. Many articles are collected in Alfred Thayer Mahan, *The Interest of America in Sea Power, Present and Future* (London: Sampson Low and Marsden, 1897). After Mahan's death appeared another digest of his early writings in *Mahan on Naval Warfare* (Boston: Little, Brown, 1918 and 1923).

54. Mahan, "Anglo-American Union," July 1894, in Mahan, *Interest of America*, 118–19.

55. Mahan to James Thursfield, January 10, 1896, in Mahan, *Letters and Papers*, 2:441.

56. Mahan, *Mahan on Naval Warfare*, 64; and Mahan to George Syndenham Clark, September 30, 1894, in Mahan, *Letters and Papers*, 2:336. See also George W. Melville, "Views of Commodore George W. Melville," Senate Document No. 188, *Cong. Rec.*, 55th Cong., 2nd sess. (1898).

57. Mahan, *Mahan on Naval Warfare*, 55.

58. John Schofield and Barton Alexander, "Report on Pearl Harbor," May 8, 1873, published in the *American Historical Review* 30 (April 1925), 560–65; and Mahan to George Sydenham Clarke, November 5, 1892, in Mahan, *Letters and Papers*, 2:84.

59. Mahan, *Mahan on Naval Warfare*, 50–52, 68–69, 75; and Mahan, *Interest of America*, 39–44.

60. Melville, "Views of Melville," 19.

61. Mahan, *Interest of America*, 40–42.

62. Melville, "Views of Melville," 15.

63. See Introduction, note 1.

64. Melville, "Views of Melville," 24.

65. Mahan, *Interest of America*, 146, 161–62.

66. Melville, "Views of Melville," 3, 32–33; and Mahan, *Interest of America*, 47–49.

67. Mahan, *Interest of America*, 26.

68. Theodore Roosevelt to James Kyle, January 4, 1898, "Departmental Letters," Volume 1, 207–9, Entry 19, RG 24; Report of Admiral George Melville, January 11, 1898, *Cong. Rec.*, 55th Cong., 2nd sess. (1898), 6266; John Harman, "The Political Importance of Hawai`i," *North American Review* 160 (March 1895): 375–76; Testimony of Admiral

David Porter, Senate Documents, No. 23, 55th Cong., 1st sess. (1897), 13; and Melville, "Views of Melville," 15–19.

69. Hayes, "War Plans." Range is also affected by such factors as hull design, wind and wave action, and currents.

70. Herrick, *American Naval Revolution*, 223; and Harris, *Age of the Battleship*, 26.

71. Melville, "Views of Melville," 25. However, even if a foreign navy could recoal at Hawai`i, a strike on the West Coast would require deck coaling to make the 4,400-mile round-trip with a fuel reserve and without recoaling at another harbor.

72. Roosevelt to Kyle, January 4, 1898, "Departmental Letters," Entry 61, RG 24, NARA; T.C. Mendenhall (Supervisor of the U.S. Coast Guard) to Cushman Davis, January 2, 1894, Davis Papers, Minnesota Historical Society; and John Proctor, "Hawai`i and the Changing Front of the World," *Forum* 24 (1897): 41–42.

73. See map in *Cong. Rec.*, 55th Cong., 2nd sess. (1898), 6609.

74. Secretary of the Navy Paul Merton to Ernest Roberts (chairman of a subcommittee, presumably for rivers and harbors, of the House Committee on Naval Affairs), January 17, 1905, Subject File 439 (Surveys), Records of the General Board of the Navy, Operational Archives Branch, NHC. Attached to Merton's letter is an extract from a letter from the captain of the *New Orleans*, who reported earlier in January 1905 that only small boats were able to land stores for the thirty-person naval garrison.

75. The Necker situation is ably summarized in Commodore R. B. Bradford to the Consul-General, Honolulu, January 16, 1899, in folder marked "Hawai`i," ZE (Places) Subfile, Historical Reference (Z) File, in the Operational Archives Branch, NHC.

76. Using 1890s measurements (for that is what contemporaries would have done), San Francisco to Yokohama was 5,442 miles via Honolulu, 4,577 miles via Kiska, and 4,535 miles direct on the Great Circle route. These data are in the chart "North Pacific Distances," printed in the *Cong. Rec.*, 55th Cong., 2nd sess. (1898), 6609. Different figures were sometimes used, owing to the source of the data (perhaps British charts vice American) and whether U.S. miles were used or nautical miles.

77. Lieutenant Commander W. H. Emory to Commander in Chief, Asiatic Station, December 31, 1895, Area Files, RG 45, M-625B, roll 360, frames 0429–32. Although Emory preferred the Honolulu route, the *Petrel* lacked the coal capacity to reach Hawai`i from Yokohama or Hakodate. It appears that the orders home were cancelled and the gunboat remained on the Asiatic station (see "USS *Petrel* (Gunboat # 2, PG-2), 1889–1920," NHC home page: http://www.history.Navy.mil/photos/sh-usn/usnsh-p/pg2.htm). The *Petrel* arrived in the Pacific in 1891 and normally sailed to Bering Sea to patrol the Pribilof Islands to catch fur seal poachers. The gunboat normally returned to the Asiatic station in August or September.

78. Fiske, *Midshipman to Rear Admiral*, 181–83.

79. Stephen M. White, "The Proposed Annexation of Hawai`i," *Forum* 23 (1897): 723–36.

80. "Diary of Bertram Willard Edwards," seaman on the *Oregon*, available at the Spanish American War Centennial Web site, http://www.spanamwar.com/Oregonedwardsdiary1. htm.

81. Hayes, "War Plans."

82. Mahan, *Influence of Sea Power*, 329.

83. Mahan, "Hawai`i and Our Future Sea Power," in *Interest of America*, 47–49.

84. Harman, "Political Importance of Hawai`i," 376; comments by Cushman Davis in connection with the Senate consideration of the Hawaiian annexation treaty, *New York Tribune*, January 12–13, 1898; John Tyler Morgan, "The Duty of Annexing Hawai`i," *Forum* 25 (1898): 11–16; Melville, "Views of Melville," 18; Mahan to Roosevelt, May 1, 1897, in Mahan, *Letters and Papers*, 2:505; Hilary Herbert, "Plea for the Navy," *Forum* 24 (1897): 1–15; Roosevelt to Frye, March 31, 1898, in Elting E. Morison, ed., *The Letters of Theodore Roosevelt*, vol. 1, *The Years of Preparation, 1868–1898* (Cambridge: Harvard University Press, 1951), 806.

85. Senate Reports, no. 336, *Cong. Rec.*, 54th Cong., 1st sess. (1896), February 25, 1896, 1–2.

86. Kenneth Earl Hamburger, "The Technology, Doctrine, and Politics of U.S. Coastal Fortifications, 1880–1945" (PhD diss., Duke University, 1986), 126; and Roger F. Sarty, *Coast Artillery, 1815–1914* (Bloomfield, Ont.: Museum Restoration Service, 1988), 36–38.

87. Hamburger, "Technology, Doctrine, and Politics," 80, 83, 102. For an interesting view of sectional differences in the building of the New Navy, see Peter Trubowitz, "Geography and Strategy: The Politics of American Naval Expansion," in *The Politics of Strategic Adjustment: Ideas, Institutions, and Interests*, ed. Peter Trubowitz, Emily O. Goldman, and Edward Rhodes (New York: Columbia University Press, 1998).

88. Senate Documents, No. 336, 54th Cong., 1st sess. (February 16, 1896), 41. In fact, the weight of gun and carriage was 108 tons, and the cycle time was 26 seconds to lower the gun, and 21 seconds to raise it, with perhaps 10–15 seconds, depending on the skill of the crew, to load a new round. This produced a rate of fire of about 60–65 seconds per round. See Charles W. Snell, "A Brief General History of the Construction of the Endicott System of Seacoast Defenses in the Continental United States, 1885–1912," unpublished paper, Historic Preservation Team, National Park Service, Denver Service Center, November 1975, 15.

89. Senate Documents, No. 336, 54th Cong., 1st sess., 47, 58–59.

90. Quoted in Hamburger, "Technology, Doctrine, and Politics," 105.

91. Quoted in Snell, "Brief General History," 18.

92. Ibid.

93. Senate Documents, No. 336, 54th Cong., 1st sess., 49.

94. Hamburger, "Technology, Doctrine, and Politics," 118.

95. Seager, *Alfred Thayer Mahan*, 368–73; Sprout and Sprout, *Rise of American Naval Power*, 270–75; and Hagan, *This People's Navy*, 213–25.

96. Hayes, "War Plans."

97. Emanuel Raymond Lewis, *Seacoast Fortifications of the United States* (San Francisco: Presidio Press, 1970/1979), 100.

98. Ibid., 113. The sole remaining example of this gun and gun carriage is at the U.S. Army Ordnance Museum at Aberdeen, Maryland. Adjusting fire to hit moving ships at maximum range obviously would have been quite difficult.

99. Cooling, *Benjamin Franklin Tracy*, chart, 157. Walker's remark was made two years earlier in 1896; the naval balance was even more adverse at that time; see Senate Documents, No. 336, 54th Cong., 1st sess., 54.

100. My sketch of German war planning, if not all of my inferences, relies on Holger H. Herwig's outstanding work, *Politics of Frustration: The United States in German Naval Planning, 1889–1941* (Boston: Little, Brown, 1976), 30–31.

101. Ibid., 43.

102. Ibid., 44–66.

103. Sarty, *Coast Artillery*, 38; and Hamburger, "Technology, Doctrine, and Politics," 102–3.

104. Regarding the *Prat*, see Francis X. Holbrook and John Nikol, "The Chilean Crisis of 1891–1892," *The American Neptune* (October 1978): 291–300.

105. *Cong. Rec.*, 53rd Cong. 2nd sess. (1894), 2535; and 49th Cong., 2nd sess. (1887), 1811.

106. *Cong. Rec.*, 53rd Cong. 2nd sess. (1894), 2536.

107. *Cong. Rec.*, 54th Cong. 1st sess. (1895–96), 36, 112, 277–78, 643, 3233, 3812, 3935–43; 55th Cong., 2nd sess. (1898), app., 656–57.

108. Senate Documents, No. 336, 54th Cong., 1st sess., 58.

109. Hilary Herbert, "The Fifty Million Appropriation and Its Lessons," *Forum* 25 (1898): 269; Melville, "Views of Melville," 10; and Herbert, "Plea for the Navy," 10–11.

110. Hamburger, "Technology, Doctrine, and Politics," 131–35. Hamburger concludes that after the war, Mahan saw the value of coastal defenses. I think he was willing to tolerate them to release the Navy from port defense.

111. Seager, *Alfred Thayer Mahan*, 248–53.

112. Mahan to Ellen Evans Mahan, June 28, 1893, in Mahan, *Letters and Papers*, 2:113.

113. Seager, *Alfred Thayer Mahan*, 253, quoting Mahan to Luce, May 6, 1909.

Chapter 12. The Republican Party Embraces Annexation

1. *Cong. Rec.*, 53rd Cong., 3rd sess. (1895), 2247.

2. Ibid., 2247.

3. Ibid., 3250.

4. Ibid., 3108.

5. Ibid., 2249, 2462, 3110–11, 3118–19, 3121–22; and *Cong. Rec.*, 54th Cong., 1st sess. (1896), 3141, 3193–94, 3196, 3240–43.

6. *Cong. Rec.*, 53rd Cong., 3rd sess. (1895), 3124; and *Cong. Rec.*, 54th Cong., 1st sess. (1896), 6326, 6357.

7. *Cong. Rec.*, 53rd Cong., 3rd sess. (1895), 2253, 2247, 2259, 3108, 3110–11, 3118–19, 3121–22; and *Cong. Rec.*, 54th Cong., 1st sess. (1896), 3193–94, 3196, 3240–43, 3248, 3250, 4564–69, 4594–97, 4653–54.

8. *Cong. Rec.*, 53rd Cong., 3rd sess. (1895), 3121.

9. Ibid., 3118–19.

10. Ibid., 2249.

11. Ibid., 2252–53.

12. Ibid., 2247–69; and *Cong. Rec.*, 54th Cong., 1st sess. (1896), 3193–77, 4554–64, 6326–57.

13. Lodge to Cushman Davis, March 22, 1895, Box 6, Davis Papers, Minnesota Historical Society.

14. *Cong. Rec.*, 53rd Cong., 3rd sess. (1895), 622–30, at 630.

15. Walker to Herbert, April 28, May 28, 1894, Walker Papers, NHC.

16. Andrade, *Unconquerable Rebel*, 150–68; and Loomis, *For Whom Are the Stars*, 103–69.

17. *Cong. Rec.*, 53rd Cong., 3rd sess. (1895), 1205 (Kyle), 1206–20.

18. Ibid., 1277, 1329, 1408–11.

19. Lodge to Anna Lodge, March 6–7, 1895, Lodge Papers, Massachusetts Historical Society.

20. *Cong. Rec.*, 53rd Cong., 3rd sess. (1895), 1277, 1329, 1408–11. For the atmospherics in the Senate, see Barbara Tuchman, *The Proud Tower: A Portrait of the World Before the War, 1890–1914* (New York: The MacMillan Company, 1966), 135.

21. *Cong. Rec.*, 53rd Cong., 3rd sess. (1895), 3082–84. See also Lodge to Anna Lodge, March 6–7, 1895, Lodge Papers, Massachusetts Historical Society. For an elaboration of Lodge's views, see Henry Cabot Lodge, "Our Blundering Foreign Policy," *Forum* 19 (March 1895): 8–17.

22. Ibid.

23. John T. Woolley and Gerhard Peters, "Republican Party Platform of 1896," in *The American Presidency Project* [online] Santa Barbara, CA. Available at http://www.presidency.ucsb.edu/ws/?pid=29629.

24. An excellent overview is David M. Pletcher, *The Diplomacy of Involvement: American Economic Expansion across the Pacific, 1784–1900* (Columbia: University of Missouri Press. 2001).

25. Marcy to David L. Gregg, no. 2, September 22, 1853, "Instructions to Hawai`i," M-77, roll 99, NARA.

26. The literature of the China market is enormous. See in particular Charles S. Campbell Jr., *Special Business Interests and the Open Door* (New Haven, CT: Yale University Press, 1951); Walter LaFeber, *The New Empire: An Interpretation of American Expansion, 1860–1898* (Ithaca, NY: Cornell University Press, 1963); Thomas J. McCormick, *China Market: America's Quest for Informal Empire, 1893–1901* (Chicago: Quadrangle Books, 1967); and William Appleman Williams, *The Roots of the Modern American Empire* (New York: Random House, 1969).

27. See Richard Hofstadter, *Social Darwinism in American Thought* (Philadelphia: University of Pennsylvania Press, 1944/1955); Albert Weinberg, *Manifest Destiny* (Baltimore, MD: Johns Hopkins University Press, 1935), 212ff; and LaFeber, *New Empire*, ch. 2.

28. Alfred Thayer Mahan, *The Problem of Asia and Its Effect upon International Policies* (Boston: Little, Brown, 1900), 29–30.

29. Quoted in Hofstadter, *Social Darwinism*, 1955 rev. ed., 180.

30. Mahan, "Hawai`i and Our Future Sea Power," March 1893, in *Interest of America in Sea Power*, 33–34.

31. Quoted in Campbell, *Transformation of American Foreign Relations*, 148.

32. Josiah Strong, *Our Country: Its Possible Future and Its Present Crisis* (New York: American Home Missionary Society, 1885), 174–75. For similar thoughts by an arch-annexationist, see John Tyler Morgan, "The Territorial Expansion of the United States," *The Independent*, July 7, 1898; copy in Morgan Papers, LC.

33. Davis to Cordenio Severance, May 5, 1898, Davis Papers, Minnesota Historical Society.

34. The best analysis is Stuart Anderson, *Race and Rapprochement: Anglo-Saxonism and Anglo-American Relations, 1895–1904* (East Brunswick, NJ: Fairleigh Dickinson University Press, 1981). Eric T. L. Love makes a persuasive analysis of the race issue with respect to Hawai`i in: *Race Empire: Racism and U.S. Imperialism, 1865–1900* (Chapel Hill: University of North Carolina Press, 2004), and in "White is the Color of Empire," in *Race, Nation, and Empire in American History*, ed. James T. Campbell, Matthew Pratt Guterl, and Robert G. Lee, 75–102 (Chapel Hill: University of North Carolina Press, 2007). A fine overview of British-American relations is Charles S. Campbell Jr., *From Revolution to Rapprochement: The United States and Great Britain, 1783–1900* (New York: Wiley, 1974). Campbell's *Anglo-American Understanding, 1898–1908* (Baltimore: Johns Hopkins University Press, 1957), is the standard work on the gradual harmonization of the two countries' national interests in the 1890s.

35. Mahan, "Hawai`i and Our Future Sea Power," 33–34; "The Future in Relation to American Naval Power," 161–62; and "A 20th Century Outlook," 263; all in *Interest of America in Sea Power*.

36. For an analysis of American destiny, see the *St James Gazette*, November 15, 1897, clipping in John Bassett Moore Papers, LC. See also Charles A. Boutelle (Chairman of the

House Committee on Naval Affairs) to Admiral George Belknap, February 11, 1894, Belknap Papers, LC; anonymous editorial, "Expansion not Imperialism," *Outlook*, October 22, 1898, 464–66; Charles J. Swift, "Practical and Legal Aspects of Annexation," *Overland Monthly* 25 (1895): 586–96; and Murat Halstead, "American Annexation and Armament," *Forum* 24 (1897): 56–66.

37. Bluford Wilson to Walter Q. Gresham, July 24, 1893, Gresham Papers, LC.

38. J. U. Pierce to Lodge, July 9, 1898, Lodge Papers, Massachusetts Historical Society.

39. Quoted in Hofstadter, *Social Darwinism*, 1955 rev. ed., 170.

40. Kristin Hoganson's *Fighting for American Manhood: How Gender Politics Provoked the Spanish-American and Philippine-American Wars* (New Haven, CT: Yale University Press, 1998), masterfully illuminates gender as a powerful influence on foreign policy around the time of Hawaiian annexation. Among many other recent works, see Gail Bederman, *Manliness & Civilization: A Cultural History of Gender and Race in the United States, 1880–1917* (Chicago: University of Chicago Press, 1995); and Edward P. Crapol, ed., *Women and American Foreign Policy: Lobbyists, Critics, and Insiders* (Westport, CT: Greenwood Press, 1987).

41. Robert A. Diamond, ed., *Guide to U.S. Elections* (Washington, DC: Congressional Quarterly, 1975): 928. The Republicans registered striking gains in the mid-1890s, primarily because voters identified the Democratic Party with the Depression of 1893. In 1891–93, for example, the Republican Party held only 88 House seats to 235 for the Democrats but by 1897 had achieved a sizable majority. In the Senate, Republicans held a slim lead in 1891–93, lost it in during 1893–95, and regained it in 1895.

42. Dwight Coy, "Cushman K. Davis and American Foreign Policy" (PhD diss., University of Minnesota, 1965): 312–13.

43. Davis to Cordenio Severance, May 5, 1898, Davis Papers, Minnesota Historical Society.

44. Quote from Davis Rpt, 16. See also New York *Tribune*, January 12 and 13, 1898; Coy, "Cushman K. Davis," 60–61, 143–44, 168–69.

45. Sketch drawn from letters, press clippings, photographs, and other materials in the Hitt Papers, LC.

46. Quote from unattributed press clipping in Hitt Papers, LC.

47. *St. Louis Republic*, December 15, 1896, clipping in Hitt Papers, LC.

48. *Chicago Record*, May 20, 1897, clipping in Hitt Papers, LC.

49. *Chicago Evening Post*, January 29, 31, 1898, clippings in Hitt Papers, LC. Hitt made these remarks during the Senate debate of the 1897 annexation treaty.

50. William O. Smith to Henry Cooper, March 15, 1897, HMW.

51. The standard biography of Morgan is Joseph A. Fry, *John Tyler Morgan and the Search for Southern Autonomy* (Knoxville: University of Tennessee Press, 1992). See also Joseph A. Fry, "John Tyler Morgan's Southern Expansionism," *Diplomatic History* 9 (Fall 1985): 329–46; and O. Lawrence Burnette, "John Tyler Morgan and Expansionist Sentiment in the New South," *Alabama Review* 18 (July 1965): 163–82.

52. Thomie Morgan to John Tyler Morgan, February 7, 1897, Morgan Papers, LC.

53. *New York Tribune*, November 19, 1897.

54. Spaulding to Morgan, May 5, 1894; William Bates to Morgan, January 20, 1895; Rowland Mahoney to Morgan, February 9, 1895; W. H. Dimond to Morgan, February 12, 1895; Bellamy Stover to Morgan, July 18, 1895, all in Morgan Papers, LC.

55. State Department Memorandum, "Political Complexion of the Senate," June 22, 1898, Day Papers, LC. Because virtually no senators changed position on annexation after the summer of 1897, this analysis is valid for 1897 as well.

56. Smith to Cooper, March 26, 1897, HMW.

57. Quoted in Ernest R. May, *Imperial Democracy: The Emergence of America as a Great Power* (New York: Harcourt, Brace & World, 1961), 112. I have used several anecdotes taken from May's fine sketch of McKinley.

58. John Davis Long, *The New American Navy*, 2 vols. (New York: Outlook Company, 1903), 2:143.

59. May, *Imperial Democracy*, 112–13.

60. Quoted in John Tebbell and Sara Miles Watts, *The Press and the Presidency: From George Washington to Ronald Reagan* (New York: Oxford University Press, 1985), 298.

61. May, *Imperial Democracy*, 112.

62. Quoted in LaFeber, *New Empire*, 328.

63. Clark, *My Quarter Century*, 424–25.

64. Harold U. Faulkner, *Politics, Reform and Expansion 1890–1900* (New York: Harper & Row, 1959), 261. Richard F. Hamilton argues persuasively that this "backbone" statement never occurred. Hamilton, "McKinley's Backbone," *Presidential Studies Quarterly* 36, no. 3 (September 2006): 482–92.

65. *New York Times*, May 1, 1898, has a lengthy sketch of Long.

66. Long, *American Navy*, II, 174.

67. Long to James Harrison Wilson, April 14, 1897, Long Papers, Massachusetts Historical Society. See also Long to Henry Lee Higginson, April 10, 1897, and Long to Roosevelt, April 6 and 8, 1897, Long Papers, Massachusetts Historical Society.

68. Long to Pierce Long, March 30, 1897; Long to Lodge, March 30, 1897, Long Papers, Massachusetts Historical Society.

69. Lester B. Shippee, "William Rufus Day," in *American Secretaries of State*, vol. 9, ed., S. F. Bemis, 27–114 (New York: Alfred A. Knopf, 1928); and Joseph McLean, *William Rufus Day* (Baltimore, MD: Johns Hopkins University Press, 1946), ch. 1–2.

70. Smith to Cooper, March 26, March 15, 1897, HMW.

71. Quoted in an internal memo describing John W. Foster's dinner for Foreign Minister Cooper in Washington in late 1896; Foreign Affairs 1896, FO-EX.

72. Theodore E. Burton, *John Sherman* (Boston: Houghton, Mifflin, 1906), 386–429; and Louis M. Sears, "John Sherman," in *The American Secretaries of State and Their Diplomacy*, vol. 9, ed. Samuel F. Bemis, 3–26 (New York: Alfred A. Knopf, 1928).

73. Hatch to Cooper, October 7, 1896, HMW; Lodge to Roosevelt, December 2, 1896, in Henry Cabot Lodge, ed., *Selections from the Correspondence of Theodore Roosevelt and Henry Cabot Lodge, 1884–1918*, 2 vols. (New York: Charles Scribner's Sons, 1925), 1:240.

74. Cooper to Hatch, December 9, 1896, HMW.

75. Hatch to Cooper, January 26 and 31, 1897, HMW.

76. Kohlsaat was one of three men—Mark Hanna and Myron T. Herrick were the others—whom William Day enlisted to rescue McKinley from financial disaster. In a typically kind gesture, McKinley had cosigned nearly $100,000 worth of loans for a friend. When the friend went bankrupt, McKinley, then governor of Ohio, allowed his three friends to bail him out (Herman H. Kohlsaat, *From McKinley to Harding: Personal Recollections of Our Presidents* [New York: Charles Scribner's Sons, 1923], 10–17).

77. Smith to Dole, February 26, 1897, HMW.

78. Hatch to Cooper, February 27, 1897, HMW.

79. Thurston, *Memoirs of the Hawaiian Revolution*, 562; Frank Hastings to Cooper, January 15, 1897, HMW.

80. Richard S. Offenberg, "The Political Career of Thomas Brackett Reed" (PhD diss., New York University, 1963), 162–63.

81. Hatch to Cooper, January 20 and 26, 1897, HMW.

82. Hatch to Cooper, April 2, 1897, HMW.

83. William O. Smith, "Memorandum" (of meeting with President McKinley), March 25, 1897; Smith to Cooper, March 26, 1897; Hatch to Cooper, March 26, 1897; and Hatch to Dole, March 27, 1897, all in HMW.

84. Hatch to Cooper, April 2, 1897, HMW.

85. Hatch to Dole, March 27, 1897, HMW.

86. Smith to Cooper, March 26, 1897, HMW.

87. Hatch to Cooper, April 2, 1897, HMW.

Chapter 13. Japanese Immigration: From Lifeline to Threat

1. James McClain, *Japan: A Modern History* (New York: Norton, 2002), 292–96.

2. The standard works on Japan's drive to eliminate the treaties are Michael R. Auslin, *Negotiating with Imperialism: The Unequal Treaties and the Culture of Japanese Diplomacy* (Cambridge, MA: Harvard University Press, 2006); and Louis G. Perez, *Mutsu Munemitsu and the Revision of the Unequal Treaties* (Cranbury, NJ: Associated University Presses, 1999). For overall foreign policy, see Akira Iriye, *Japan and the Wider World: From the Mid-Nineteenth Century to the Present* (London and New York: Longman, 1997), 1–22; and Ian Nish, *Japanese Foreign Policy, 1869–1942: Kasumigaseki to Miyakezaka* (London:

Routledge & Kegan Paul, 1977). An older but still useful work is Stevens, *American Expansion in Hawai`i.*

3. Perez, *Mutsu Munemitsu,* esp. ch. 7 and 8.

4. Quoted in Nish, *Japanese Foreign Policy,* 273.

5. Satow to Salisbury, no. 205, November 5, 1896, FO 881/6970X; and Sidney Giffard, *Japan Among the Powers, 1890–1990* (New Haven, CT: Yale University Press, 1994).

6. Minutes of the Executive Council, September 4, 1894, quoted in William A. Russ Jr., "Hawaiian Labor and Immigration Problems before Annexation," *Journal of Modern History* 15, no. 3 (September 1943): 212.

7. Moriyama, *Imingaisha,* 30–32.

8. Odo and Sinoto, *Pictorial History,* 23; and Hazama and Komeiji, *Okage Sama de,* 25.

9. *PCA,* November 11, 1897.

10. Okahata, *A History of the Japanese in Hawai`i,* 110. Moriyama notes that the three-year contracts of this final group did not end until June 27, 1897 (*Imingaisha,* 30).

11. Moriyama, *Imingaisha,* 50, table 9. The ordinance was issued first as an Imperial Government regulation and, in 1896, in expanded form as a law.

12. Hazama and Komeiji, *Okage Sama de,* 25.

13. Internal correspondence shows that the convention was still in force. For example, during the spring 1897 immigration crisis, Hatch recorded that "the Labor convention will prove to be of inestimable value to us. It is most fortunate that it has never been terminated" (Hatch to Cooper, May 21, 1897, HMW).

14. Odo and Sinoto, *Pictorial History,* 38–41.

15. Ernest K. Wakukawa, *A History of the Japanese in Hawai`i* (Honolulu: Toyo Shoin, 1938), 90–91.

16. Moriyama, *Imingaisha,* 113.

17. Soga Yasutaro, February 1896, quoted in Kimura, *Issei,* 12.

18. Minutes of the Executive Council, April 2, 1894, quoted in Russ, "Hawaiian Labor and Immigration Problems," 214.

19. Moriyama, *Imingaisha,* 98.

20. Dole thought "we may find it necessary to try and procure a modification of our Japanese treaty on the point of the right of the Japanese to come in" (Dole to Hatch, December 3, 1896, Dole Papers, AH).

21. Cooper to Hatch, March 3, 1896, Hatch Papers, AH. For the limit per ship, see April 23, 1896, Minutes of the Executive Council (1896-Immigration), FO-EX, AH.

22. Letter of December 30, 1896, Minutes of the Executive Council (1896-Immigration), FO-EX.

23. Minutes of the Executive Council, March 11, April 24, May 19, and November 2, 1896, Executive and Advisory Council, 1896, AH; Cooper to Hatch, March 3, 1896, Hatch

Papers, AH; Russ, "Hawaiian Labor and Immigration Problems," 212–20. See also Thurston interview with the *New York Sun*, October 15, 1894, clipping in C-240, Moore Papers, LC.

24. Schmitt, *Historical Statistics of Hawai`i*, 25, 97; William D. Alexander, "History of Immigration to Hawai`i," in Thrum, *Hawaiian Annual, 1896*, 119–20; Odo and Sinoto, *Pictorial History of the Japanese*, 18–19.

25. Moriyama, *Imingaisha*, 214n23.

26. Hatch to Cooper, February 19, 1896, HMW.

27. Cooper to Hatch, March 3, 1896, Hatch Papers, AH.

28. Undated and unsigned memo, 1896, Foreign Affairs 1896, FO-EX. This memo summarizes the conversation at the dinner.

29. Minutes of the Executive Council, November 12, 1896, quoted in Russ, *Hawaiian Republic*, 133.

30. Dole to Hatch, December 3, 1896, and January 7, 1897, Dole Papers, AH.

31. Smith to Hatch, December 10, 1896, Hatch Papers, AH.

32. Alexander to Hastings, December 9, 1896, quoted by Russ, *Hawaiian Republic*, 129.

33. Dole to Hatch, December 3, 1896, President's Letters, FO-EX. Irwin was traveling to Washington, so Dole passed him the request through Hatch.

34. Hatch to Cooper, January 26, 1897, HMW.

35. Cooper to Hatch, January 7, 1897, FO-EX.

36. Mills to Rockhill, February 8, 1897, "Despatches from United States Consuls in Honolulu, Hawai`i, 1820–1903," RG 59, M-144, roll 20, NARA.

37. This crude calculation slightly overstates the number of voting age males. The census data lists males of up to 15 years and over 15. It is impossible to calculate the number of males 20 years and older, but one can come close. In the case of Japanese, there were 19,212 males in the 1896 census. Of these, 1,054 were Hawaiian-born; virtually all of these were born to immigrants arriving in the convention years of 1885–94 and were therefore children. This gives a crude total of 18,156 Japanese males of voting age. Similar calculations were done for Chinese and Caucasians from Europe and North America. See Thrum's *Hawaiian Annual, 1898*, 46; Robert C. Schmitt, *Demographic Statistics of Hawai`i, 1778–1965* (Honolulu: University of Hawai`i Press, 1968), 74–75; Coman, "Contract Labor," 64; and Odo and Sinoto, *Pictorial History*, 18–19.

Chapter 14. The U.S.–Japan Crisis of 1897

1. The Ōkuma sketch relies heavily on Oka Yoshitake, *Five Political Leaders of Modern Japan* (Tokyo: University of Tokyo Press, 1984), 49, 72–73; and Smimasa Idditti, *The Life of Marquis Shigenobu Ōkuma* (Tokyo: Hokusei Press, 1940).

2. Offenberg, *Political Career of Thomas Brackett Reed*, 162–63.

3. Hatch to Cooper, April 13, 1897, HMW.

4. Hawes to Salisbury, April 29, 1897, p. 12, FO 58/309.

5. Mills to Olney, no. 191, February 1, 1897, Despatches; and Olney to Secretary of the Navy, February 16, 1897, Area 9 File, RG 45, NARA.

6. Cooper to Hatch, March 23, 1897, HMW.

7. *Yamato Shimbun*, March 9, 13, 18, 20, 1897.

8. *Yamato Shimbun*, March 25, 1897. The *Shinshu Maru* and *Sakura Maru* incidents were somehow not reported to Washington until late March, probably because repeated outbreaks of measles among the passengers forced two extensions of the quarantine period. A final determination about entry could not be made until late March. See Mills to Rockhill, March 22, 1897, "Despatches to Consuls in Honolulu," RG 59, M-144, roll 20, NARA.

9. *Yamato Shimbun*, April 1, 1897.

10. Commander S. Hansday [?] (signature nearly illegible) to Long, March 23, 1897, Area 9 File, RG 45, NARA. Quote from Akira Iriye, *Pacific Estrangement: Japanese and American Expansion, 1897–1911* (Cambridge, MA: Harvard University Press, 1972), 50. Shimamura overestimated the number of Japanese.

11. Long to Sicard, March 29, 1897, Long Papers, Massachusetts Historical Society. See also John A. S. Grenville, "American Naval Preparations for War with Spain, 1896–1898," *Journal of American Studies* 12 (1967–68): 3638; and Michael Vlahos, "The Naval War College and the Origins of War-Planning Against Japan," *Naval War College Review* 33 (1980): 23–41. The revised war plan can be found in "War Portfolios," file 425, Subject File, Records of the General Board of the Navy, Naval History Division, Washington Navy Yard, Washington, DC.

12. Long to commander-in-chief, Pacific Station, March 30, 1897, "Letters to Stations," entry 59, RG 24, NARA; Long to Beardslee, March 30, 1897, Area 9 File, RG 45, NARA. See also Beardslee to Long, April 7, 1897, and E. P. Wood to Long, April 12, 1897, both in "Letters to Stations," entry 59, RG 24, NARA.

13. Satow to Salisbury, no. 70, April 10, 1897, p. 4, FO 58/309.

14. Satow to Salisbury, April 11, 1897, p. 92, FO 46/486.

15. FO internal memo, April 11, 1897, p. 30, FO 58/309. Lord Salisbury wrote: "We should do all we can to prevent the annexation and therefore we will lie very quiet."

16. Ōkuma to Hoshi, April 14, 1897, copy in "Notes from the Japanese Legation in the United States," RG 59, M-163, roll 6, NARA.

17. Hoshi to Sherman, June 21, 1897, "Notes from Japan," RG 59, M-163, roll 6, NARA. For background on Ōkuma's instructions to Hoshi, see Satow to Salisbury, no. 70, April 10, 1897, p. 4; FO 58/309; and Satow to Salisbury, no. 75, April 15, 1897, p. 130, FO 46/483.

18. Burton, *John Sherman*, 386–429; and Sears, "John Sherman," 3–26.

19. Satow to Salisbury, no. 75, April 15, 1897, p. 130, FO 46/483. Satow said Ōkuma instructed Hoshi again on April 15.

20. Satow to Salisbury, April 22, 1897, in Ian Ruxton, ed., *The Semi-Official Letters of British Envoy Sir Ernest Satow from Japan and China (1895–1906)* (Morrisville, NC: Lulu Press, 2007), 88.

21. Appleton to Long, March 31, 1897, in Gardner Weld Allen, ed., *The Papers of John Davis Long, 1897–1904* (Boston: Massachusetts Historical Society, 1939), 10.

22. Long to Appleton, April 2, 1897, Long Papers, Massachusetts Historical Society.

23. Long to Julia M. Castle, March 16 and April 6, 1897, Long Papers, Massachusetts Historical Society.

24. Long to Joseph M. White, April 8, 1897; Long to A. L. Castle, April 13, 1897; Long to Hartwell, April 13, 1897; and Long to George Miner, April 13, 1897, Long Papers, Massachusetts Historical Society.

25. Long to Hartwell, March 31 1897; and Long to Appleton, April 2, 1897, Long Papers, Massachusetts Historical Society.

26. Hatch to Cooper, April 13 and 14, 1897, HMW. The hints were in the letter from the skipper of the *Alert* to Long (Hansday to Long, March 23, 1897, Area 9 File, RG 45, NARA) and in Mills to Rockhill, March 22, 1897, "Despatches to Consuls in Honolulu," RG 59, M-144, roll 20, NARA.

27. *New York Times*, November 26, 1896. Foster did some legal work for the Pacific Cable Company. The *New York Times* reported that "Mr. Foster's trip to the islands was not alone to urge extension and enlargement of the Pacific Cable Company's concession, but that he went also in the interest of the Republican Party to ascertain the extent of annexationist sentiment at the present time" (*New York Times*, November 29, 1896).

28. *New York Times*, March 27, 1897. For the text, see John Watson Foster, "Paper Read before the National Geographic Society of Washington, Friday, March 26, 1897, by Hon. John W. Foster," Senate Document No. 23, *Cong. Rec.*, 55th Cong. 1st sess. (April 5, 1897).

29. Foster, *Diplomatic Memoirs*, Vol. II, 166, 172.

30. Elisha Allen to Frank Hastings, April 14, 1897; and James Swan to Hastings, April 19, 21, 1897, HMW.

31. *Pittsburgh Dispatch*, April 4, 1897, clipping in Hitt Papers, LC.

32. *Chicago Tribune*, April 9, 1897, clipping in Hitt Papers, LC.

33. Dun to Sherman, no. 477, April 12, 1897, "Despatches from United States Ministers to Japan, 1855–1910," RG 59, M-133, roll 70, NARA. Dun's report mirrored that of the Hawaiian consul in Yokohama (Eldridge to Cooper, April 12, 1897, Hatch Papers, AH).

34. Hatch to Cooper, April 13, 1897, HMW.

35. *Yamato Shimbun*, April 14, 1897.

36. Sherman to Mills, no. 170, April 19, 1897, "Instructions to Hawai`i," RG 59, M-77, roll 100, NARA.

37. McNair to Long, April 21, 1897, "Translations of Cipher Messages," entry 19; Long to Sherman, April 21, 1897, Area 9 File, both in RG 45, NARA; Roosevelt to McKinley, April 22, 1897, Roosevelt Papers, LC; Roosevelt to Beardslee, April 22, 1897, "Letters to Stations," entry 59, RG 24, NARA.

38. For Sewall's views see *Kennebec Journal*, September 5, 1894; New York *Sun*, October 25, 1894, and November 1, 1894; and *Portland (ME) Daily Press*, June 28, 1894. There is an excellent chapter on Sewall in Burlin, *Imperial Maine and Hawai`i*, 233–60.

39. Quote from an interview in the *Hawaiian Star*, July 13, 1898. Enclosure in Sewall to Day, no. 184, July 18, 1898, "Despatches from Hawai`i," RG 59, T-30, roll 31, NARA.

40. Hatch to Cooper, April 24, 1897, HMW.

41. Roosevelt to Henry White, April 30, 1897, in Morison, *Letters of Roosevelt*, 606.

42. Mahan to Roosevelt, May 1, 1897; and Mahan to Roosevelt, May 6, 1897, in Seager and Maguire, *Letters of Mahan*, II, 505, 507.

43. Roosevelt to Mahan, May 3, 1897, in Morison, *Letters of Roosevelt*, 607–8.

44. Roosevelt to A. S. Hartwell, June 7, 1897, in Morison, *Letters of Roosevelt*, 622; and Long to A. L. Castle, June 12, 1897, Long Papers, Massachusetts Historical Society.

45. Roosevelt to Mahan, May 3, 1897, in Morison, *Letters of Roosevelt*, 607–8.

46. Ibid.

47. Beardslee to Long, May 5, 1897, Area 9 File, RG 45, NARA; and *Cong. Rec.*, 55th Cong., 1st sess. (1897), 776. At Long's instruction, the commander of the Pacific Station completed the survey in early 1898 (Long to commander in chief, Pacific Station, July 28, 1897, and March 19, 1898, "Letters to Stations," Entry 59, RG 24).

48. *Washington Post*, May 12, 1897; and *Washington Star*, May 12, 1897.

49. Although the development bill died because of disagreement over the technical features of the dredging scheme, and because the foreign affairs committee had not yet been formally convened, Congress later authorized additional engineering studies to resolve the technical problems; *Washington Post*, May 12, 1897; *Washington Star*, May 12, 1897; and *Cong. Rec.*, 55th Cong., 1st sess. (1897), 1024.

50. *Washington Star*, May 12, 1897.

51. *Omaha Bee*, May 13, 1897.

52. Mills to Sherman, May 5, 1897, "Despatches from Hawai`i," RG 59, T-30, roll 28, NARA. An endorsement indicates that this dispatch arrived in Washington on 18 May. See also Beardslee to Long, May 5, 1897, Area 9 File, RG 45, NARA. This missive was also received May 18.

53. Hatch to Day, May 22, 1897, "Notes from the Hawaiian Legation," RG 59, T-160, roll 4, NARA.

54. Roosevelt to Goodrich, May 28, 1897, in Morison, *Letters of Roosevelt*, 617–18.

55. In May the Navy again refused to let Admiral Beardslee send any ships home for maintenance (Beardslee to Long, June 15, 1897, Area 9 File, RG 45, NARA).

56. Hatch to Dole, June 18, 1897, FO-Dole file, AH.

57. Foster, *Diplomatic Memoirs*, 2:172–73.

58. There is no indication in the Long, Roosevelt, Lodge, Sherman, Hitt, or Davis papers that any of them knew of it until June 9. Because Foster asked the Hawaiians for general suggestions for a draft treaty, Hatch said, "It was evident that he [Foster] knew more than he was at liberty to tell us" (Hatch to Dole, June 18, 1897, FO-Dole file, AH).

59. Cooper to Hatch, June 18, 1897, FO-EX, AH. Cooper and Sewall discussed the Japanese question several times after the minister's June 3 arrival. Cooper said, "He told me afterwards that Mr. McKinley had requested him to get this information and send it to him at once."

60. On May 29 the Navy Department ordered Beardslee to keep his entire flotilla in Hawai`i. Instead of sending the *Marion* to San Francisco for overhaul, temporary repairs were made in Honolulu. Beardslee to Long, June 15, 1897, Area 9 File, RG 45, NARA, refers to the May 29 order.

61. Thurston, *Memoirs of the Hawaiian Revolution*, 573.

62. Theodore Roosevelt, "To Be Prepared for War Is the Most Effectual Means to Promote Peace: Address of the Hon. Theodore Roosevelt before the Naval War College" (Washington, DC: Government Printing Office, 1897) 24, 5, 19, 6.

63. Long and Senator William P. Frye both declined to address the War College before Roosevelt was invited in late May. See Long to Goodrich, April 12 and May 17, 1897; and Long to John B. Herreshoff, May 27, 1897, Long Papers, Massachusetts Historical Society.

64. Goodrich to Stephen B. Luce, May 27, 1897, Luce Papers, LC. Goodrich had advance knowledge of the topic of the address.

65. Roosevelt to Goodrich, June 8, 1897, "Letters of the Assistant Secretary of the Navy," Official Correspondence, February–August 1897, entry 124, RG 80, NARA.

66. Mills to Sherman, no. 211, May 22, 1897, nos. 212, 213, May 24, 1897, "Despatches from Hawai`i," RG 59, T-30, roll 28, NARA. Endorsements on the faces of the three dispatches indicate that they arrived June 7 in Washington. Sewall arrived in Honolulu on June 3 and presented his credentials on June 7.

67. Mills to Sherman, no. 212, May 24, 1897, "Despatches from Hawai`i," RG 59, T-30, roll 28, NARA.

68. Ibid.

69. Mills to Sherman, no. 211, May 22, 1897, "Despatches from Hawai`i," RG 59, T-30, roll 28, NARA. For Akiyama's arrival and an analysis of his mission, see Mills to Sherman, May 5, 1897, ibid.; Beardslee to Long, May 5, 1897, Area 9 File, RG 45, NARA; and Wakukawa, *Japanese People in Hawai`i*, 93.

70. Mills to Sherman, no. 213, May 24, 1897, "Despatches from Hawai`i," RG 59, T-30, roll 28, NARA. Quote from George C. Potter, Secretary, Ministry of Foreign Affairs, to Charles Wilder, Hawaiian Consul General at San Francisco, May 27, 1897, HMW. In the note, Potter asks Wilder to wire the Shimamura quote to Hatch in Washington. Potter quotes Shimamura as saying that there is "no court where cases in International Law are tried; only tribunal is the strong arm and the strong vessel." See also the *Pacific Commercial Advertiser* (Honolulu), May 25, 1897, clipping in Sewall to Sherman, no. 3, June 20, 1897, RG 59, T-30, roll 29, NARA.

71. Cooper relayed gossip from an acquaintance, Chester Doyle, who spoke in Japanese with Akiyama. Doyle said Akiyama was tipsy and talkative. Akiyama supposedly said if Hawai`i refused compensation "the payment would be forced." Cooper recorded: "This conversation took place in the Japanese language and if I were a little more certain of its scope and authenticity I would be inclined to take the matter up here, but we have taken no further notice of it than to anticipate that perhaps Mr. Shimamura's instructions may go that extent" (Cooper to Hatch, May 22, 1897, HMW).

72. Mills to Sherman, no. 213, May 24, 1897, RG 59, T-30, roll 28, NARA.

73. See handwritten endorsement on Mills to Sherman, no. 213, May 24, 1897, RG 59, T-30, roll 28, NARA.

74. Roosevelt to Mahan, June 9, 1897, in Morison, *Letters of Roosevelt*, 622; Roosevelt to Goodrich, June 8, 1897, "Letters of the Assistant Secretary," entry 124, RG 80, NARA. Beginning with Thomas A. Bailey's article ("Japan's Protest against the Annexation of Hawai`i," *Journal of Modern History* 3 [1931]: 46–61), historians have noted the 1897 confrontation between Japan and the United States. Charles Neu (*The Troubled Encounter: The United States and Japan* [New York: John Wiley and Sons, 1975], 34–35), Iriye (*Pacific Estrangement*, 49–55), Russ (*Hawaiian Republic*, 130–77), and Campbell (*Transformation of American Foreign Relations*, 230–34), among others, noted a connection between American decision making and Japanese policy. The most comprehensive analysis is William Michael Morgan, "The Anti-Japanese Origins of the Hawaiian Annexation Treaty of 1897," *Diplomatic History* 6, no. 4 (1982), doi:10.1111/j.1467-7709.1982. tb00790.x.

75. George Frisbie Hoar, *Autobiography of Seventy Years*, 2 vols. (New York, 1903), 2:307–8.

76. Kinney to Dole, June 9, 1897, HMW. Kinney's overview of political developments shows that the Hawaiian Legation had no idea that a treaty was imminent. Hatch said he heard nothing about a treaty between early May, when Foster solicited their input for a draft, and June 11, when Day asked the commissioners to sign (Hatch to Dole, June 18, 1897, HMW).

77. Hatch to Cooper, June 9, 1897, HMW.

78. Day to Hatch, June 11, 1897; and Hatch to Dole, June 18, 1897, HMW.

79. Thomas Cridler to Hatch, two notes of June 15, 1897, HMW.

80. Long to Beardslee, June 10, 1897, "Confidential Letters Sent," vol. 2, page 316, entry 20, RG 45, NARA. This telegram has been overlooked by historians and has occasionally been confused with two similar telegrams sent in July. On July 10, 1897, Sherman sent Sewall in Honolulu a telegram similar to the one Long sent June 10, and Long himself sent another version to his naval commander. See Sherman to Sewall, July 10, 1897, "Instructions to Hawai`i," RG 59, M-77, roll 100, NARA.

81. Long to Beardslee, June 10, 1897, "Confidential Letters Sent," vol. 2, page 316, entry 20, RG 45, NARA.

82. Adee memorandum, June 9, 1897, "Notes from Japan," RG 59, M-163, roll 6, NARA.

83. Sherman to Hoshi, June 16, 1897, "Notes to Foreign Legations in the United States from the Department of State, 1834–1906," RG 59, M-99, roll 66, NARA.

84. Hatch to Dole, June 18, 1897, FO-Dole file, AH.

85. Hoshi to Sherman, June 15, 1897, printed in the *New York Times*, July 6, 1897.

86. Junesay Iddittie, *The Life of Marquis Shigenobu Ōkuma* (Tokyo: The Hokusei Press, 1956), 296.

87. Sketch of Hoshi drawn from "Hoshi Toru, National Diet Library Portraits of Modern Japanese Historical Figures," National Institute of Informatics, http://ci.nii.ac.jp/naid/110000273667/en/; Kawake Kisaburo, *Press and Politics in Japan* (Chicago: University of Chicago Press, 1921), 92–94, 127–28; and *New York Times*, June 6, 1896; July 6 and October 5, 1897; January 12 and September 8, 1898; November 22 and December 24, 1900; and June 22 and September 11, 1901.

88. Iddittie, *Life of Marquis Shigenobu Ōkuma*, 314.

89. Ōkuma described these instructions to the British chargé d'affaires. See Gerald Lowther to Lord Salisbury (Robert Cecil), no. 129, June 26, 1897, p. 102, FO 58/309.

90. Hatch to Cooper, May 17, 1897, HMW. Hatch also said, "If, however, the Japanese representatives follow any extreme course of action in Honolulu that would undoubtedly help annexation along; mere recital of the facts without comment would be all that is necessary."

91. Hatch to Cooper, June 9, 1897, HMW.

92. Cooper thought that, despite Japanese warships in Hawai`i, "everything points to a satisfactory and peaceful settlement" (Cooper to Peter Denniston, June 2, 1897, Foreign Office Letter Books, vol. 78, AH). From Yokohama, Eldridge wrote that "better counsels and cooler heads are prevailing." In late May, Eldridge reported that "intense irritation" with the proposed Dingley tariff provisions, which Japan thought aimed squarely at it, diverted attention from Hawai`i (Eldridge to Cooper, May 4 and May 21, 1897, "Hawaiian Officials Abroad—Consul at Yokohama," FO-EX, AH).

93. Hoshi to Ōkuma, June 17, 1897, *Nihon Gaiko Bunsho* (Japanese Diplomatic Documents), U.S.-Hawai`i Annexation, vol. 22, 978; Iddittie, *Life of Marquis Shigenobu Ōkuma,* 298; John J. Stephan, *Hawai`i under the Rising Sun* (Honolulu: University of Hawai`i Press, 1984), 18–19.

94. Roosevelt to Day, June 15, 1897, Box 7, Day Papers, LC; and Roosevelt to Caspar Goodrich, June 16, 1897, in Morison, *Letters of Roosevelt*, 626.

95. Roosevelt to Long, June 23, 1897, in Morison, *Letters of Roosevelt*, 631.

96. Ōkuma to Hoshi, June 19, 1897, *Nihon Gaiko Bunsho* (Japanese Diplomatic Documents), U.S.-Hawai`i Annexation, vol. 22, 985–86; Iddittie, *Life of Marquis Shigenobu Ōkuma,* 298.

97. Lowther to Salisbury, no. 129, June 26, 1897, p. 102, FO 58/309.

98. FO memo (written by Thomas Sanderson) for Salisbury, April 11, 1897, p. 30; FO to Kato, May 17, 1897, p. 33; Pauncefote to Salisbury, June 21, 1897, p. 70, all in FO 58/309.

99. Hoshi to Sherman, June 19, 1897, "Notes From Japan." Also printed in the *New York Times*, July 6, 1897.

100. Roosevelt to Long, June 28, 1897, Letters of the Assistant Secretary of the Navy, February–August 1897, Entry 124, RG 80, NARA. Because telegraph nodes were high priority targets, Roosevelt also directed the *Marion* to ascertain the landing points of any undersea telegraph cables between O`ahu and the other Hawaiian islands. Roosevelt apparently did not know that no interisland cables existed (Roosevelt to Commanding Officer, USS *Marion*, June 25, 1897, Entry 61, RG 24).

101. "Plans of Campaign Against Spain and Japan," War Portfolios, file 425, Subject File, Records of the General Board of the Navy, Operational Archives, Naval History Division, Washington Navy Yard, Washington, DC. See also Roosevelt to Goodrich, June 16, 1897, in Morison, *Letters of Roosevelt*, 626: "Although there doesn't seem any immediate likelihood of trouble with Japan at present, still I have been studying your letter in connection with a possible Japanese problem with very great interest.... The determining factor in any war with Japan would be the control of the sea, and not the presence of troops in Hawai`i. If we smash the Japanese Navy, definitely and thoroughly, then the presence of a Japanese army corps in Hawai`i would merely mean the establishment of Hawai`i as a half-way post for that army corps on its way to our prisons. If we didn't get control of the seas then no troops that we would be able to land could hold Hawai`i against the Japanese. In other words, I think our objective should be the Japanese fleet."

102. George E. Belknap, "Address at Naval War College, July 1897," C-2, Belknap Papers, LC.

103. Roosevelt to the Secretary of State, July 1, 1897, Entry 61, RG 24. The *Fuji* and the *Yashima* were Japan's first two battleships, built in Britain. Mahan had mentioned to Roosevelt in May 1897 that the *Fuji* and the *Yashima* were nearing completion. The warships compared favorably with America's three modern battleships, the *Indiana* and the *Massachusetts*, completed on the East Coast, and the *Oregon*, built in San Francisco. The *Maine* and the *Texas* were second-class battleships.

104. Sherman to Hoshi, June 25, 1897, enclosed in Sherman to Sewall, June 26, 1897, Instructions to Hawai`i, RG 59, M-77, roll 100, NARA.

105. Long to Roosevelt, July 3, 1897, Long Papers, Massachusetts Historical Society.

106. Sewall to Sherman, no. 3, June 20, 1897, RG 59, T-30, roll 29, NARA. Marginal notes show this message was received July 3 but not read by Long until at least July 6, when Alvey Adee suggested McKinley ought to see it, or likely July 7 or 8. Quote from Sewall to Sherman, June 24, 1887, RG 59, T-30, roll 29, NARA.

107. Hoshi to Sherman, July 10, 1897, enclosed in Day to Sewall, July 17, 1897, Instructions to Hawai`i, RG 59, M-77, roll 100, NARA .

108. Long to Commander in Chief, Pacific Squadron, July 12, 1897, "Confidential Letters Sent," vol. 2, p. 314–15, Entry 20, RG 45; Sherman to Sewall, cipher telegram, July 10, 1897, RG 59, M-77, roll 100, NARA. The orders said a Japanese landing "is not expected, and you will use the greatest discretion and caution in your activities and conversation not to precipitate it, and not act except in the face of overt hostility on the part of the Japanese." Day told Sewall that the dispatch of July 10 was sent "more as an act of abundant caution than any belief that the suggested emergency was likely to occur." Adee used nearly the same language two weeks later (Day to Sewall, July 17; Adee to Sewall, August 4, 1897, RG 59, M-77, roll 100, NARA).

109. William A. Russ wrongly argues that Day and Adee tried to undo Sherman's July 10 warning order on the grounds that the secretary, "enfeebled by age and long service, was unduly alarmed" (*Hawaiian Republic*, 162). Long sent nearly identical orders on June 10 and July 12, so Sherman's cable was not an aberration.

110. *Japan Times*, quoted in *Literary Digest* 15, no. 9 (May 22, 1897): 114.

111. *Mainichi Shimbun*, quoted in *Literary Digest* 15, no. 9 (June 1897): 262–63.

112. N. W. McIvor (Consul General at Yokohama) to Day, Aug 19, 1897, Day Papers, LC.

113. Robert Erwin Johnson, *Far China Station: The U.S. Navy in Asian Waters, 1800–1898* (Annapolis, MD: Naval Institute Press, 1979), 255–56.

114. Long to CO USS *Oregon* (in San Francisco), July 13, 1897, "Confidential Letters Sent," vol. 2, page 317, Entry 20, RG 45, NARA.

115. Long to McNair (in Yokohama), July 14, 1897, Translations of Cipher Messages," Entry 19, RG 45, NARA. Long's message was sent just after the arrival of another alarming message from Sewall (Sewall to Sherman, June 29, 1897 [received July 14], T-30, roll 29, NARA).

116. Long to Commander in Chief, Pacific Squadron, July 20, 1897, "Confidential Letters Sent," vol. 2, page 318, Entry 20, RG 45, NARA.

117. Admiral Merrill Miller to Long, August 25, 1897, M-625, roll 317, NARA. Long also ordered a strategic survey of Pearl River Lagoon, to include the amount and probable cost of the land necessary to build a major naval base. Completed in early 1898, the survey was

forwarded to Long just before the outbreak of war with Spain (Long to Beardslee, July 28, 1897, and Long to Miller, March 19, 1898, "Letters to Stations," Entry 59, RG 45, NARA).

118. Roosevelt messaged the captains of the *Petrel*, May 5, 1897, the *Yorktown*, September 4, 1897, the *Philadelphia*, September 20, 1897, the *Olympia*, October 8, 1897, the *Philadelphia*, October 20, 1897, the *Machias*, December 11, 1897, and the *Baltimore*, January 24, 1898. He also cabled Admiral Dewey, February 28, 1897; "Departmental Letters," Entry 61, RG 24, NARA.

119. Roosevelt to the captains of the *Philadelphia*, September 20, 1897, and the *San Francisco*, October 7, 1897, "Departmental Letters," Entry 61, RG 24, NARA. Assistant Secretary of the Navy William McAdoo had previously obtained reports on the *Naniwa*, the protected cruiser *Suma*, and the torpedo boat *Tatsuda*. See McAdoo to the captain of the *Olympia*, October 27 and November 4, 1896, "Departmental Letters," Entry 61, RG 24, NARA.

120. Roosevelt to Mare Island Navy Yard, September 20, 21, 22, and 23, 1897, "Translations of Cipher Messages," Entry 19, RG 45, NARA. The quote is from the September 21 message. See also Admiral Miller to Long, September 4 and 13, 1897, M-625, roll 317, NARA. The Navy received the September 4 message on September 20. See also Sewall to Sherman, no. 35, September 4, 1897, T-30, roll 29, NARA.

121. Roosevelt to Mare Island Navy Yard, September 29, 1897, "Translations of Cipher Messages," Entry 19, RG 45, NARA. This order was likely spurred by an earlier message from the *Oregon* mentioning that the presence of Japanese stewards would be "very undesirable should there be any trouble with Japan" (Barker to Long, July 22, 1897, M-625, roll 317, NARA). For the *Yorktown* order, see McNair to SecNav, September 22, 1897, "Translations of Cipher Messages," entry 19, RG 45, NARA. The *Naniwa* departed September 7, 1897, according to the *Yamato Shimbun* of that date.

122. Roosevelt to Lodge, August 3, 1897, Morison, *Letters*, 1:637–38. Roosevelt said Long thought the speech was too inflammatory and "he gave me as heavy a wigging as his invariable courtesy and kindness would permit." For the speech, see the *New York Tribune*, July 27, 1897.

123. Roosevelt to Lodge, September 15, 1897; Roosevelt to James Harrison Wilson, September 15, 1897; Roosevelt to Lodge, September 21, 1897; and Roosevelt to W. W. Kimball, September 22, 1897, all in Morison, *Letters of Roosevelt*, 676–85. See also Roosevelt to Admiral Kirkland, September 21, 1897, "Confidential Letters Sent," vol. 2, page 322, Entry 20, RG 45, NARA.

124. Sherman to Hoshi, August 14, 1897, "Notes to Japan," RG 59, NARA.

125. *Philadelphia Press*, August 19, 1897, clipping in Sherman Papers, LC.

126. Seddon to Joseph Chamberlain, June 23, p. 136; July 30, 1897, p. 218; FO draft reply to Seddon, August 1897, p. 222, all in FO 58/309. The final version simply said the United States would not tolerate interference.

127. Colonial Office memo attached to Seddon to Chamberlain, June 23 and July 30, 1897, FO 58/309.

128. Lowther to Salisbury, no. 143, July 10, 1897, p. 154, 156, FO 58/309.

129. Satow letter of November 25, 1897, quoted in Ruxton, ed., *Semi-Official Letters*, 88.

130. "Permitted Memo of Asiatic Labor for 1897," Board of Immigration records, AH. Photocopy in author's possession. In its early 1897 meetings, the Board of Immigration meetings stuck closely to the hard-line formula of two Chinese per Japanese in preauthorizing contracts for 1,585 Chinese and 725 Japanese. After Japan's protest, 1,298 Japanese were approved but no Chinese.

131. Irwin to Cooper, January 26, 1898, HMW.

132. Russ, *Hawaiian Republic*, 146–177; and Bailey, "Japan's Protest," 46–61.

133. In *The Nation Within*, Tom Coffman charges that Hawai`i provoked the crisis with Japan to push the United States into annexation. He argues that the huge increase in Japanese immigrants immediately after annexation shows that fear of immigration was a phony pretext. At least four factors disprove Coffman's contention. First, Hawai`i did not invent the immigration issue in 1897 but struggled to control the inflow for years, even during the hostile Cleveland administration. Second, annexation dramatically changed the context for immigration. With American ownership, which no one imagined could ever be challenged, immigration, even voting rights for Asians, presented no threat to political control. The islands would never become a Japanese colony. Therefore, immigration was no longer threatening. Third, because the Newlands resolution forbade Chinese immigration, many more Japanese were needed in the short term. Finally, a spur to increased Japanese immigration was the fear that Congress would ban Japanese as well as Chinese when writing laws organizing Hawai`i as a territory. This is why Hawaiian officials vainly sought, as part of treaty negotiations with John Watson Foster in the spring of 1897, exemption from U.S. restraints on Asian immigration to preserve plantation labor supplies.

134. Pauncefote to Salisbury, no. 186, June 18, 1897, p. 48, FO 58/309.

Chapter 15. Annexation Consummated: The Spanish-American War and Hawai`i

1.   Sketch drawn from clippings in the Hitt Papers (LC) and from Clark, *My Quarter Century*; Offenberg, "Political Career of Thomas Brackett Reed"; Henry Cabot Lodge, "Thomas Brackett Reed," manuscript in the Lodge Papers, Massachusetts Historical Society; Robert L. Beisner, *Twelve against Empire: The Anti-Imperialists, 1898–1900* (New York: McGraw, 1968), 203–11; and Tuchman, *Proud Tower*, ch. 3.

2.   Quoted in Tuchman, *Proud Tower*, 118, 130.

3. Albert Shaw, "Empire Can Wait: Speaker Reed's View of Annexation," *Review of Reviews* 17 (January–June 1898), 77–78. This is a commentary on Reed's December 1897 article in *The Illustrated American.*

4. Tuchman, *Proud Tower,* 117.

5. Clark, *My Quarter Century,* 282.

6. Davis to Kellogg, December 11, 16, and 27, 1897; and June 30, 1898, Davis Papers, Minnesota Historical Society.

7. Clippings in scrapbooks in the Hitt Papers, LC. The one contrary account comes from Barbara Tuchman, *Proud Tower,* 141: "With no favorites and no near rivals, he [Reed] ruled alone. Careful not to excite jealousy, he avoided even walking in public with a member."

8. *New York Herald,* November 26, 1897, clipping attached on p. 329, FO 58/309.

9. *New York Tribune,* December 16 and November 19, 1897.

10. Hatch to Cooper, June 18, 1897, HMW.

11. Davis to Lodge, September 25, 1897, Lodge Papers, Massachusetts Historical Society.

12. Davis to Kellogg, December 11, 16, 1897, Davis Papers, Minnesota Historical Society.

13. *Washington Times,* November 28, 1897. Hitt saw McKinley three times the previous week.

14. Roosevelt to McKinley, January 19, 1898, Roosevelt Papers, LC; and Roosevelt to Mahan, December 13, 1897, *Letters and Papers of Alfred Thayer Mahan,* 1:741–43.

15. Roosevelt to William Laffan [*Sun* editor], December 13, 1897, Roosevelt Papers, LC.

16. Roosevelt to William Chanler, December 23, 1897, in Morison, *Letters of Roosevelt,* 746–47; and Roosevelt to Speck von Sternberg, January 17, 1898, in ibid., 763.

17. *Washington Post,* February 27, 1898; and *The Nation* 66 (February 1898): 80.

18. George Frisbie Hoar, *Autobiography of Seventy Years,* 2 vols. (New York: Charles Scribner's Sons, 1903), 2:307–8.

19. *Washington Evening Star,* January 12, 1898.

20. Davis to Kellogg and Severance, December 27 and 16, 1897, Davis Papers, Minnesota Historical Society.

21. John Addison Porter to Hitt, January 25, 1898, Hitt Papers, LC; Damon, *Dole and His Hawai`i,* 321.

22. *Washington Post,* January 31, 1898.

23. *Journal of the Executive Proceedings of the Senate,* 31 (55th Cong.), Part One, 465, 470, 485, 489, 495, 500, 502.

24. *New York Tribune,* January 12 and 13, 1898.

25. Davis to Kellogg and Severance, December 27, 1897, Davis Papers, Minnesota Historical Society.

26. *New York Tribune,* January 19, 1898.

27. *Chicago Evening Post,* January 29, 31, 1898, clippings in Hitt Papers, LC.

28. "Address before the Commercial Club of Boston," February 19, 1898, Belknap Papers, LC.

29. *New York Times*, January 15, 1898; and *New York Tribune*, January 15, 1898. The Senate Web site lists (for the 55th Congress) 44 Republicans, 5 Silver Republicans, 34 Democrats, 5 Populists, and 2 Silver Party.

30. Pauncefote to Salisbury, no. 23, February 3, 1898, FO 58/319; and Hatch to Cooper, January 21, 1898, HMW.

31. Presented to senators Hoar and Pettigrew in December 1897, the petitions were discussed by the Senate. As we have seen, numerous surveys showed no annexationists changed sides after mid-1897.

32. *Washington Post*, January 8, 1898.

33. Smith to Cooper, March 26, 1897, HMW.

34. *New York Tribune*, February 2, 1898.

35. *Washington Post*, February 7, 1898; and Hatch to Cooper, February 6 and 10, 1898, HMW.

36. Hatch to Cooper, February 18 and March 2, 3, and 6, 1898, HMW; Davis to Whitelaw Reid, March 12, 1898, Davis Papers, Minnesota Historical Society; and Pauncefote to Salisbury, no. 71, March 17, 1898, p. 12, FO 58/319.

37. Hatch to Cooper, February 25, 18, 1898, HMW; and *New York Times*, March 14, 1898.

38. Foster, *Diplomatic Memoirs*, 2:173.

39. Osborne, *Annexation Hawai`i*, 107.

40. Hatch to Cooper, March 2, 3, and 6, 1898, HMW; Hatch to Dole, March 6, 1898, cited by Tate, *U.S. and Hawaiian Kingdom*, 293; Davis to Kellogg, December 11 and 16, 1897, Davis Papers, Minnesota Historical Society.

41. *Journal of the United States Senate*, 55th Cong., 2nd sess., 164; and Davis Rpt.

42. Davis Rpt, 31, 37. See also appendix 6 (113–16), a reprint of a January 7, 1893, article from the *Commercial Advertiser*.

43. Davis Rpt, 61.

44. Ibid., 98.

45. Ibid., 30–31, 99.

46. Ibid., 100, 98.

47. "Very Confidential from British Ambassador," received March 8, 1898; the reply is an undated memorandum with the notation "The above was read to Sir Julian Pauncefote on March 16, 1898, by direction of the President. [Signed] Day" (both in Day Papers, LC).

48. *Cong. Rec.*, 55th Cong., 2nd sess. (1898), 2917. See also 3880, 3892, 3977.

49. Roosevelt to Mahan, March 21, 1898, Morison, *Letters of Roosevelt*, 797.

50. Hatch to Cooper, March 26 and May 13, 1898, HMW.

51. Davis to Lodge, April 3, 1898, Lodge Papers, Massachusetts Historical Society; and Davis to Kellogg, April 14, 1898, Davis Papers, Minnesota Historical Society.

52. Hatch to Cooper, April 28, May 4, 1898, HMW.

53. Herrick, *American Naval Revolution*, 223–25; and Roosevelt to Mahan, March 14, 1898, quoted in Morison, *Letters of Roosevelt*, 793–94.

54. *Cong. Rec.*, 55th Cong., 2nd sess. (1898), 3179, 3188–89, 3191, 3197–3200, 3223, 3477.

55. Campbell, *Transformation of American Foreign Relations*, 280–82. Official confirmation arrived May 7.

56. *Cong. Rec.*, 55th Cong., 2nd sess. (1898), 4600.

57. Russ, *Hawaiian Republic*, 300. Minister Hatch claimed a "very dangerous state of luke-warmness in regard to annexation" in a rant protesting the rejection of his weird suggestion that Hawai`i should proclaim neutrality if war broke out to give McKinley an excuse to occupy the islands to protect them from Spain (Hatch to Cooper, April 14, 1898, HMW). Cooper wrote that officials in Honolulu believed it better to remain silent than to declare neutrality, which might insult the United States. Cooper's argument was sound. Hatch was simply venting his displeasure about the rejection of his idea. In previous and subse-quent correspondence, he never mentioned "lukewarmness." Just two weeks before, he told Cooper that he was more confident of eventual annexation than at any time since the opening of Congress (Hatch to Cooper, March 26, 1898, HMW).

58. Russ, *Hawaiian Republic*, 288–91.

59. Sewall to Day, June 8, 1898, "Despatches"; and Albertine Loomis, "Summer of 1898," *Hawaiian Journal of History* 13 (1979): 94–98.

60. Hawaiian *Star*, June 16, 1898, quoted in Russ, *Hawaiian Republic*, 292.

61. Hatch to Cooper, May 13, 1898, HMW.

62. *New York Times*, May 31, 1898.

63. Hatch to Cooper, May 13 and 26, 1898, HMW.

64. House Report no. 1355, "Annexation of the Hawaiian Islands," *Cong. Rec.*, 55th Cong., 2nd sess. (May 17, 1898).

65. Ibid., 2–4, 13.

66. FO internal memo, August 5, 1897, p. 191; FO internal memo, August 6, 1897, p. 204; FO draft reply to German ambassador, August 1897, p. 208; FO internal memo, August 9, 1897, p. 202; and Colonial Office memo to FO, August 24, 1897, p. 243, all in FO 58/309.

67. Hay to Day, May 3 and 9, 1898, Day Papers, LC. See also Osborne, *Annexation Hawai`i*, 125–26.

68. *New York Tribune*, May 15 and 29, and June 2, 1898.

69. *Chicago Chronicle*, May 20, 1898; *Rockford (IL) Republic*, May 20, 1898; and *New York Tribune*, May 17, 1898.

70. *Chicago Inter-Ocean*, May 20, 1898, clipping in Hitt Papers, LC.

71. Day and Hitt were reacting to John Tyler Morgan's warning to McKinley about Democrat Alexander Dockery's proposal to defer annexation until after the war. Morgan complained: "If Mr. Reed can find a footing on this pretext, the annexation of Hawai`i will never be

accomplished" (Morgan to McKinley, May 23, 1898, enclosed in John Addison Porter to Day, May 23, 1898, Day Papers, LC). Morgan was flat wrong that McKinley faced a choice among annexation, occupation, or abandoning use of Hawai`i. There was a fourth option: continue to resupply via the islands. Dockery eventually voted for the joint resolution. At a private dinner, Day and Hitt discussed whether threatening executive action might convince Reed to bow to the inevitable (*New York Tribune*, June 5, 1898; and Sallie R. Hitt to Day, May 23, 1898, Day Papers, LC). It is very doubtful that Day and Hitt pressured Reed in this fashion, for the speaker knew that the Navy was using Hawai`i freely and that nothing would stop that use.

72. *New York Sun*, June 2, 1898; Thurston, *Memoirs of the Hawaiian Revolution*, 578. Quote from *Washington Evening Star*, May 31, 1898. For Reed's final capitulation, see *Cong. Rec.*, 55th Cong., 2nd sess. (1898), 5646, 5760–61, 5765–66.

73. George Lyman to Lodge, June 9, 1898, Lodge Papers, Massachusetts Historical Society.

74. Hatch to Cooper, June 12, 1898, HMW.

75. The best analysis of the debates is Osborne, *Annexation Hawai`i*. Osborne scrutinized the debates and concluded that commercial not strategic factors were the main reason for annexation (p. 127). While my interpretation is the reverse, Osborne's well-argued and comprehensive analysis of the debates is the best we have. I simply give less weight to the Asian trade argument. I agree completely with Osborne's main premise that the anti-annexationist movement was "based upon a reverence for America's republican tradition and an inveterate hostility to colonialism." See also Thomas J. Osborne, "Trade or War? America's Annexation of Hawai`i Reconsidered," *Pacific Historical Review* 50 (August 1981): 285–307.

76. *New York Sun*, June 12, 1898.

77. *Cong. Rec.*, 55th Cong., 2nd sess. (1898), 5771.

78. Ibid., 5772.

79. Ibid., 5916.

80. Ibid., 5989.

81. Ibid., 5785.

82. Ibid., 5916, 5835, 5897, 5927, 5931; appendix, 665.

83. Hitt's speech and the related debate are in ibid., 5770–776. For mention of the military strategists and the security argument, see ibid., 5785, 5795, 5828–30, 5838–40, 5872, 5895, 5903, 5915–20, 5928, 5931, 5983, 5988, 5990, 6003.

84. In particular, see ibid., 5775, 5830–31, 5894–97, 5706–7, 5917, 5931.

85. Ibid., 5773–74, 5786, 5930–31. Selected comments regarding the Japan threat are found in ibid., 5773–74, 5785–86, 5828–30, 5839, 5895–97, 5706–7, 5917, 5981.

86. Ibid., 5829. The Imperial Japanese Navy was superior to the American Navy in the Pacific but roughly equal overall.

87. Ibid., appendix, 656–57.
88. Ibid., appendix, 656, 660.
89. Ibid., 5911.
90. Ibid., 5915, 5918.
91. Ibid., 5931.
92. Ibid., 5879.
93. Ibid., 5927.
94. Ibid., 5990.
95. Ibid., 5892.
96. Ibid., 6003.
97. Honolulu, Records of Foreign Service Posts of the United States, RG 84, NARA (January 1, 1897 through June 30, 1898). The legation, headed by the minister and located in a different building, handled diplomatic and political matters. The consul-general handled the rest of the correspondence and purely consular matters.
98. *Chicago Record*, May 20, 1898, clipping in Hitt Papers, LC.
99. *Cong. Rec.*, 55th Cong., 2nd sess. (1898), 5828, 5830, 6708.
100. The four were Hugh Dinsmore, who, as Hitt's counterpart, would lead the antiannexationists in the deliberations, Champ Clark, John Sharp Williams, and William Howard (*House Reports*, 55th Cong. 2nd sess., no. 1355, part 2, "Views of the Minority," May 17, 1898).
101. Osborne, *Annexation Hawai`i*, 135. While Osborne's work is the most detailed and persuasive account of the antiannexationists, and it has significant implications for the broader anti-imperialist movement, the standard work for that movement is still Beisner, *Twelve against Empire*.
102. *Cong. Rec.*, 55th Cong., 2nd sess. (1898), 6018–19.
103. Ibid.; Margaret Leech, *In the Days of McKinley* (New York: Harper and Brothers, 1959), 212–13; and Beisner, *Twelve against Empire*, 208.
104. Davis believed several senators apparently had made a secret deal to postpone annexation if other senators agreed to pass the war revenue bills quickly in March and April 1898 (Davis to Kellogg and Severance, June 24, 1898, Davis Papers, Minnesota Historical Society).
105. *Cong. Rec.*, 55th Cong., 2nd sess. (1898), 6018.
106. Ibid., 1024ff; and Snowbarger, "Development of Pearl Harbor," 361–69.
107. *Cong. Rec.*, 55th Cong., 2nd sess. (1898), 6707–8.
108. Davis to Kellogg and Severance, June 24, 30, 1898, Davis Papers, Minnesota Historical Society; Lodge to John Hay, and to W. Murray Crane, both June 18, 1898, Lodge Papers, Massachusetts Historical Society; and Lodge to William Chandler, June 18, 1898, Chandler Papers, LC.
109. Hatch to Cooper, July 1, 1898, HMW.

110. For the final vote, see *Cong. Rec.*, 55th Cong., 2nd sess. (1898), 6712. Of the 26 senators not voting, 14 were yeas and 12 nays. There was one vacancy (Oregon) about to be filled with a Republican. The two Silver Republicans supported annexation and are counted with the Republican votes. Senator Richard Kenney of Delaware, a Democrat, was not present and no one claimed a pair with him. See also "Political Complexion of the Senate," memorandum of June 22, 1898, Day Papers, LC.

Conclusion: Local Power, Eclectic Imperialism, Enhanced Security

1.   See chapter 14, note 133, for a discussion.

Selected Bibliography

Unpublished Papers

Alvey Adee Papers. Library of Congress.
Albert Barker Papers. Naval Historical Foundation, Washington Navy Yard.
George Belknap Papers. Library of Congress.
William Chandler Papers. Library of Congress.
Grover Cleveland Papers. Library of Congress.
Henry Cooper Papers. State Archives of Hawai`i.
Cushman Davis Papers. Minnesota Historical Society.
William Day Papers. Library of Congress.
Sanford Dole Papers. State Archives of Hawai`i.
Joseph Dolph Papers. Oregon Historical Society.
John Watson Foster Papers. Library of Congress.
Walter Q. Gresham Papers. Library of Congress.
Benjamin Harrison Papers. Library of Congress.
Alfred Hartwell Papers. State Archives of Hawai`i.
Francis Hatch Papers. State Archives of Hawai`i.
Robert Hitt Papers. Library of Congress.
Lili`uokalani Diary. University of Hawai`i.
Henry Cabot Lodge Papers. Massachusetts Historical Society.
John D. Long Papers. Massachusetts Historical Society.
Stephen Luce Papers. Library of Congress.
William McKinley Papers. Library of Congress.
John Bassett Moore Papers. Library of Congress.

John Tyler Morgan Papers. Library of Congress.

Richard Olney Papers. Library of Congress.

Whitelaw Reid Papers. Library of Congress.

Theodore Roosevelt Papers. Library of Congress.

Carl Schurz Papers, Library of Congress.

John Sherman Papers. Library of Congress.

William O. Smith Papers. State Archives of Hawai`i.

Lorrin Thurston Papers. State Archives of Hawai`i.

John G. Walker Papers. Library of Congress.

John G. Walker Papers. Naval Historical Center, Washington Navy Yard.

Unpublished U.S. Government Records in the National Archives

Record Group 24, Records of the Bureau of Naval Personnel

Logs of Ships and Stations, 1801–1946, Logs of U.S. Naval Ships, 1801–1915
Logs of the *Adams*
Logs of the *Boston*
Logs of the *Philadelphia*

Records of the Bureau of Navigation
Entry 55, "Letters to Commandants of Navy Yards and Stations"
Entry 57, "Letters to Officers Commanding Squadrons and Vessels"
Entry 59, "Letters to Stations and Squadrons and Shore Establishments"
Entry 60, "Letters to Ships"
Entry 61, "Departmental Letters"

Record Group 37, Cartographic Records of the United States Naval Hydrographic Office
Record Group 38, Records of the Chief of Naval Operations

Records of the Deputy Chief of Naval Operations
Entry 38, "Letters Received by the Office of Naval Intelligence"
Entry 90, "Letters from Naval Attaches"
Naval Attache Reports

Record Group 45, Naval Records Collection of the Office of Naval Records and Library

Records of the Naval War Board, 1898
Entry 194, "Naval War Board Correspondence, 1898"
Entry 370, "Letters Sent by Captain Albert S. Barker, 1898"
Entry 371, "Letters and Telegrams Sent by the Naval War Board, 1898"
Entry 372, "Letters and Telegrams Sent by the Strategy Board, 1898"

Records of the Secretary of the Navy
Entry 19, "Translations of Cipher *Messages* Sent"
Entry 20, "Confidential Letters"
Entry 40, "Translations of Cipher Messages Received"

Subject File, 1763–1910
Area Files
Area 9 (Eastern Pacific) file, 1887–1898
Area 10 (Western Pacific) file, 1887–1898

Record Group 59, General Records of the Department of State (microcopy number in parentheses)

Despatches from United States Consuls in Honolulu, Hawai`i, 1820–1903 (M-144)
Despatches from United States Ministers in Hawai`i, 1843–1900 (T-30)
Despatches from United States Ministers to Great Britain, 1791–1906 (M-30)
Despatches from United States Ministers to Japan, 1855–1910 (M-133)
Diplomatic Instructions of the Department of State (M-77)
Entry 872, "Miscellaneous Memoranda of Conversations with the Secretary of State"
Japan: Kanagawa—Consular Despatches, 1861–1897 (M-135)
Japan: Nagasaki—Consular Despatches, 1860–1906 (M-131)
Japan: Yokohama—Consular Despatches, 1860–1906 (M-136)
Notes from the Hawaiian Legation in the United States to the Department of State, 1841–1899 (T-160)
Notes to Foreign Legations in the United States from the Department of State, 1834–1906 (M-99)

Record Group 80, General Records of the Department of the Navy

Records of the Assistant Secretary of the Navy
Entry 124, "Letters of the Assistant Secretary"

Record Group 84, Records of the Foreign Service Posts of the Department of State

Records of the United States Consular Post, Honolulu
Entry 1, "Despatches to the Department of State"
Entry 3, "Miscellaneous Letters Sent"
Entry 4, "Miscellaneous Letters Received"

Unpublished Government Records in the Washington Navy Yard (Naval History Division, Operational Archives, Washington Navy Yard, Washington, DC)

Records of the General Board of the Navy

General Board Studies
"Coaling Station in Aleutian Islands" (33-03, 11-438, November 25, 1903)
"Development of Pearl Harbor as a Naval Station" (28-04, 111-228, September 29, 1904)
"Hilo vs. Pearl Harbor as a Naval Station" (5-04, 111-30, February 17, 1904)
"Naval Bases for Defense of Panama Canal" (29-04, 111-236, September 29, 1904)

Historical Reference (Z) Files, ZE (Places) subfile
Hawai`i folder
Japan folder

Subject File
403—Coast and Harbor Defense
404—Naval Stations
415—Surveys
425—War Plans
429—Harbors

Unpublished Records in the State Archives of Hawai`i

Foreign and Executive Files, 1893–1898

Council of State, Republic of Hawai`i
Minutes, 1895–1900
President's Letters, 1894–1900

Diplomatic Representatives, Warships, etc., 1878–1898
Executive and Advisory Councils, 1893, 1897, 1898
Annexation, 1893
Military Reports, 1893

Executive and Advisory Council, Provisional Government and Republic
Letter Books, 1893–1895
Minutes, 1893–1895
Proceedings, 1893–1894

Executive Council, Provisional Government and Republic
Letter Books, 1893–1900
Minutes, 1893–1900.

Foreign Officials in Hawai`i
Consul General for Japan, 1893, 1894, 1897
British Commissioner, 1893, 1897
U.S. Minister and Consuls, 1893–1898

Hawaiian Officials Abroad, 1893–1898
Consul at Nagasaki, 1897
Files of Hawaiian Minister and Commissioners in Washington, 1893
    (files originally maintained in Washington)
Hawaiian Minister at Washington, letters sent, 1893
Hawaiian (Treaty) Commissioners at Washington, letters sent, 1893
Immigration, 1893, 1897
Minister at Tokyo, 1897, 1898
Minister at Washington, 1893–1898
Vice Consul at Kobe, 1897

Letters from Foreign Agents at Home and Hawaiian Minister's Agents Abroad
Hawaiian Legation at Washington, 1885–1897

Miscellaneous Foreign Correspondence, 1897
Numbered Miscellaneous and Consular Books
No. 12–Japan, diplomatic and miscellaneous, 1873–1900
No. 19–Hawaiian Legation, Washington, 1873–1887, v. 1
No. 20–Hawaiian Legation, Washington, 1888–1898, v. 2
No. 31–Correspondence with Japanese Minister, 1869–1900

Pacific Cable, 1897
President's File, 1894–98
Correspondence, 1898
Mainland trip clips

Unpublished Records in the U.K. National Archives, Kew

Foreign Office Records

FO 46: Japan: General Correspondence
FO 46/482   Japan: Diplomatic, January–March 12, 1897
FO 46/483   Japan: Diplomatic, March 12–May, 1897
FO 46/484   Japan: Diplomatic, June–September 21, 1897
FO 46/486   Japan: Diplomatic telegrams and paraphrases, 1897

FO 58: General Correspondence, Pacific Islands
FO 58/258   Hawai`i, 1891
FO 58/259   Hawai`i, 1891–92
FO 58/263   Hawai`i, 1892
FO 58/270   Hawai`i, 1893
FO 58/279   Hawai`i, 1893
FO 58/288   Hawai`i, 1894
FO 58/304   Hawai`i, 1895–96
FO 58/309   Hawai`i, 1897
FO 58/319   Hawai`i, 1898

FO 115   United States of America: General Correspondence
FO 115/914   United States, August–September 1892
FO 881   Japan: Confidential Print
FO 881/6970X   Report on Japan's 1896 naval budget

Published U.S. Government Documents

Foreign Relations of the United States, 1894, Appendix II, "Affairs in Hawai`i" (1895).

House Executive Document no. 1, part 1, *Cong. Rec.,* 53rd Cong., 3rd sess. (1895). Contains the Blount Report as well as other Senate and House documents.

House Executive Document no. 47, *Cong. Rec.,* 53rd Cong., 2nd sess. (1893). The Blount Report. (This is reprinted in the Morgan Report, vol. 2, 1251–1958.)

House Executive Document no. 48, *Cong. Rec.,* 53rd Cong., 2nd sess. (1894).

House Executive Document no. 282, *Cong. Rec.,* 53rd Cong., 3rd sess. (1895).

House Report no. 1355, "Annexation of the Hawaiian Islands," *Cong. Rec.,* 55th Cong., 2nd sess. (May 17, 1898). The Hitt Report.

Senate Report no. 227, *Cong. Rec.,* 53rd Cong., 2nd sess. (1894). The Morgan Report.

Senate Report, no. 336, *Cong. Rec.,* 54th Cong., 1st sess. (February 16, 1896).

Senate Report no. 681, "Annexation of Hawai`i," *Cong. Rec.,* 55th Cong., 2nd sess. (March 16, 1898). The Davis Report.

Senate Report no. 1265, "Nicaragua Canal," *Cong. Rec.,* 55th Cong., 2nd sess. (June 20, 1898).

Index

coastal security: fears of Cervera compel Navy to divert warships from Caribbean, 165–66, 169; German war planning against the United States illustrates recoaling problem, 167–68; Hawai`i's strategic value as main cause of annexation, 161, 236, 238–39; linkage of naval expansion and port fortification, 161–66; raids versus invasion, 167–69

Colborn, John: agrees to support new constitution if appointed to cabinet, 77; consults with soon-to-be rebels, 81; opposes promulgation, 81–82, 260n40; returns to royalist fold, 86

Committee of Safety: contacts with Stevens, 85–89, 95; decides to replace monarchy with provisional government, 89, 261–62n54; formed, 85

Congress, U.S.: analysis of passage of Newlands resolution, 228–36; appreciates Hawai`i's strategic value, 172–77; bipartisan support in for naval expansion and coastal fortification, 173; election of 1896 gives Republicans both houses, 179; investigates revolution and restoration, 136–38; queries removal of the *Philadelphia*, 173–74; supplants executive as shaper of Hawaiian policy, 172; surveys show House or Senate majorities for annexation, 205, 220, 222–23, 289n55. *See also* annexation; Republican Party

Constitution of 1887 (Hawai`i): forced on king, 26, 57; provisions, 145

Constitution of 1893 (Hawai`i), 62, 78–83

Constitution of 1894 (Hawai`i), 143–45

Convention of 1886, 44–45, 49, 291n13

Cook, James, 9, 11

Cooper, Henry: biographical information, 85; declines to talk with Blount, 122; as foreign minister during immigration crisis, 194–95, 200, 296n59, 298n92; heads Committee of Safety, 85; proclaims new government, 96, 98; supports U.S. resupply effort to Philippines, 226, 305n57; visits McKinley at Canton, 185; visits Wiltse on *Boston*, 83, 261n47

Cornwell, William, 80

Crapol, Edward, 288n40

Cuba: huge sugar exporter, 29, 32; troubles draw attention from annexation, 185, 204–5, 221–23, 225

D

Damon, Samuel: negotiates surrender of the queen, 101–2, 267n60; serves in the provisional government, 98, 102, 132, 134, 143

Davies, Theo, 82, 109, 116

Davis, Cushman Kellogg: biographical information, 178–80; forces Senate vote on Newlands joint resolution, 235; gives primary importance to Hawai`i's strategic value, 221–24, 239; leads annexationists in Senate, 181, 221, 235; views of Japan, 221, 224

Davis Report, 221–24, 239; main theme is Hawai`i's military value, 224

Day, William R.: appointed assistant secretary of state, 184; assumes more responsibility as Sherman's health weakens, 185; takes charge of annexation, 184, 202, 204, 208, 214–15, 228, 289n55, 300nn108–9, 305–6n71

About the Author

WILLIAM MICHAEL MORGAN is professor of strategic studies and director of the Regional Studies Program at the Marine Corps War College in Quantico, Virginia. After service in the Marine Corps, he earned a PhD in history from the Claremont Graduate University. His thirty-one-year career with the U.S. Foreign Service included overseas assignments in South Africa, Venezuela, and Hungary, as well as three assignments in Japan.